鳥 山 明

It's our final volume! I tried to keep the end low-key, almost as if the story might keep going. What do you think of it? Thanks to all of you who stuck with me through 42 volumes [counting from the beginning of **Dragon Ball**–Ed.] and to everyone who sent fan mail and presents. I'm sorry I haven't been able to reply. Thank you from the bottom of my heart!! Goodbye.
—Akira Toriyama, 1995

Widely known all over the world for his playful, innovative storytelling and humorous, distinctive art style, **Dragon Ball** creator Akira Toriyama is also known in his native Japan for the wildly popular **Dr. Slump**, his previous manga series about the adventures of a mad scientist and his android "daughter." His hit series **Dragon Ball** ran from 1984 to 1995 in Shueisha's **Weekly Shonen Jump** magazine. He is also known for his design work on video games such as **Dragon Warrior**, **Chrono Trigger** and **Tobal No. 1**. His recent manga works include **Cowa!**, **Kajika**, **Sand Land**, **Neko Majin**, and a children's book, **Toccio the Angel**. He lives with his family in Japan.

DRAGON BALL Z VOL. 26
SHONEN JUMP Manga Edition

STORY AND ART BY
AKIRA TORIYAMA

English Adaptation/Gerard Jones
Translation/Lillian Olsen
Touch-up Art & Lettering/Wayne Truman
Design/Sean Lee
Editor/Jason Thompson

DRAGON BALL © 1984 by BIRD STUDIO. All rights reserved.
First published in Japan in 1984 by SHUEISHA Inc., Tokyo.
English translation rights arranged by SHUEISHA Inc.

Some art has been modified from the original Japanese edition.

In the original Japanese edition, DRAGON BALL and DRAGON BALL Z
are known collectively as the 42-volume series DRAGON BALL. The
English DRAGON BALL Z was originally volumes 17–42 of the Japanese
DRAGON BALL.

Printed in the U.S.A.

Published by VIZ Media, LLC
P.O. Box 77010
San Francisco, CA 94107

14
First printing, June 2006
Fourteenth printing, January 2019

SHONEN JUMP MANGA

Vol. 26

DB: 42 of 42

STORY AND ART BY
AKIRA TORIYAMA

THE MAIN CHARACTERS

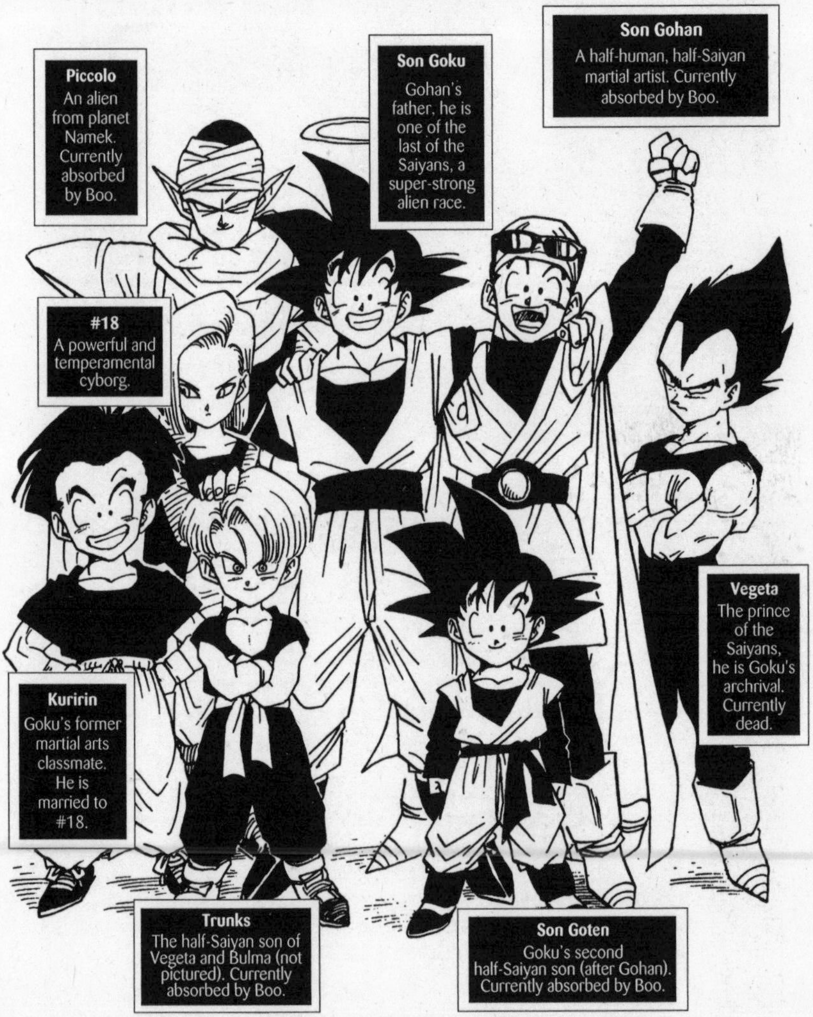
Piccolo
An alien from planet Namek. Currently absorbed by Boo.
Son Goku
Gohan's father, he is one of the last of the Saiyans, a super-strong alien race.
Son Gohan
A half-human, half-Saiyan martial artist. Currently absorbed by Boo.
#18
A powerful and temperamental cyborg.
Vegeta
The prince of the Saiyans, he is Goku's archrival. Currently dead.
Kuririn
Goku's former martial arts classmate. He is married to #18.
Trunks
The half-Saiyan son of Vegeta and Bulma (not pictured). Currently absorbed by Boo.
Son Goten
Goku's second half-Saiyan son (after Gohan). Currently absorbed by Boo.

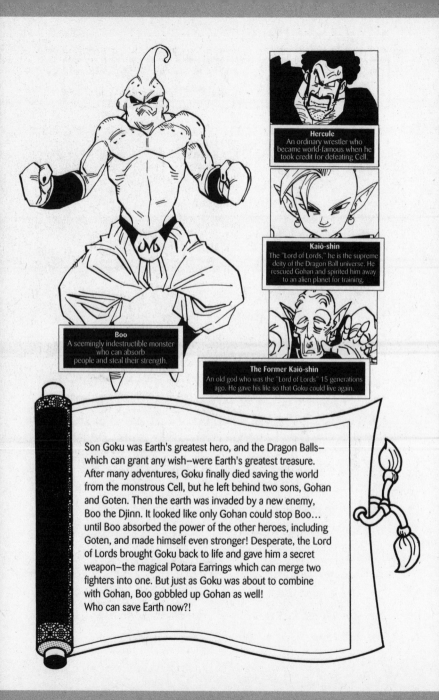

Hercule
An ordinary wrestler who became world-famous when he took credit for defeating Cell.

Kaiô-shin
The "Lord of Lords," he is the supreme deity of the Dragon Ball universe. He rescued Gohan and spirited him away to an alien planet for training.

The Former Kaiô-shin
An old god who was the "Lord of Lords" 15 generations ago. He gave his life so that Goku could live again.

Boo
A seemingly indestructible monster who can absorb people and steal their strength.

Son Goku was Earth's greatest hero, and the Dragon Balls—which can grant any wish—were Earth's greatest treasure. After many adventures, Goku finally died saving the world from the monstrous Cell, but he left behind two sons, Gohan and Goten. Then the earth was invaded by a new enemy, Boo the Djinn. It looked like only Gohan could stop Boo... until Boo absorbed the power of the other heroes, including Goten, and made himself even stronger! Desperate, the Lord of Lords brought Goku back to life and gave him a secret weapon—the magical Potara Earrings which can merge two fighters into one. But just as Goku was about to combine with Gohan, Boo gobbled up Gohan as well!
Who can save Earth now?!

DRAGON BALL Z 26

CONTENTS

IT'S THE CONTENTS !

DRAGON BALL ドラゴンボール

DBZ:309
The Ultimate Combination!!

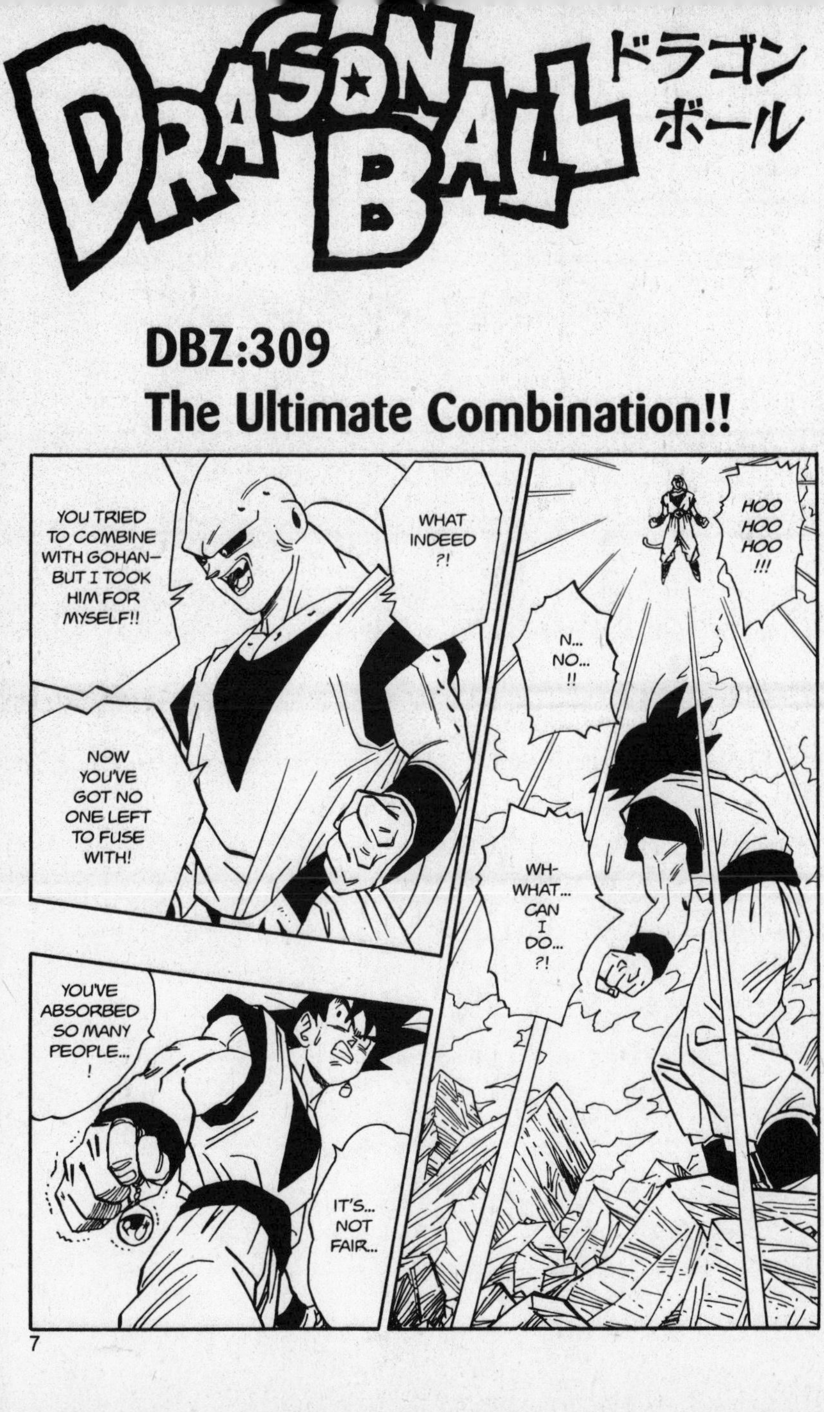
HOO HOO HOO!!!
N... NO...!!
WH-WHAT... CAN I DO...?!
WHAT INDEED?!
YOU TRIED TO COMBINE WITH GOHAN—BUT I TOOK HIM FOR MYSELF!!
NOW YOU'VE GOT NO ONE LEFT TO FUSE WITH!
YOU'VE ABSORBED SO MANY PEOPLE...!
IT'S... NOT FAIR...

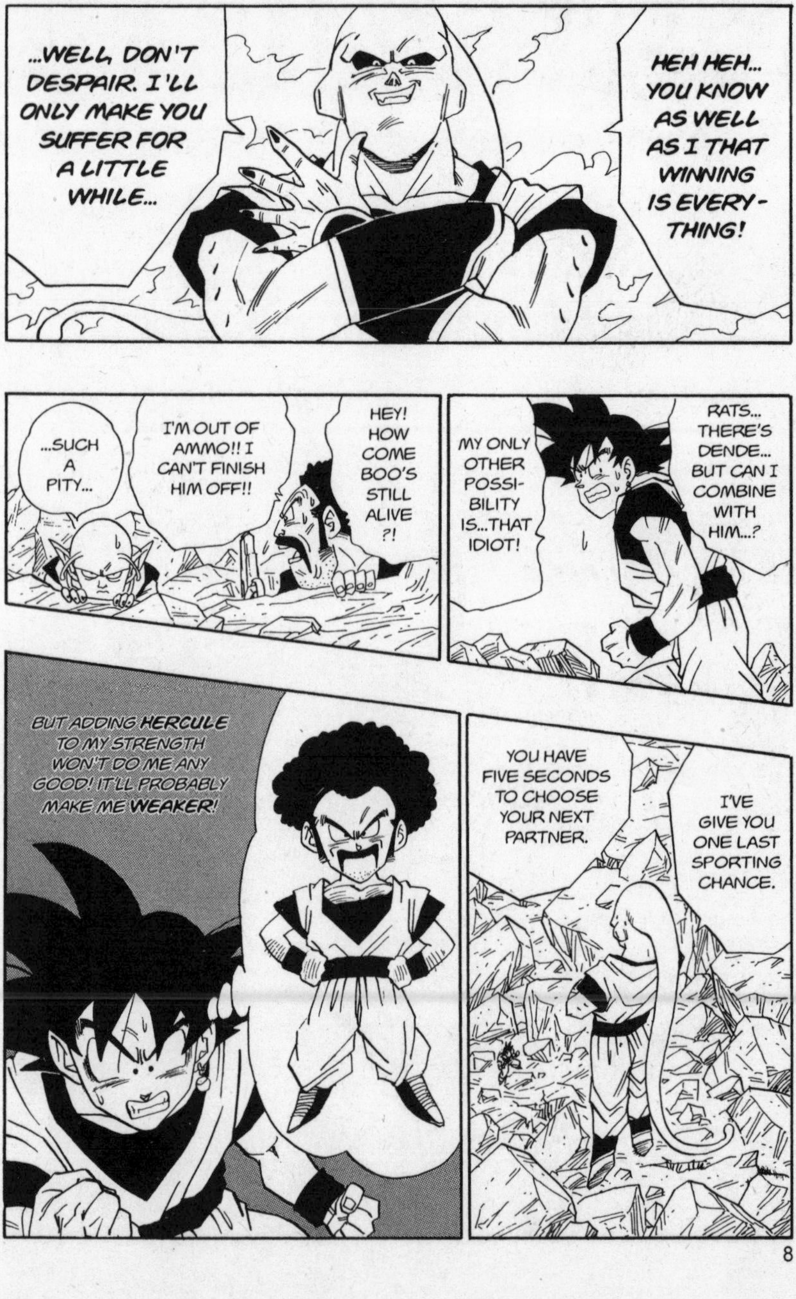
HEH HEH... YOU KNOW AS WELL AS I THAT WINNING IS EVERY-THING!
...WELL, DON'T DESPAIR. I'LL ONLY MAKE YOU SUFFER FOR A LITTLE WHILE...
RATS... THERE'S DENDE... BUT CAN I COMBINE WITH HIM...?
MY ONLY OTHER POSSI-BILITY IS...THAT IDIOT!
HEY! HOW COME BOO'S STILL ALIVE ?!
I'M OUT OF AMMO!! I CAN'T FINISH HIM OFF!!
...SUCH A PITY...
I'VE GIVE YOU ONE LAST SPORTING CHANCE.
YOU HAVE FIVE SECONDS TO CHOOSE YOUR NEXT PARTNER.
BUT ADDING HERCULE TO MY STRENGTH WON'T DO ME ANY GOOD! IT'LL PROBABLY MAKE ME WEAKER!

READ THIS WAY

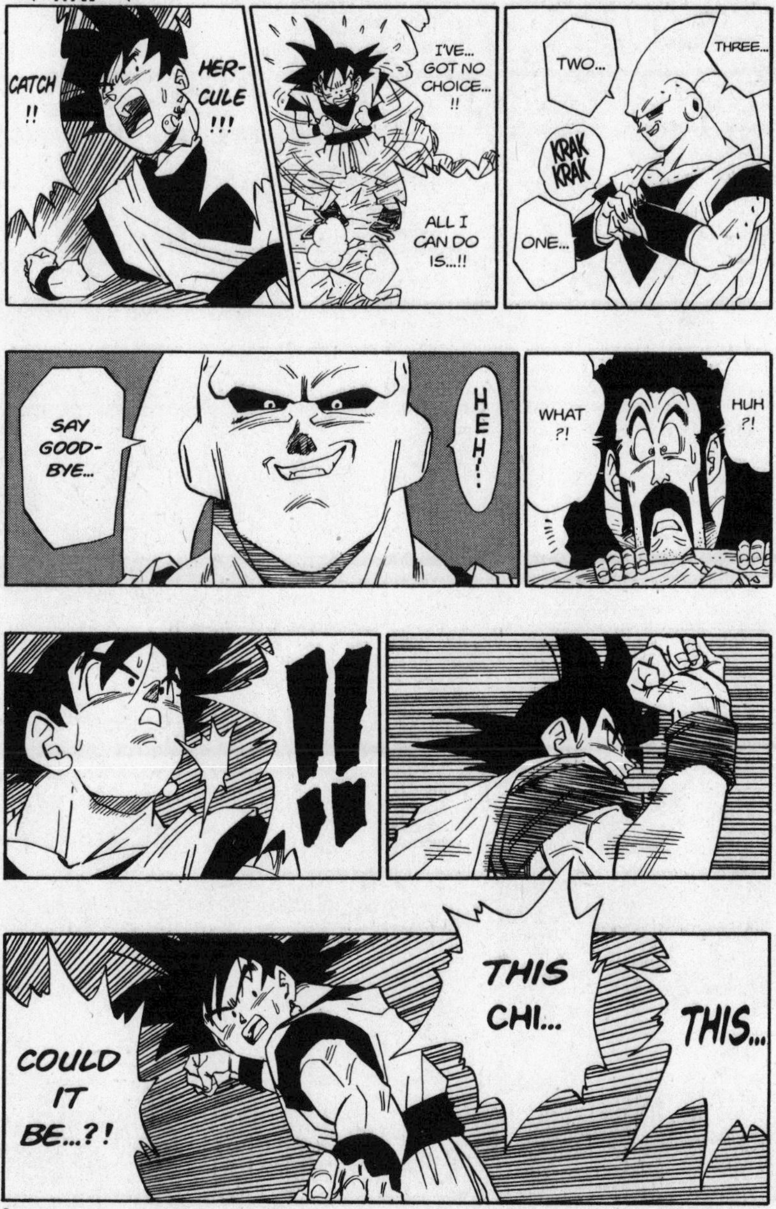
THREE...
TWO...
KRAK KRAK
ONE...
I'VE... GOT NO CHOICE... !!
ALL I CAN DO IS...!!
HER-CULE !!!
CATCH !!
HUH ?!
WHAT ?!
HEH!!
SAY GOOD-BYE...
!!
THIS...
THIS CHI...
COULD IT BE...?!

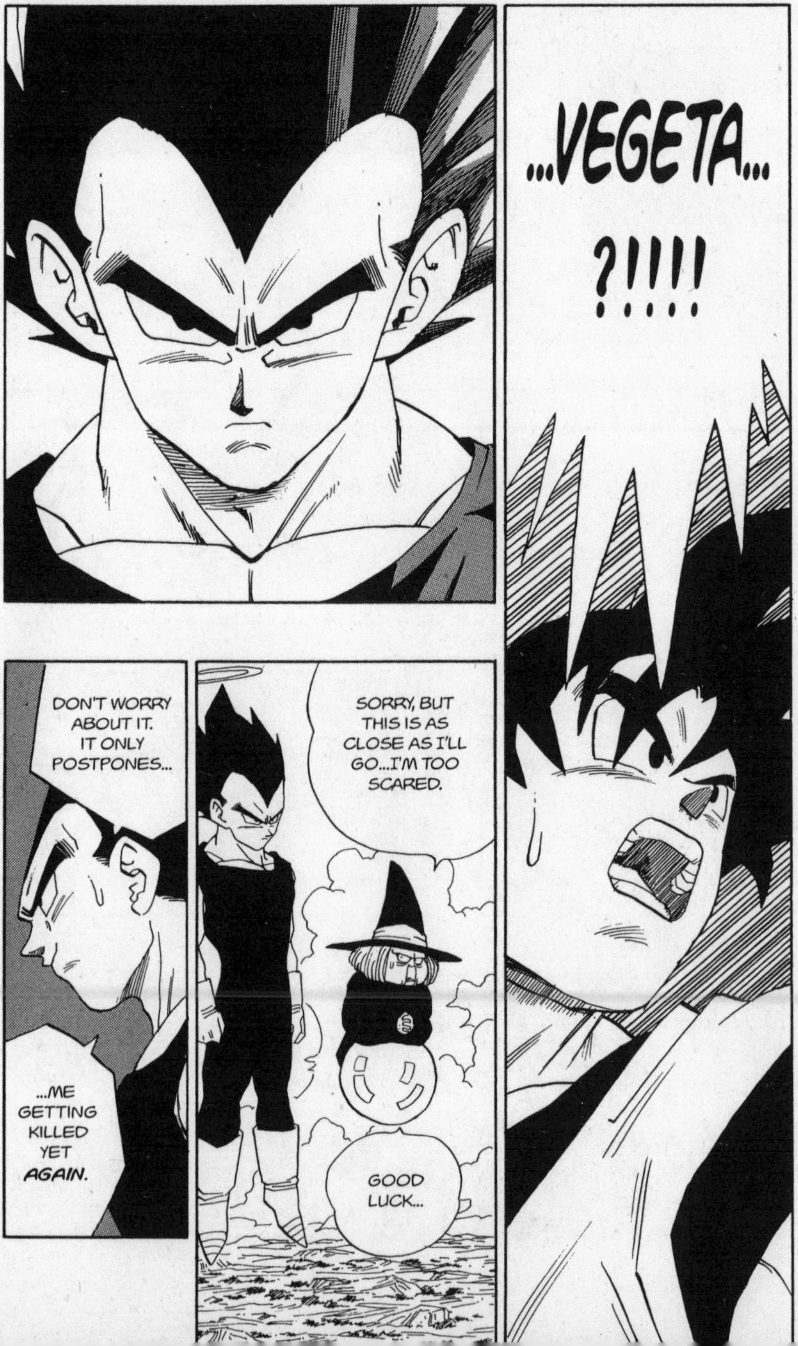
...VEGETA... ?!!!!
SORRY, BUT THIS IS AS CLOSE AS I'LL GO...I'M TOO SCARED.
GOOD LUCK...
DON'T WORRY ABOUT IT. IT ONLY POSTPONES...
...ME GETTING KILLED YET *AGAIN*.

READ THIS WAY

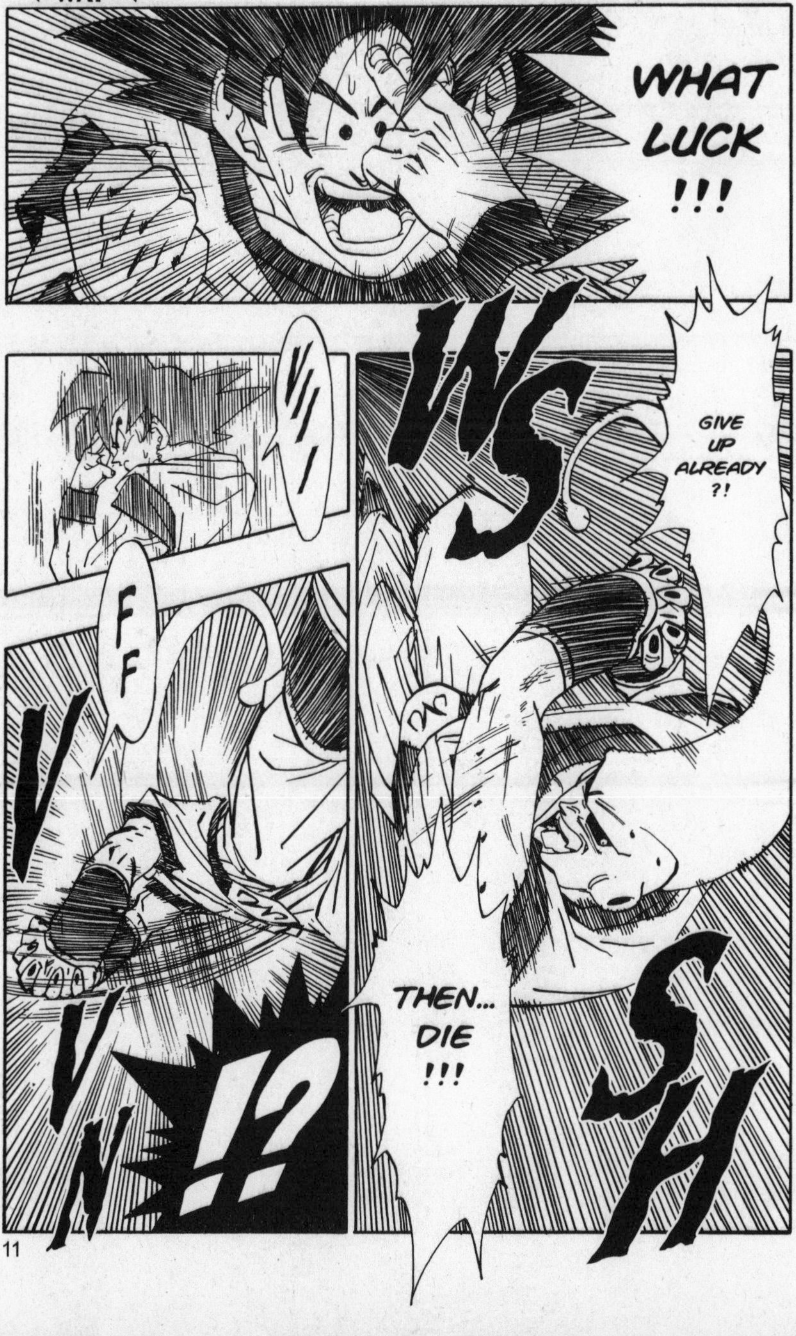
WHAT LUCK !!!
WS
GIVE UP ALREADY ?!
THEN... DIE !!!
SH
FF
V
VN
!?

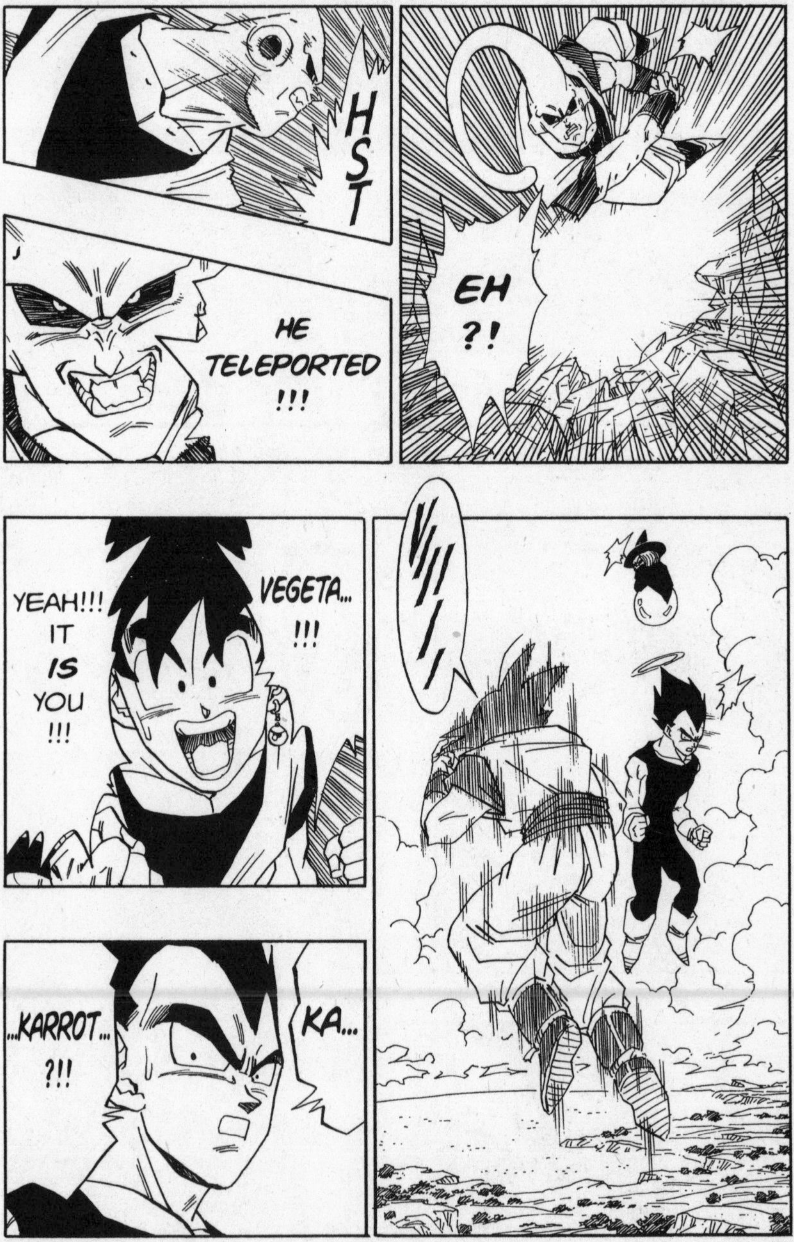
EH ?!
HST
HE TELEPORTED !!!
VEGETA... !!!
YEAH!!! IT IS YOU !!!
KA...
...KARROT... ?!!

READ THIS WAY

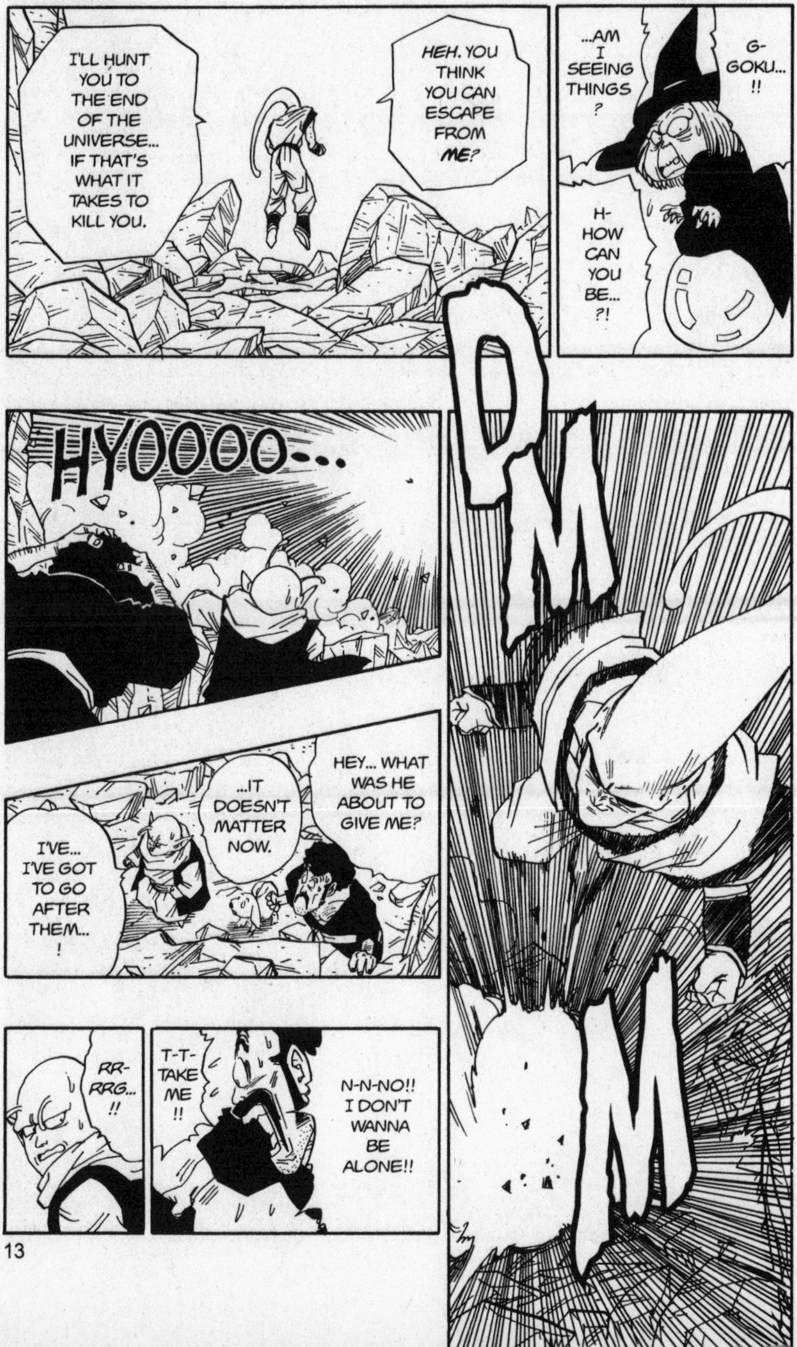
G-GOKU...!!
...AM I SEEING THINGS?
H-HOW CAN YOU BE...?!
HEH. YOU THINK YOU CAN ESCAPE FROM *ME?*
I'LL HUNT YOU TO THE END OF THE UNIVERSE... IF THAT'S WHAT IT TAKES TO KILL YOU.
DMM
HYOOOO-...
HEY... WHAT WAS HE ABOUT TO GIVE ME?
...IT DOESN'T MATTER NOW.
I'VE... I'VE GOT TO GO AFTER THEM...!
N-N-NO!! I DON'T WANNA BE ALONE!!
T-T-TAKE ME!!
RR-RRG...!!

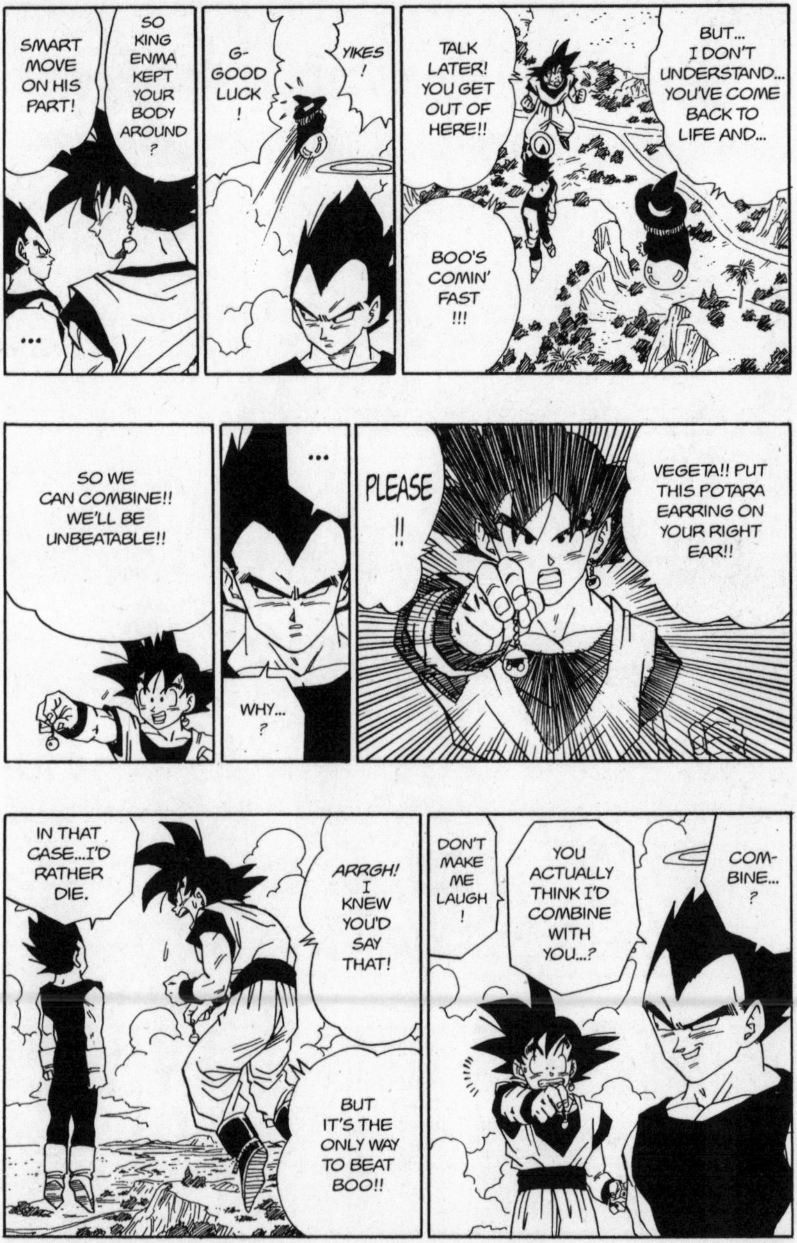
BUT... I DON'T UNDERSTAND... YOU'VE COME BACK TO LIFE AND...
TALK LATER! YOU GET OUT OF HERE!!
BOO'S COMIN' FAST!!!
YIKES!
G-GOOD LUCK!
SO KING ENMA KEPT YOUR BODY AROUND?
SMART MOVE ON HIS PART!
...
VEGETA!! PUT THIS POTARA EARRING ON YOUR RIGHT EAR!!
PLEASE!!
...
WHY...?
SO WE CAN COMBINE!! WE'LL BE UNBEATABLE!!
COMBINE...?
YOU ACTUALLY THINK I'D COMBINE WITH YOU...?
DON'T MAKE ME LAUGH!
ARRGH! I KNEW YOU'D SAY THAT!
BUT IT'S THE ONLY WAY TO BEAT BOO!!
IN THAT CASE...I'D RATHER DIE.

READ THIS WAY

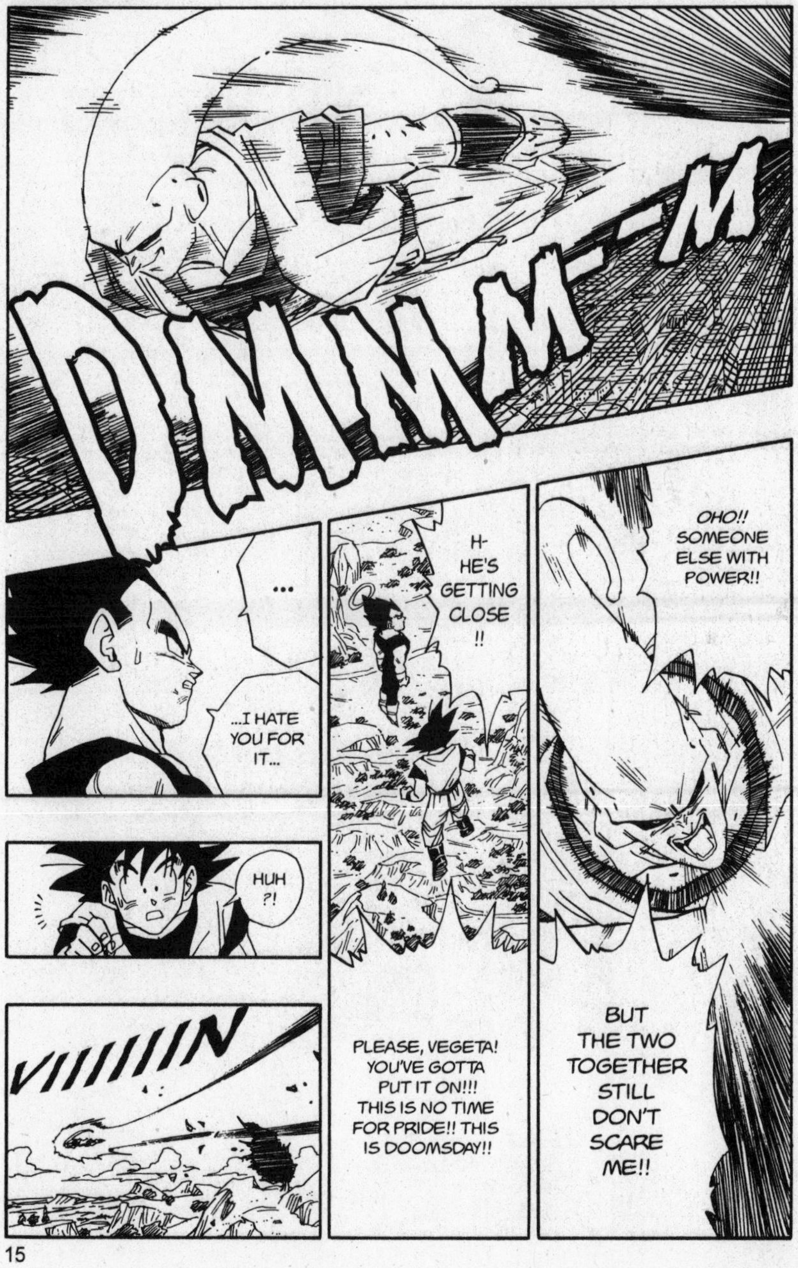
DMMMM--M
OHO!! SOMEONE ELSE WITH POWER!!
BUT THE TWO TOGETHER STILL DON'T SCARE ME!!
H-HE'S GETTING CLOSE!!
PLEASE, VEGETA! YOU'VE GOTTA PUT IT ON!!! THIS IS NO TIME FOR PRIDE!! THIS IS DOOMSDAY!!
...
...I HATE YOU FOR IT...
HUH?!
VIIIIIIN

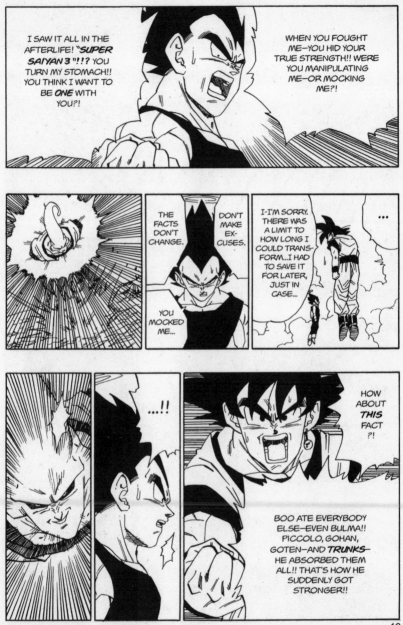

WHEN YOU FOUGHT ME—YOU HID YOUR TRUE STRENGTH!! WERE YOU MANIPULATING ME—OR MOCKING ME?!
I SAW IT ALL IN THE AFTERLIFE! "SUPER SAIYAN 3"!!? YOU TURN MY STOMACH!! YOU THINK I WANT TO BE ONE WITH YOU?!
I-I'M SORRY. THERE WAS A LIMIT TO HOW LONG I COULD TRANSFORM...I HAD TO SAVE IT FOR LATER, JUST IN CASE...
...
DON'T MAKE EXCUSES.
THE FACTS DON'T CHANGE.
YOU MOCKED ME...
HOW ABOUT THIS FACT?!
BOO ATE EVERYBODY ELSE—EVEN BULMA!! PICCOLO, GOHAN, GOTEN—AND TRUNKS—HE ABSORBED THEM ALL!! THAT'S HOW HE SUDDENLY GOT STRONGER!!
...!!

READ THIS WAY

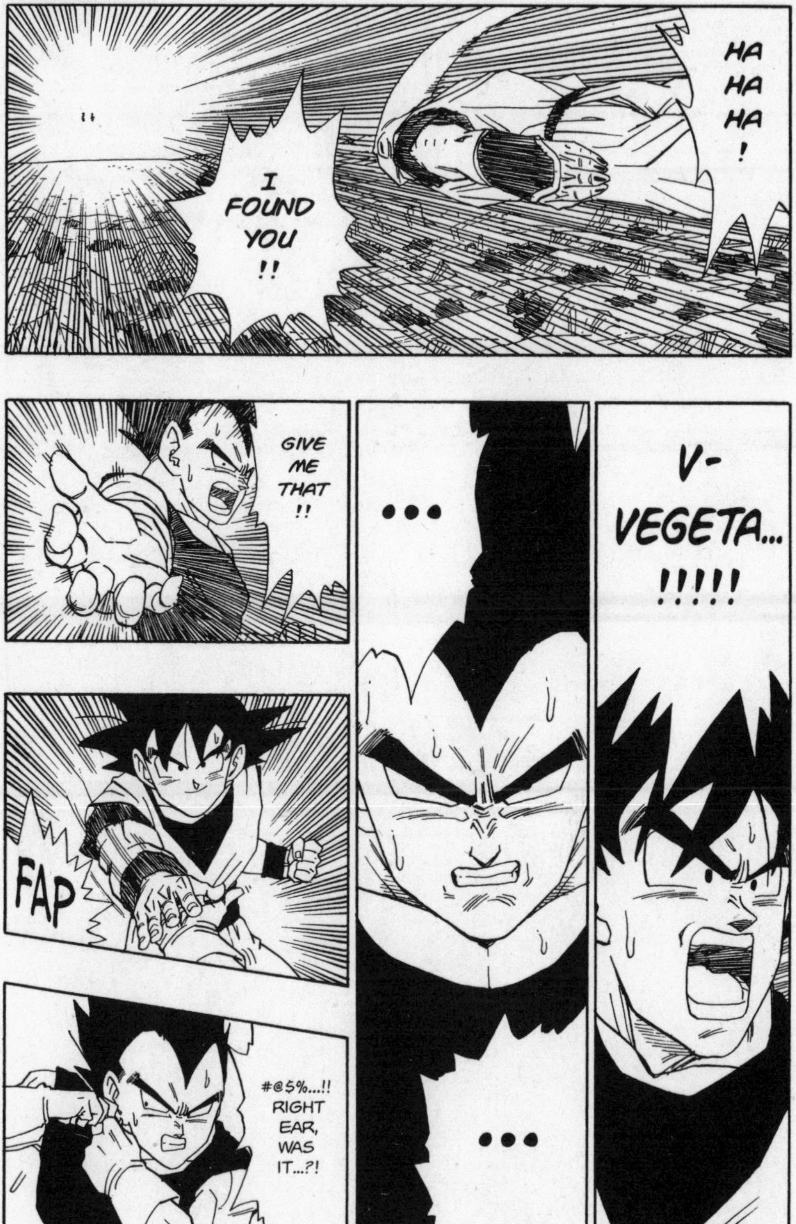
HA HA HA!
I FOUND YOU!!
V-VEGETA...!!!!!
...
...
GIVE ME THAT!!
FAP
#@$%...!! RIGHT EAR, WAS IT...?!

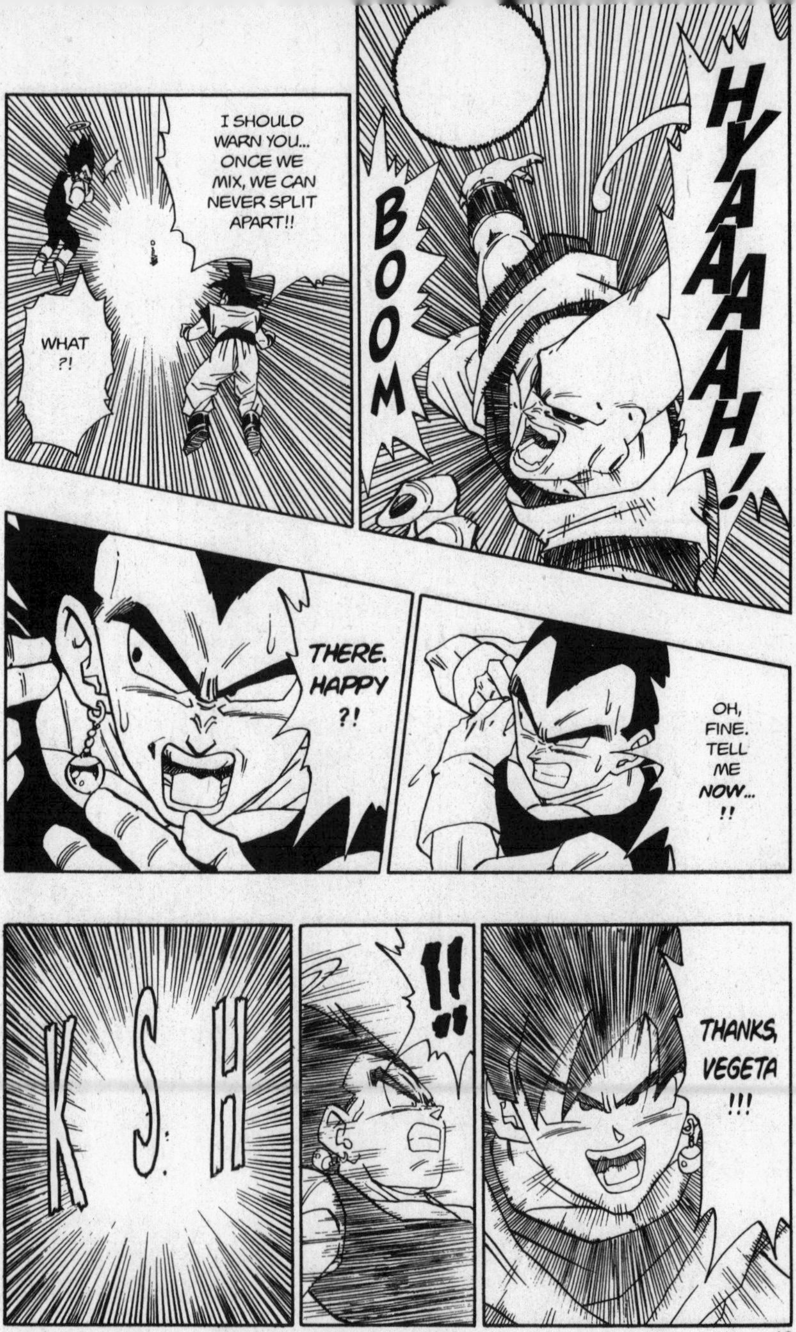
HYAAAAAH!
BOOM
I SHOULD WARN YOU... ONCE WE MIX, WE CAN NEVER SPLIT APART!!
WHAT ?!
OH, FINE. TELL ME NOW... !!
THERE. HAPPY ?!
THANKS, VEGETA !!!
!!
KSH

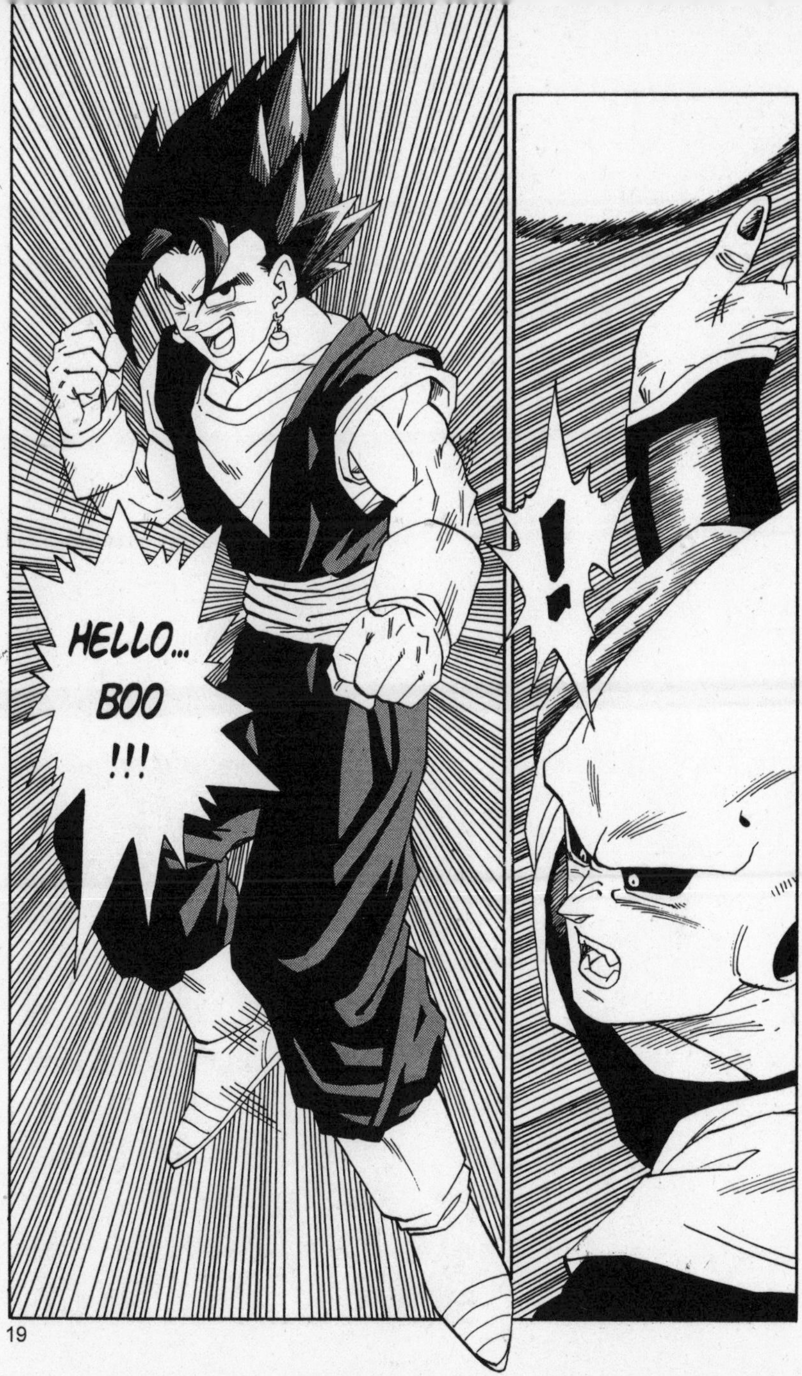
!
HELLO... BOO !!!

DBZ:310 · The Ultimate Fighter

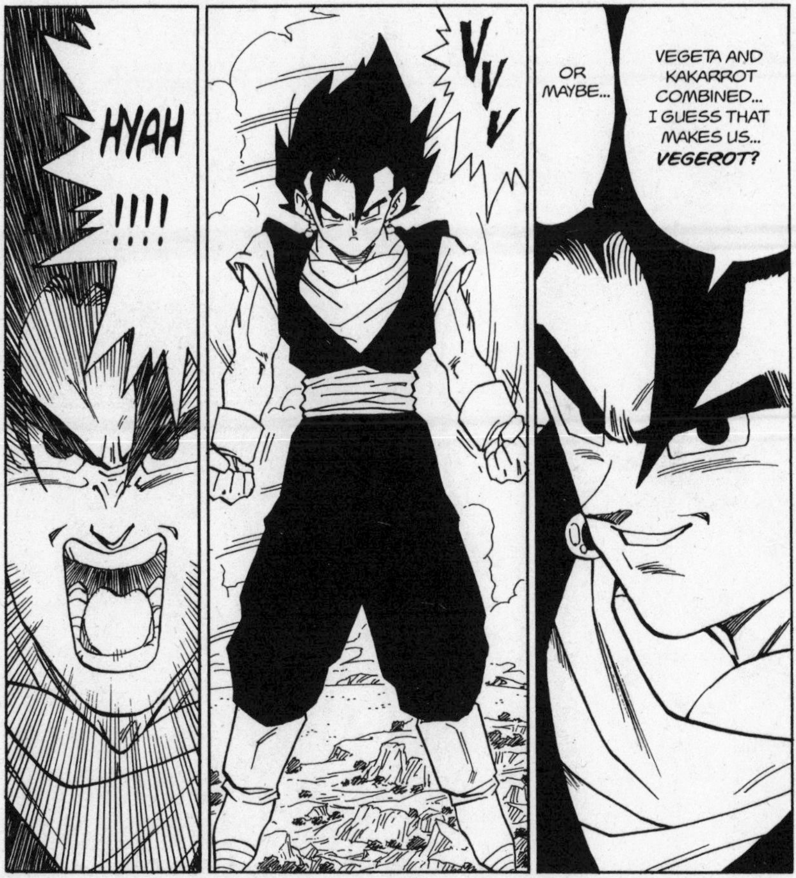
VEGETA AND KAKARROT COMBINED... I GUESS THAT MAKES US... *VEGEROT?*
OR MAYBE...
VVV
HYAH !!!!

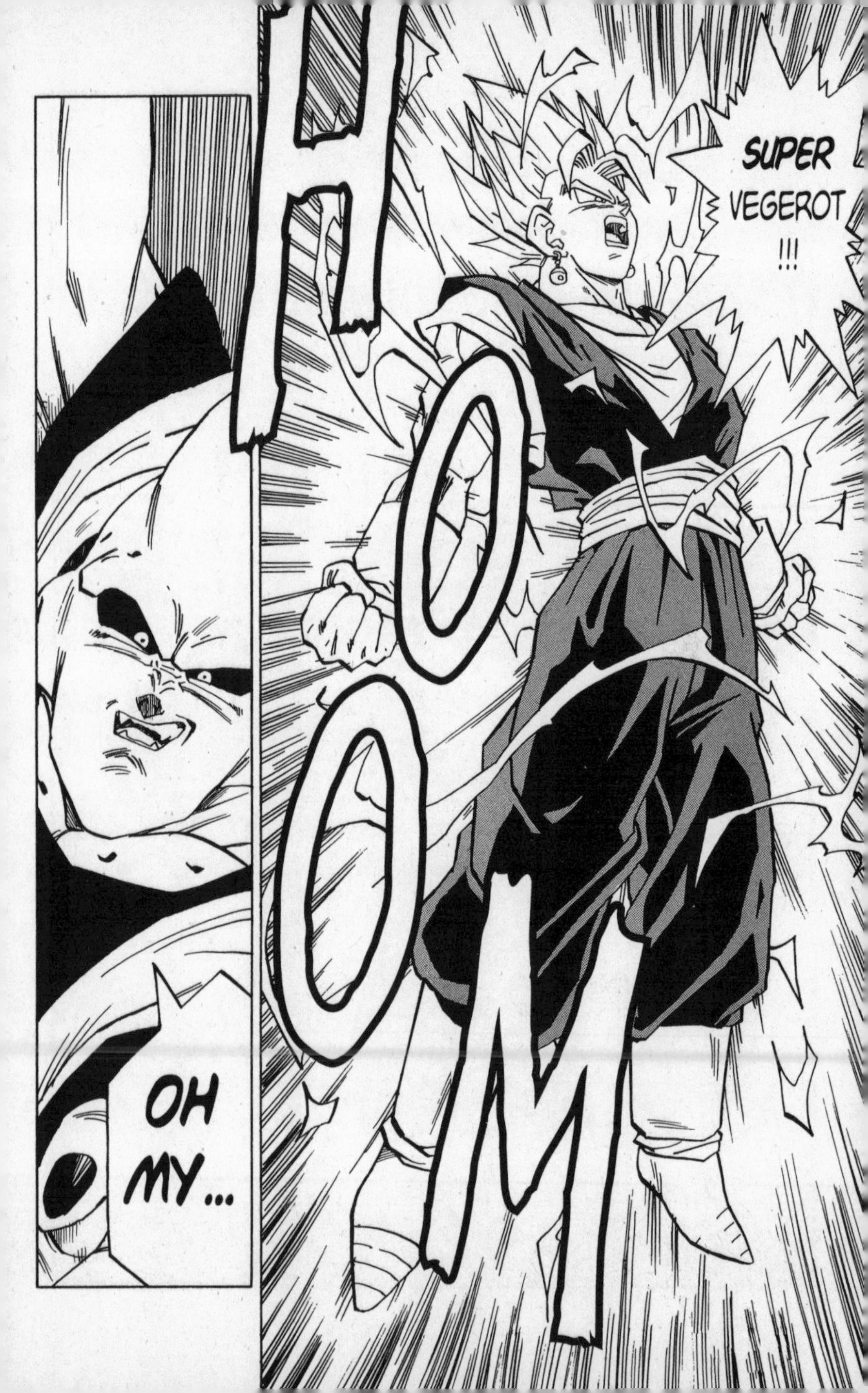
SUPER VEGEROT !!!
HOOOM
OH MY...

READ THIS WAY

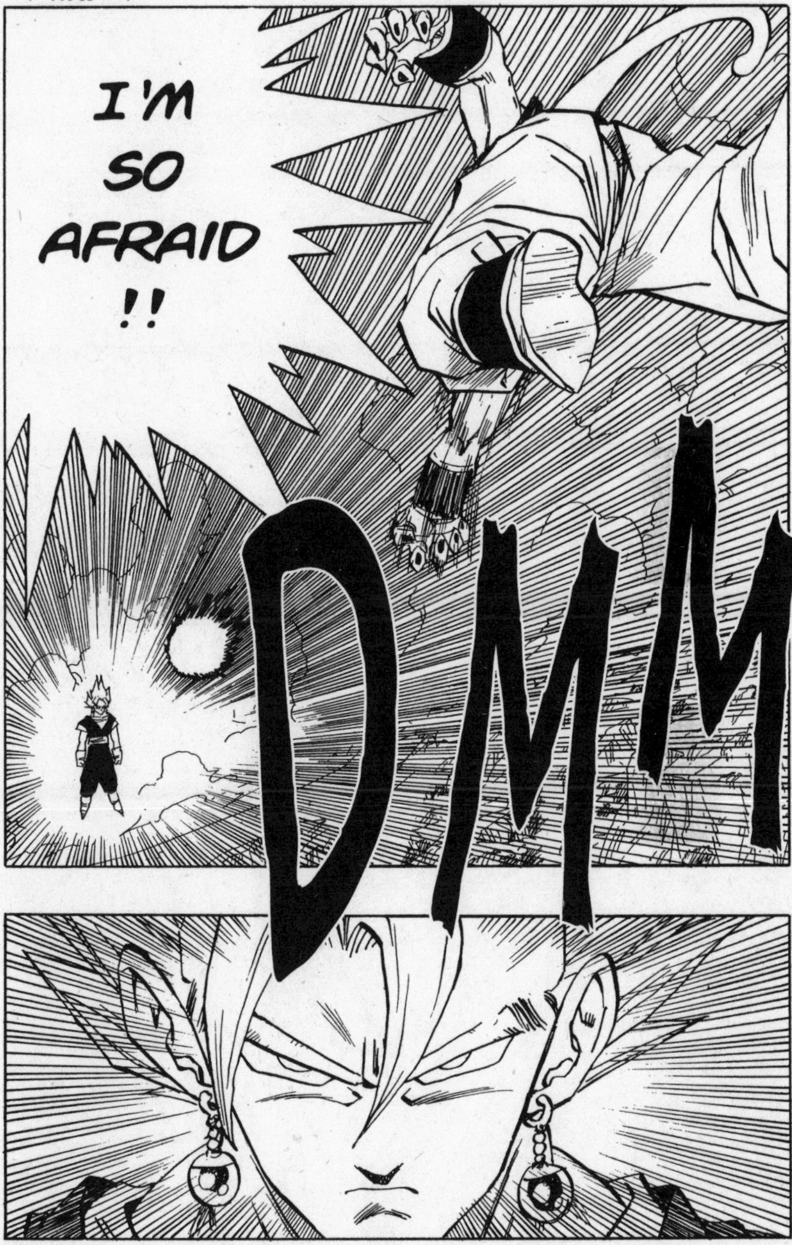
I'M SO AFRAID !!
DMM

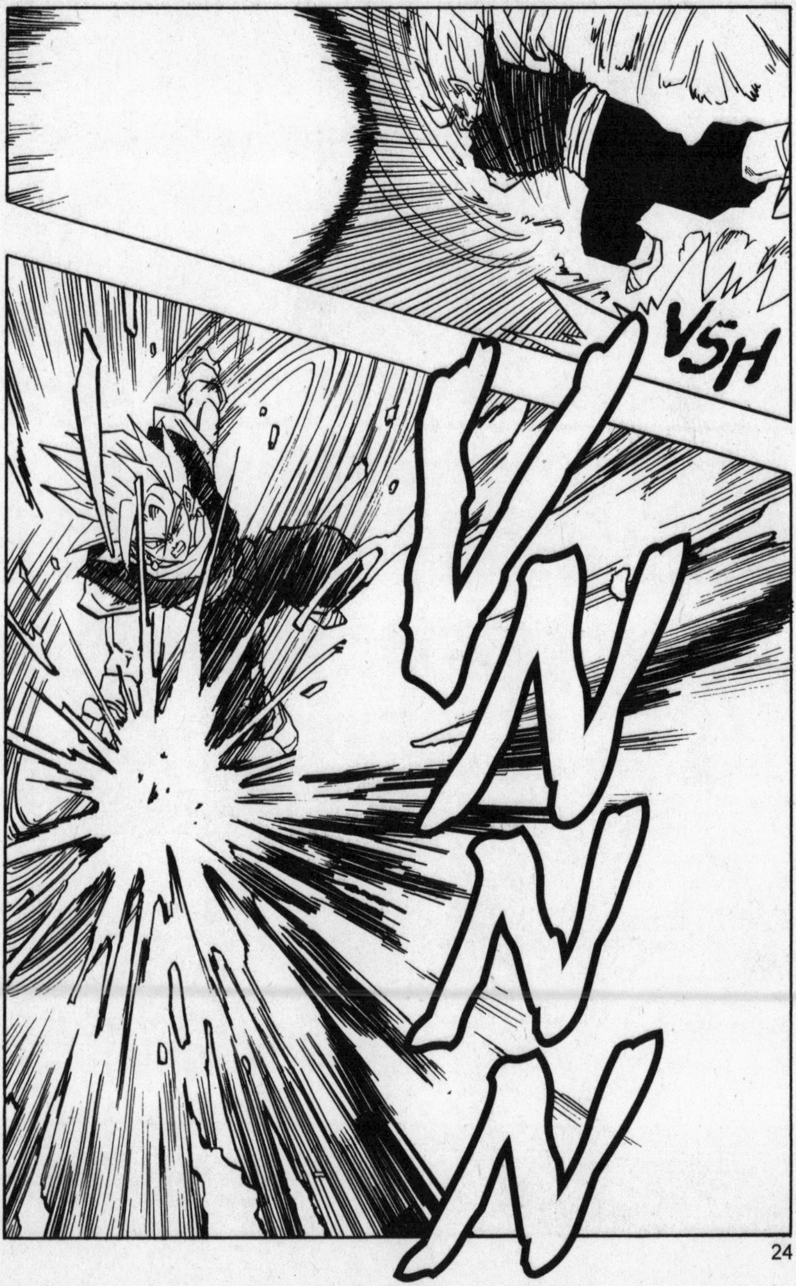
VSH
VWNNN

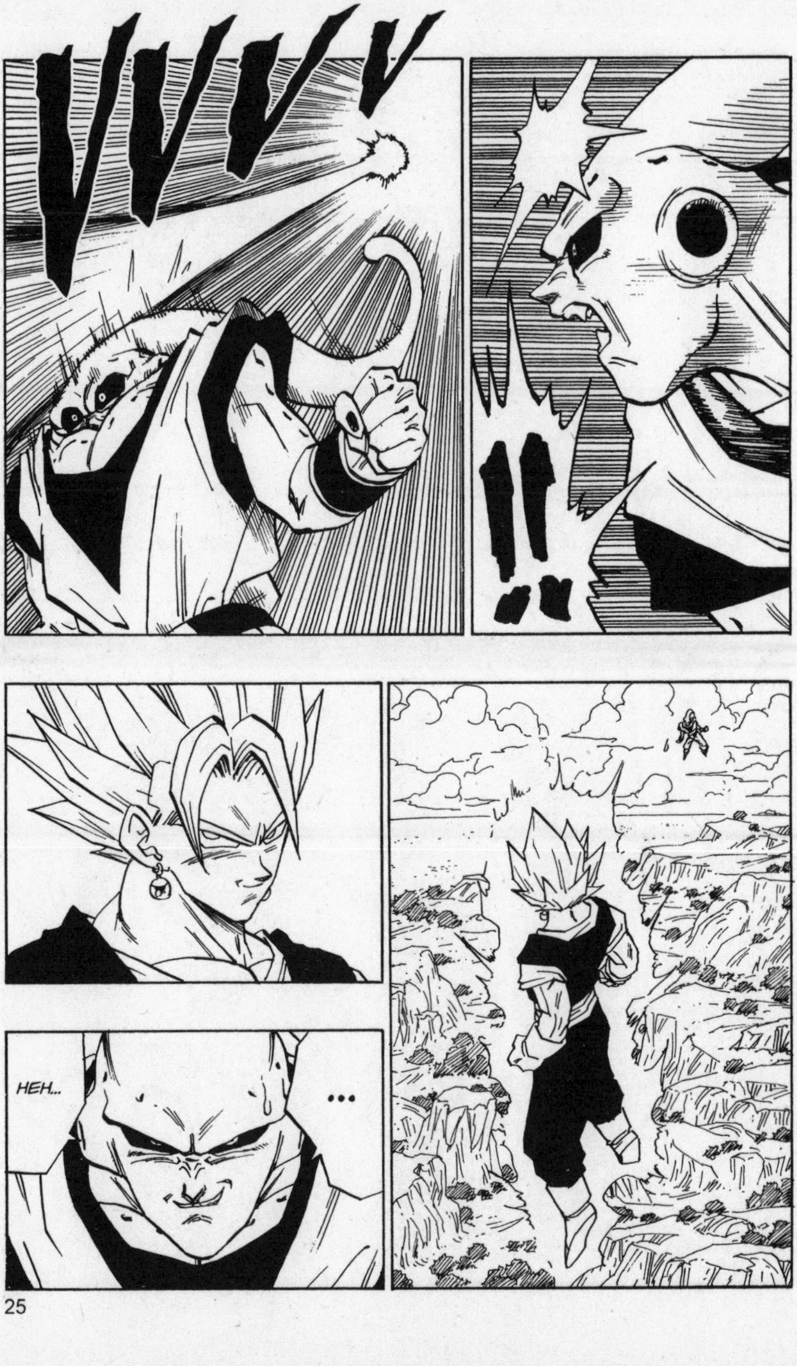
VVVV
!!
...
HEH...

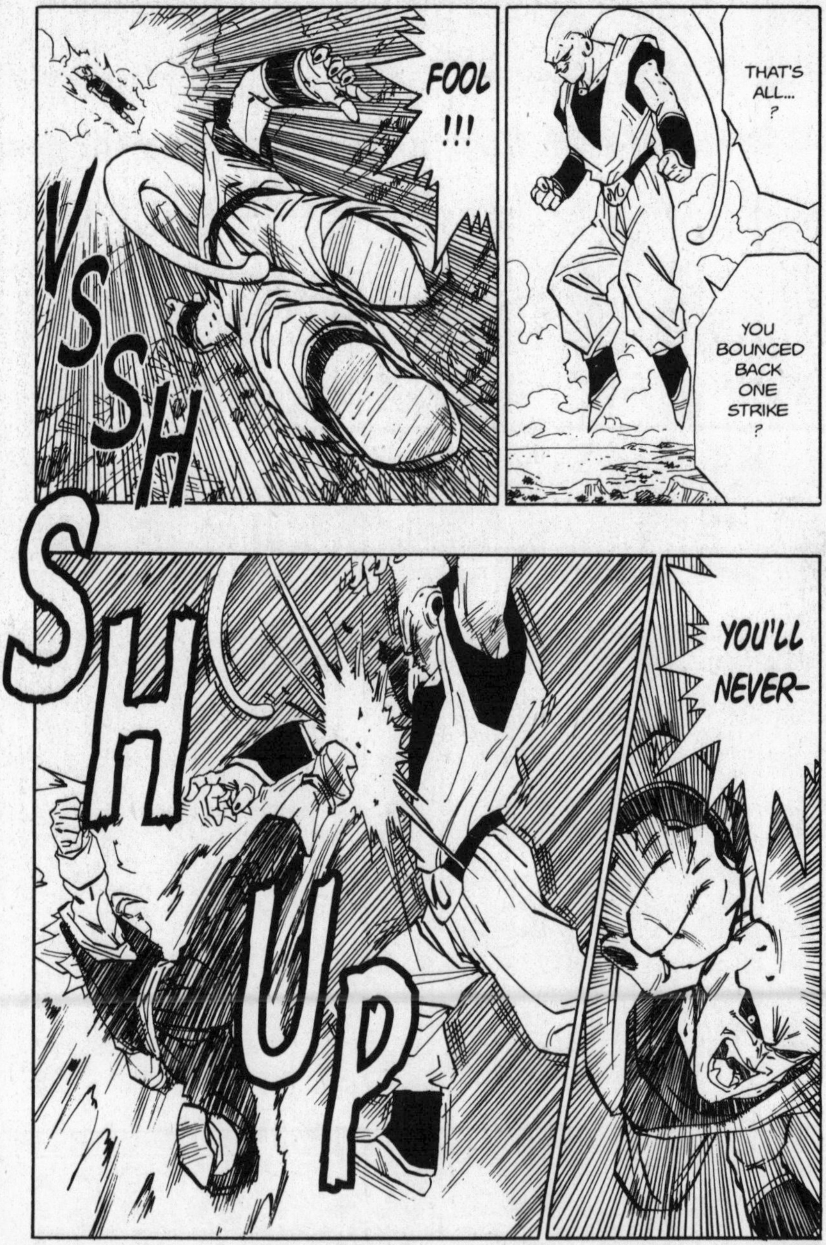
THAT'S ALL... ?
YOU BOUNCED BACK ONE STRIKE ?
FOOL !!!
VSSH
YOU'LL NEVER-
SHUP

READ THIS WAY

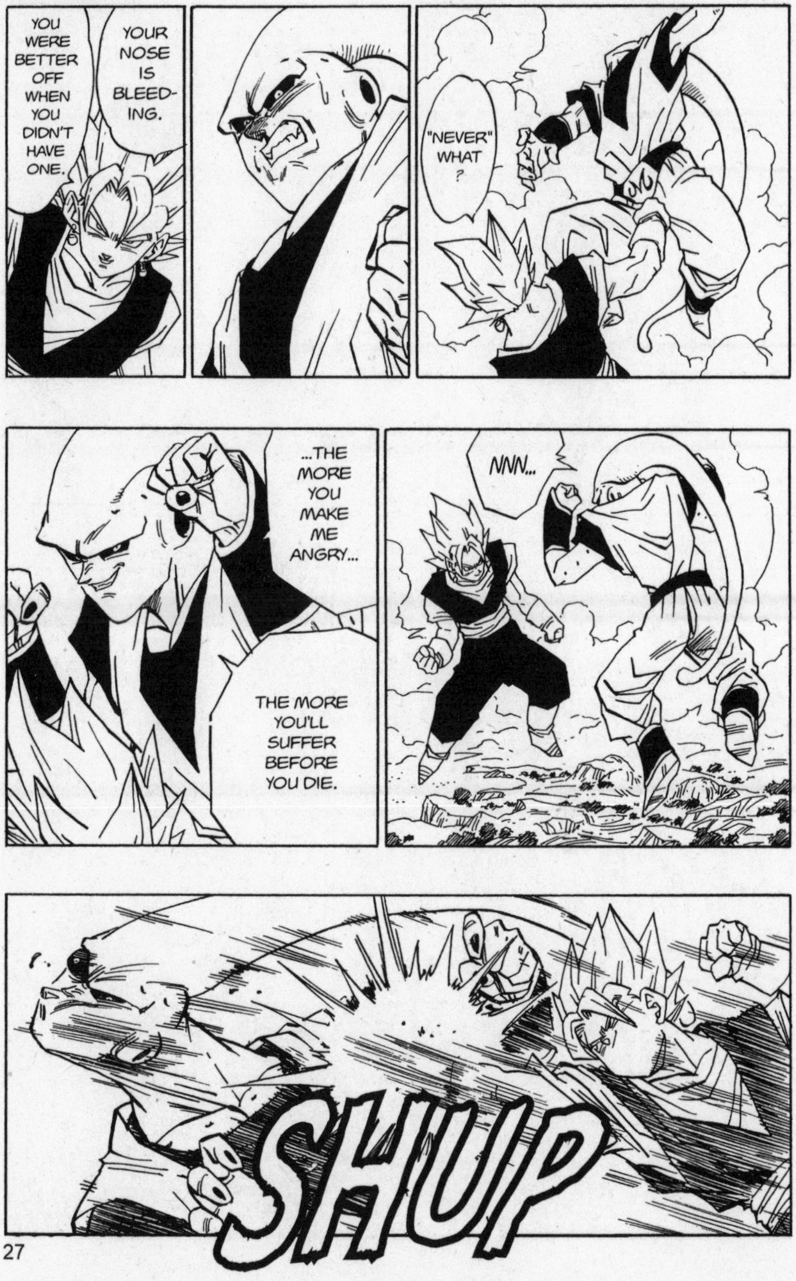

"NEVER" WHAT?
YOUR NOSE IS BLEEDING.
YOU WERE BETTER OFF WHEN YOU DIDN'T HAVE ONE.
NNN...
...THE MORE YOU MAKE ME ANGRY...
THE MORE YOU'LL SUFFER BEFORE YOU DIE.
SHUIP

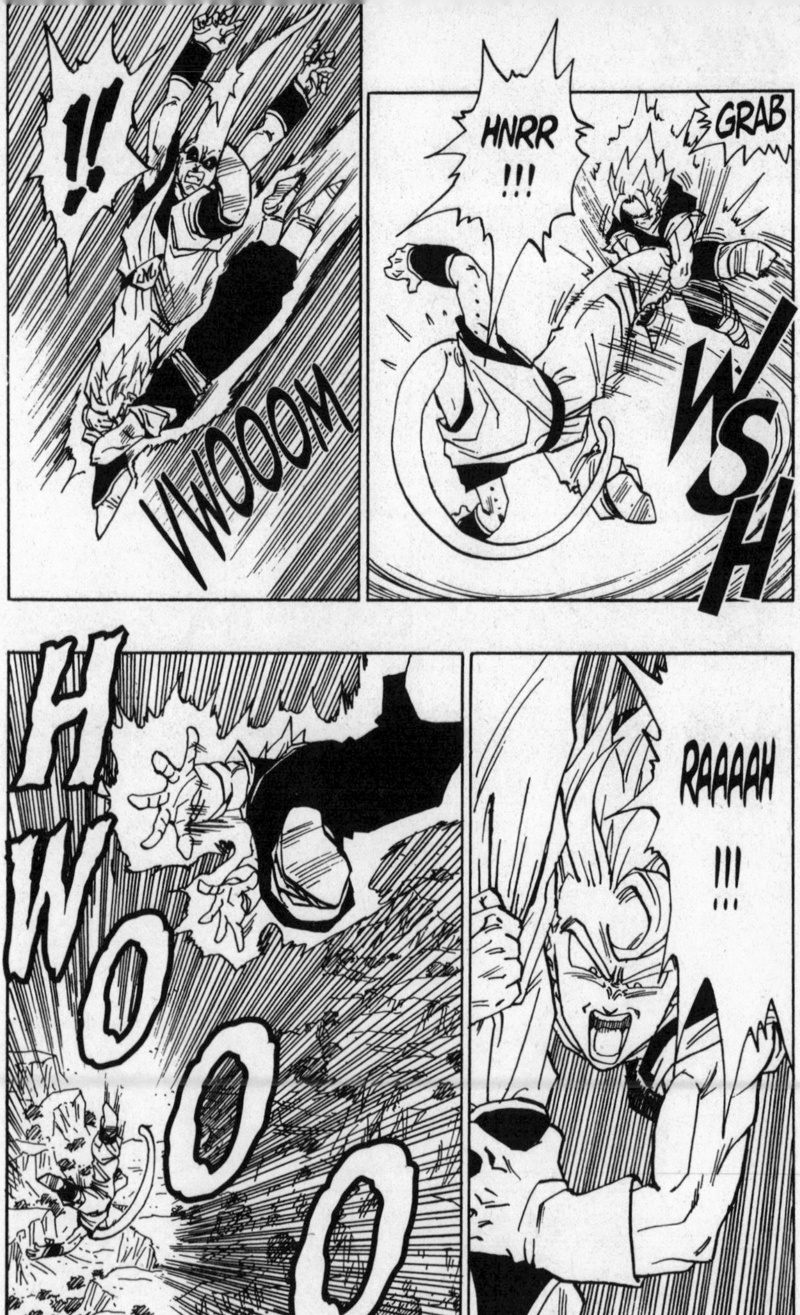
GRAB
HNRR!!!
WSH
!!
VWOOOM
RAAAAH!!!
HWOOOO

READ THIS WAY

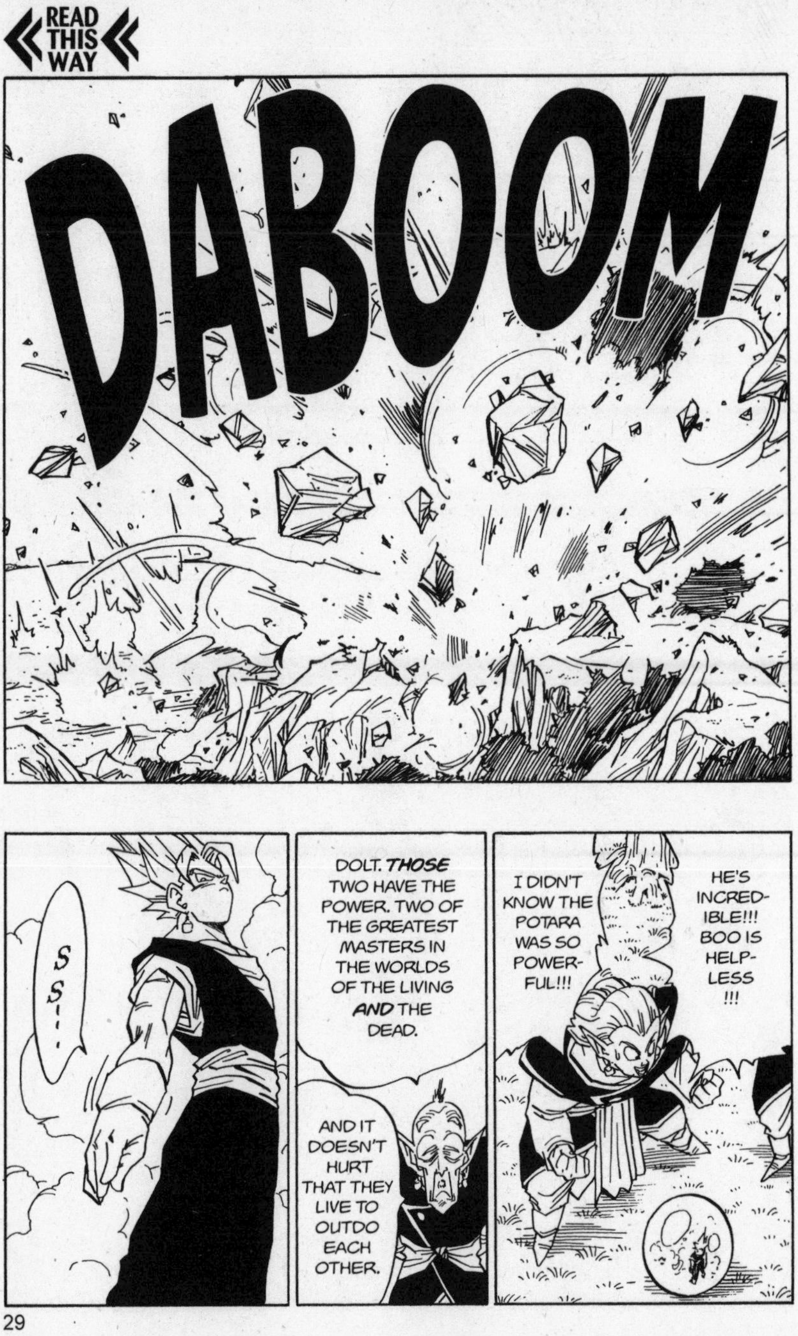
DABOOM
HE'S INCREDIBLE!!! BOO IS HELPLESS!!!
I DIDN'T KNOW THE POTARA WAS SO POWERFUL!!!
DOLT. ***THOSE*** TWO HAVE THE POWER. TWO OF THE GREATEST MASTERS IN THE WORLDS OF THE LIVING ***AND*** THE DEAD.
AND IT DOESN'T HURT THAT THEY LIVE TO OUTDO EACH OTHER.
S S...

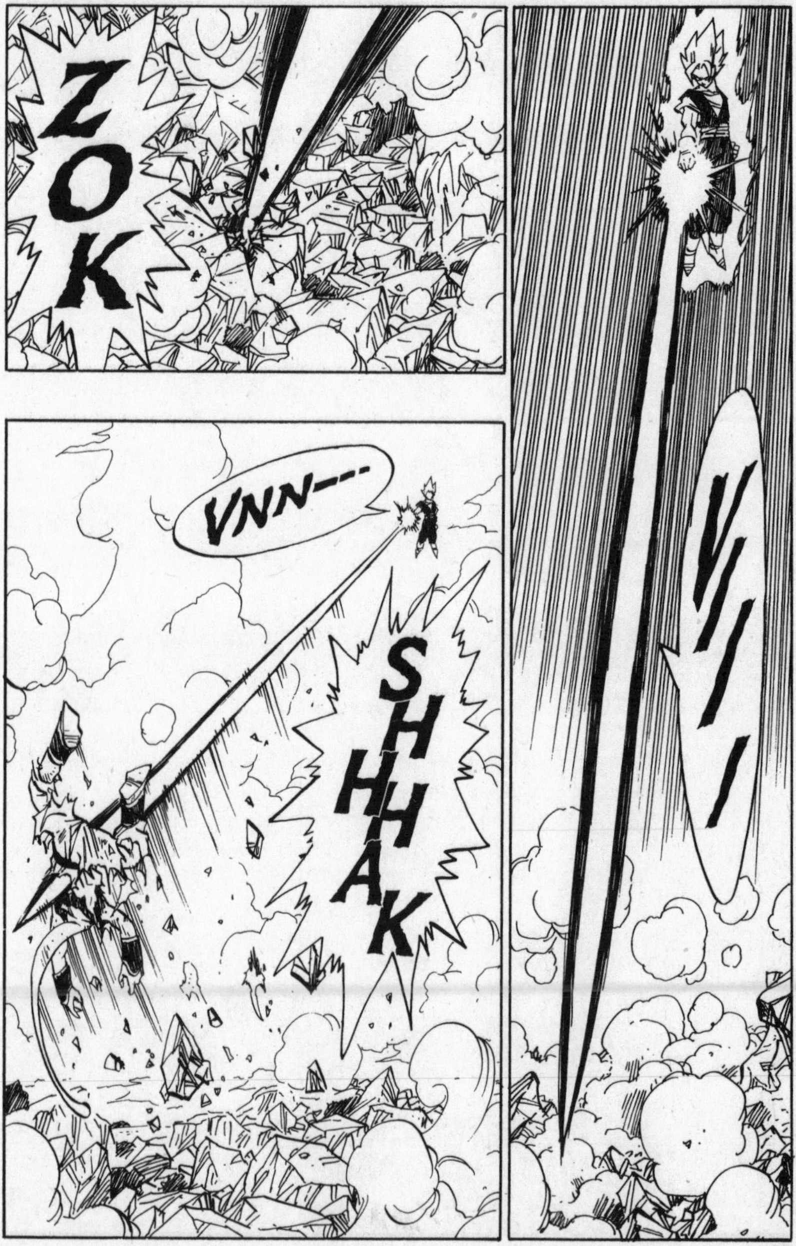
V///
ZOK
VNN---
SHHHAK

READ THIS WAY

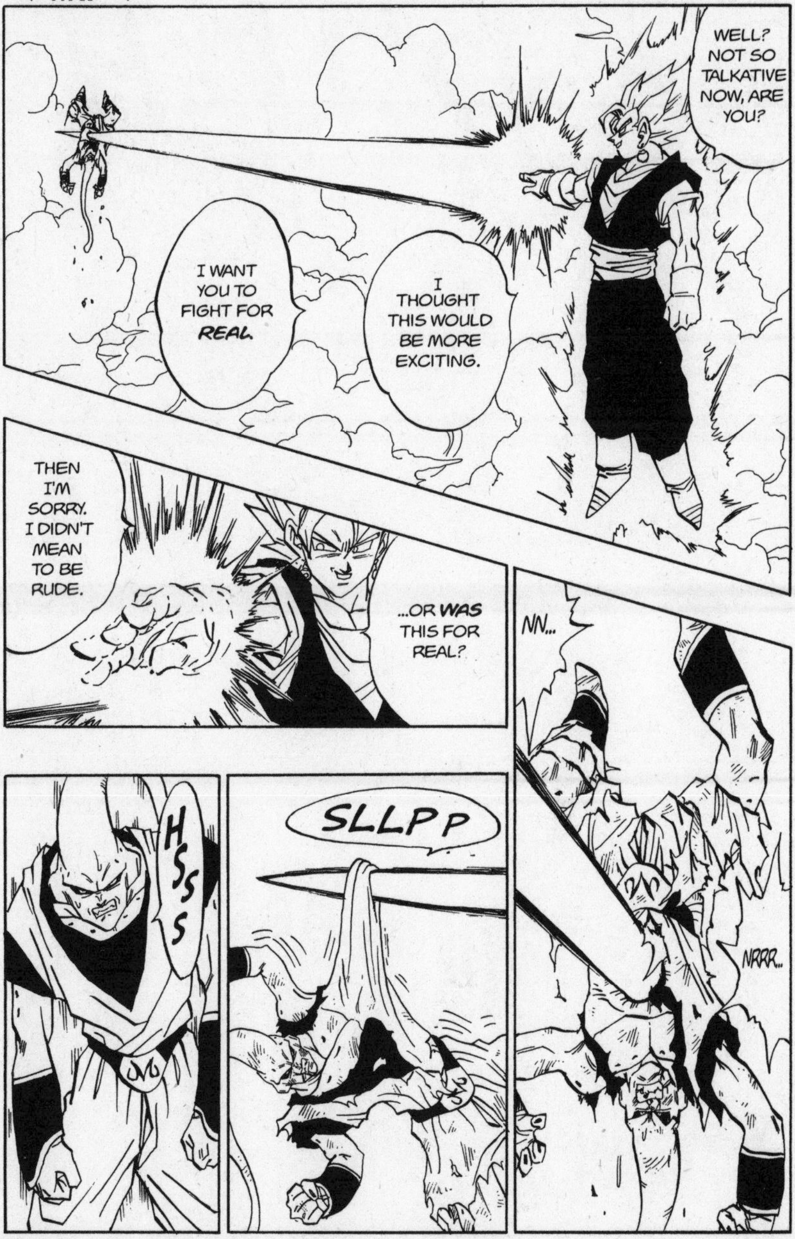
WELL? NOT SO TALKATIVE NOW, ARE YOU?
I THOUGHT THIS WOULD BE MORE EXCITING.
I WANT YOU TO FIGHT FOR *REAL*.
NN...
NRRR...
...OR *WAS* THIS FOR REAL?
THEN I'M SORRY. I DIDN'T MEAN TO BE RUDE.
SLLPP
HSSS

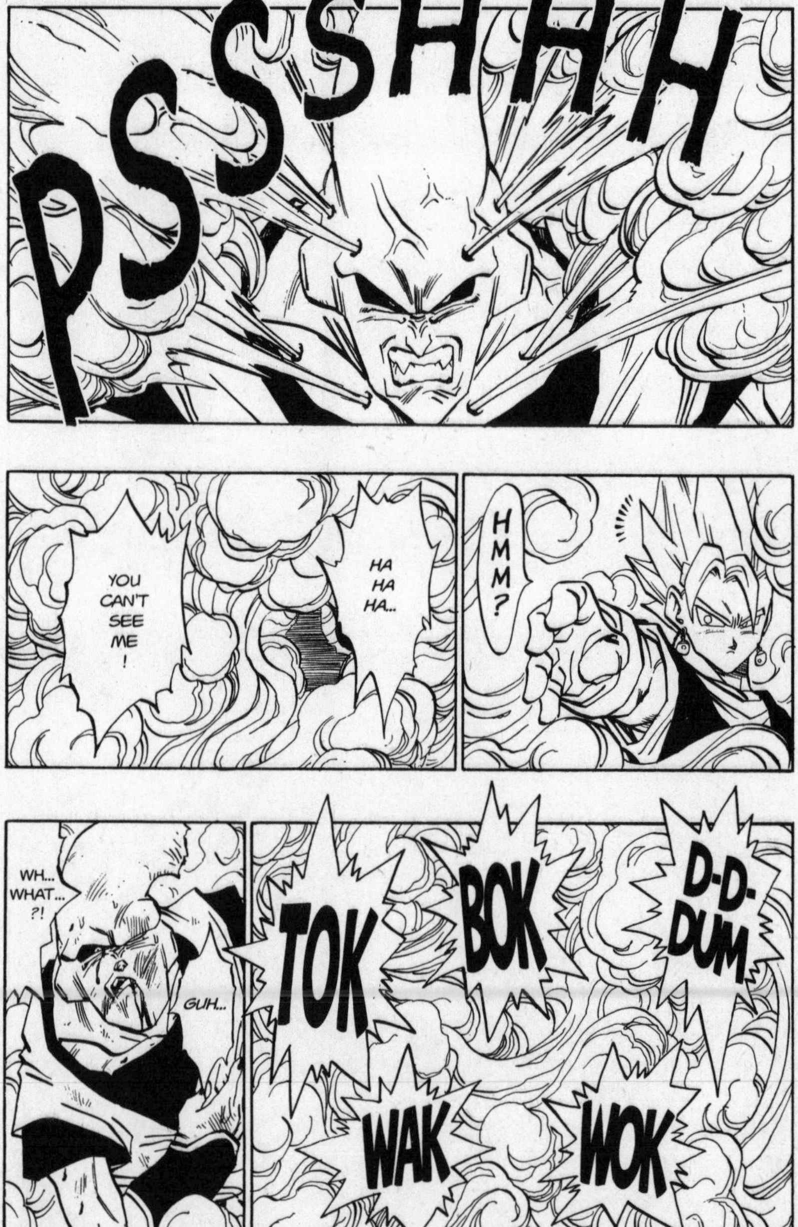
PSSHHHH
HMM?
HA HA HA...
YOU CAN'T SEE ME!
D-D-DUM
BOK
TOK
WOK
WAK
WH... WHAT...?!
GUH...

READ THIS WAY

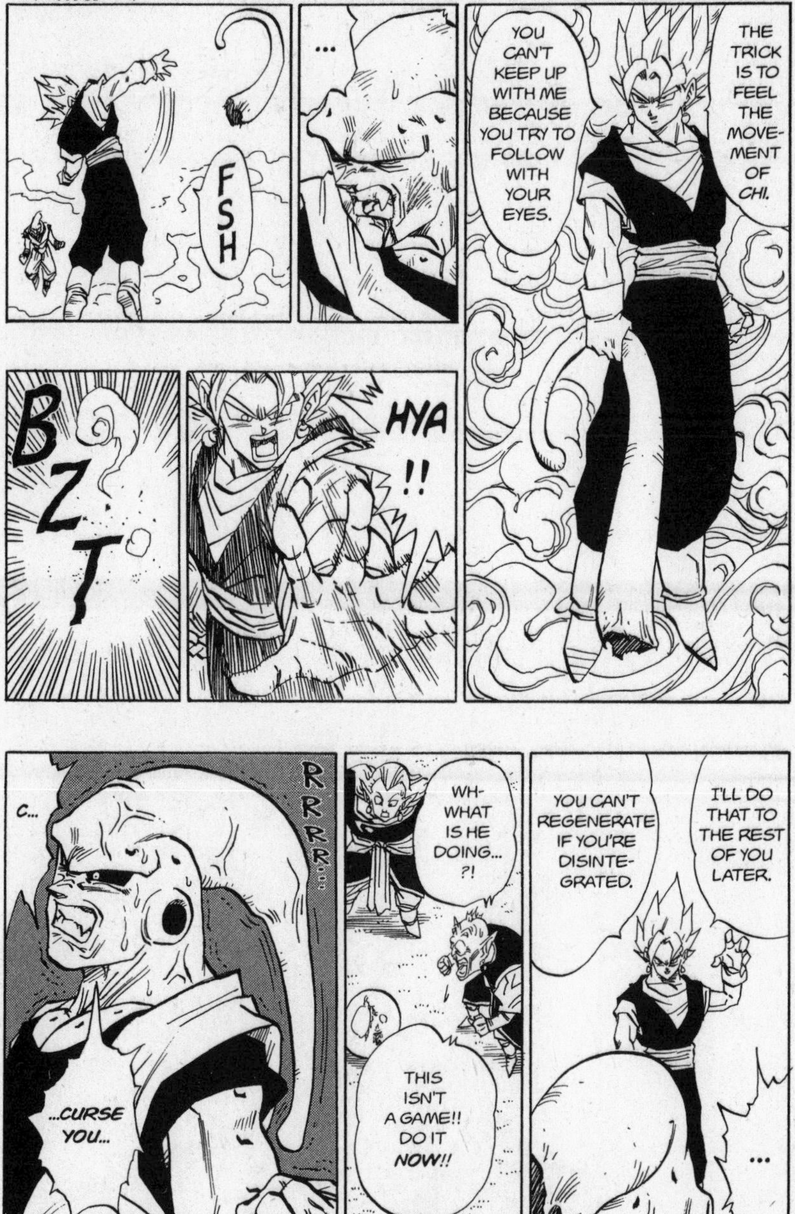

THE TRICK IS TO FEEL THE MOVEMENT OF CHI.
YOU CAN'T KEEP UP WITH ME BECAUSE YOU TRY TO FOLLOW WITH YOUR EYES.
...
FSH
HYA!!
BZT
YOU CAN'T REGENERATE IF YOU'RE DISINTEGRATED.
I'LL DO THAT TO THE REST OF YOU LATER.
...
WH-WHAT IS HE DOING...?!
THIS ISN'T A GAME!! DO IT NOW!!
RRRR...
C...
...CURSE YOU...

DBZ:311 • Vegerot's Game

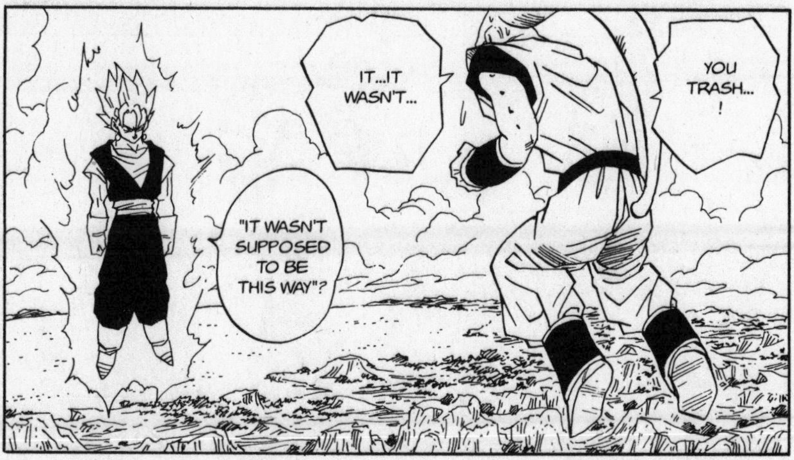
YOU TRASH... !
IT...IT WASN'T...
"IT WASN'T SUPPOSED TO BE THIS WAY"?

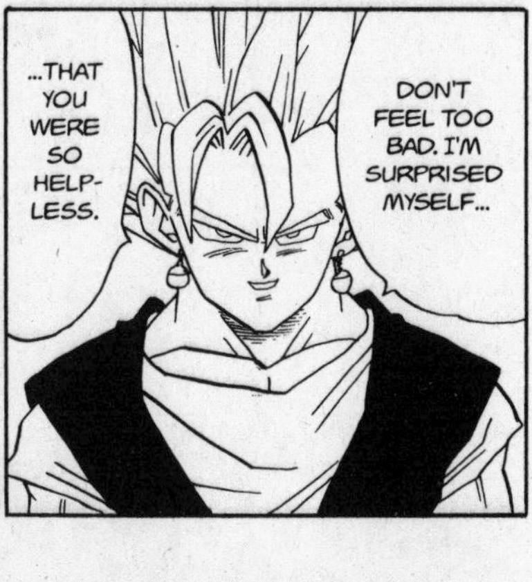
DON'T FEEL TOO BAD. I'M SURPRISED MYSELF...
...THAT YOU WERE SO HELP-LESS.

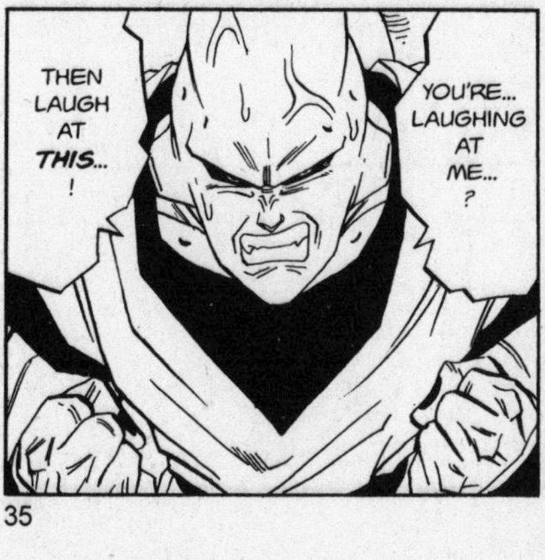
YOU'RE... LAUGHING AT ME... ?
THEN LAUGH AT ***THIS***... !

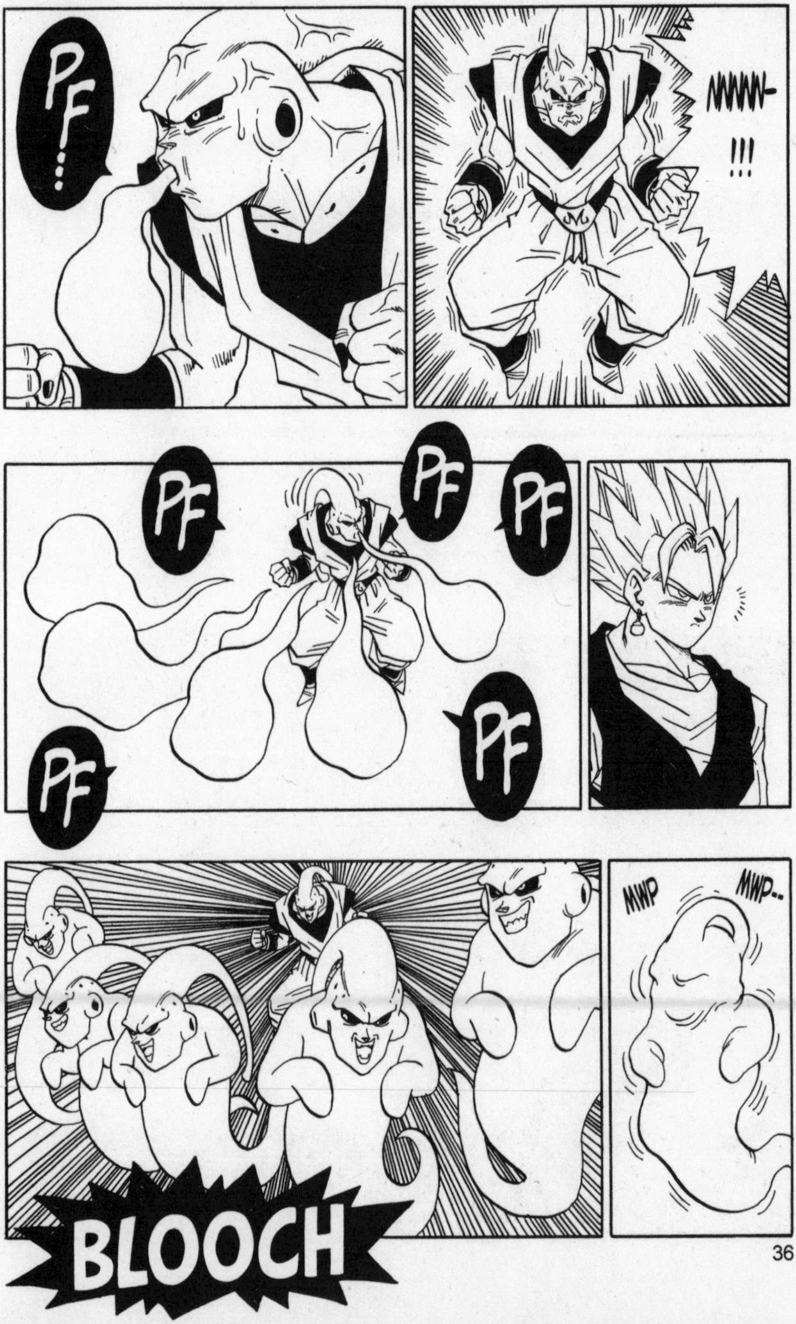
NNNNN-
!!!
PF...!
PF
PF
PF
PF
PF
MWP
MWP..
BLOOCH

READ THIS WAY

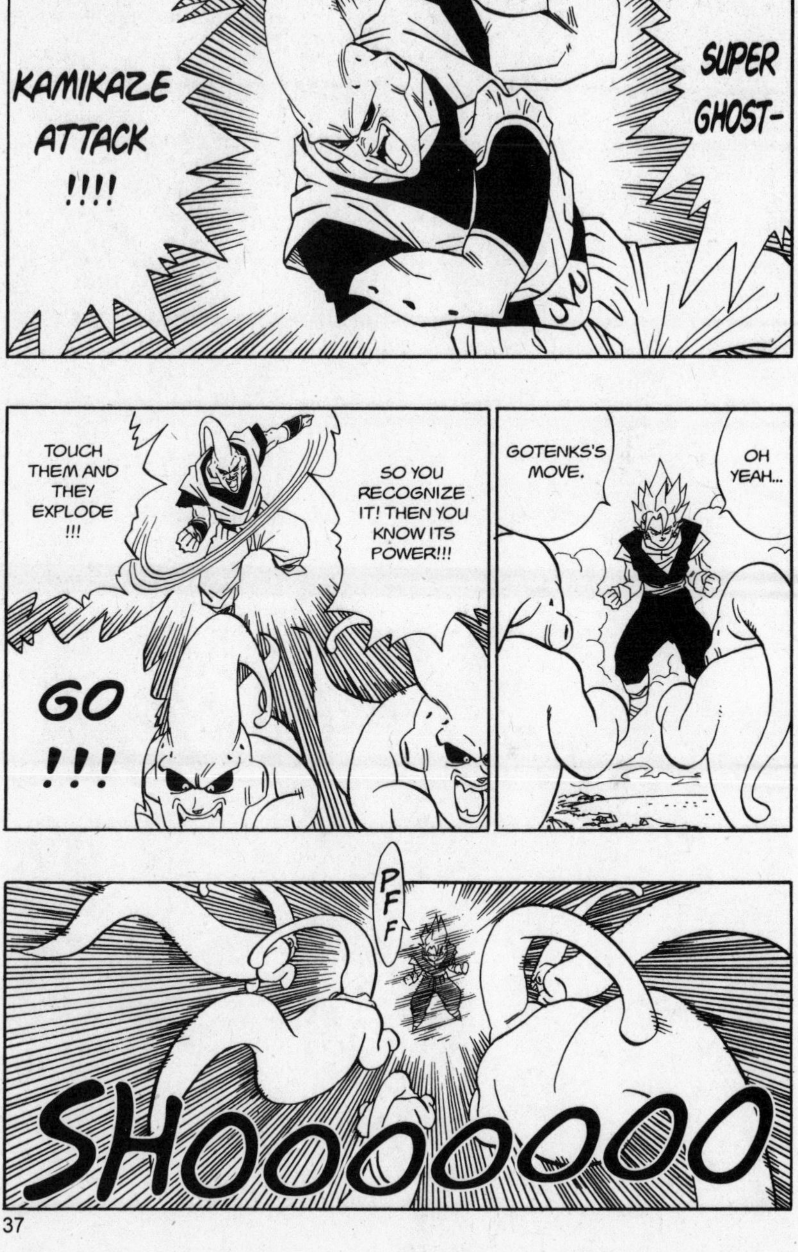
SUPER GHOST-
KAMIKAZE ATTACK !!!!
OH YEAH...
GOTENKS'S MOVE.
SO YOU RECOGNIZE IT! THEN YOU KNOW ITS POWER!!!
TOUCH THEM AND THEY EXPLODE !!!
GO !!!
PFF
SHOOOOOOO

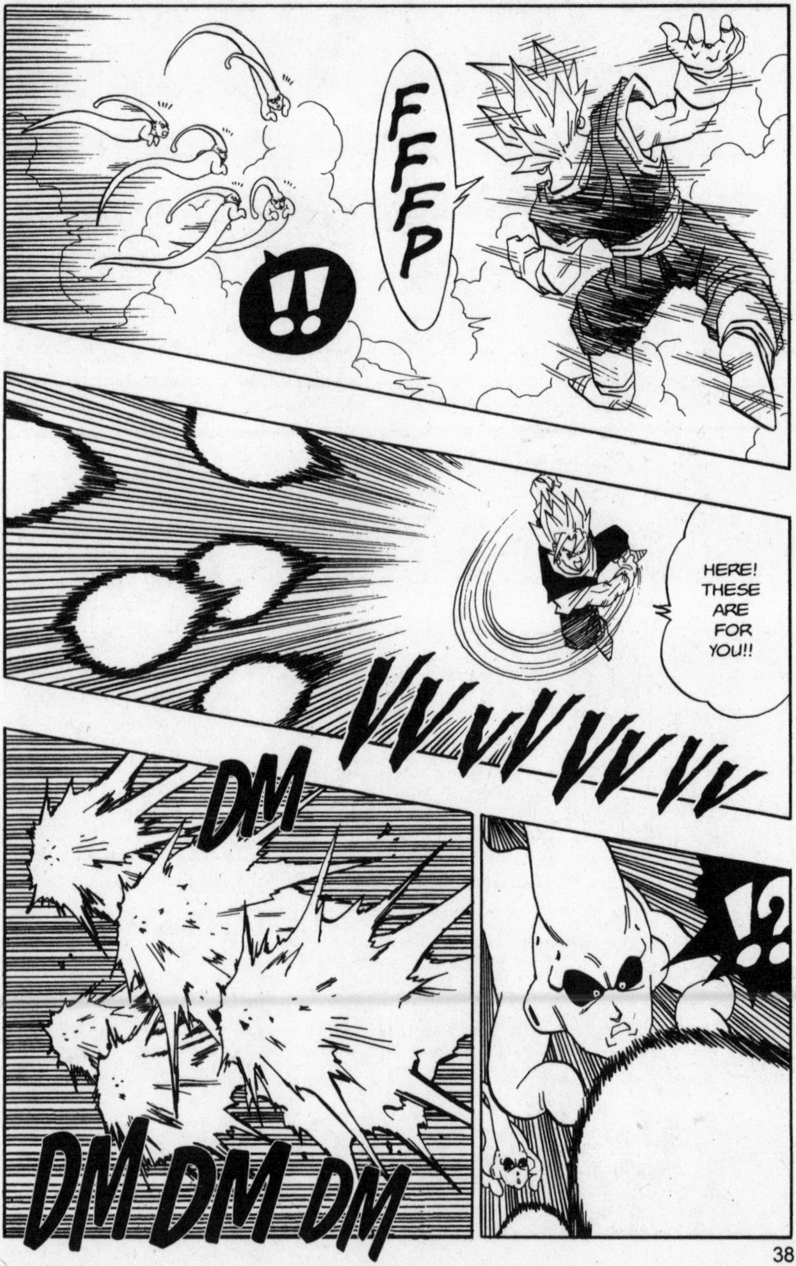

FFFP
!!
HERE! THESE ARE FOR YOU!!
VVVVVVVVVV
!?
DM
DM DM DM

READ THIS WAY

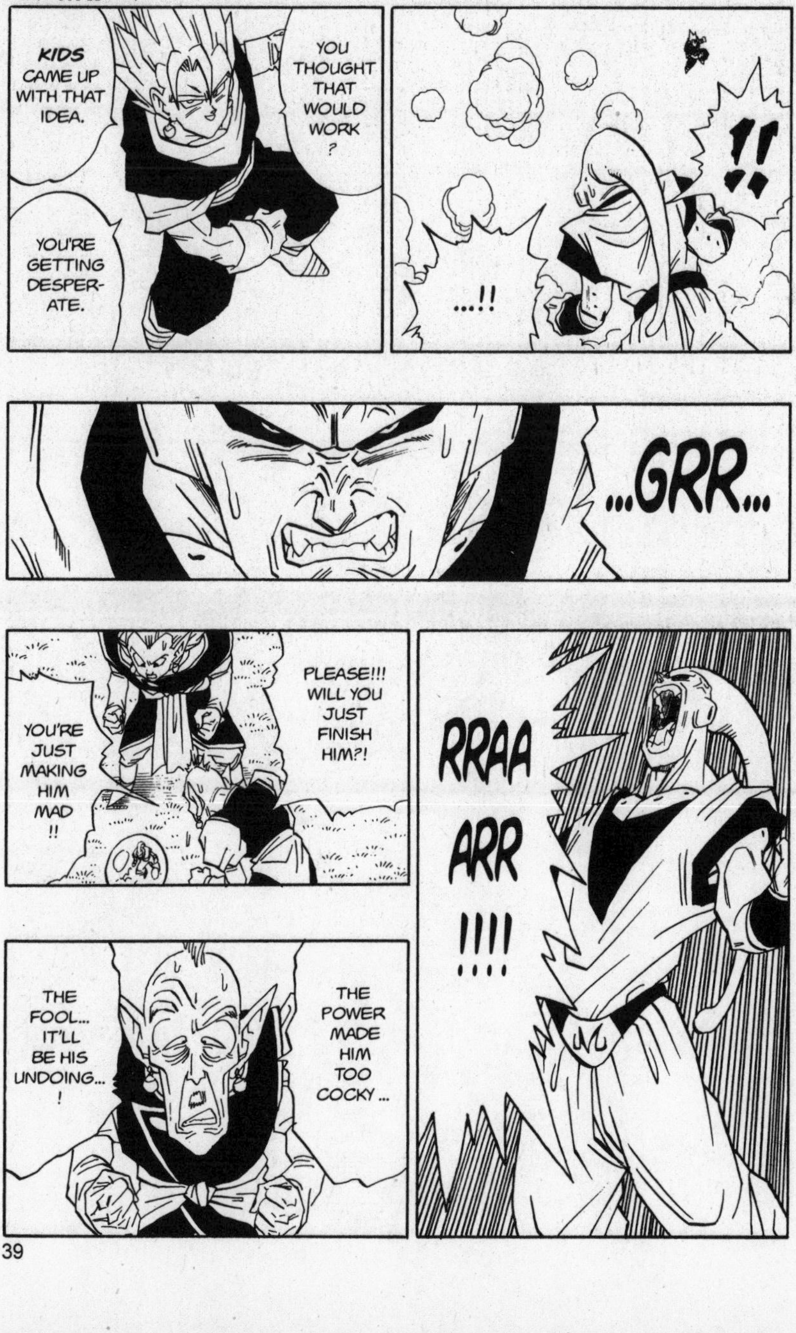

!!
...!!
YOU THOUGHT THAT WOULD WORK?
KIDS CAME UP WITH THAT IDEA.
YOU'RE GETTING DESPERATE.
...GRR...
RRAAARR!!!!
PLEASE!!! WILL YOU JUST FINISH HIM?!
YOU'RE JUST MAKING HIM MAD!!
THE POWER MADE HIM TOO COCKY...
THE FOOL... IT'LL BE HIS UNDOING...!

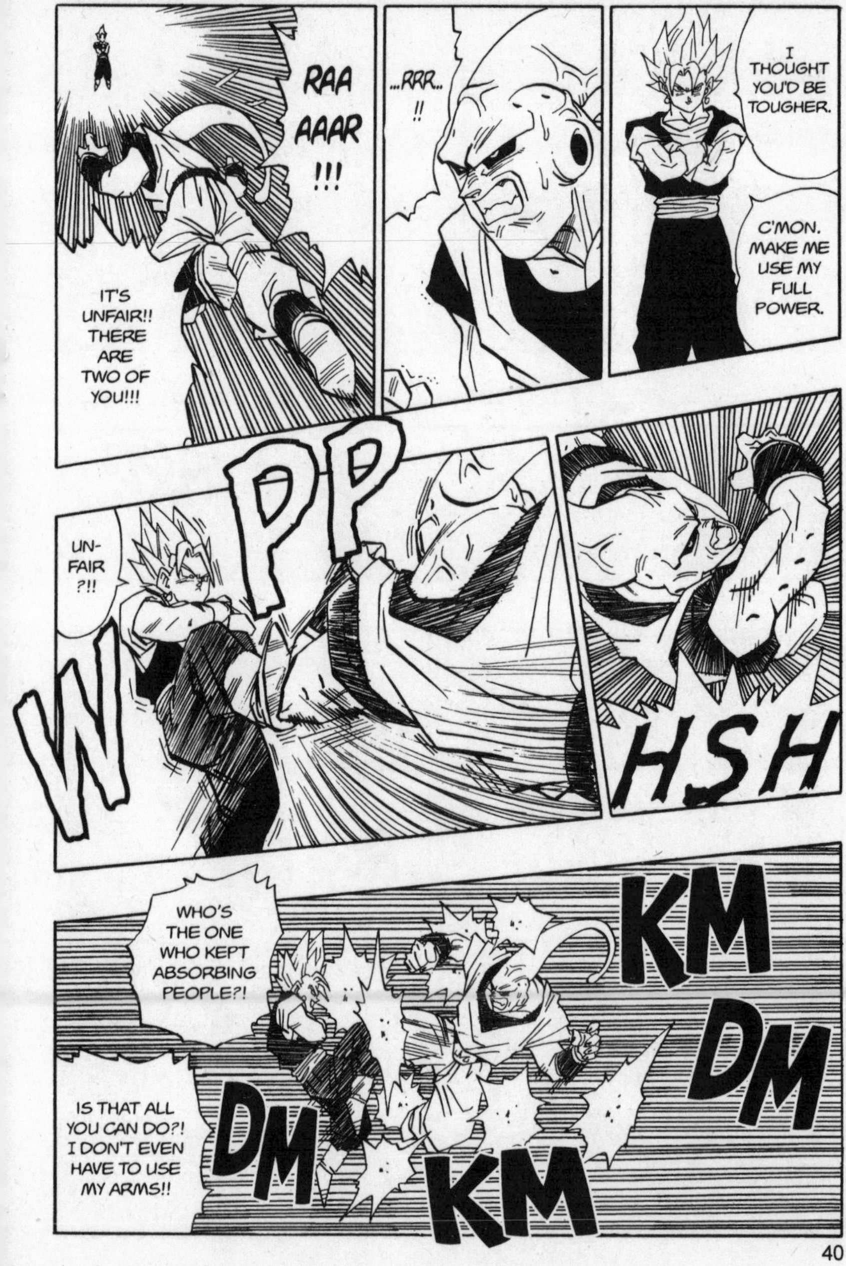
I THOUGHT YOU'D BE TOUGHER.
C'MON. MAKE ME USE MY FULL POWER.
...RRR... !!
RAA AAAR !!!
IT'S UNFAIR!! THERE ARE TWO OF YOU!!!
HSH
PP
UN-FAIR ?!!
W
KM
DM
WHO'S THE ONE WHO KEPT ABSORBING PEOPLE?!
KM
DM
IS THAT ALL YOU CAN DO?! I DON'T EVEN HAVE TO USE MY ARMS!!

READ THIS WAY

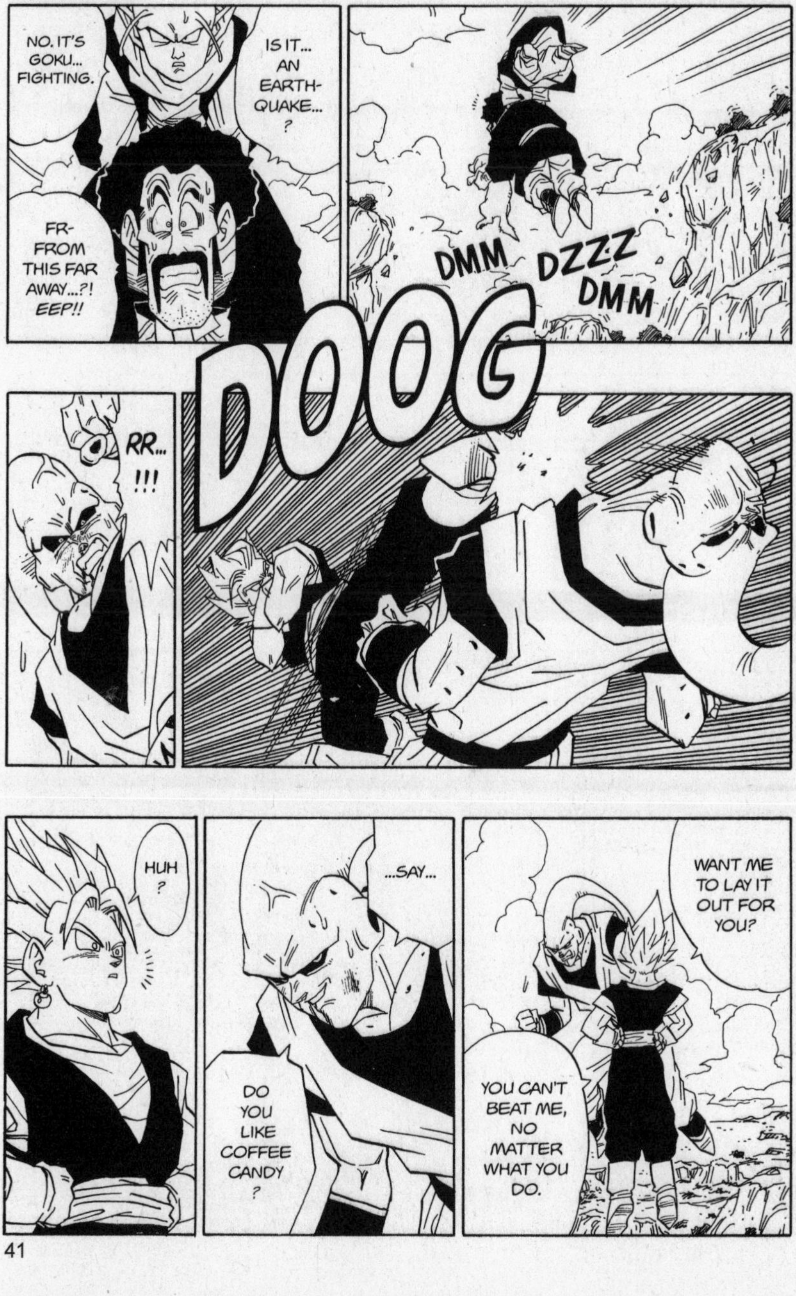

DMM DZZZ DMM
IS IT... AN EARTH-QUAKE...?
NO. IT'S GOKU... FIGHTING.
FR- FROM THIS FAR AWAY...?! EEP!!
DOOG
RR... !!!
WANT ME TO LAY IT OUT FOR YOU?
YOU CAN'T BEAT ME, NO MATTER WHAT YOU DO.
...SAY...
DO YOU LIKE COFFEE CANDY?
HUH?

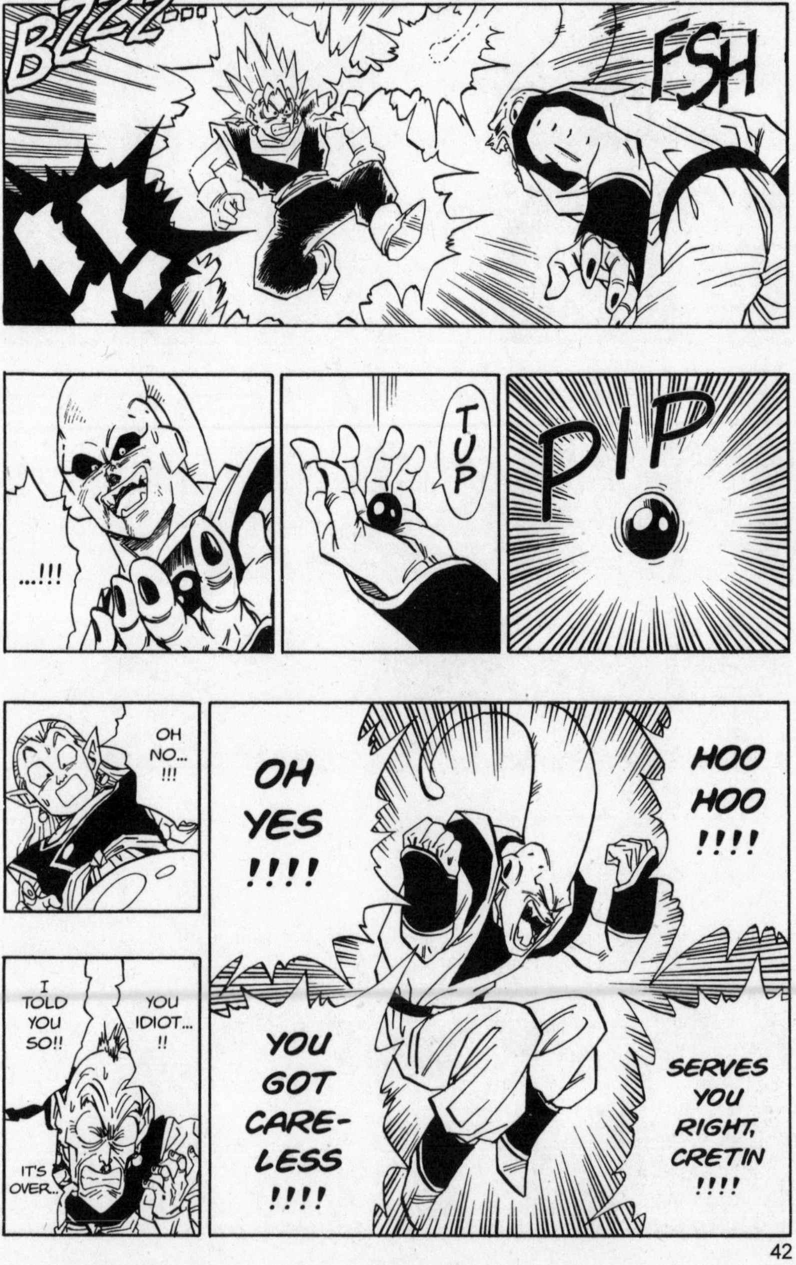
FSH
BZZZ...
PIP
TUP
...!!!
HOO HOO !!!!
OH YES !!!!
SERVES YOU RIGHT, CRETIN !!!!
YOU GOT CARE-LESS !!!!
OH NO... !!!
YOU IDIOT... !!
I TOLD YOU SO!!
IT'S OVER...

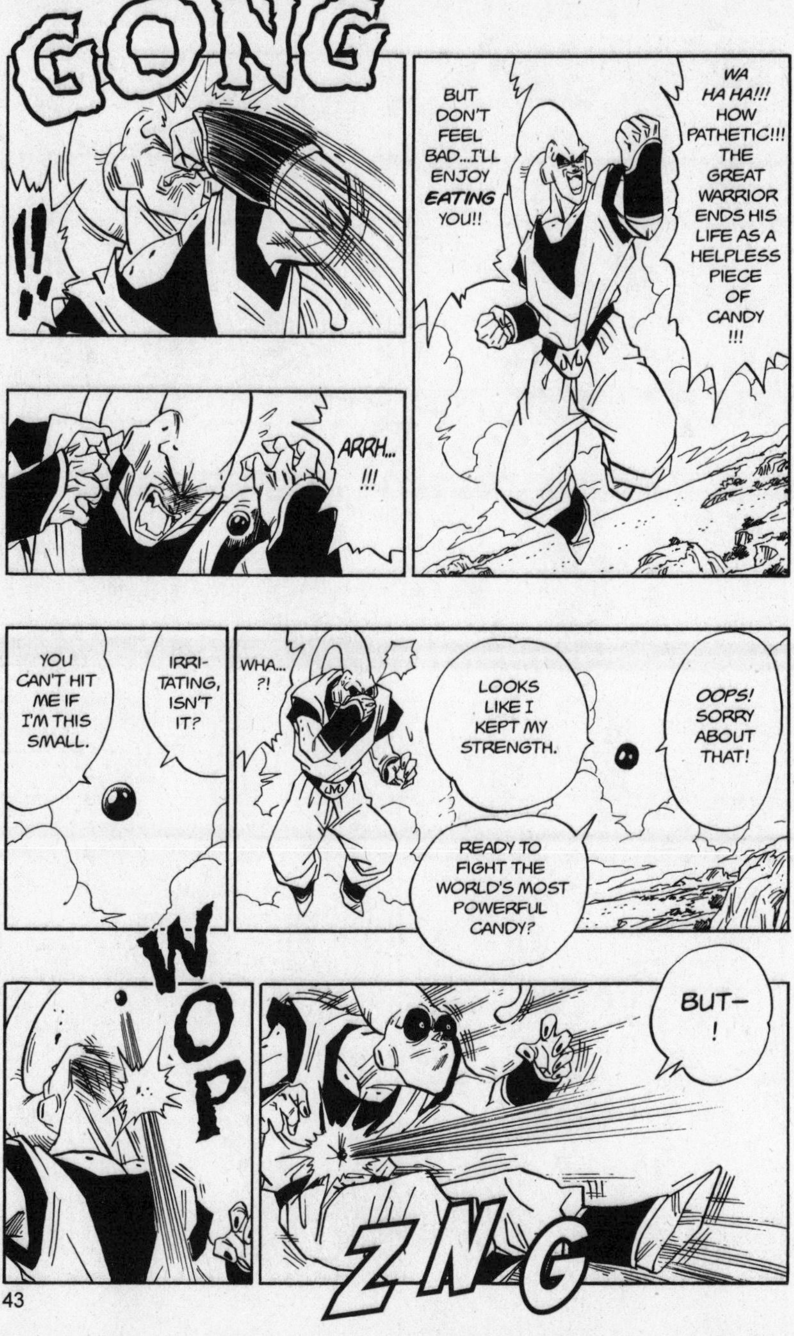
WA HA HA!!! HOW PATHETIC!!! THE GREAT WARRIOR ENDS HIS LIFE AS A HELPLESS PIECE OF CANDY !!!
BUT DON'T FEEL BAD...I'LL ENJOY **EATING** YOU!!
GONG
!!
ARRH... !!!
OOPS! SORRY ABOUT THAT!
LOOKS LIKE I KEPT MY STRENGTH.
WHA... ?!
READY TO FIGHT THE WORLD'S MOST POWERFUL CANDY?
IRRI-TATING, ISN'T IT?
YOU CAN'T HIT ME IF I'M THIS SMALL.
BUT— !
ZNG
WOP

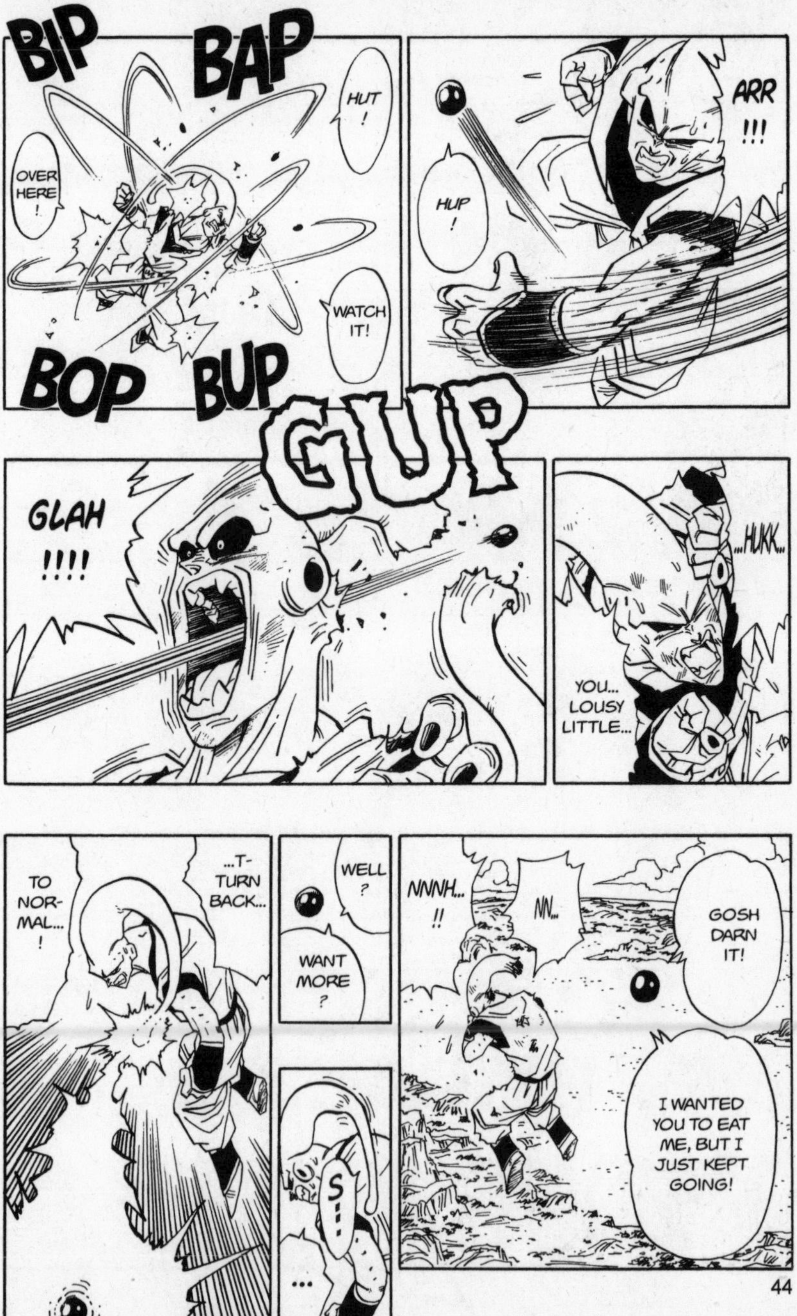
ARR!!!
HUP!
BIP
BAP
HUT!
OVER HERE!
WATCH IT!
BOP
BUP
...HUKK...
YOU... LOUSY LITTLE...
GUP
GLAH!!!!
GOSH DARN IT!
NN...
NNNH...!!
I WANTED YOU TO EAT ME, BUT I JUST KEPT GOING!
WELL?
WANT MORE?
S...!
...
...T-TURN BACK...
TO NOR-MAL...!

READ THIS WAY

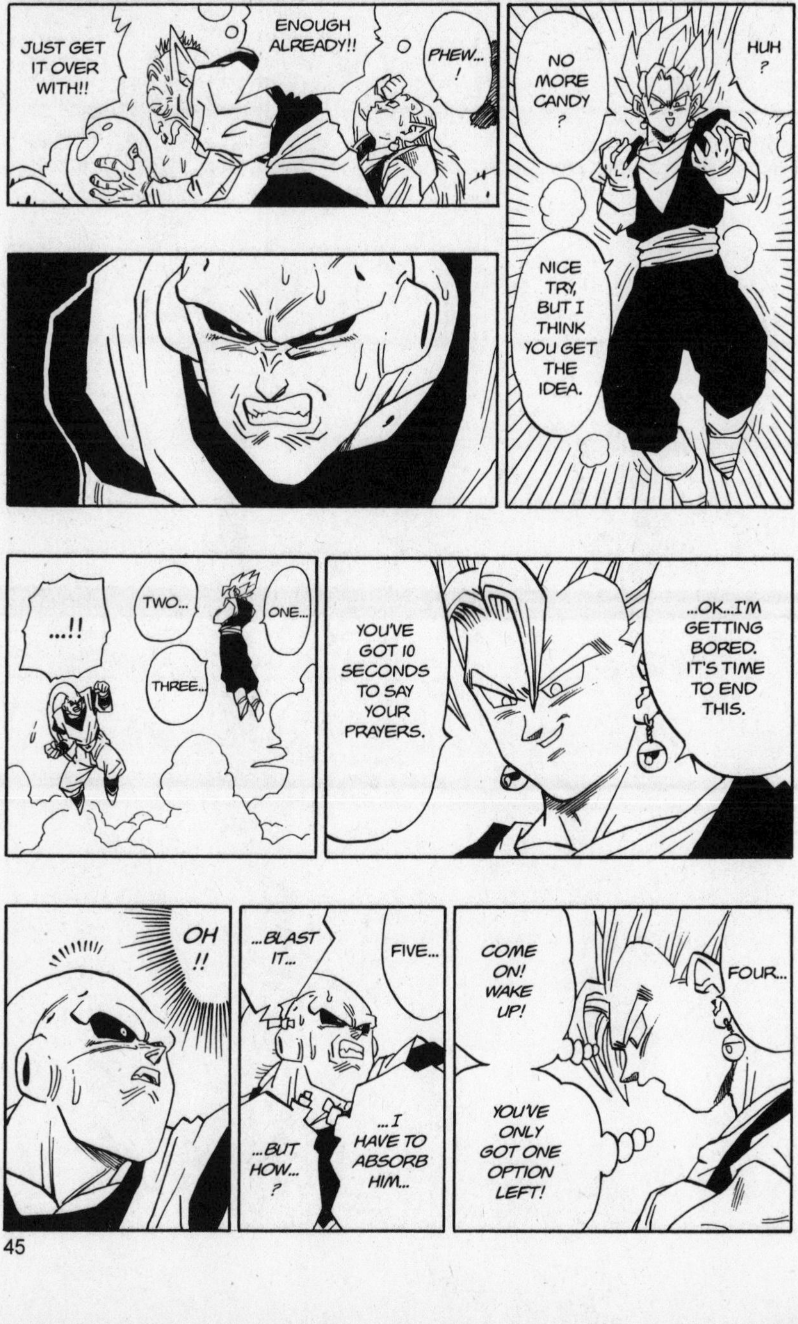
HUH ?
NO MORE CANDY ?
NICE TRY, BUT I THINK YOU GET THE IDEA.
PHEW...!
ENOUGH ALREADY!!
JUST GET IT OVER WITH!!
...OK...I'M GETTING BORED. IT'S TIME TO END THIS.
YOU'VE GOT 10 SECONDS TO SAY YOUR PRAYERS.
ONE...
TWO...
THREE...
...!!
FOUR...
COME ON! WAKE UP!
YOU'VE ONLY GOT ONE OPTION LEFT!
FIVE...
...BLAST IT...
...I HAVE TO ABSORB HIM...
...BUT HOW...?
OH !!

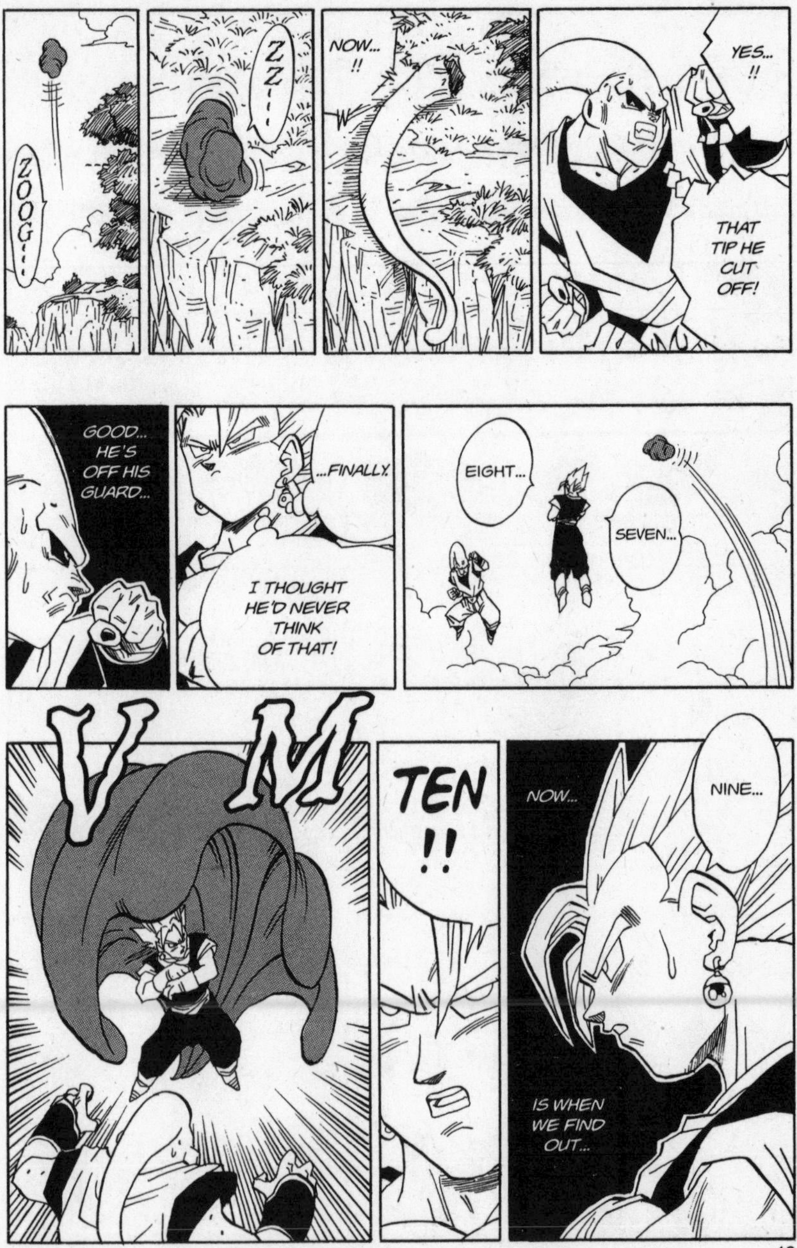
YES... !!
THAT TIP HE CUT OFF!
NOW... !!
ZZ...
ZOOG...
SEVEN...
EIGHT...
...FINALLY.
I THOUGHT HE'D NEVER THINK OF THAT!
GOOD... HE'S OFF HIS GUARD...
NINE...
NOW...
IS WHEN WE FIND OUT...
TEN !!
V M

READ THIS WAY

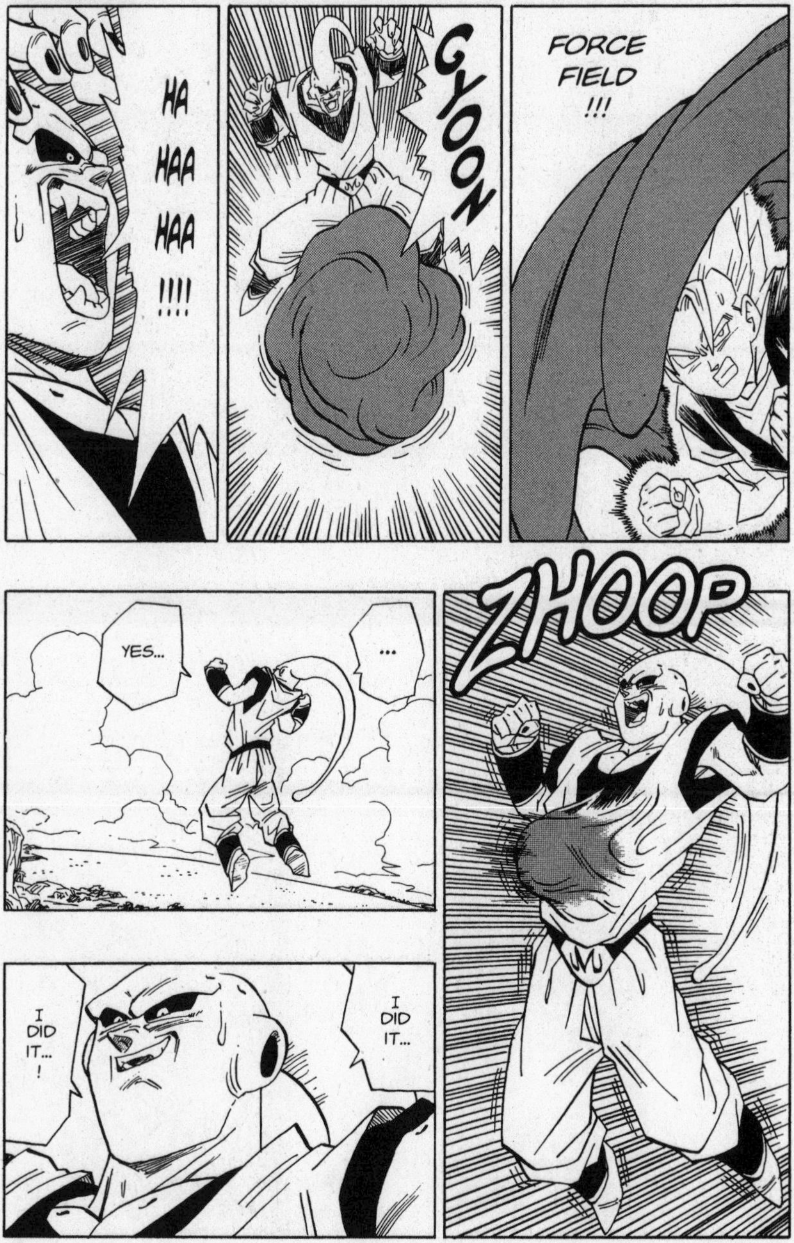
FORCE FIELD !!!
GYOON
HA HAA HAA !!!!
ZHOOP
...
YES...
I DID IT...
I DID IT... !

DBZ:312 • Two Inside Boo

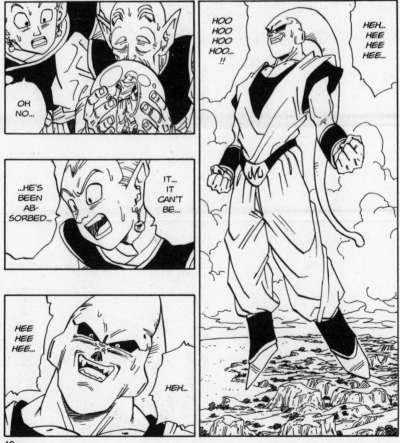

HEH... HEE HEE HEE...
HOO HOO HOO HOO... !!
OH NO...
IT... IT CAN'T BE...
...HE'S BEEN AB-SORBED...
HEE HEE HEE...
HEH...

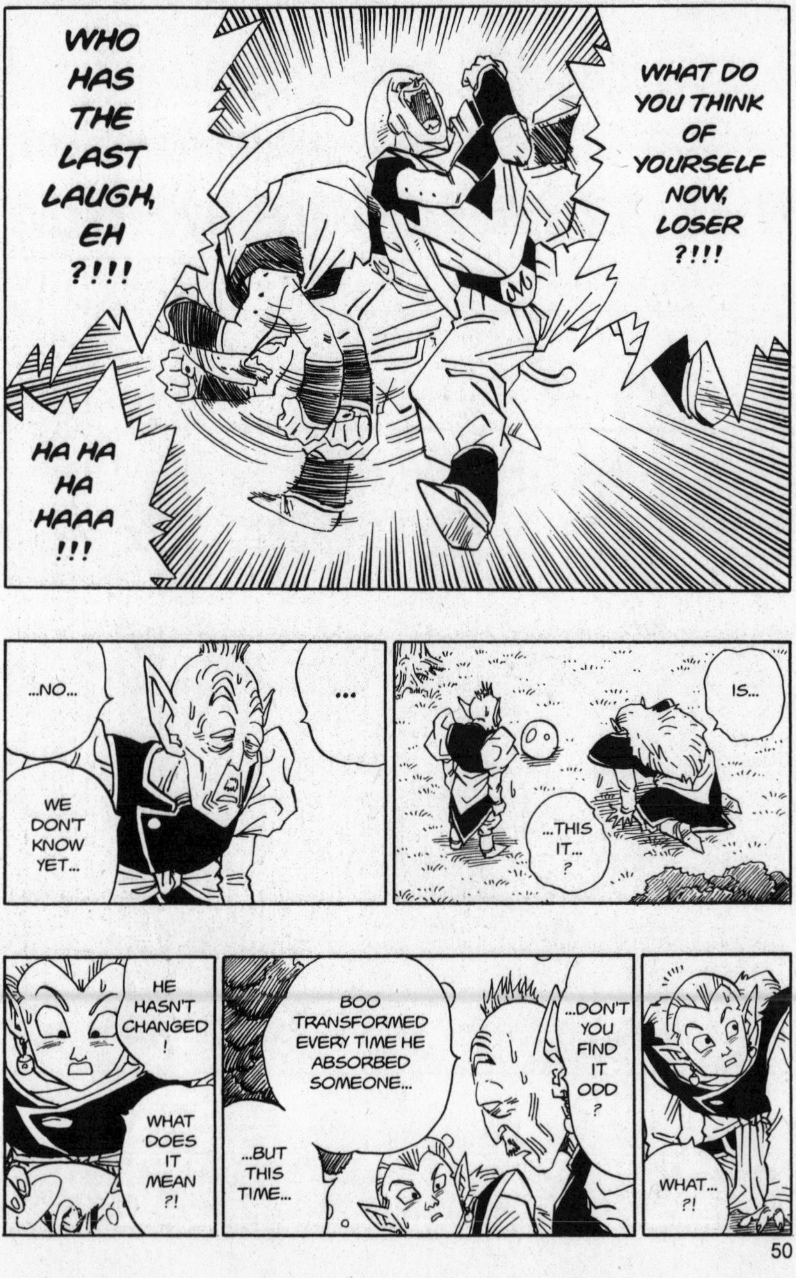
WHAT DO YOU THINK OF YOURSELF NOW, LOSER ?!!!
WHO HAS THE LAST LAUGH, EH ?!!!
HA HA HA HAAA !!!
IS...
...THIS IT... ?
...
...NO...
WE DON'T KNOW YET...
WHAT... ?!
...DON'T YOU FIND IT ODD ?
BOO TRANSFORMED EVERY TIME HE ABSORBED SOMEONE...
...BUT THIS TIME...
HE HASN'T CHANGED !
WHAT DOES IT MEAN ?!

READ THIS WAY

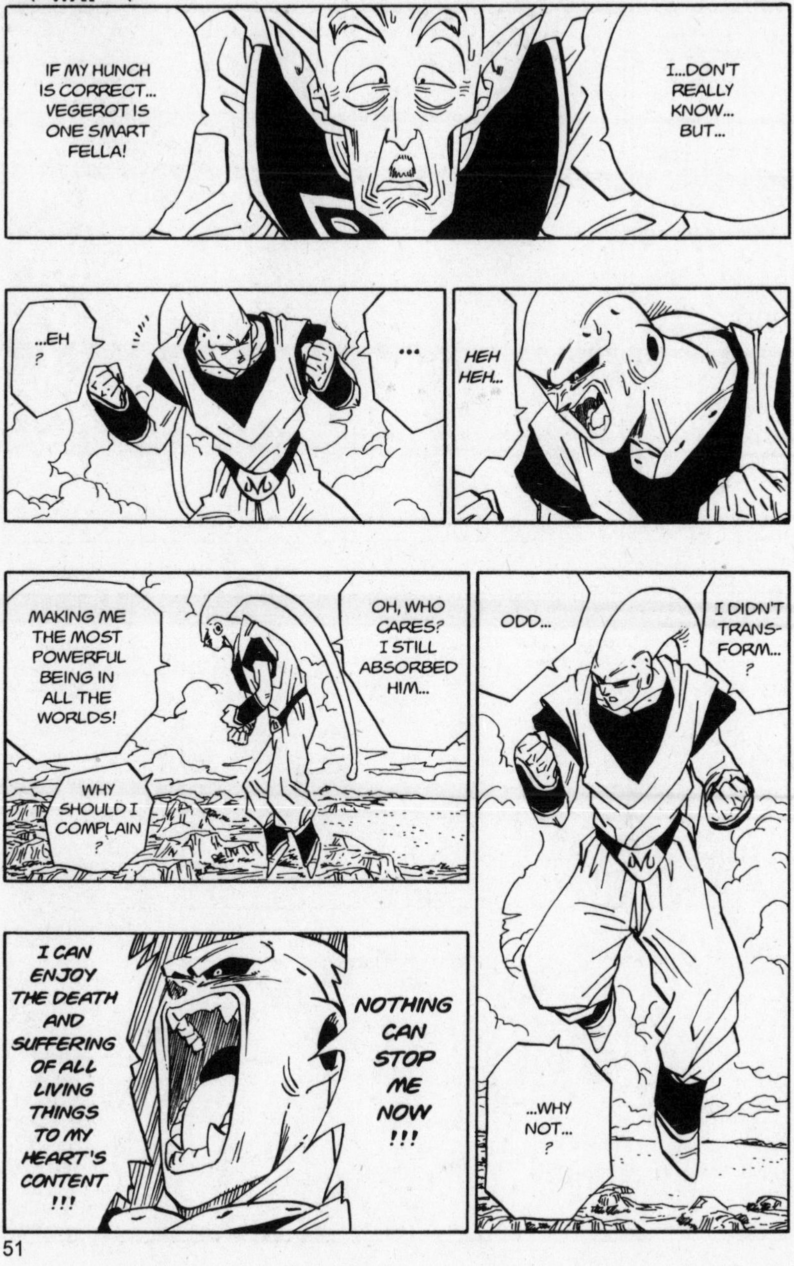

I...DON'T REALLY KNOW... BUT...
IF MY HUNCH IS CORRECT... VEGEROT IS ONE SMART FELLA!
HEH HEH...
...
...EH ?
I DIDN'T TRANS-FORM... ?
ODD...
...WHY NOT... ?
OH, WHO CARES? I STILL ABSORBED HIM...
MAKING ME THE MOST POWERFUL BEING IN ALL THE WORLDS!
WHY SHOULD I COMPLAIN ?
NOTHING CAN STOP ME NOW !!!
I CAN ENJOY THE DEATH AND SUFFERING OF ALL LIVING THINGS TO MY HEART'S CONTENT !!!

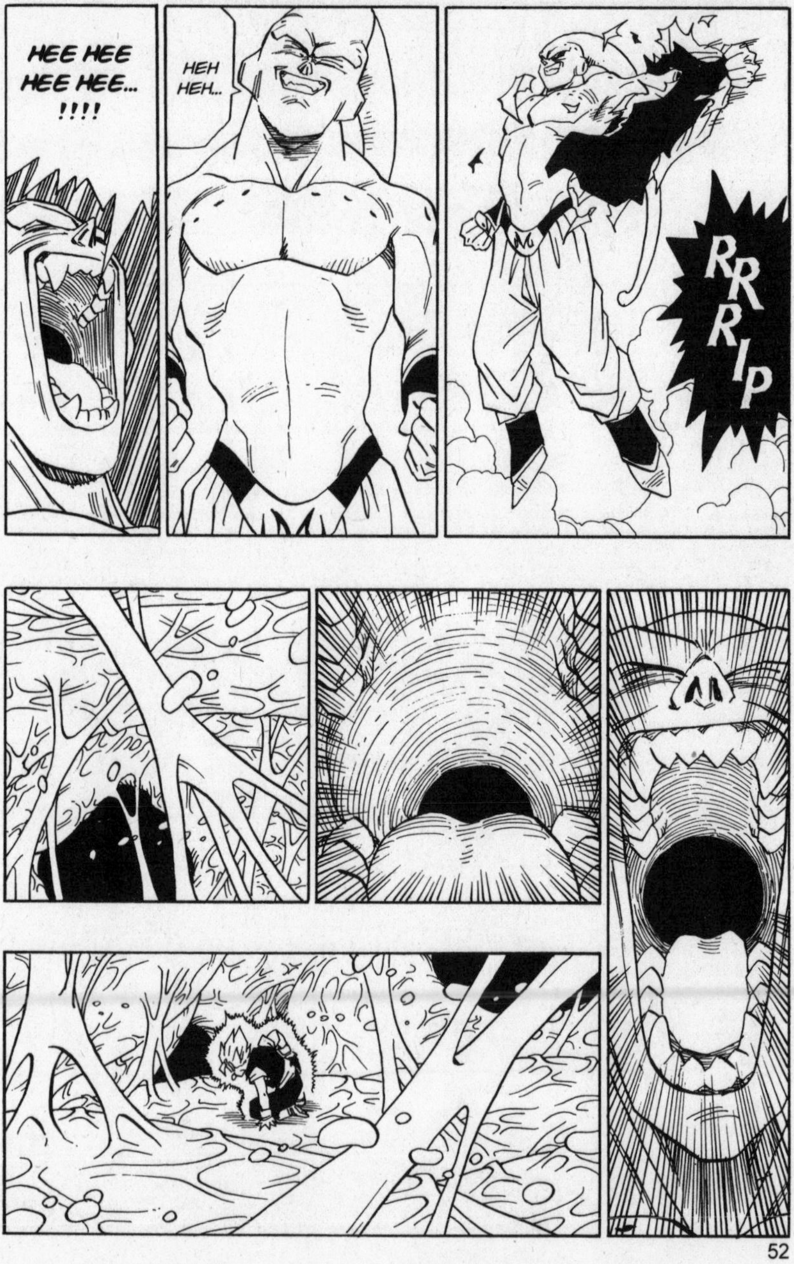
RRRIP
HEH HEH...
HEE HEE HEE HEE...
!!!!

READ THIS WAY

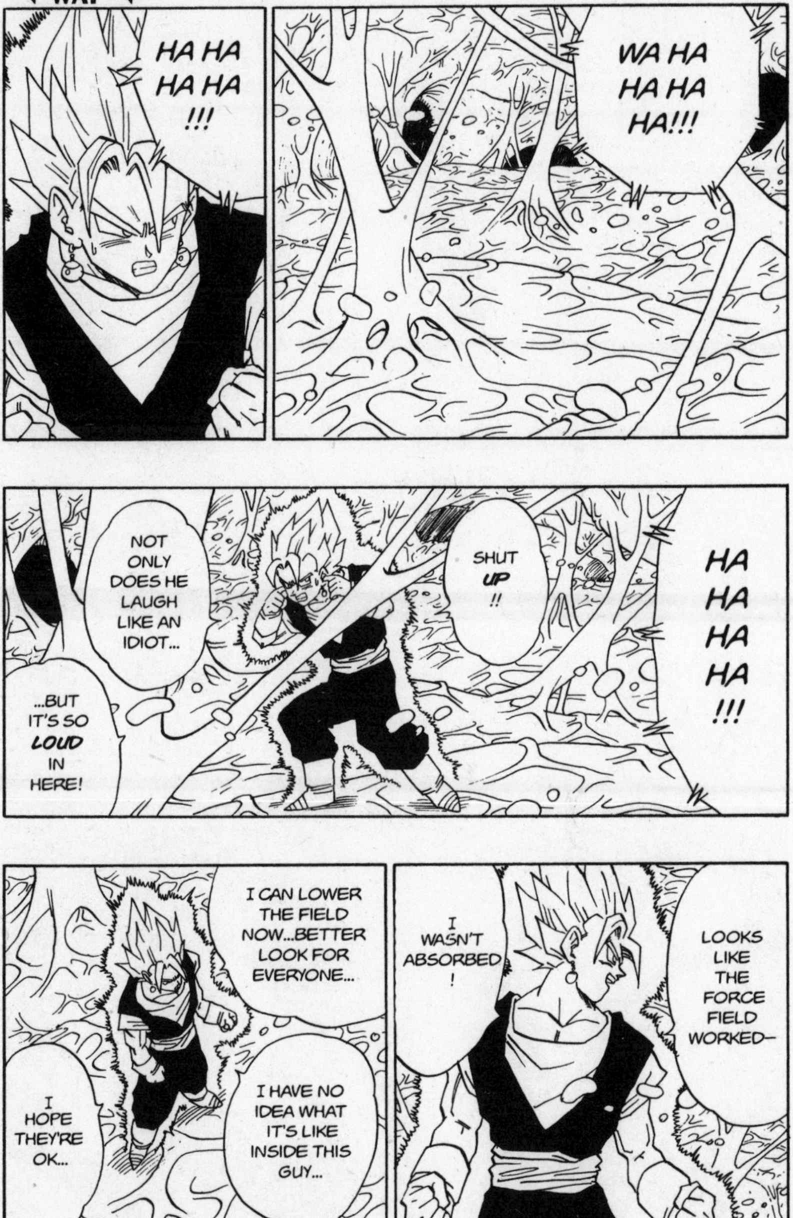
WA HA HA HA HA!!!
HA HA HA HA !!!
HA HA HA HA !!!
SHUT UP !!
NOT ONLY DOES HE LAUGH LIKE AN IDIOT...
...BUT IT'S SO LOUD IN HERE!
LOOKS LIKE THE FORCE FIELD WORKED—
I WASN'T ABSORBED !
I CAN LOWER THE FIELD NOW...BETTER LOOK FOR EVERYONE...
I HAVE NO IDEA WHAT IT'S LIKE INSIDE THIS GUY...
I HOPE THEY'RE OK...

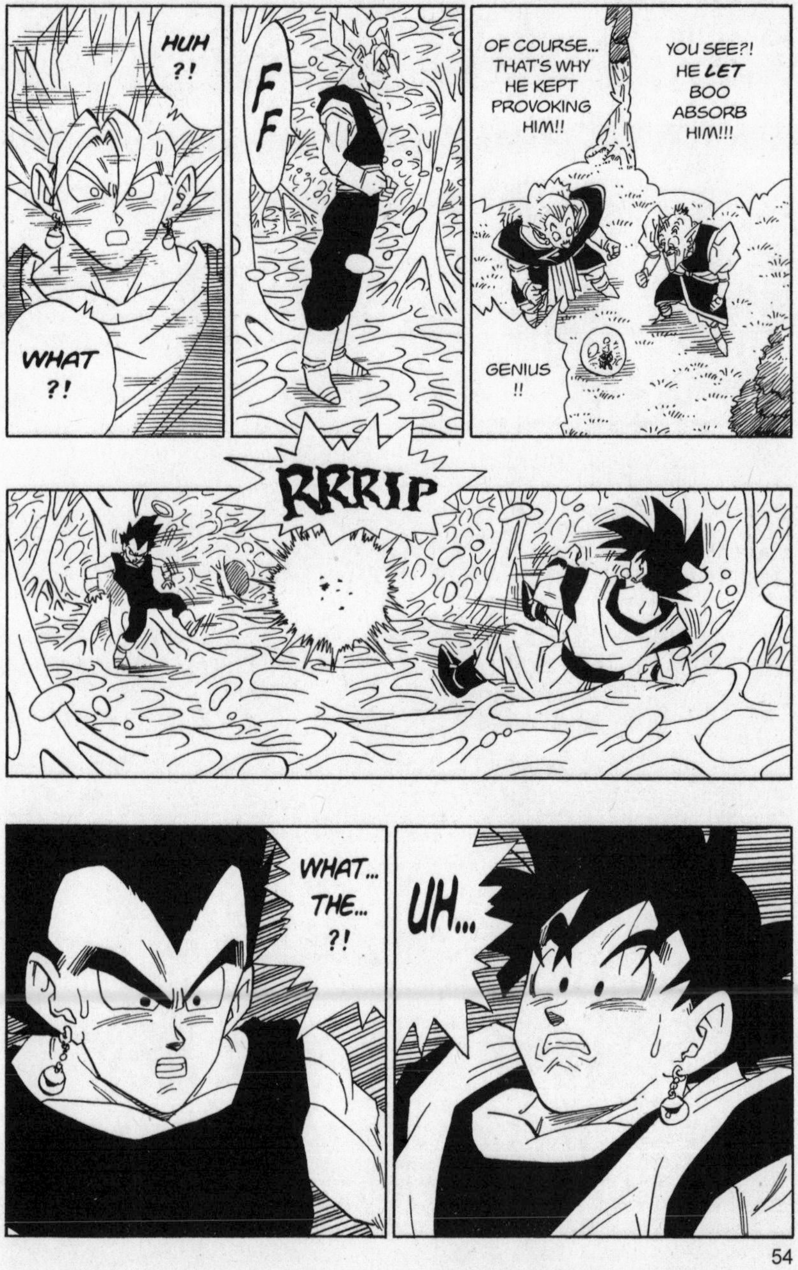
YOU SEE?! HE LET BOO ABSORB HIM!!!
OF COURSE... THAT'S WHY HE KEPT PROVOKING HIM!!
GENIUS !!
FF
HUH ?!
WHAT ?!
RRRIP
UH...
WHAT... THE... ?!

READ THIS WAY

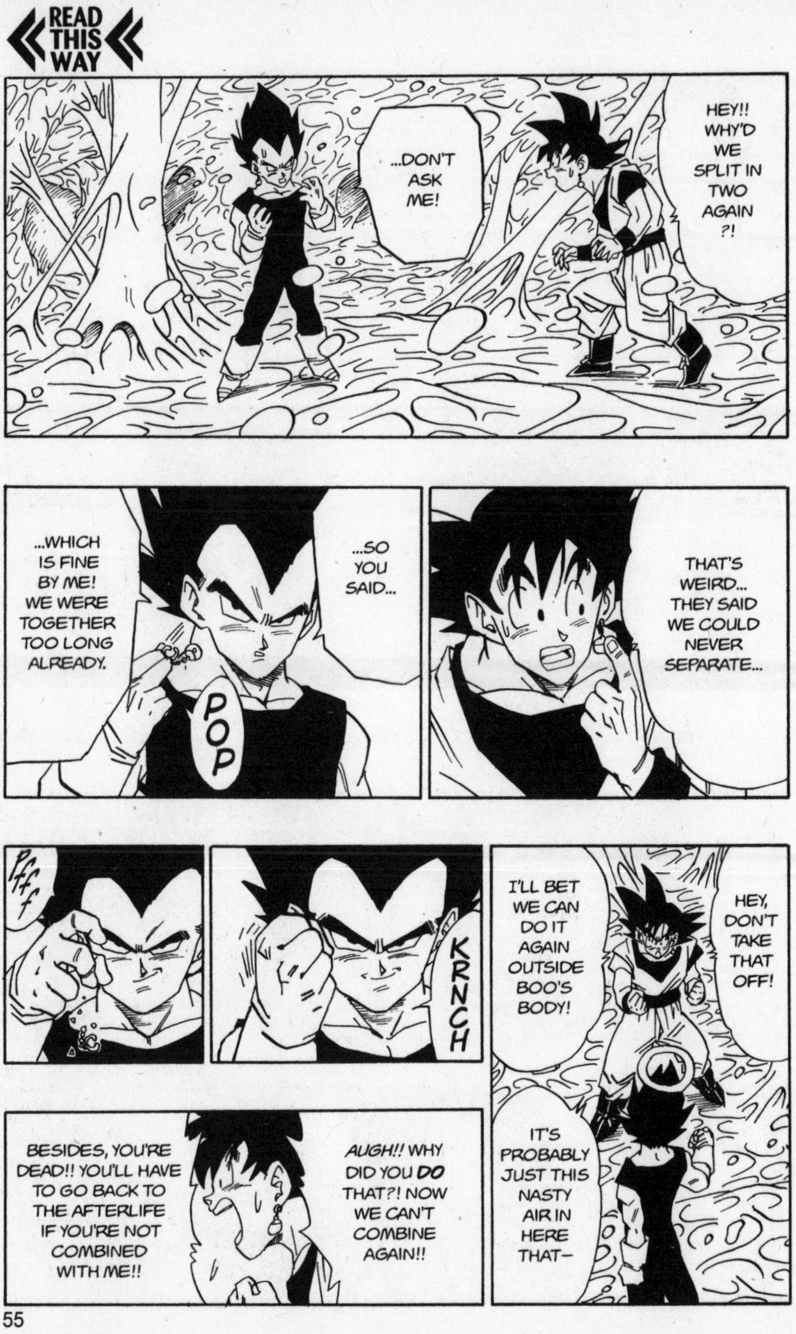
HEY!! WHY'D WE SPLIT IN TWO AGAIN ?!
...DON'T ASK ME!
THAT'S WEIRD... THEY SAID WE COULD NEVER SEPARATE...
...SO YOU SAID...
...WHICH IS FINE BY ME! WE WERE TOGETHER TOO LONG ALREADY.
POP
HEY, DON'T TAKE THAT OFF!
I'LL BET WE CAN DO IT AGAIN OUTSIDE BOO'S BODY!
IT'S PROBABLY JUST THIS NASTY AIR IN HERE THAT—
KRNCH
Pfff
AUGH!! WHY DID YOU DO THAT?! NOW WE CAN'T COMBINE AGAIN!!
BESIDES, YOU'RE DEAD!! YOU'LL HAVE TO GO BACK TO THE AFTERLIFE IF YOU'RE NOT COMBINED WITH ME!!

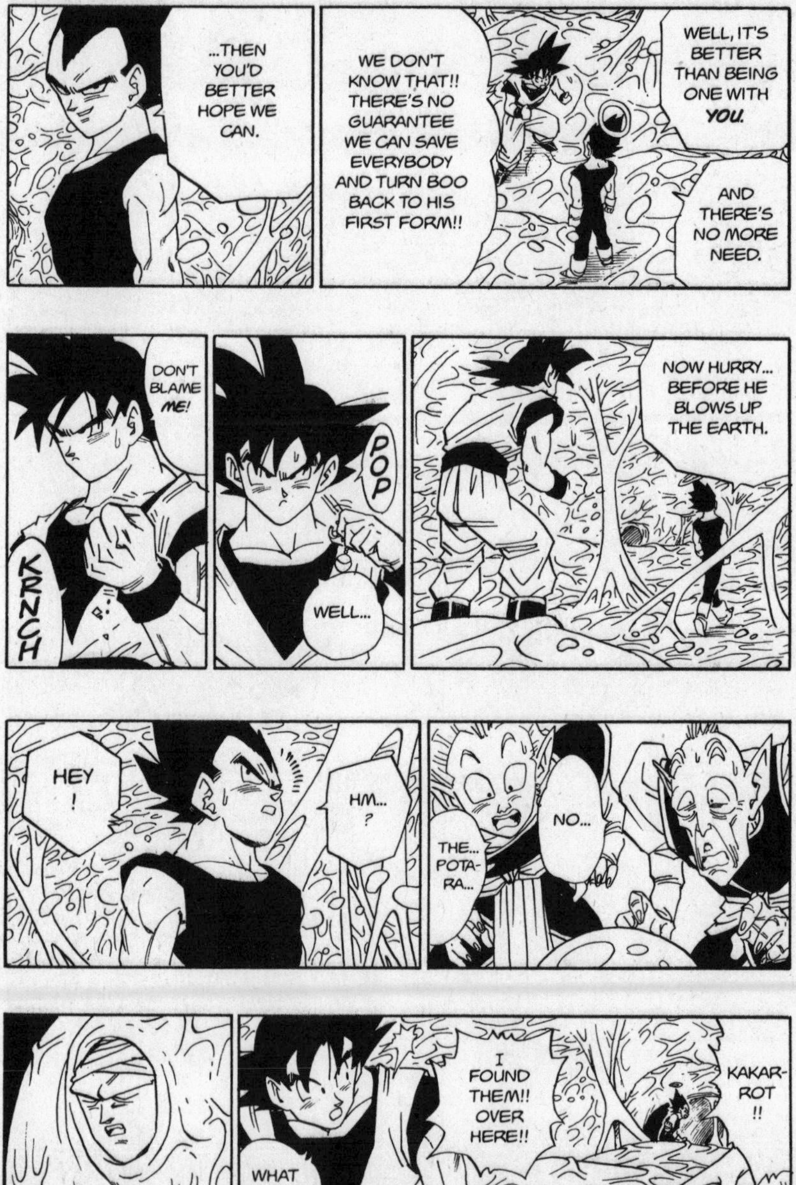
WELL, IT'S BETTER THAN BEING ONE WITH *YOU.*
AND THERE'S NO MORE NEED.
WE DON'T KNOW THAT!! THERE'S NO GUARANTEE WE CAN SAVE EVERYBODY AND TURN BOO BACK TO HIS FIRST FORM!!
...THEN YOU'D BETTER HOPE WE CAN.
NOW HURRY... BEFORE HE BLOWS UP THE EARTH.
POP
WELL...
DON'T BLAME *ME!*
KRNCH
NO...
THE... POTA-RA...
HM... ?
HEY !
KAKAR-ROT !!
I FOUND THEM!! OVER HERE!!
WHAT ?!

READ THIS WAY

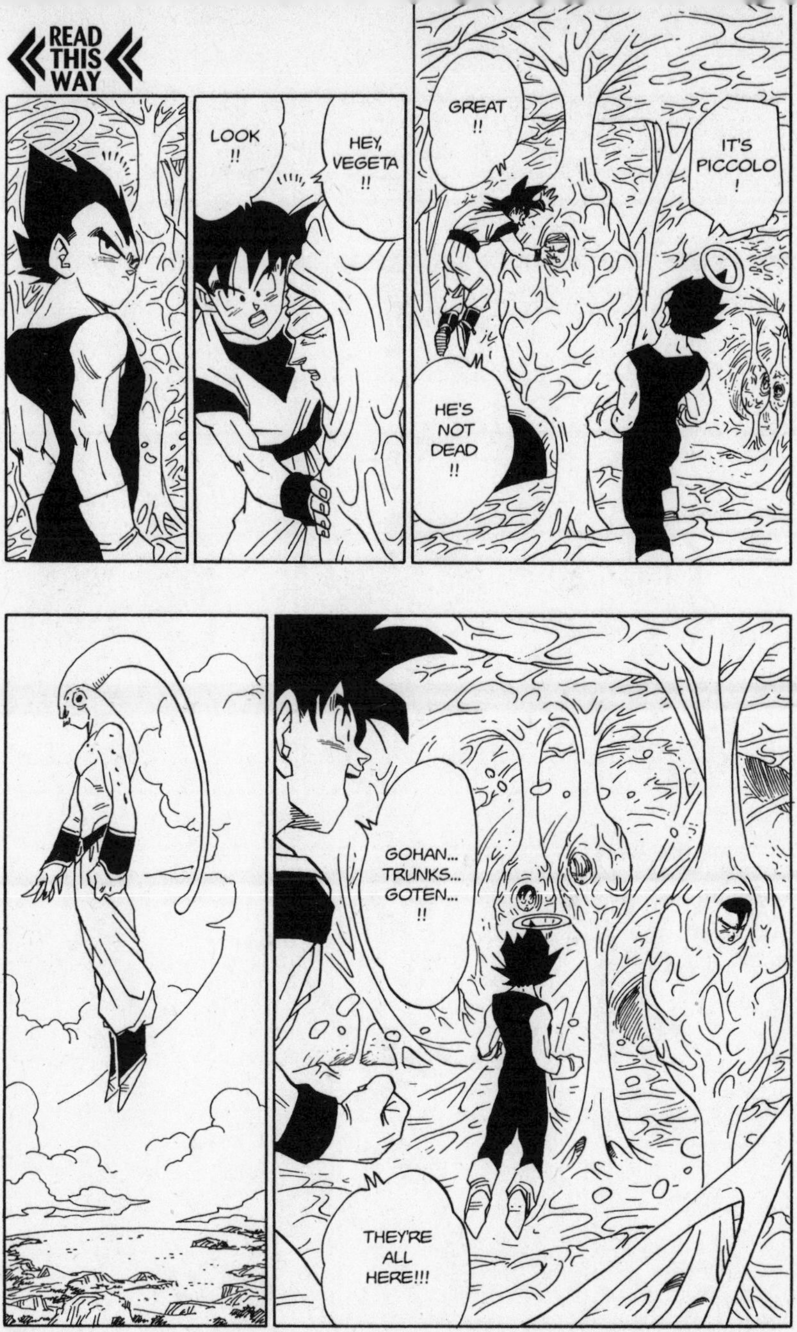
IT'S PICCOLO!
GREAT!!
HE'S NOT DEAD!!
HEY, VEGETA!!
LOOK!!
GOHAN... TRUNKS... GOTEN...!!
THEY'RE ALL HERE!!!

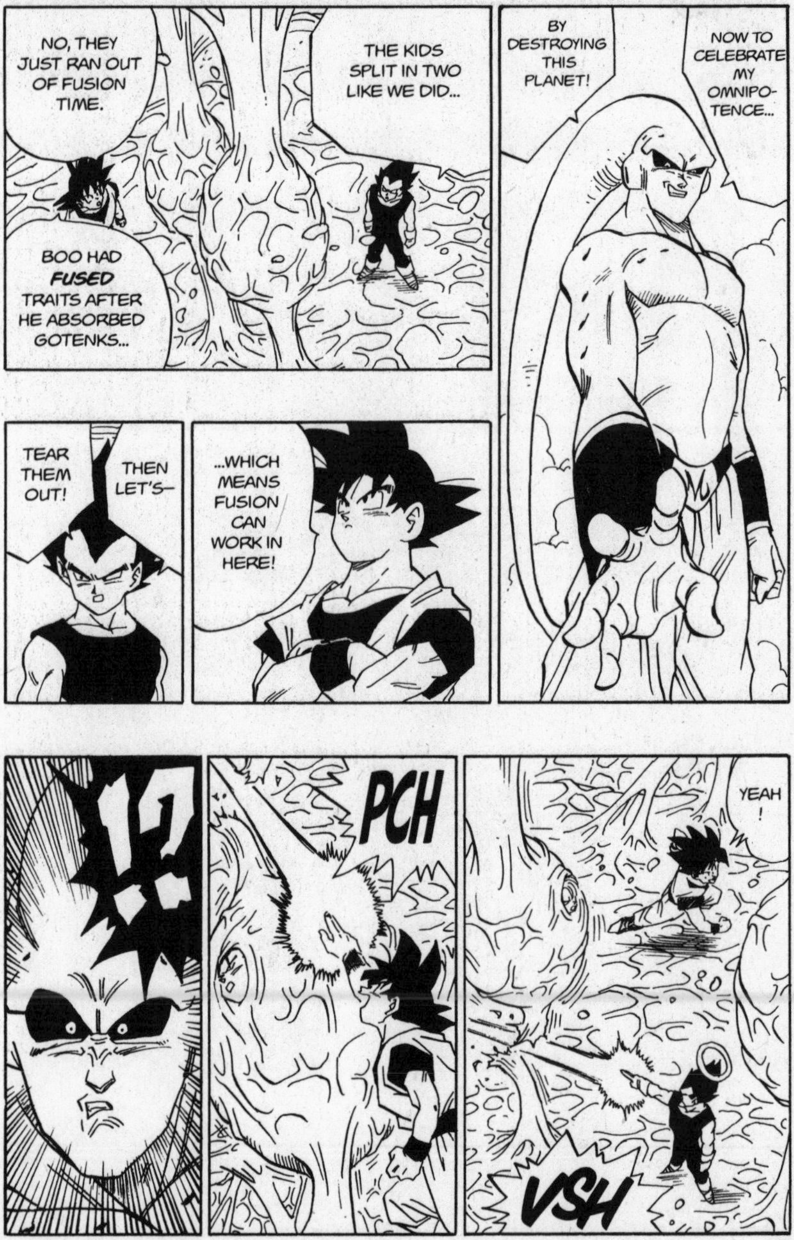
NOW TO CELEBRATE MY OMNIPOTENCE...
BY DESTROYING THIS PLANET!
THE KIDS SPLIT IN TWO LIKE WE DID...
NO, THEY JUST RAN OUT OF FUSION TIME.
BOO HAD FUSED TRAITS AFTER HE ABSORBED GOTENKS...
...WHICH MEANS FUSION CAN WORK IN HERE!
THEN LET'S—
TEAR THEM OUT!
YEAH!
VSH
PCH
!?

READ THIS WAY

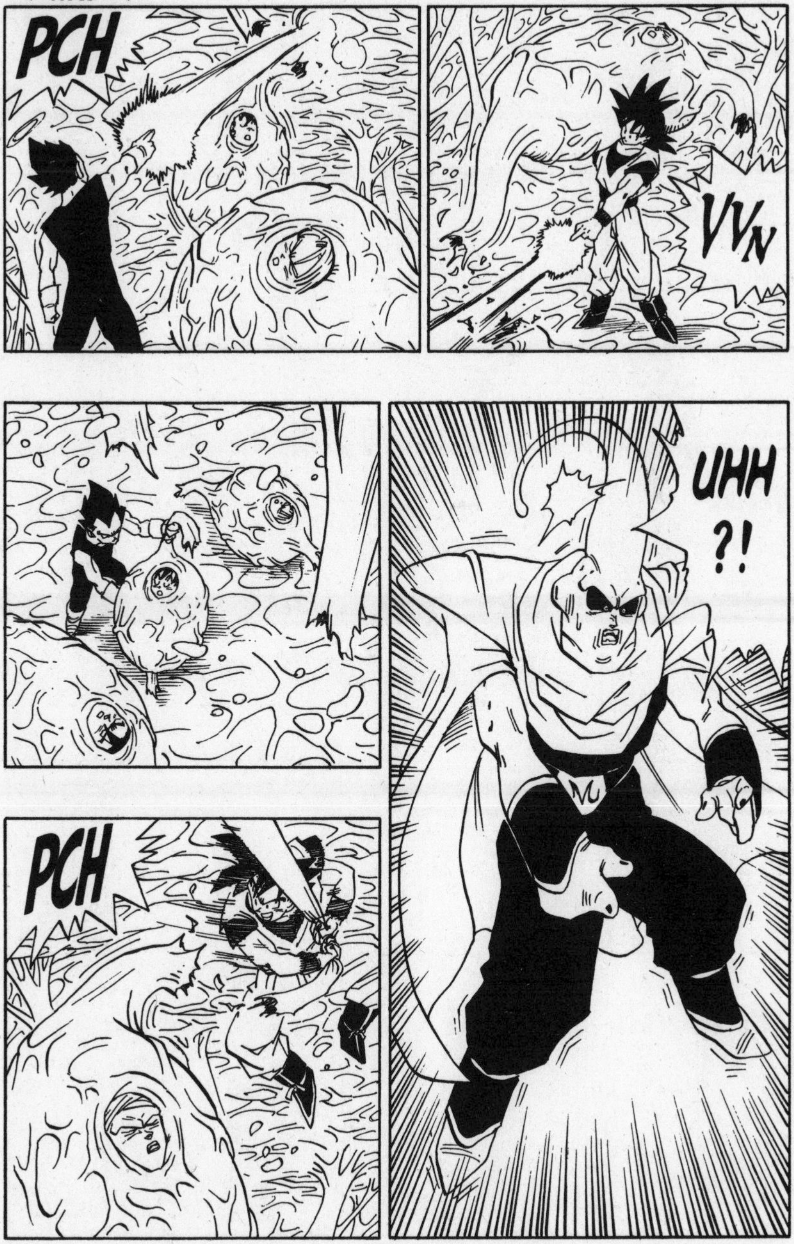
VVN
PCH
UHH ?!
PCH

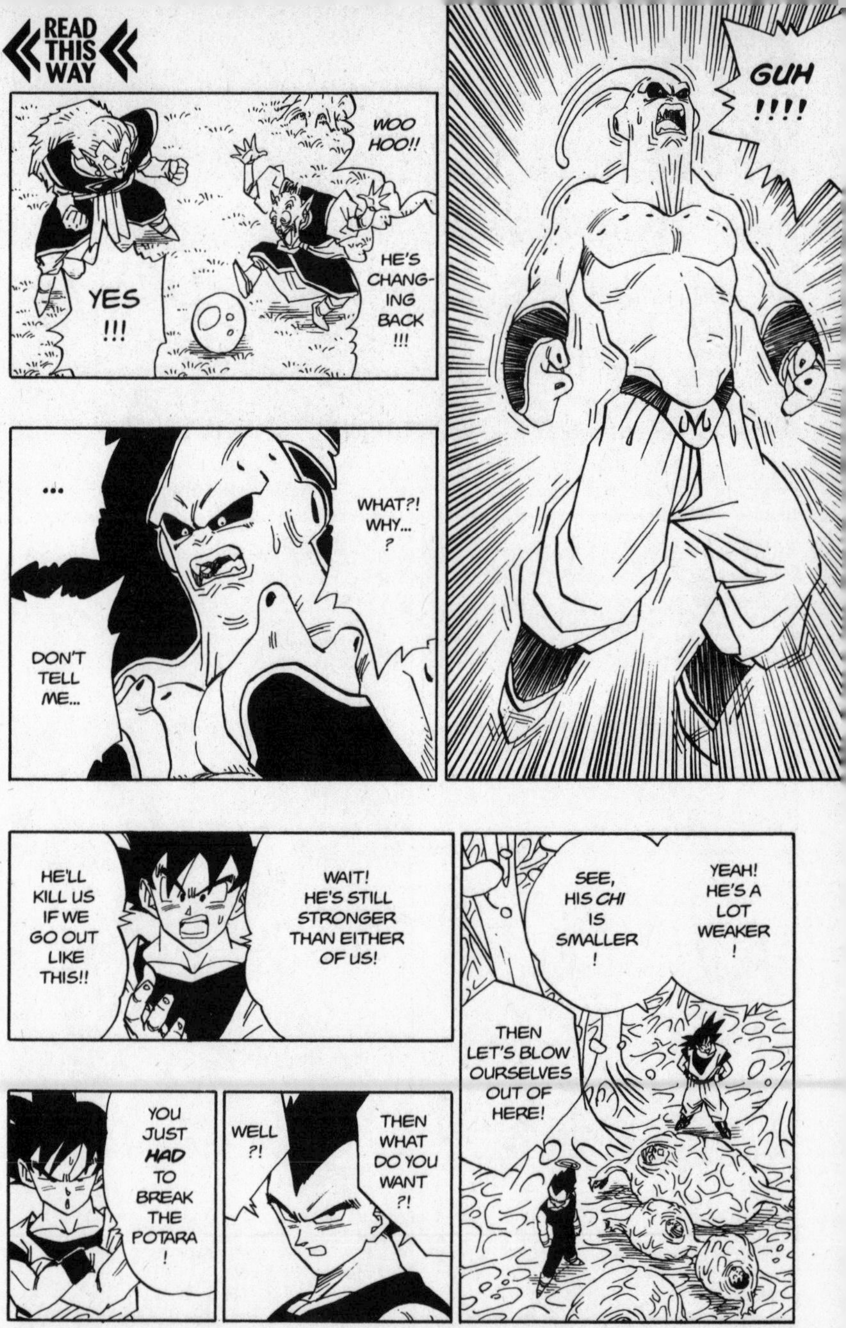
READ THIS WAY
GUH!!!!
WOO HOO!!
HE'S CHANGING-ING BACK!!!
YES!!!
WHAT?! WHY...?
...
DON'T TELL ME...
YEAH! HE'S A LOT WEAKER!
SEE, HIS *CHI* IS SMALLER!
THEN LET'S BLOW OURSELVES OUT OF HERE!
WAIT! HE'S STILL STRONGER THAN EITHER OF US!
HE'LL KILL US IF WE GO OUT LIKE THIS!!
THEN WHAT DO YOU WANT?!
WELL?!
YOU JUST **HAD** TO BREAK THE POTARA!

READ THIS WAY

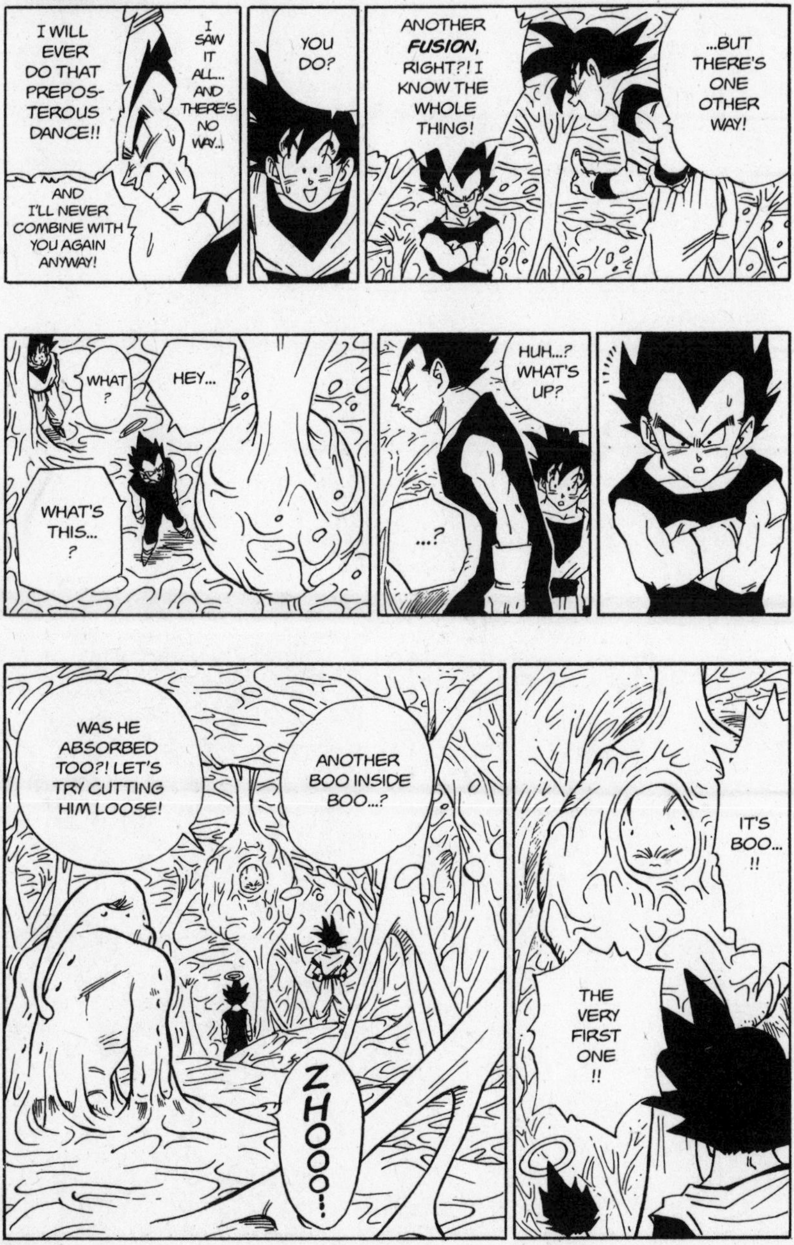
...BUT THERE'S ONE OTHER WAY!
ANOTHER ***FUSION***, RIGHT?! I KNOW THE WHOLE THING!
YOU DO?
I SAW IT ALL... AND THERE'S NO WAY...
I WILL EVER DO THAT PREPOSTEROUS DANCE!!
AND I'LL NEVER COMBINE WITH YOU AGAIN ANYWAY!
HUH...? WHAT'S UP?
...?
HEY...
WHAT ?
WHAT'S THIS... ?
IT'S BOO... !!
THE VERY FIRST ONE !!
ANOTHER BOO INSIDE BOO...?
WAS HE ABSORBED TOO?! LET'S TRY CUTTING HIM LOOSE!
ZHOOO!!

DBZ:313 · Boos Inside Boo

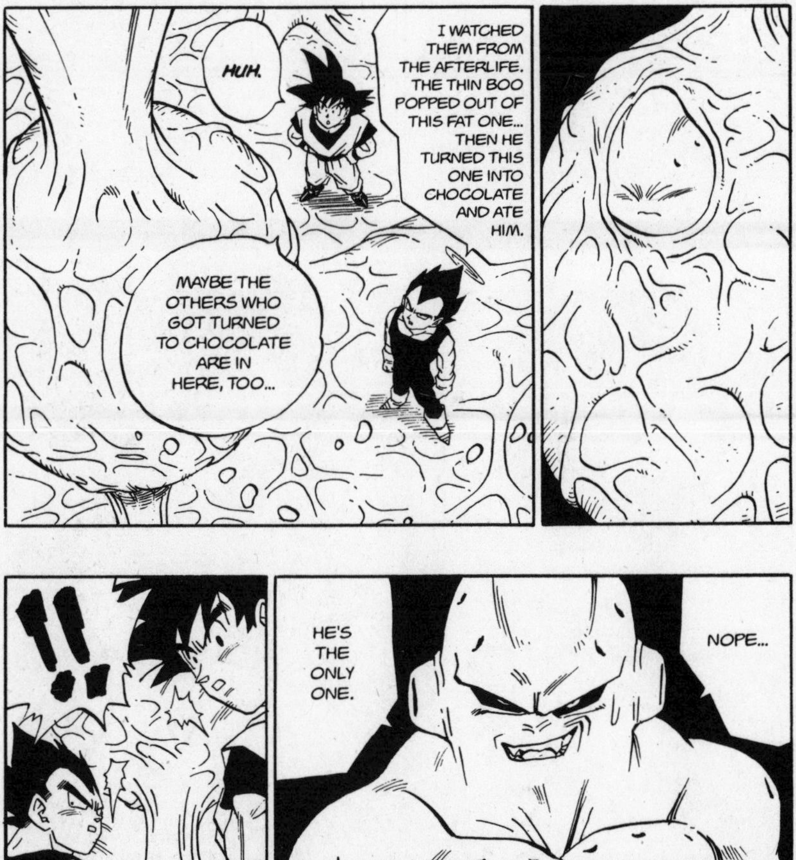
I WATCHED THEM FROM THE AFTERLIFE. THE THIN BOO POPPED OUT OF THIS FAT ONE... THEN HE TURNED THIS ONE INTO CHOCOLATE AND ATE HIM.
HUH.
MAYBE THE OTHERS WHO GOT TURNED TO CHOCOLATE ARE IN HERE, TOO...
NOPE...
HE'S THE ONLY ONE.
!!

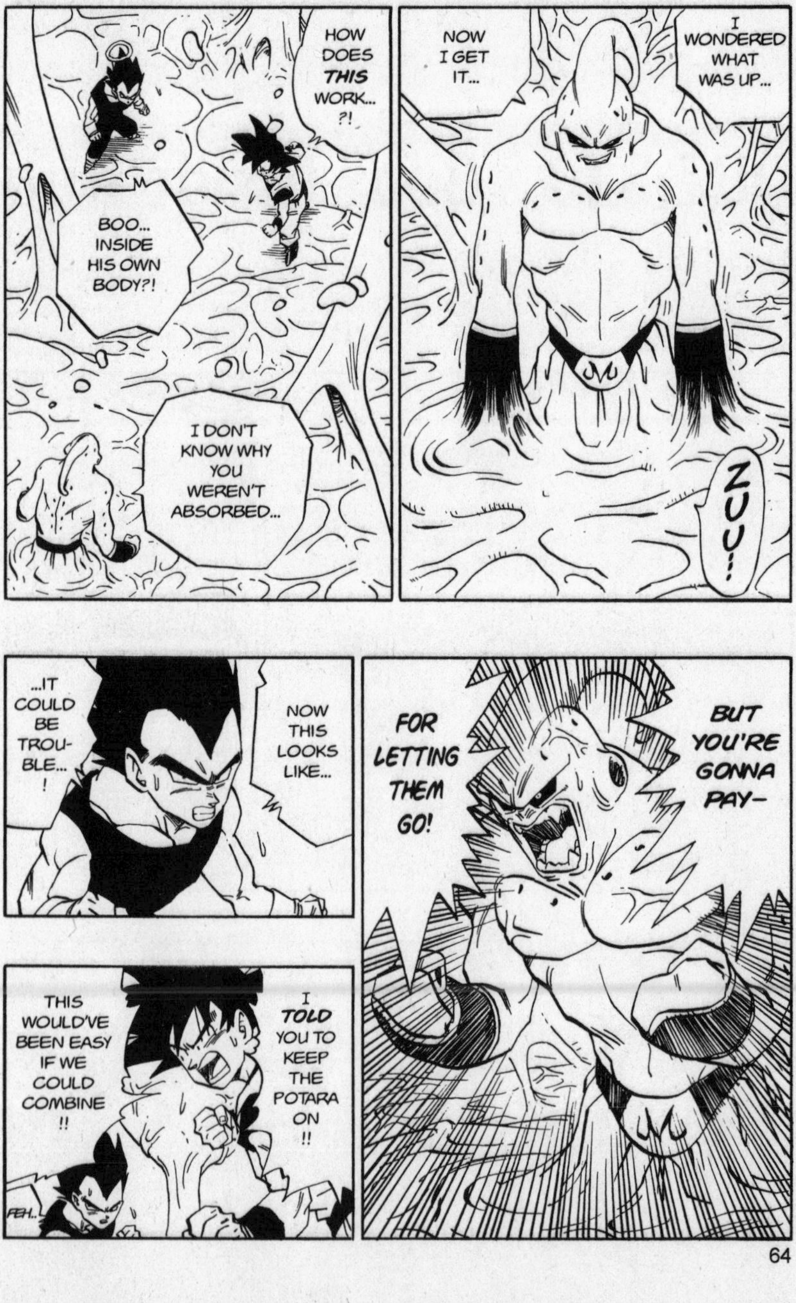
I WONDERED WHAT WAS UP...
NOW I GET IT...
ZUUU!
HOW DOES **THIS** WORK...?!
BOO... INSIDE HIS OWN BODY?!
I DON'T KNOW WHY YOU WEREN'T ABSORBED...
BUT YOU'RE GONNA PAY-
FOR LETTING THEM GO!
NOW THIS LOOKS LIKE...
...IT COULD BE TROUBLE...!
I **TOLD** YOU TO KEEP THE POTARA ON!!
THIS WOULD'VE BEEN EASY IF WE COULD COMBINE!!
FEH..

READ THIS WAY

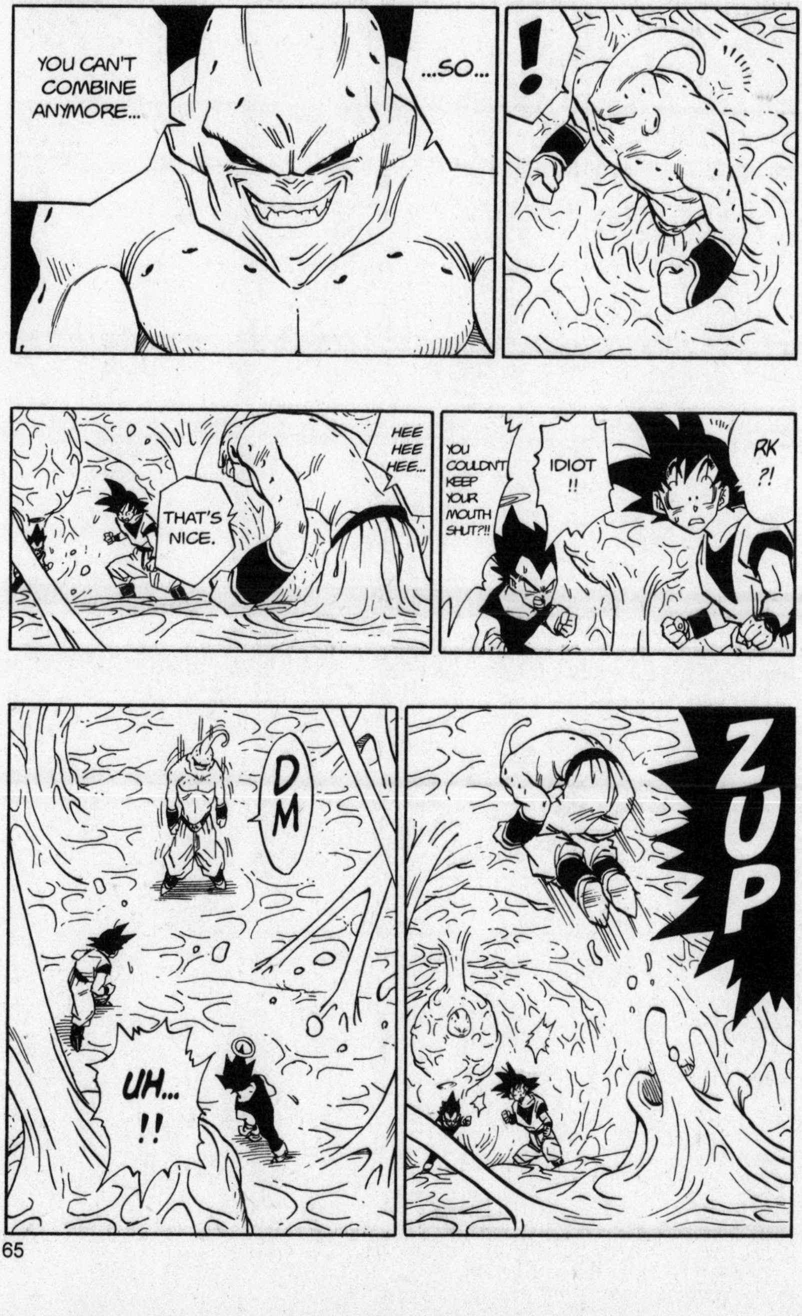
!
YOU CAN'T COMBINE ANYMORE...
...SO...
RK ?!
IDIOT !!
YOU COULDN'T KEEP YOUR MOUTH SHUT?!!
HEE HEE HEE...
THAT'S NICE.
ZUP
DM
UH... !!

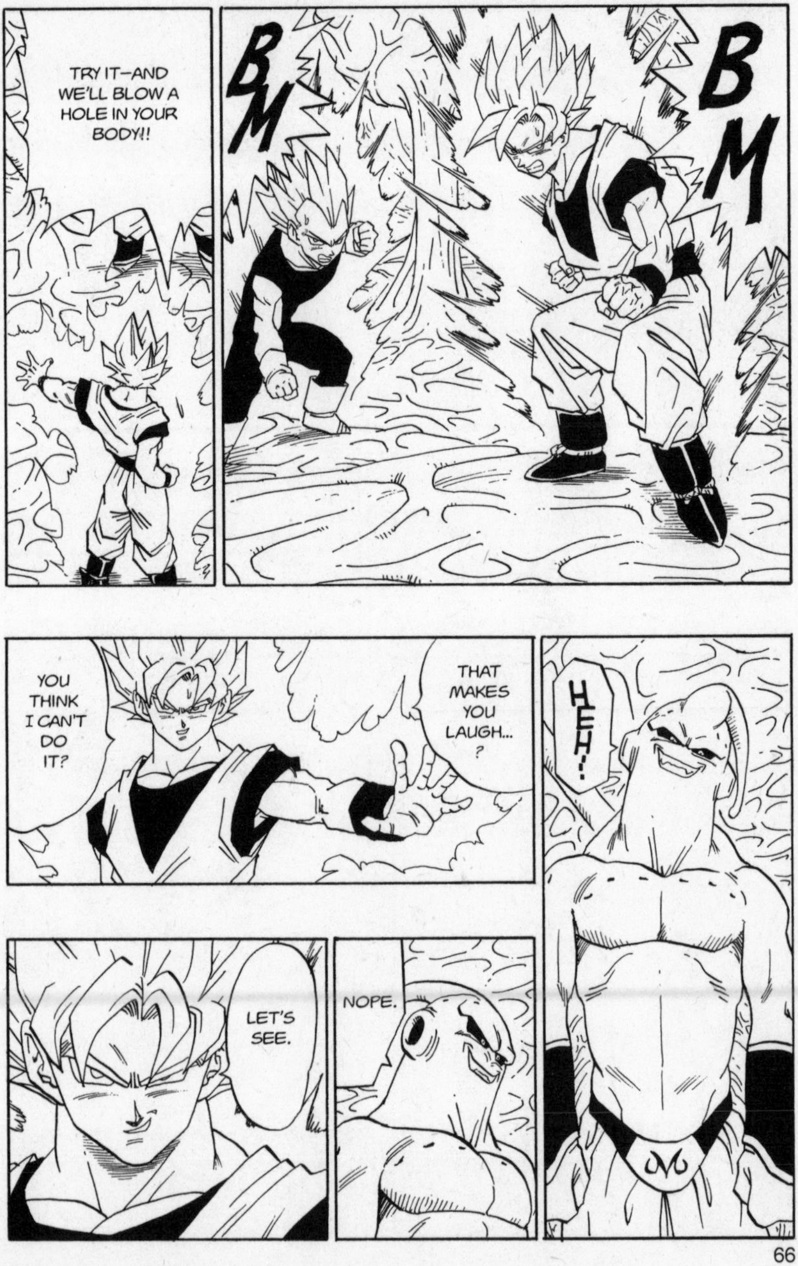
BM
BM
TRY IT—AND WE'LL BLOW A HOLE IN YOUR BODY!!
HEH!!
THAT MAKES YOU LAUGH...?
YOU THINK I CAN'T DO IT?
NOPE.
LET'S SEE.

READ THIS WAY

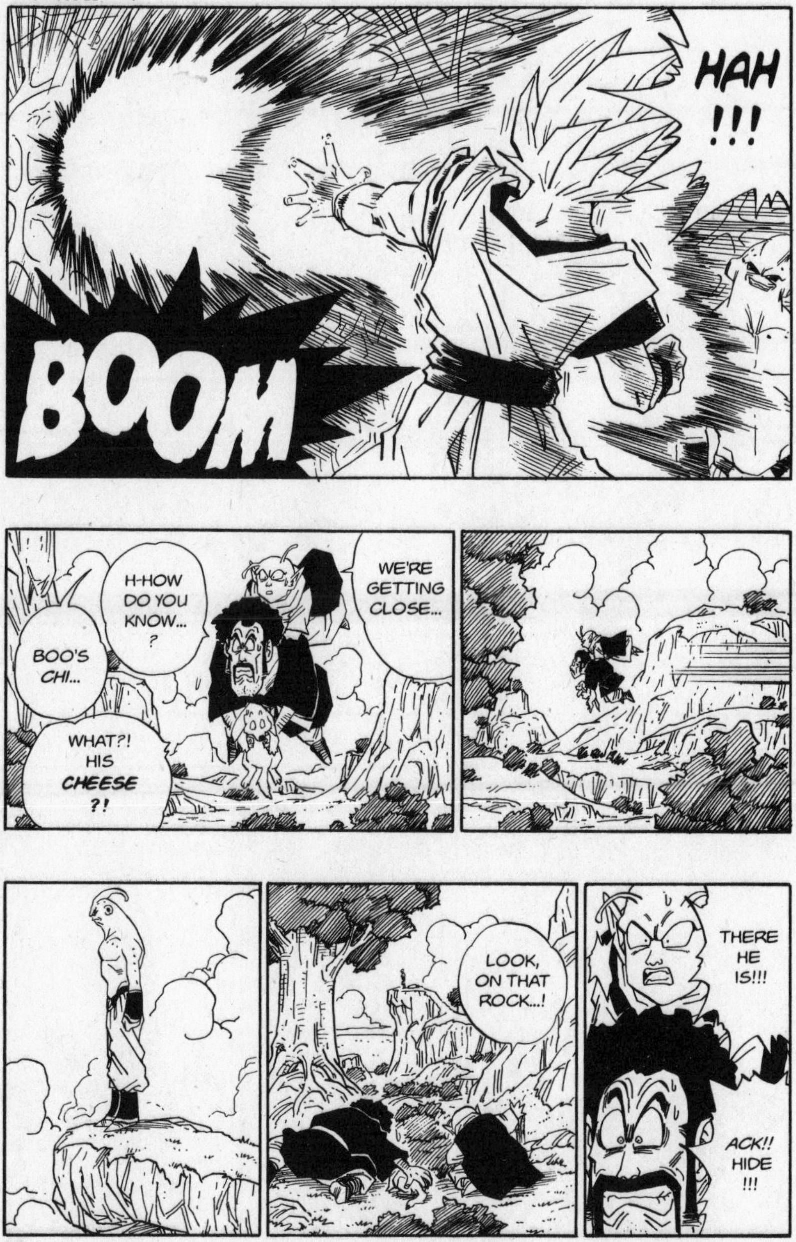
HAH !!!
BOOM
WE'RE GETTING CLOSE...
H-HOW DO YOU KNOW...?
BOO'S CHI...
WHAT?! HIS *CHEESE* ?!
THERE HE IS!!!
ACK!! HIDE !!!
LOOK, ON THAT ROCK...!

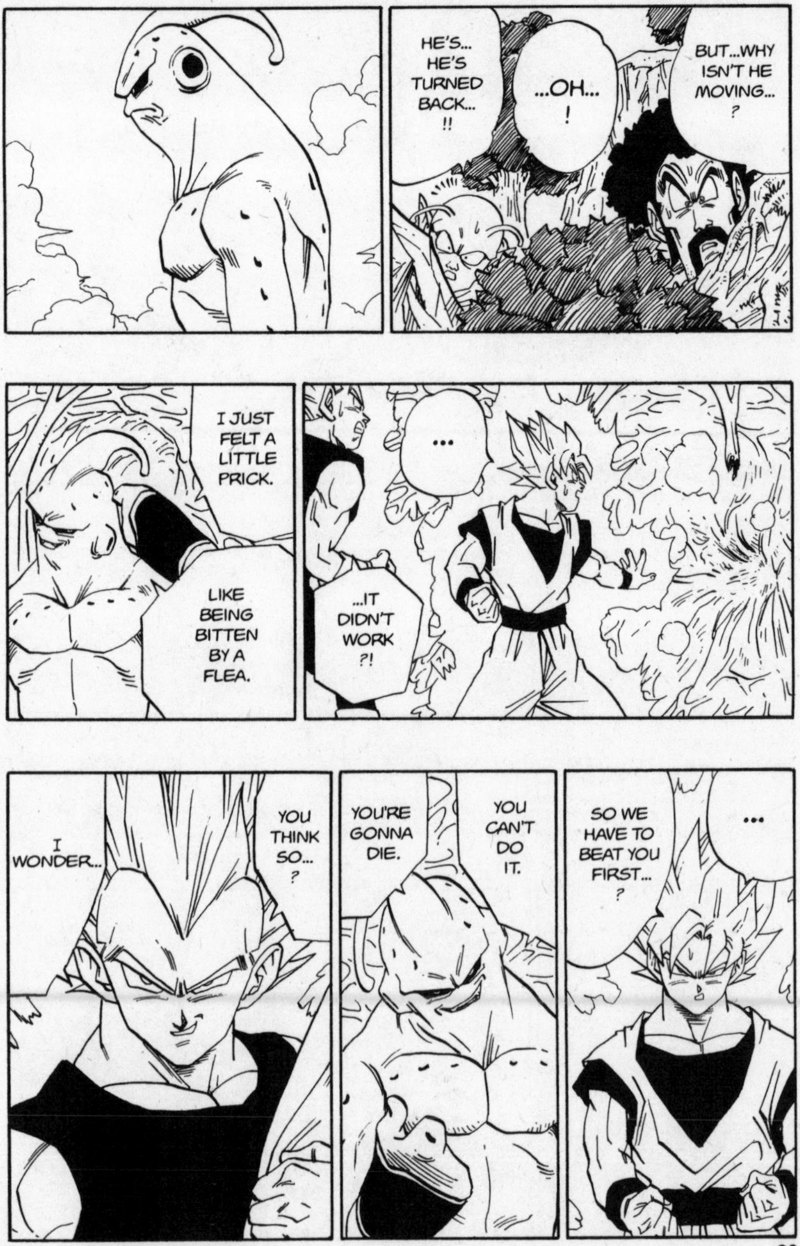
BUT...WHY ISN'T HE MOVING...?
...OH...!
HE'S... HE'S TURNED BACK...!!
...
...IT DIDN'T WORK?!
I JUST FELT A LITTLE PRICK.
LIKE BEING BITTEN BY A FLEA.
...
SO WE HAVE TO BEAT YOU FIRST...?
YOU CAN'T DO IT.
YOU'RE GONNA DIE.
YOU THINK SO...?
I WONDER...

READ THIS WAY

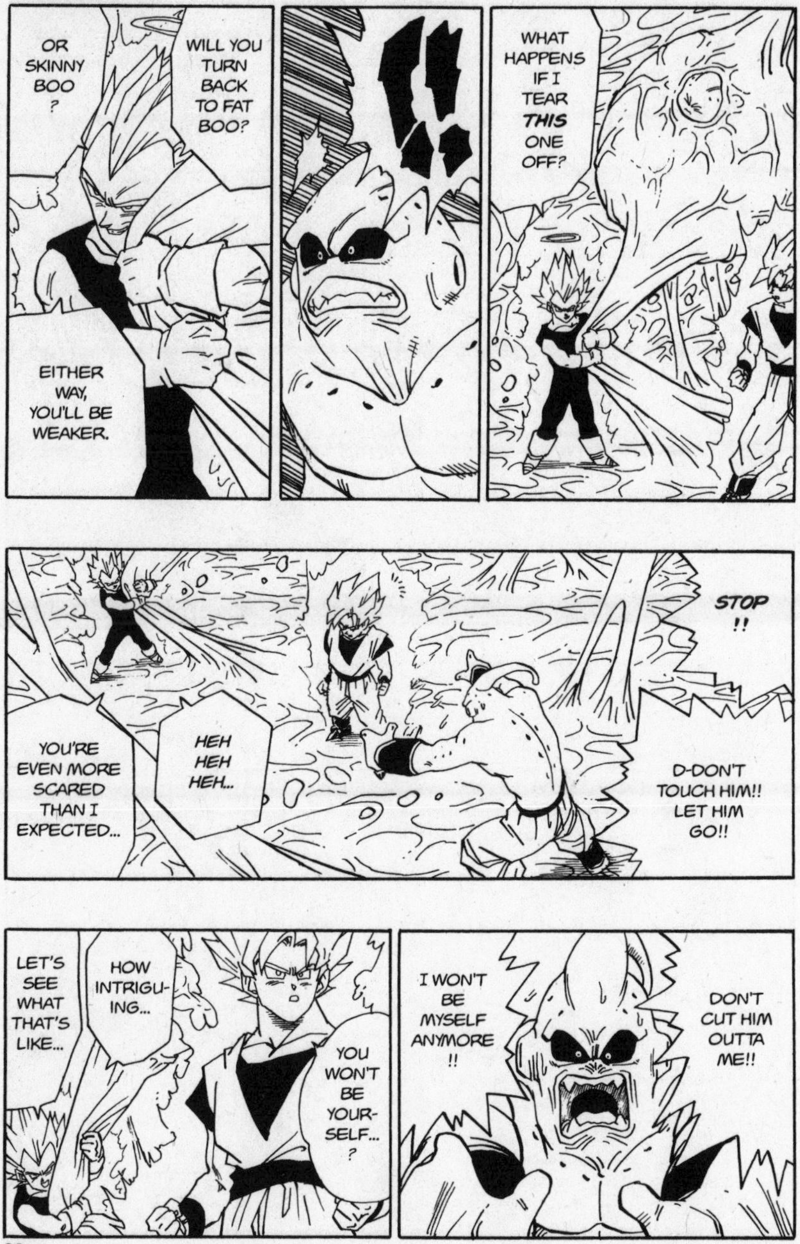
WHAT HAPPENS IF I TEAR ***THIS*** ONE OFF?
!!
WILL YOU TURN BACK TO FAT BOO?
OR SKINNY BOO?
EITHER WAY, YOU'LL BE WEAKER.
STOP !!
D-DON'T TOUCH HIM!! LET HIM GO!!
HEH HEH HEH...
YOU'RE EVEN MORE SCARED THAN I EXPECTED...
DON'T CUT HIM OUTTA ME!!
I WON'T BE MYSELF ANYMORE !!
YOU WON'T BE YOURSELF... ?
HOW INTRIGUING...
LET'S SEE WHAT THAT'S LIKE...

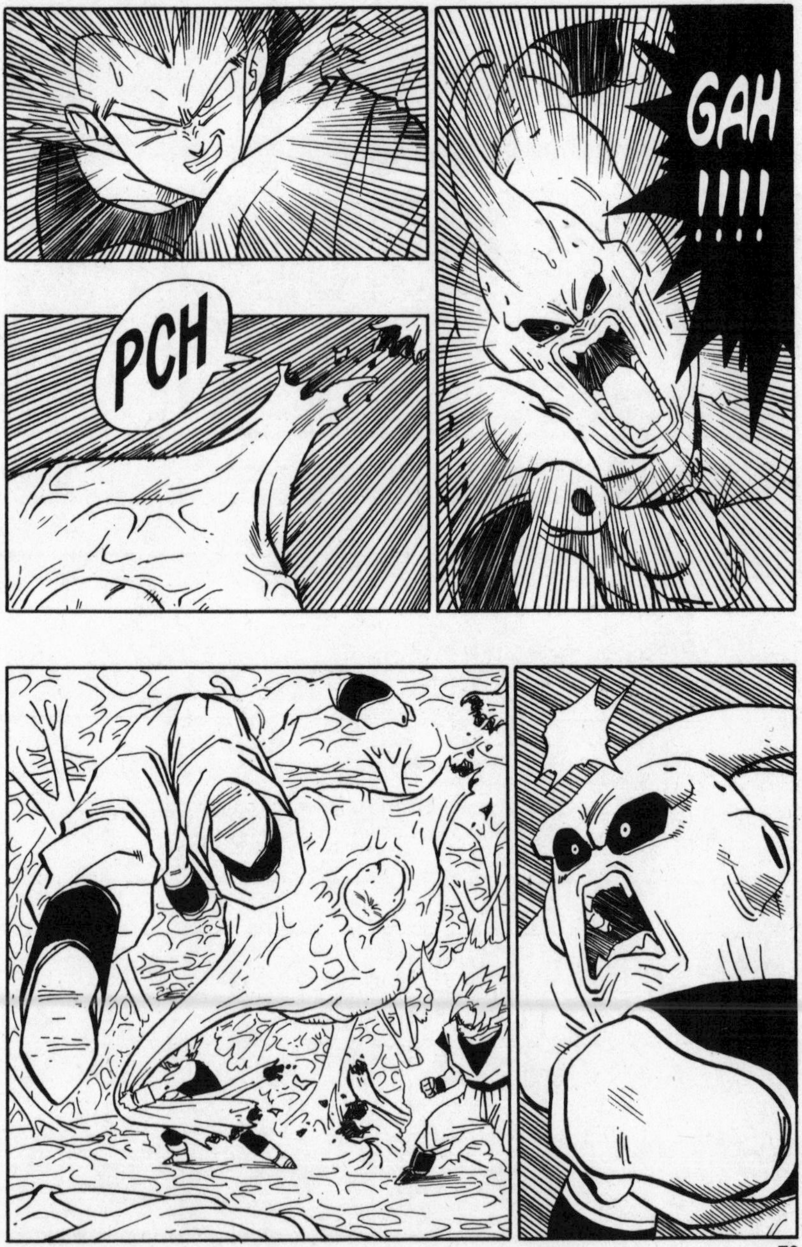
GAH !!!!
PCH

READ THIS WAY

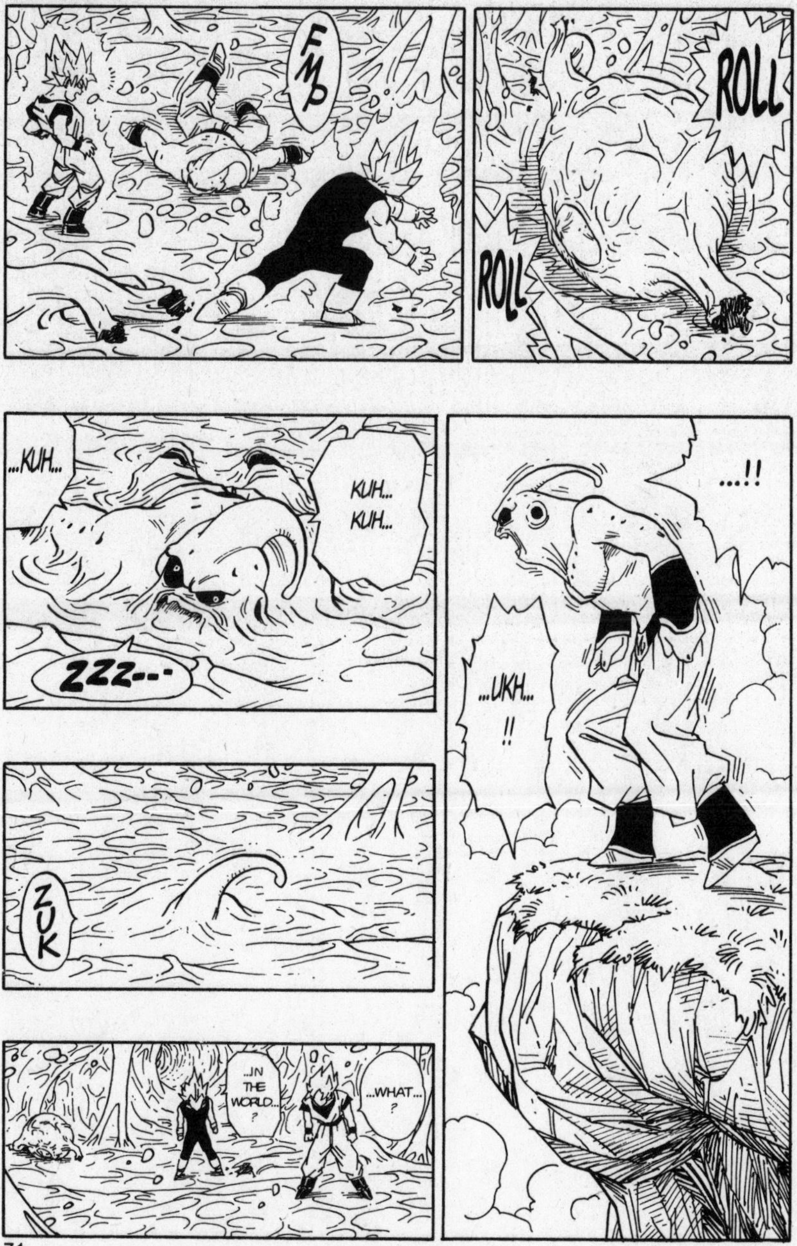

ROLL
ROLL
FMP
...!!
...UKH... !!
KUH... KUH...
...KUH...
ZZZ---
ZUK
...WHAT... ?
...IN THE WORLD... ?

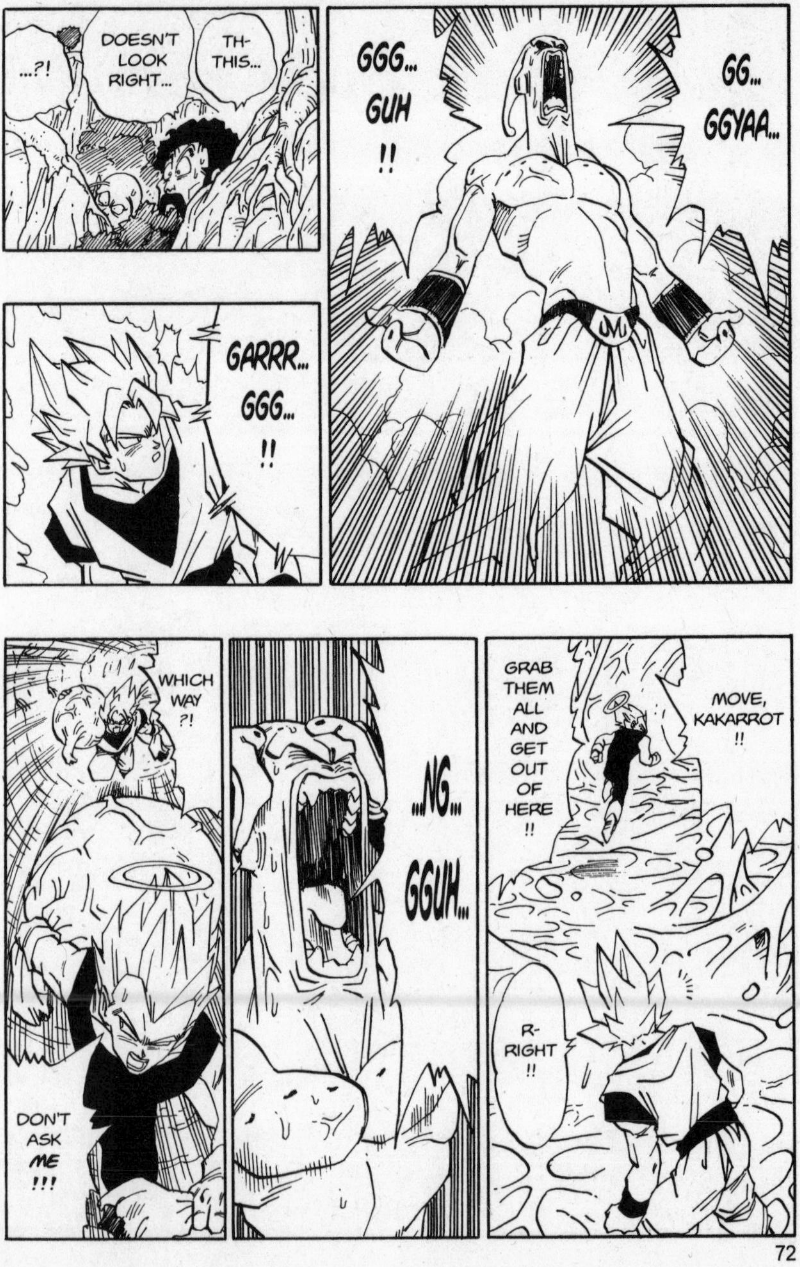
GG... GGYAA...
GGG... GUH !!
TH- THIS...
DOESN'T LOOK RIGHT...
...?!
GARRR... GGG... !!
MOVE, KAKARROT !!
GRAB THEM ALL AND GET OUT OF HERE !!
R- RIGHT !!
...NG... GGUH...
WHICH WAY ?!
DON'T ASK ME !!!

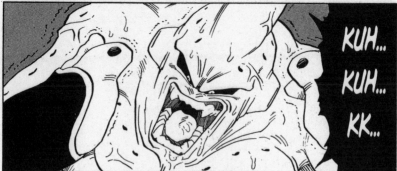

READ THIS WAY

KUH... KUH... KK...
HEY!! EVERY-THING'S GOIN' CRAZY!!
HE'S TRANS-FORMING!!
EITHER FAT OR THIN!!!
ARGH...!!!
WHERE'S THE EXIT?!
VEGETA!!! STOP!!!
SKRII
I SEE LIGHT!!
THE OUT-SIDE!!

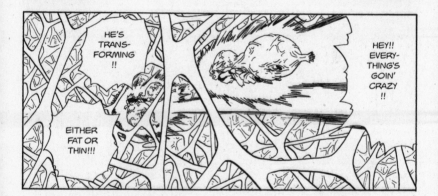

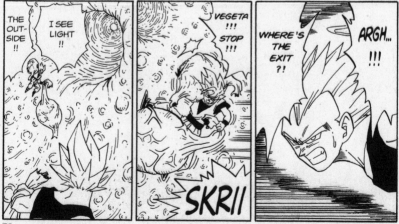

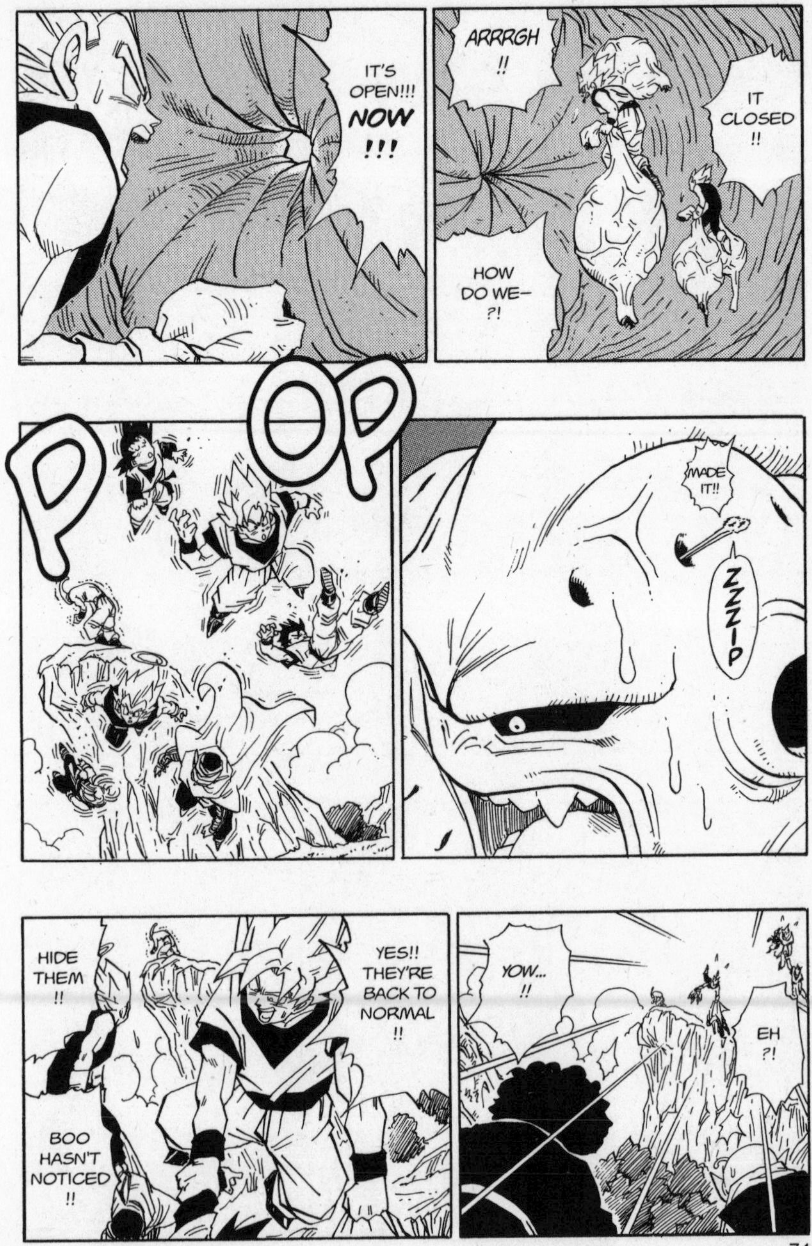
ARRRGH !!
IT CLOSED !!
HOW DO WE— ?!
IT'S OPEN!!! **NOW** !!!
MADE IT!!
ZZZIP
POP
YOW... !!
EH ?!
YES!! THEY'RE BACK TO NORMAL !!
HIDE THEM !!
BOO HASN'T NOTICED !!

READ THIS WAY

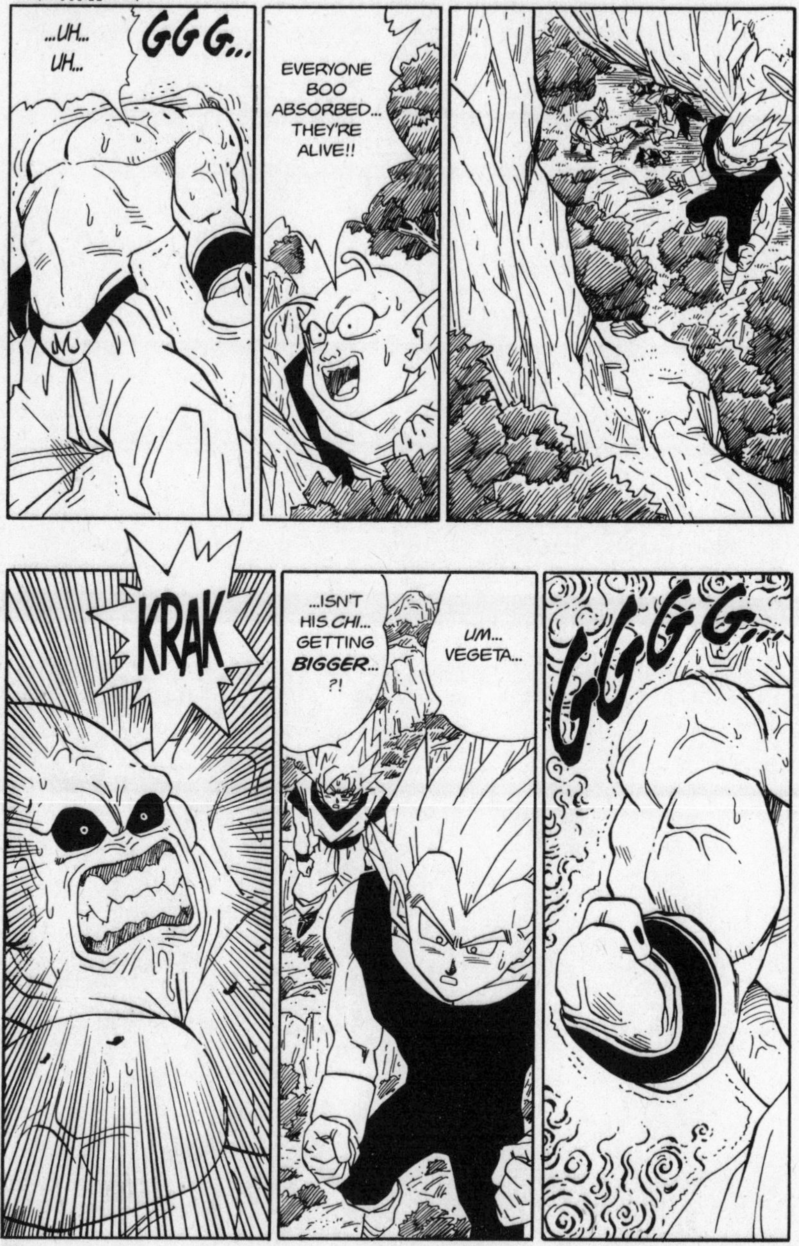
EVERYONE BOO ABSORBED... THEY'RE ALIVE!!
...UH... UH...
GGG...
GGGG...
UM... VEGETA...
...ISN'T HIS *CHI*... GETTING **BIGGER**... ?!
KRAK

DBZ:314 · The Boo of Pure Evil

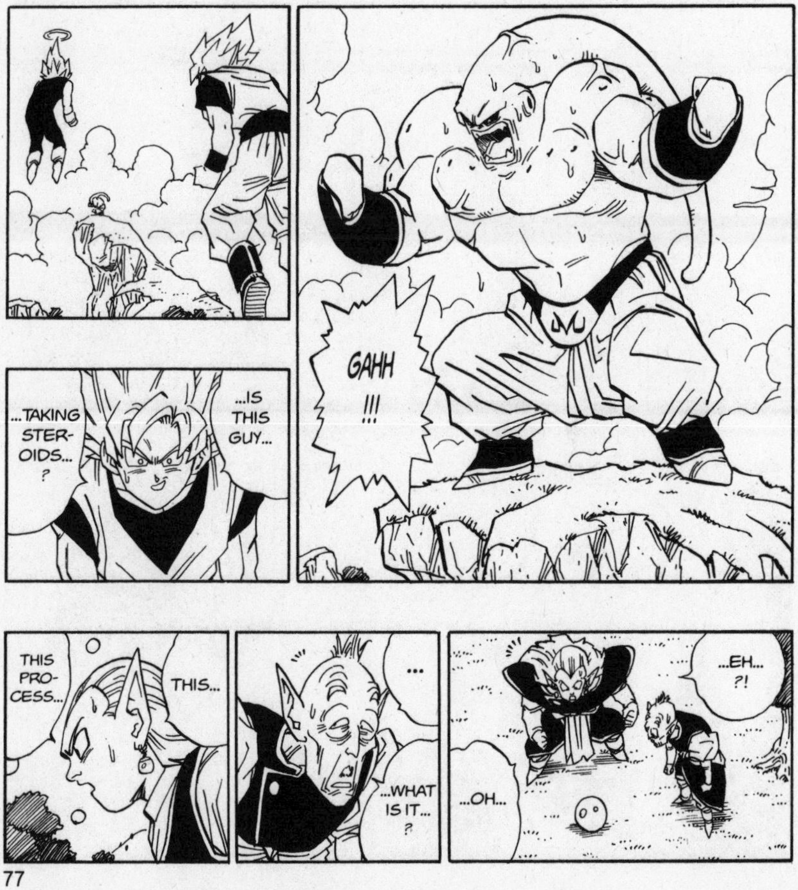
GAHH !!!
...IS THIS GUY...
...TAKING STEROIDS... ?
...EH... ?!
...OH...
...
...WHAT IS IT... ?
THIS...
THIS PROCESS...

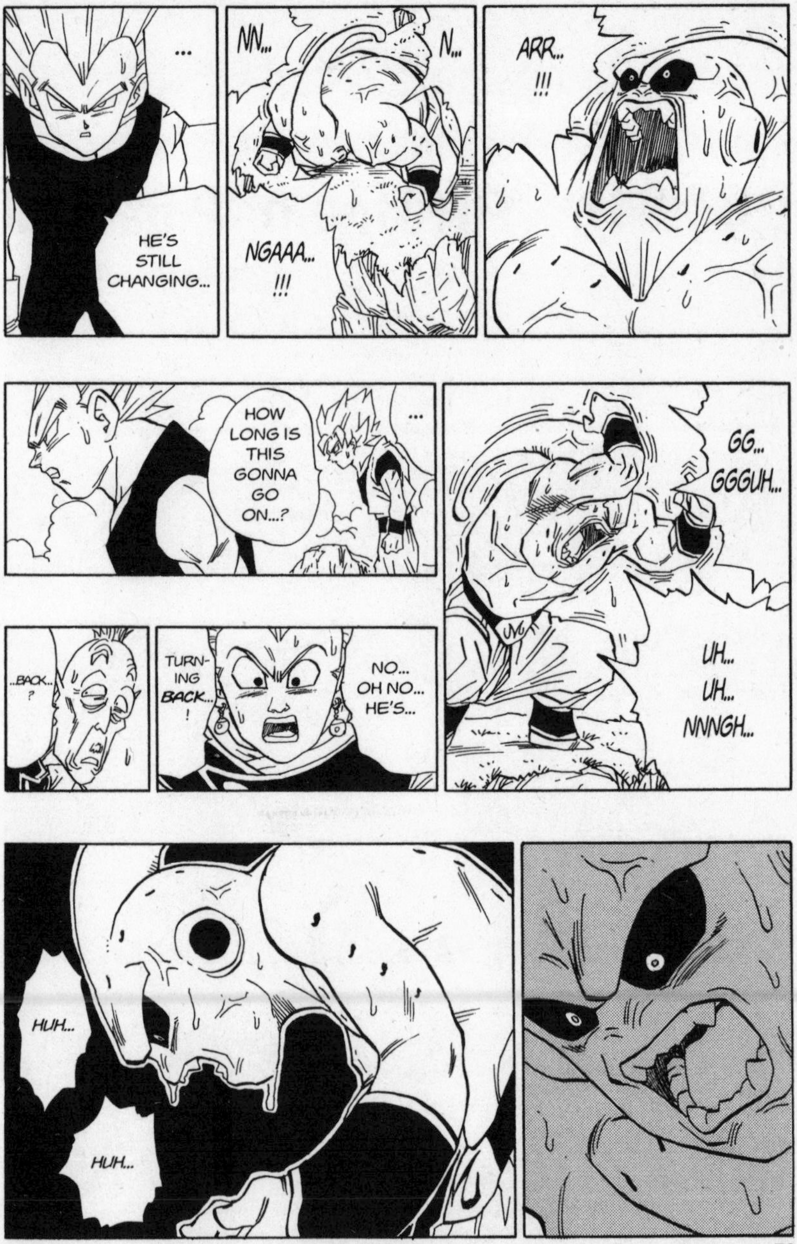
ARR... !!!
N...
NN...
NGAAA... !!!
...
HE'S STILL CHANGING...
GG... GGGUH...
UH... UH... NNNGH...
...
HOW LONG IS THIS GONNA GO ON...?
NO... OH NO... HE'S...
TURNING BACK...!
...BACK...?
HUH...
HUH...

READ THIS WAY

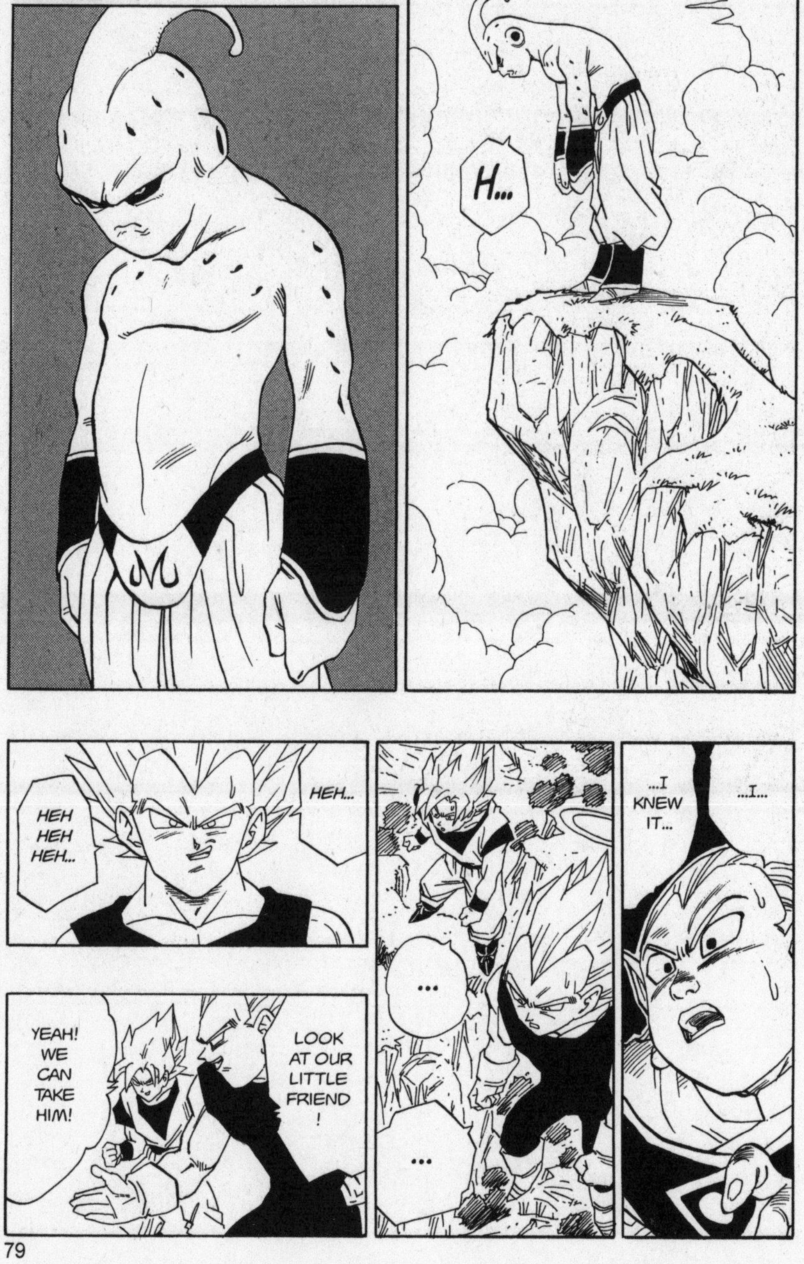
H...
...I...
...I KNEW IT...
...
...
HEH...
HEH HEH HEH...
LOOK AT OUR LITTLE FRIEND!
YEAH! WE CAN TAKE HIM!

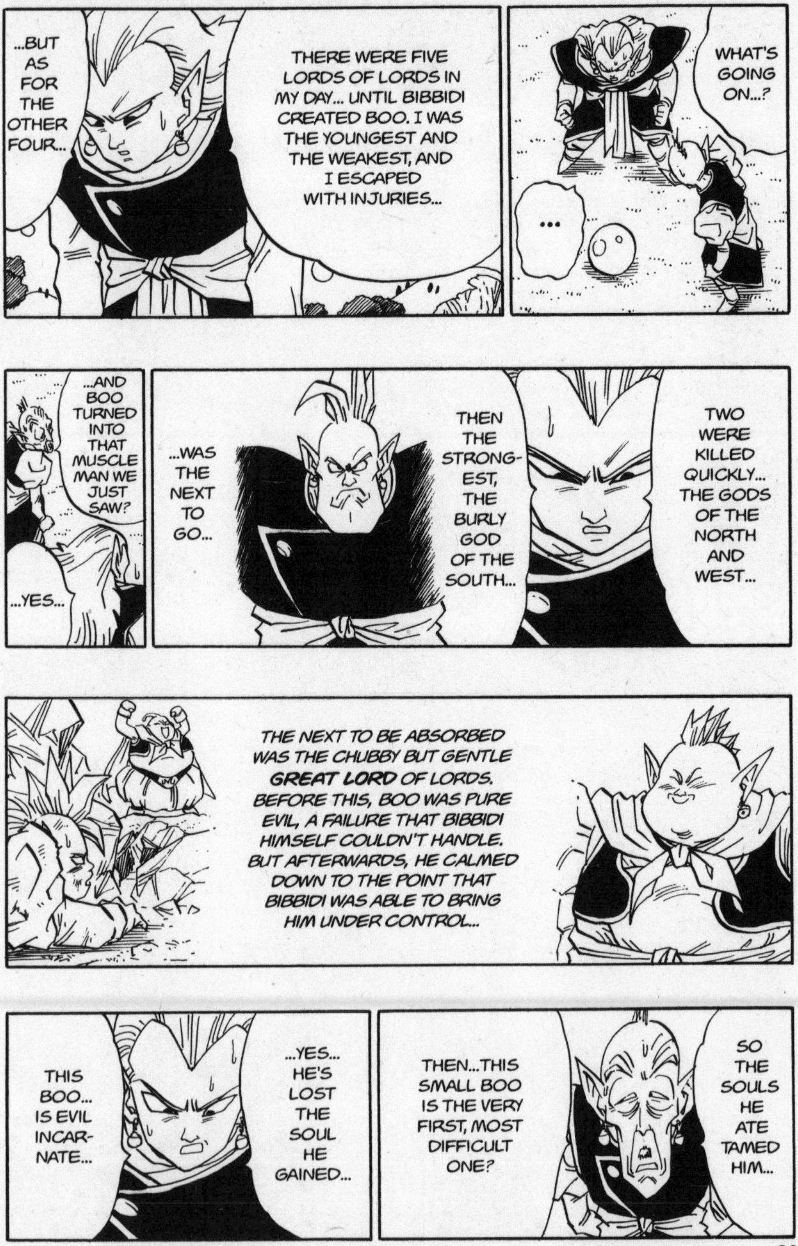
WHAT'S GOING ON...?
...
THERE WERE FIVE LORDS OF LORDS IN MY DAY... UNTIL BIBBIDI CREATED BOO. I WAS THE YOUNGEST AND THE WEAKEST, AND I ESCAPED WITH INJURIES...
...BUT AS FOR THE OTHER FOUR...
TWO WERE KILLED QUICKLY... THE GODS OF THE NORTH AND WEST...
THEN THE STRONGEST, THE BURLY GOD OF THE SOUTH...
...WAS THE NEXT TO GO...
...AND BOO TURNED INTO THAT MUSCLE MAN WE JUST SAW?
...YES...
THE NEXT TO BE ABSORBED WAS THE CHUBBY BUT GENTLE **GREAT LORD** OF LORDS. BEFORE THIS, BOO WAS PURE EVIL, A FAILURE THAT BIBBIDI HIMSELF COULDN'T HANDLE. BUT AFTERWARDS, HE CALMED DOWN TO THE POINT THAT BIBBIDI WAS ABLE TO BRING HIM UNDER CONTROL...
SO THE SOULS HE ATE TAMED HIM...
THEN...THIS SMALL BOO IS THE VERY FIRST, MOST DIFFICULT ONE?
...YES... HE'S LOST THE SOUL HE GAINED...
THIS BOO... IS EVIL INCARNATE...

READ THIS WAY

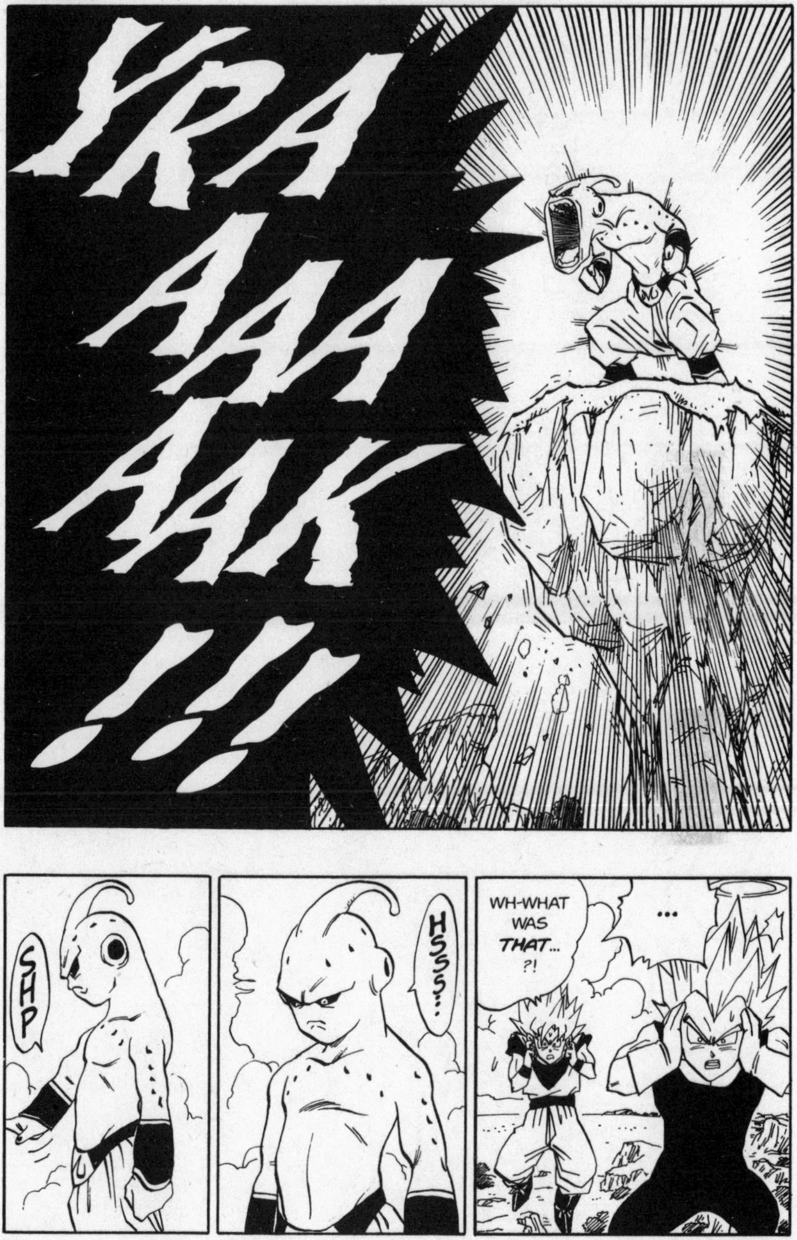
YRAAAAAAK!!!!
...
WH-WHAT WAS THAT...?!
HSSS...
SHP

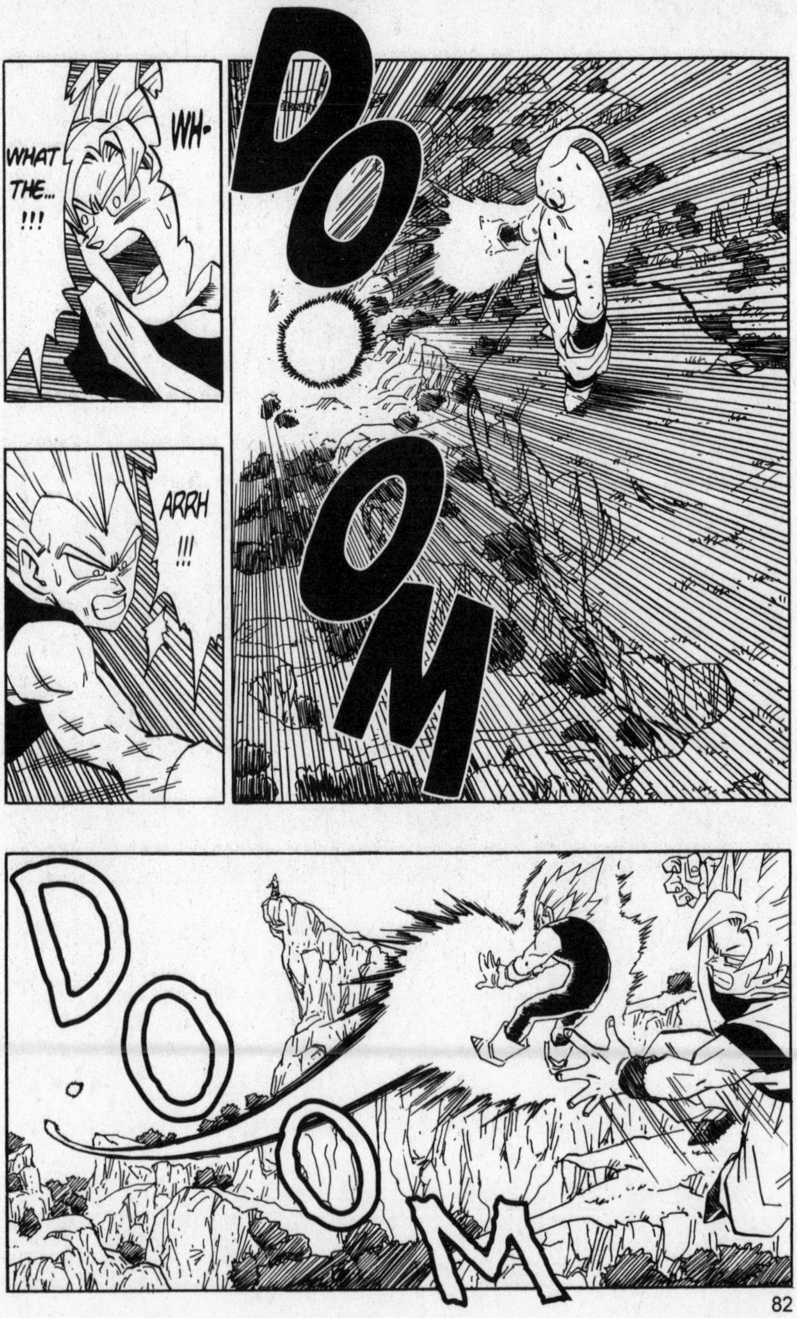
DOOM
WH-
WHAT THE... !!!
ARRH !!!
DOOOM

READ THIS WAY

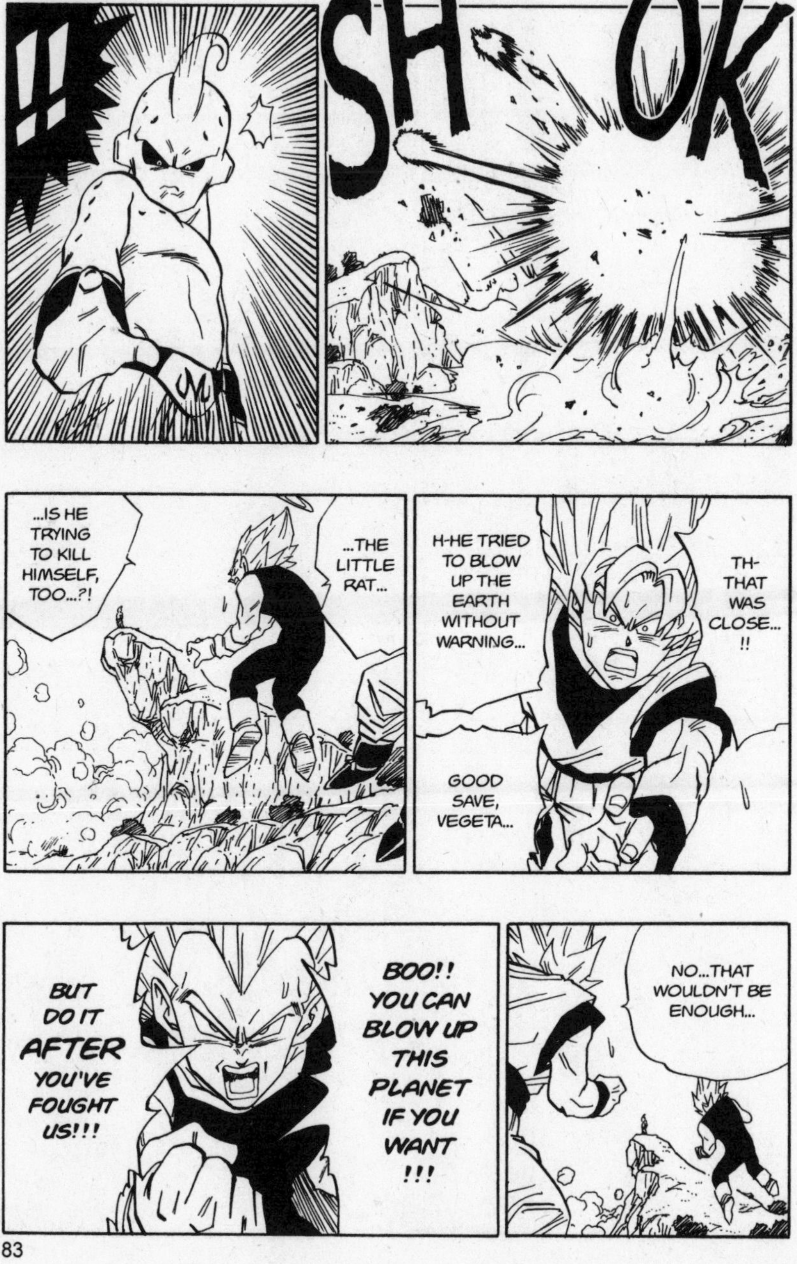

SHOOK
!!
TH-THAT WAS CLOSE...!!
H-HE TRIED TO BLOW UP THE EARTH WITHOUT WARNING...
GOOD SAVE, VEGETA...
...THE LITTLE RAT...
...IS HE TRYING TO KILL HIMSELF, TOO...?!
NO...THAT WOULDN'T BE ENOUGH...
BOO!! YOU CAN BLOW UP THIS PLANET IF YOU WANT!!!
BUT DO IT AFTER YOU'VE FOUGHT US!!!

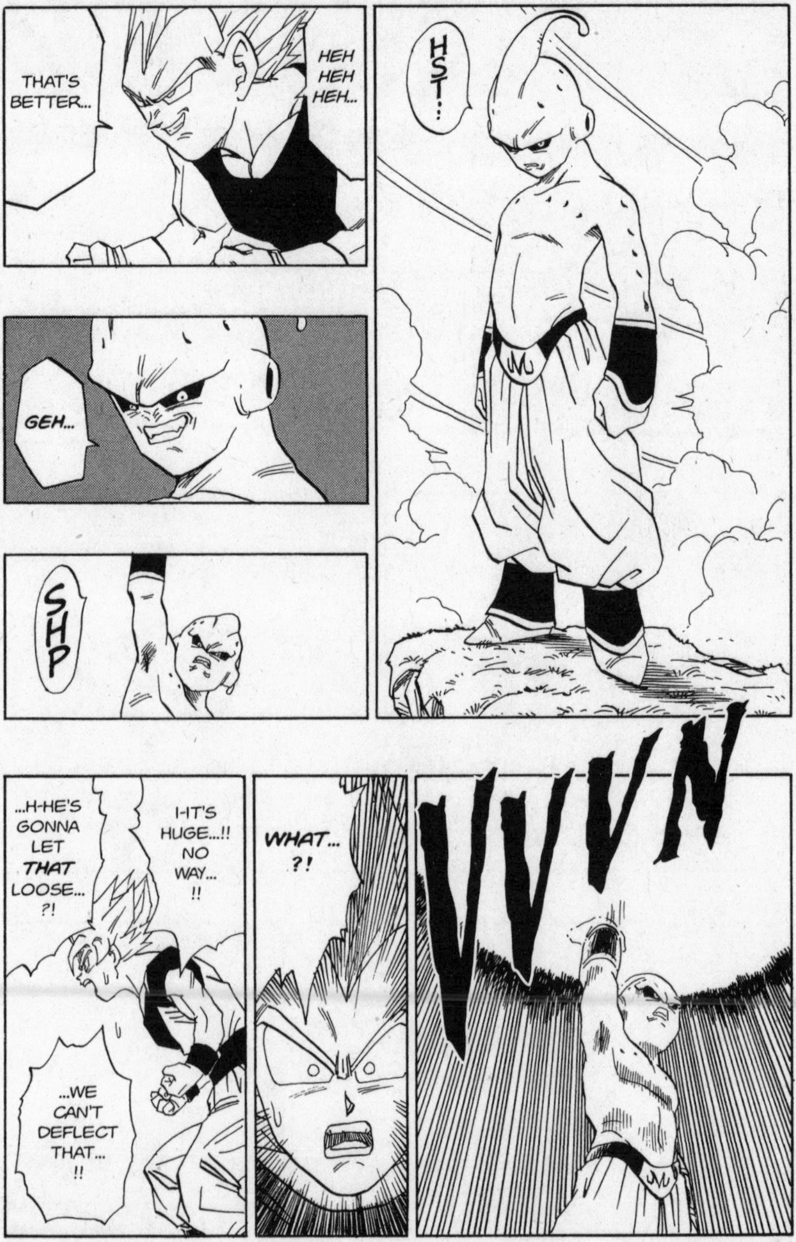
HST...
HEH HEH HEH...
THAT'S BETTER...
GEH...
SHP
VVVN
WHAT...?!
I-IT'S HUGE...!! NO WAY...!!
...H-HE'S GONNA LET THAT LOOSE...?!
...WE CAN'T DEFLECT THAT...!!

READ THIS WAY

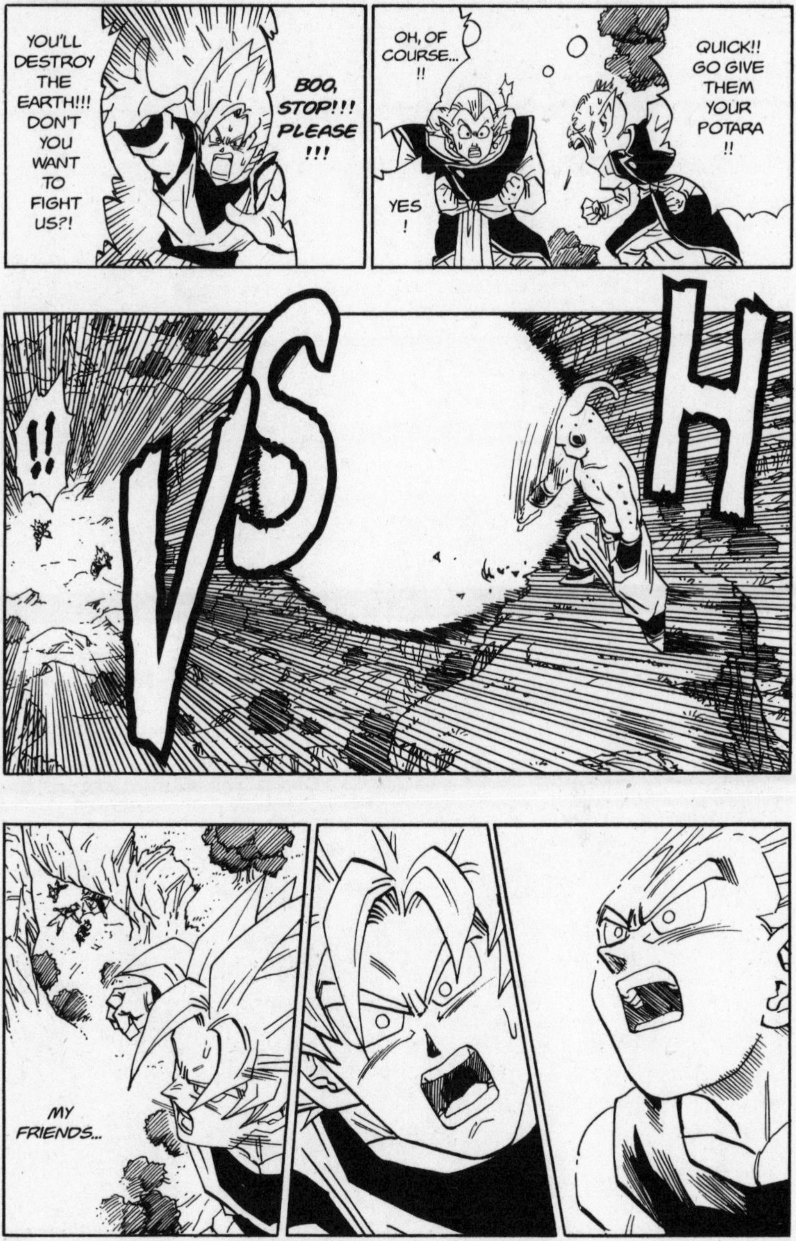

QUICK!! GO GIVE THEM YOUR POTARA !!
OH, OF COURSE... !!
YES !
BOO, STOP!!! PLEASE !!!
YOU'LL DESTROY THE EARTH!!! DON'T YOU WANT TO FIGHT US?!
VSSH
!!
MY FRIENDS...

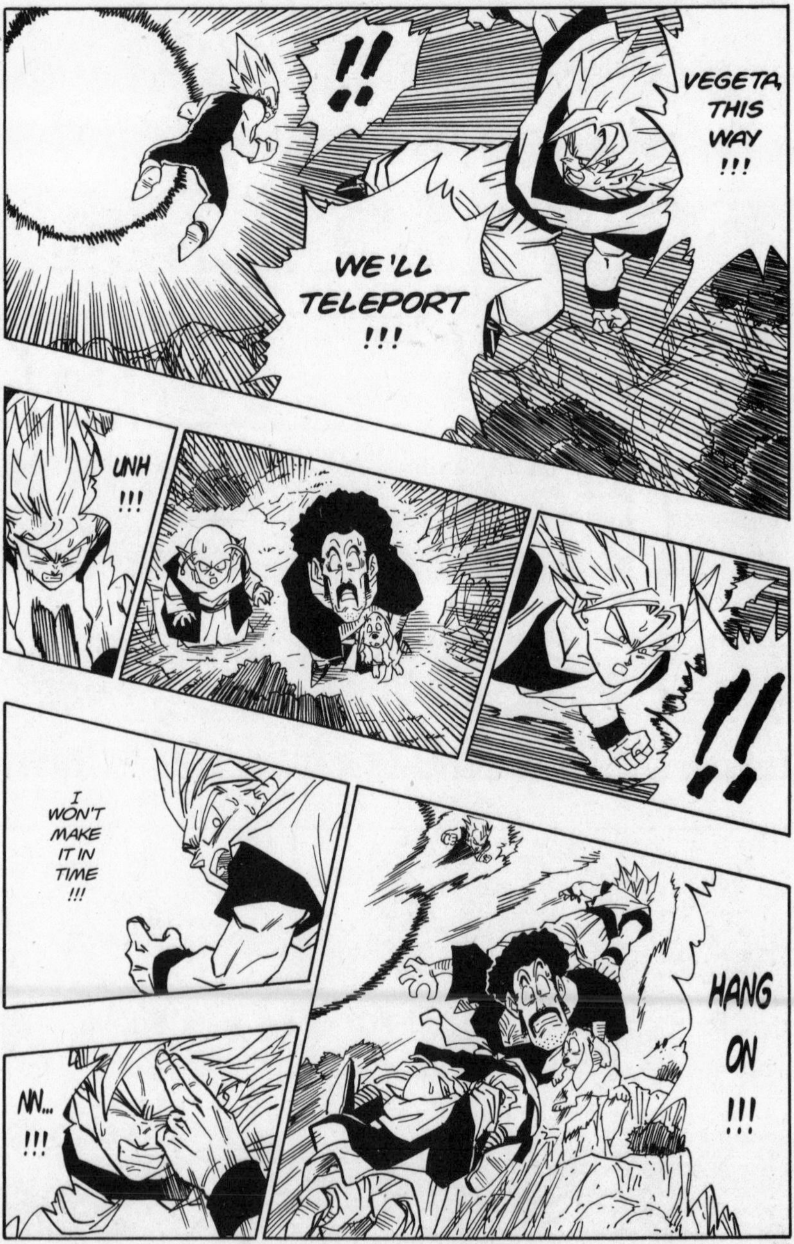
VEGETA, THIS WAY!!!
!!
WE'LL TELEPORT!!!
!!
UNH!!!
HANG ON!!!
I WON'T MAKE IT IN TIME!!!
NN...!!!

READ THIS WAY

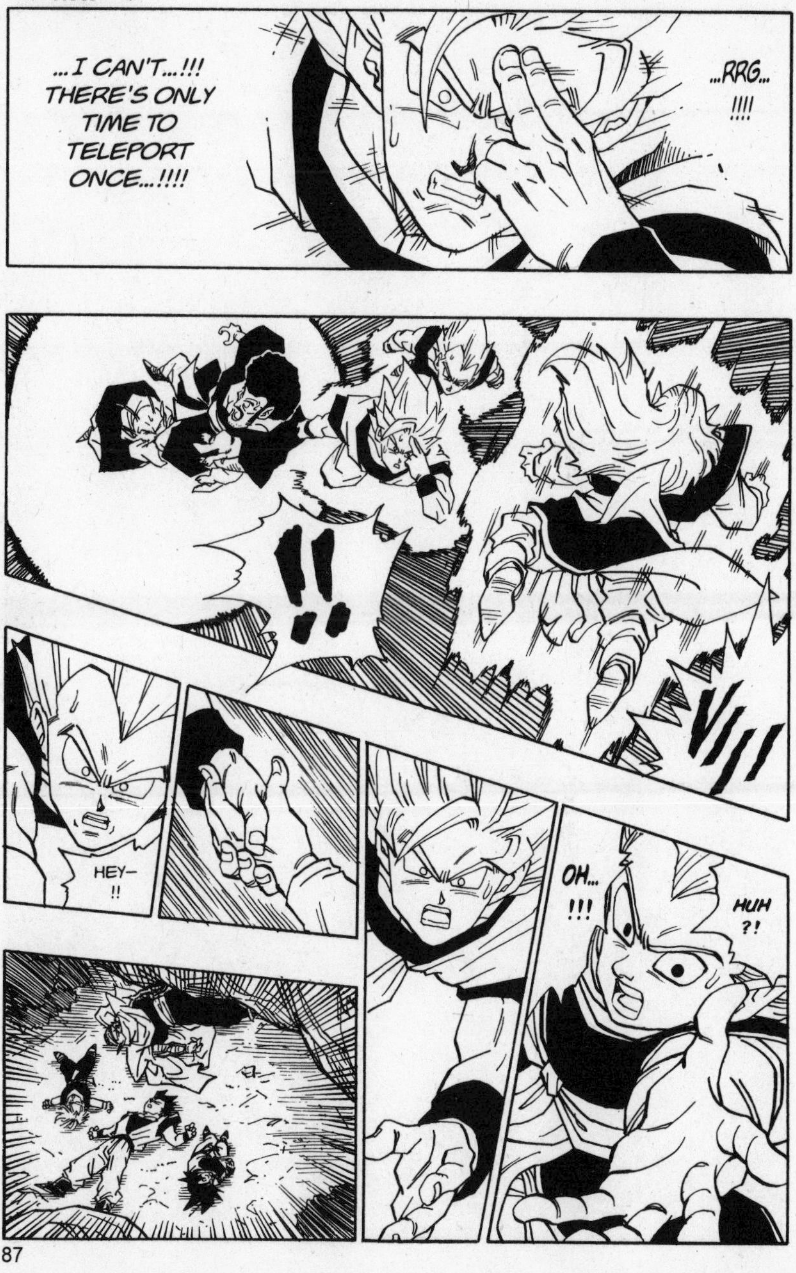

...RRG... !!!!
...I CAN'T...!!! THERE'S ONLY TIME TO TELEPORT ONCE...!!!!
!!
HUH ?!
OH... !!!
HEY— !!

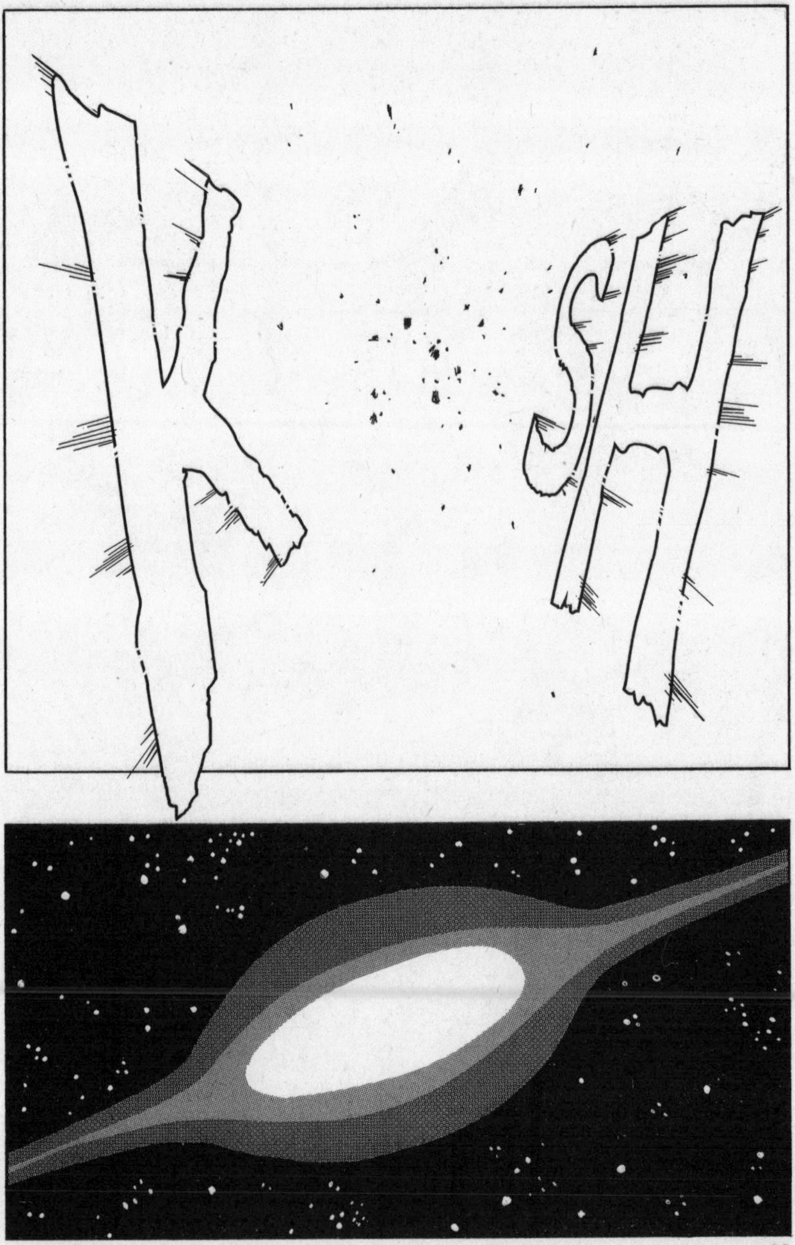
KSH

READ THIS WAY

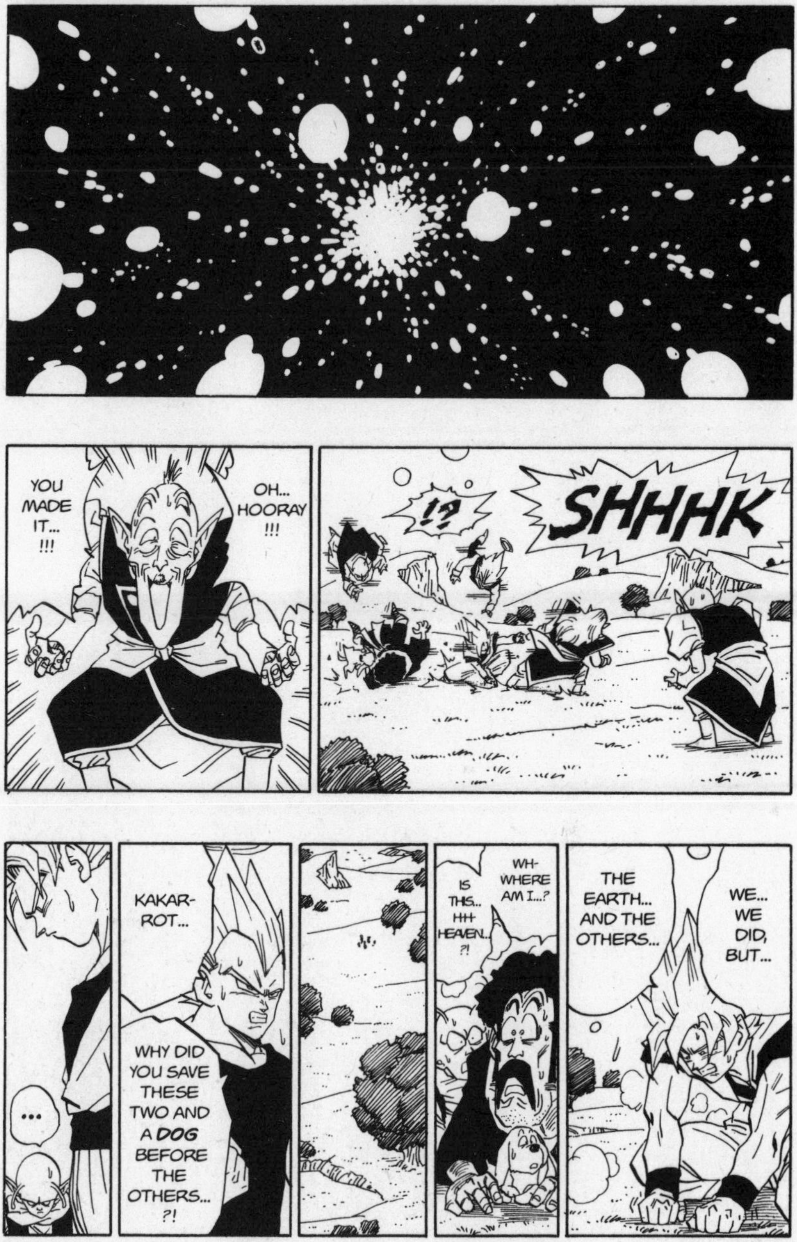
SHHHK
!?
OH... HOORAY !!!
YOU MADE IT... !!!
WE... WE DID, BUT...
THE EARTH... AND THE OTHERS...
WH-WHERE AM I...?
IS THIS... HHH HEAVEN...?!
KAKARROT...
WHY DID YOU SAVE THESE TWO AND A **DOG** BEFORE THE OTHERS...?!
...

DBZ:315 · Battle for the Universe

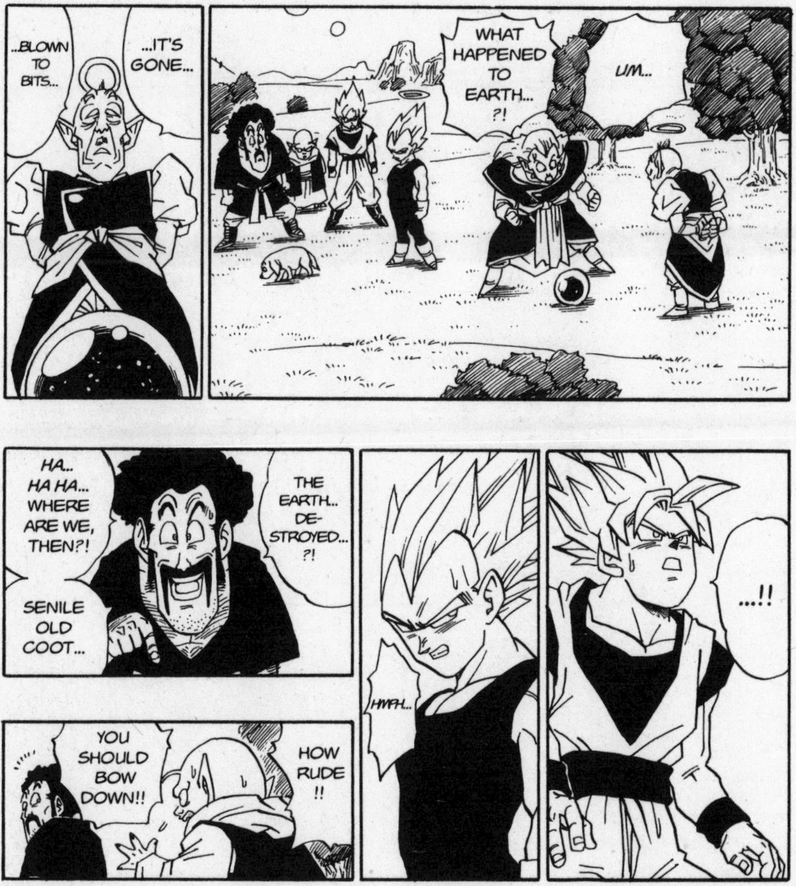
UM...
WHAT HAPPENED TO EARTH...?!
...IT'S GONE...
...BLOWN TO BITS...
...!!
HMPH...
THE EARTH... DE-STROYED...?!
HA... HA HA... WHERE ARE WE, THEN?!
SENILE OLD COOT...
HOW RUDE!!
YOU SHOULD BOW DOWN!!

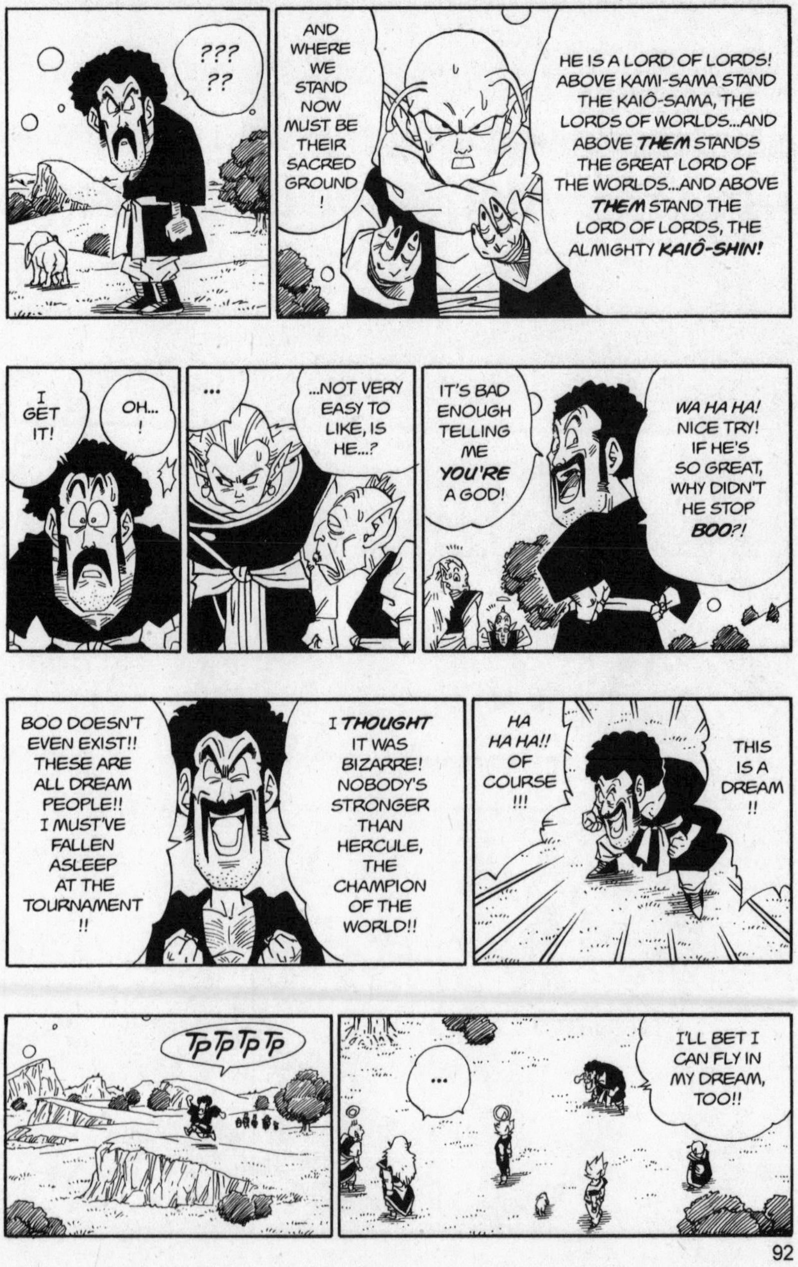
HE IS A LORD OF LORDS! ABOVE KAMI-SAMA STAND THE KAIÔ-SAMA, THE LORDS OF WORLDS...AND ABOVE *THEM* STANDS THE GREAT LORD OF THE WORLDS...AND ABOVE *THEM* STAND THE LORD OF LORDS, THE ALMIGHTY *KAIÔ-SHIN!*
AND WHERE WE STAND NOW MUST BE THEIR SACRED GROUND!
??? ??
WA HA HA! NICE TRY! IF HE'S SO GREAT, WHY DIDN'T HE STOP *BOO?!*
IT'S BAD ENOUGH TELLING ME *YOU'RE* A GOD!
...NOT VERY EASY TO LIKE, IS HE...?
...
OH...!
I GET IT!
THIS IS A DREAM!!
HA HA HA!! OF COURSE!!!
I *THOUGHT* IT WAS BIZARRE! NOBODY'S STRONGER THAN HERCULE, THE CHAMPION OF THE WORLD!!
BOO DOESN'T EVEN EXIST!! THESE ARE ALL DREAM PEOPLE!! I MUST'VE FALLEN ASLEEP AT THE TOURNAMENT!!
I'LL BET I CAN FLY IN MY DREAM, TOO!!
...
TP TP TP TP

READ THIS WAY

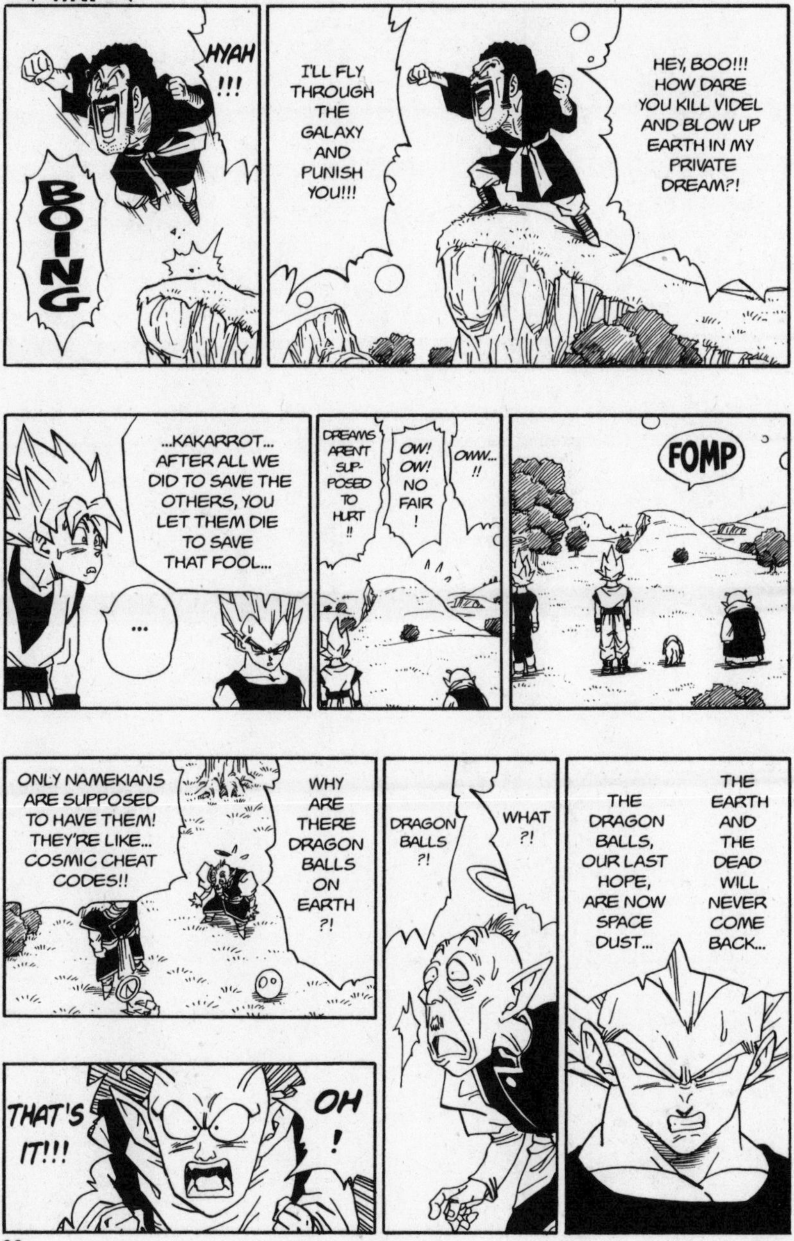

HEY, BOO!!! HOW DARE YOU KILL VIDEL AND BLOW UP EARTH IN MY PRIVATE DREAM?!
I'LL FLY THROUGH THE GALAXY AND PUNISH YOU!!!
HYAH !!!
BOING
FOMP
OWW... !!
OW! OW! NO FAIR !
DREAMS AREN'T SUP-POSED TO HURT !!
...KAKARROT... AFTER ALL WE DID TO SAVE THE OTHERS, YOU LET THEM DIE TO SAVE THAT FOOL...
...
THE EARTH AND THE DEAD WILL NEVER COME BACK...
THE DRAGON BALLS, OUR LAST HOPE, ARE NOW SPACE DUST...
WHAT ?!
DRAGON BALLS ?!
WHY ARE THERE DRAGON BALLS ON EARTH ?!
ONLY NAMEKIANS ARE SUPPOSED TO HAVE THEM! THEY'RE LIKE... COSMIC CHEAT CODES!!
OH !
THAT'S IT!!!

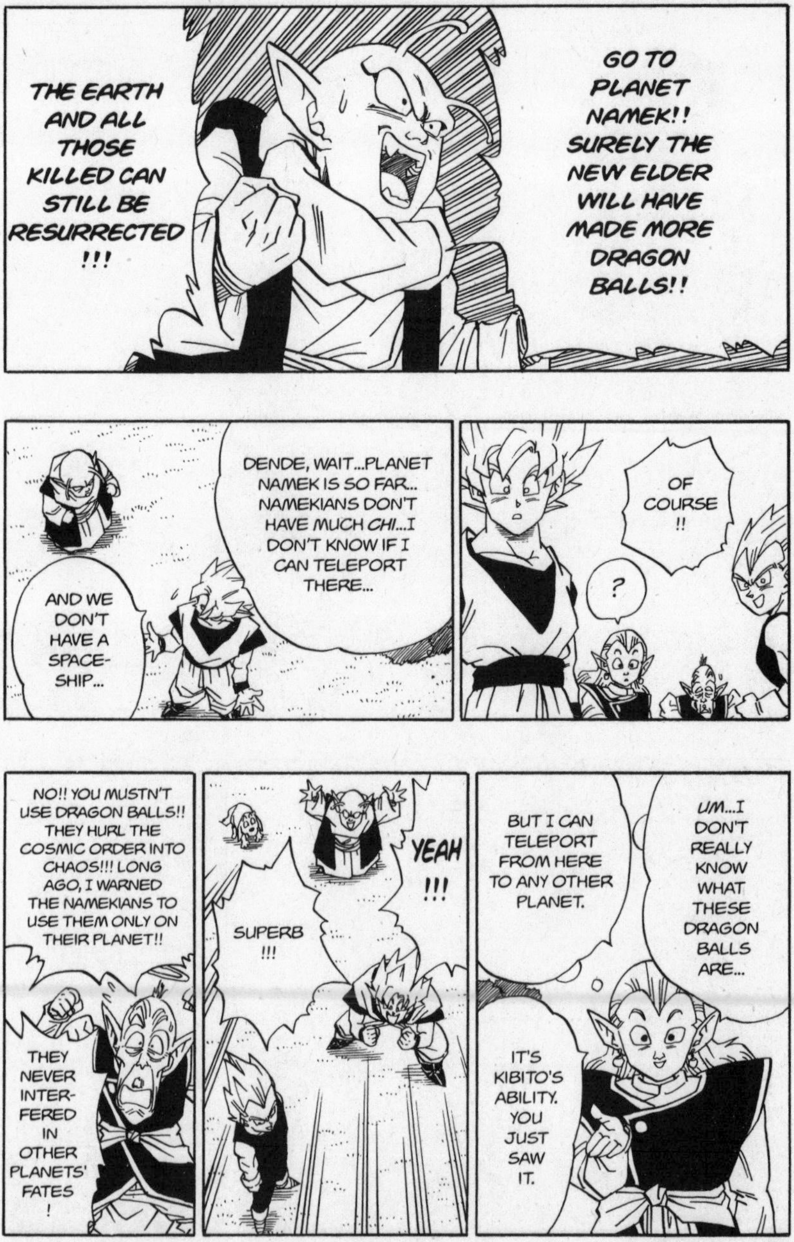
GO TO PLANET NAMEK!! SURELY THE NEW ELDER WILL HAVE MADE MORE DRAGON BALLS!!
THE EARTH AND ALL THOSE KILLED CAN STILL BE RESURRECTED !!!
OF COURSE !!
?
DENDE, WAIT...PLANET NAMEK IS SO FAR... NAMEKIANS DON'T HAVE MUCH *CHI*...I DON'T KNOW IF I CAN TELEPORT THERE...
AND WE DON'T HAVE A SPACE-SHIP...
UM...I DON'T REALLY KNOW WHAT THESE DRAGON BALLS ARE...
BUT I CAN TELEPORT FROM HERE TO ANY OTHER PLANET.
IT'S KIBITO'S ABILITY. YOU JUST SAW IT.
YEAH !!!
SUPERB !!!
NO!! YOU MUSTN'T USE DRAGON BALLS!! THEY HURL THE COSMIC ORDER INTO CHAOS!!! LONG AGO, I WARNED THE NAMEKIANS TO USE THEM ONLY ON THEIR PLANET!!
THEY NEVER INTER-FERED IN OTHER PLANETS' FATES !

READ THIS WAY

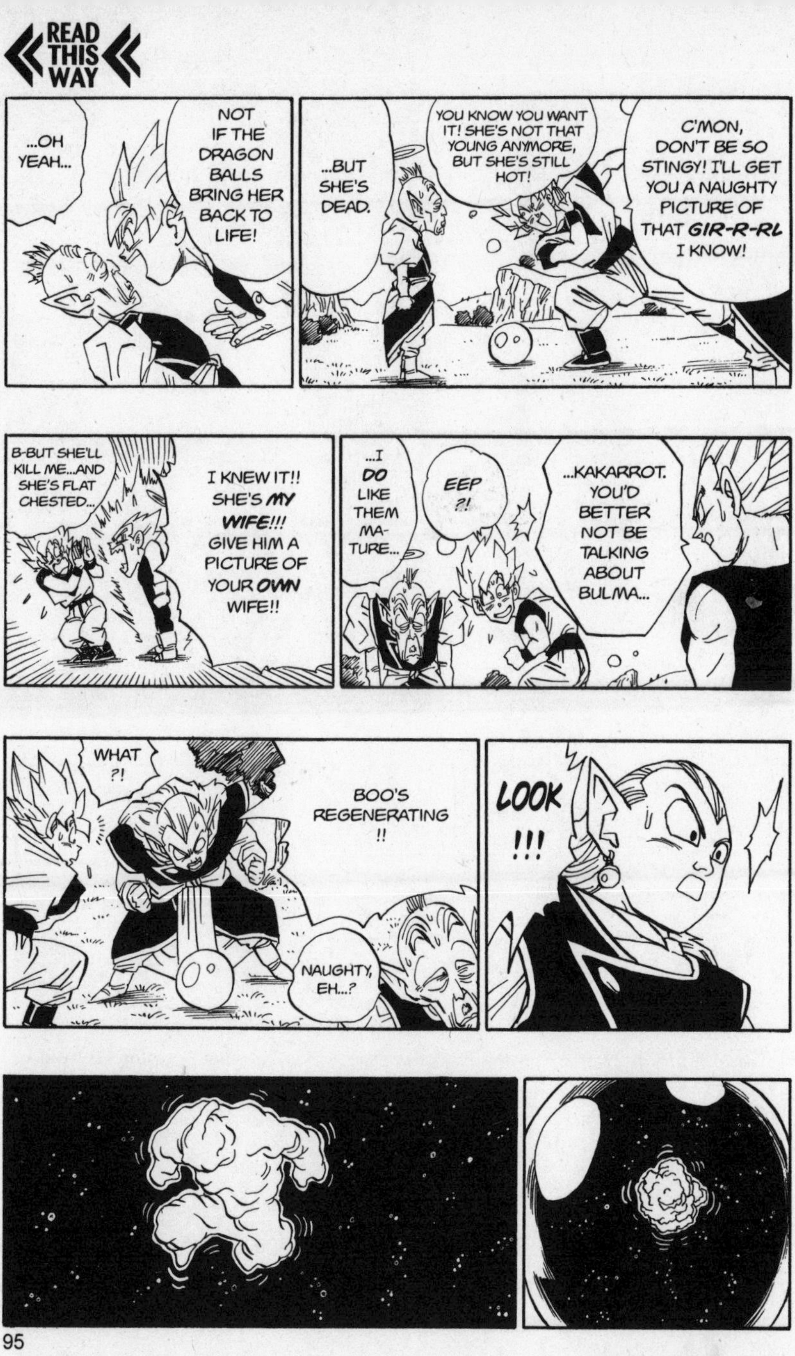
C'MON, DON'T BE SO STINGY! I'LL GET YOU A NAUGHTY PICTURE OF THAT GIR-R-RL I KNOW!
YOU KNOW YOU WANT IT! SHE'S NOT THAT YOUNG ANYMORE, BUT SHE'S STILL HOT!
...BUT SHE'S DEAD.
NOT IF THE DRAGON BALLS BRING HER BACK TO LIFE!
...OH YEAH...
...KAKARROT. YOU'D BETTER NOT BE TALKING ABOUT BULMA...
EEP ?!
...I DO LIKE THEM MA-TURE...
I KNEW IT!! SHE'S MY WIFE!!! GIVE HIM A PICTURE OF YOUR OWN WIFE!!
B-BUT SHE'LL KILL ME...AND SHE'S FLAT CHESTED...
LOOK !!!
BOO'S REGENERATING !!
WHAT ?!
NAUGHTY, EH...?

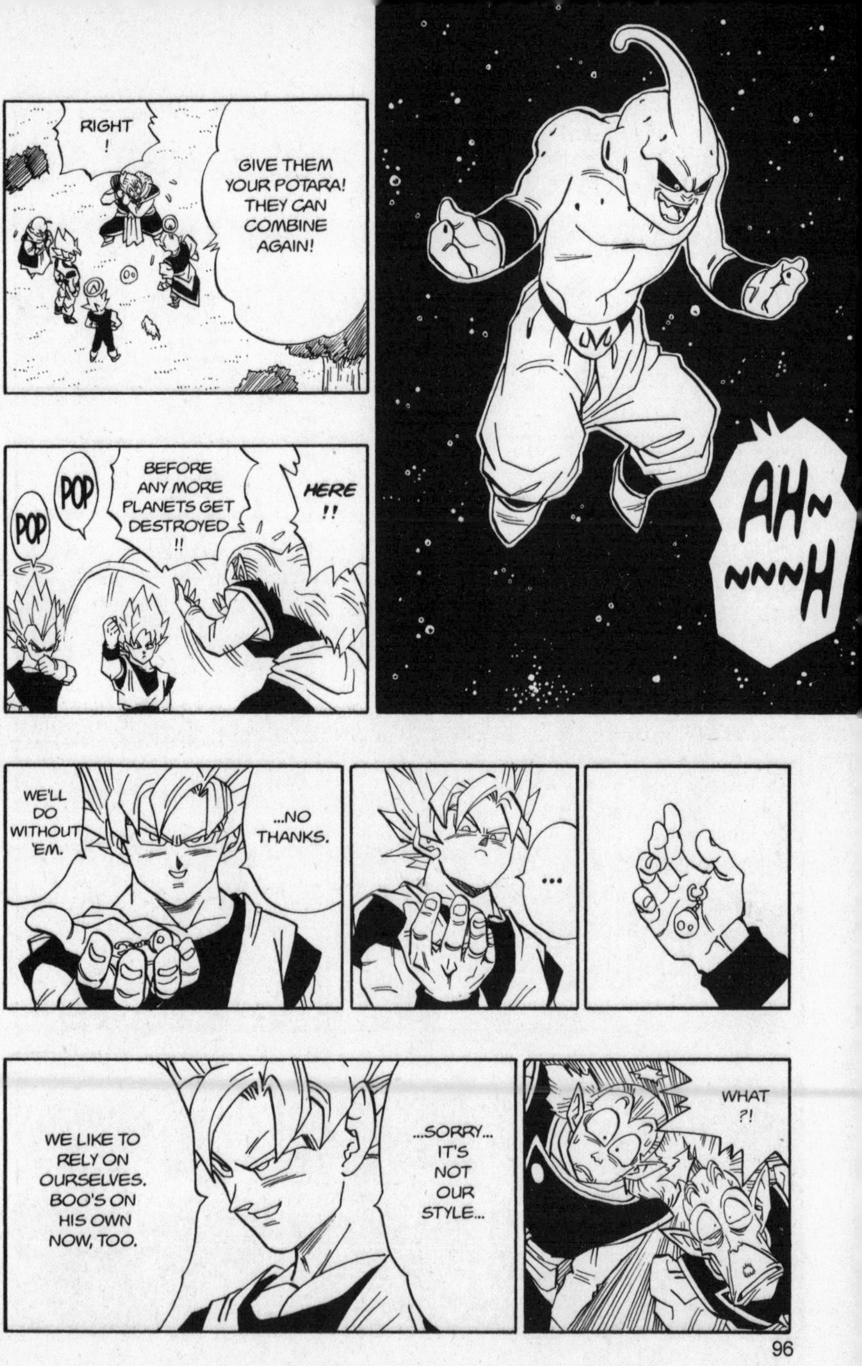
AH~NNNH
GIVE THEM YOUR POTARA! THEY CAN COMBINE AGAIN!
RIGHT !
HERE !!
BEFORE ANY MORE PLANETS GET DESTROYED !!
POP
POP
...
...NO THANKS.
WE'LL DO WITHOUT 'EM.
WHAT ?!
...SORRY... IT'S NOT OUR STYLE...
WE LIKE TO RELY ON OURSELVES. BOO'S ON HIS OWN NOW, TOO.

READ THIS WAY

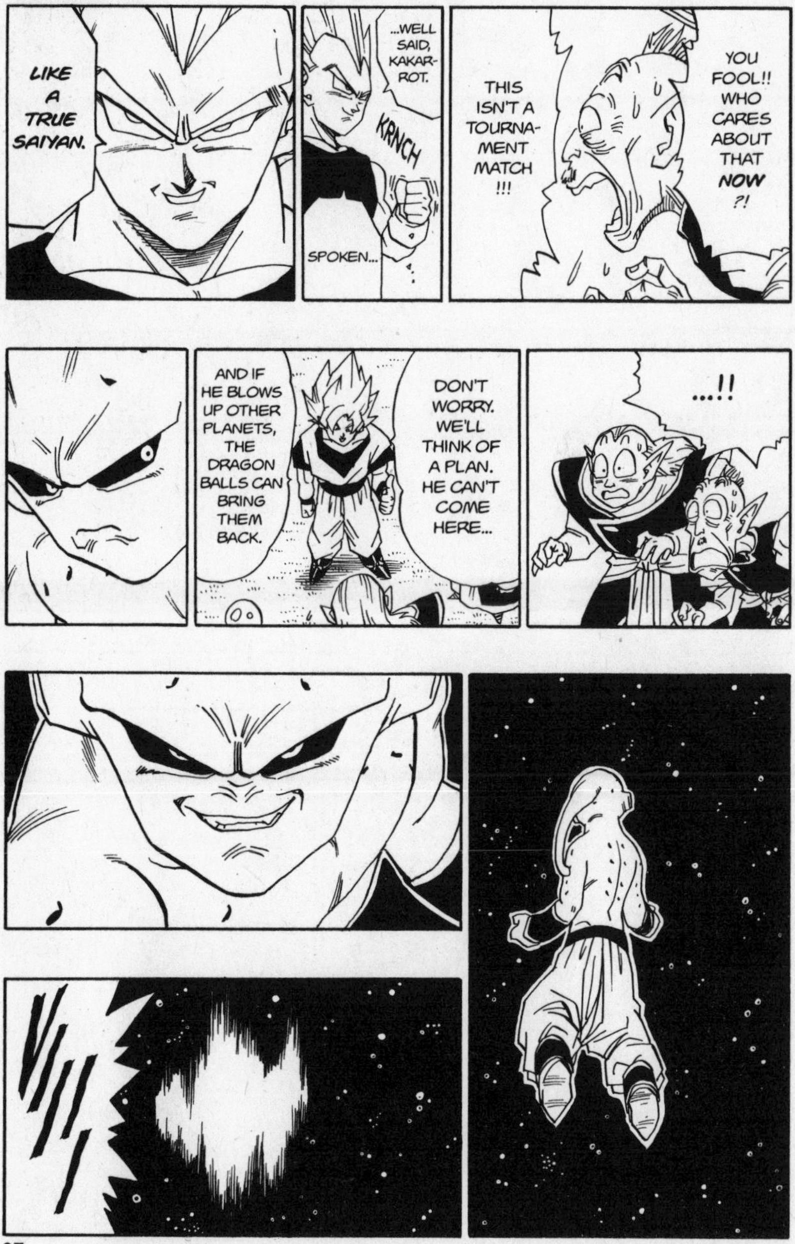
YOU FOOL!! WHO CARES ABOUT THAT NOW?!
THIS ISN'T A TOURNAMENT MATCH!!!
...WELL SAID, KAKARROT.
KRNCH
SPOKEN...
LIKE A TRUE SAIYAN.
...!!
DON'T WORRY. WE'LL THINK OF A PLAN. HE CAN'T COME HERE...
AND IF HE BLOWS UP OTHER PLANETS, THE DRAGON BALLS CAN BRING THEM BACK.

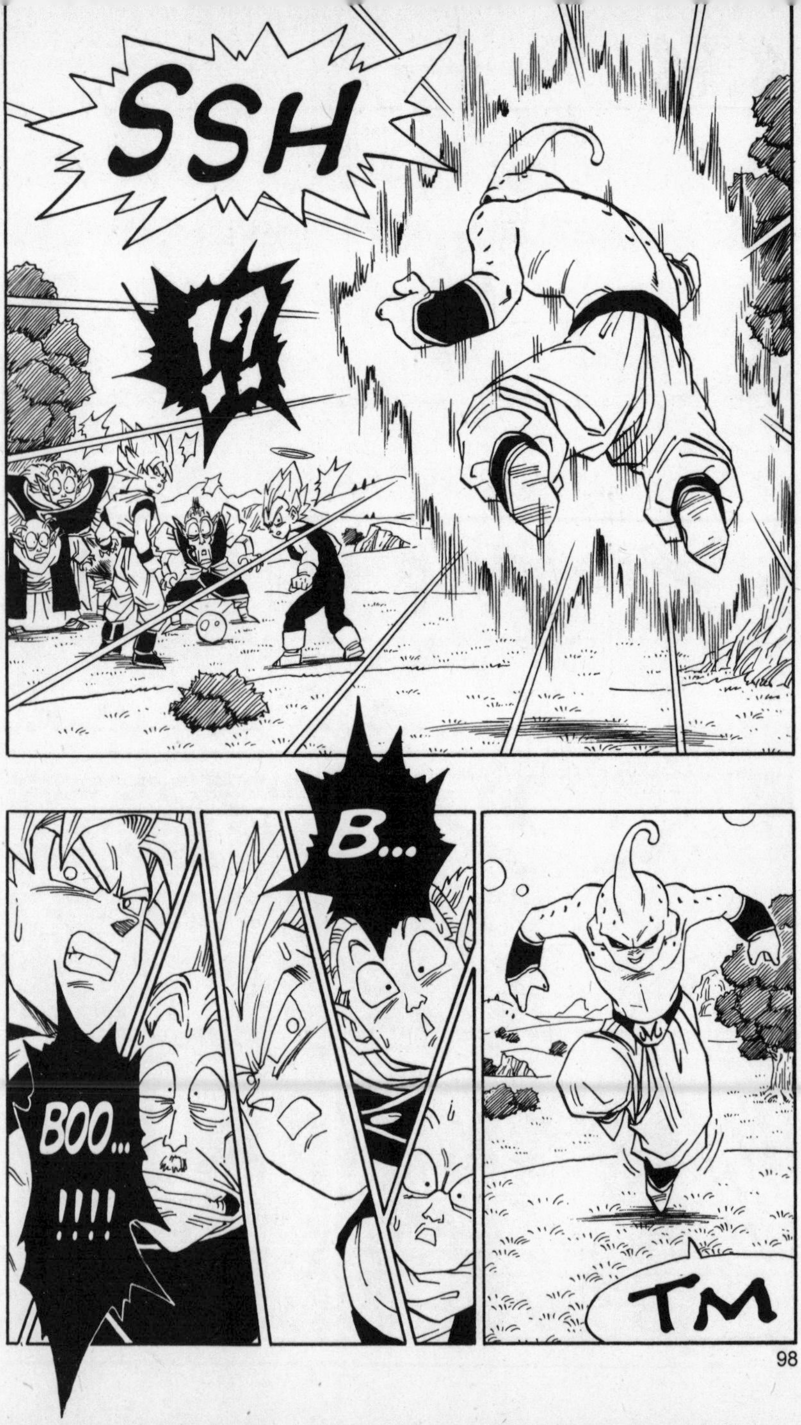

SSH
!?
TM
B...
BOO...
!!!!!

READ THIS WAY

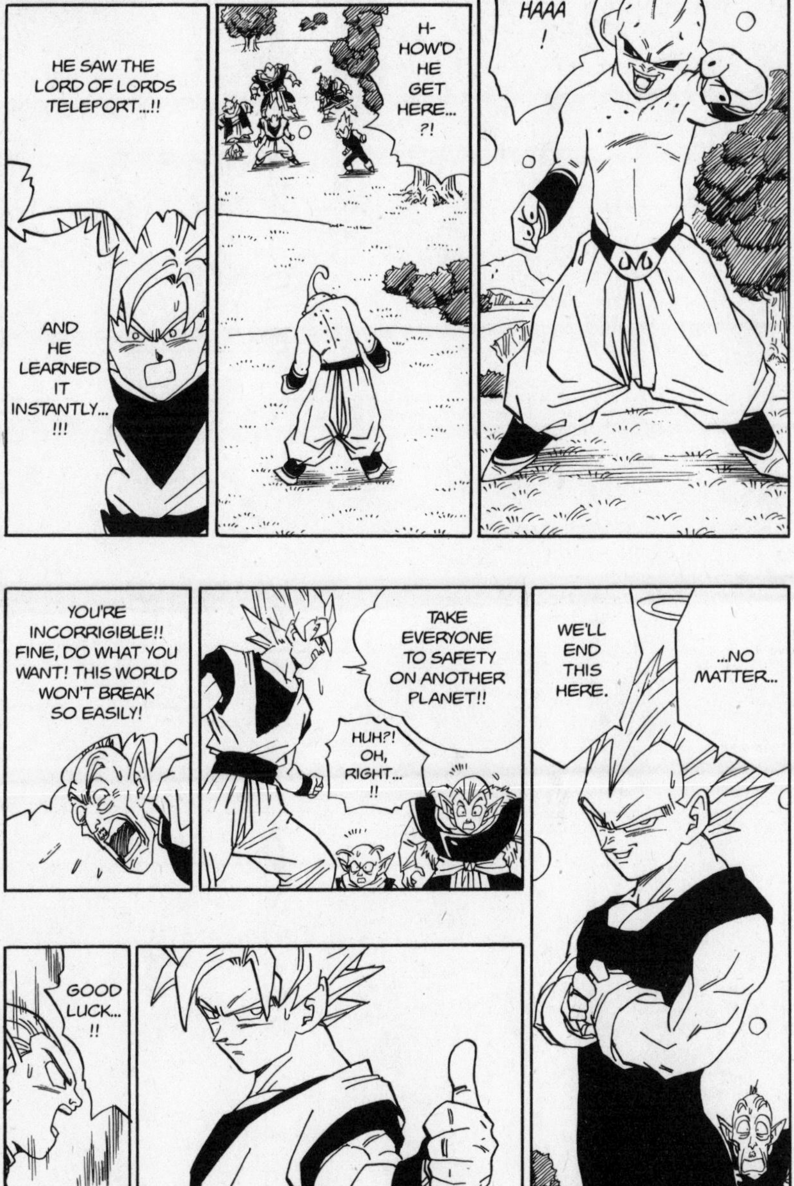

HA HAAA!
H- HOW'D HE GET HERE...?!
HE SAW THE LORD OF LORDS TELEPORT...!!
AND HE LEARNED IT INSTANTLY...!!!
...NO MATTER...
WE'LL END THIS HERE.
TAKE EVERYONE TO SAFETY ON ANOTHER PLANET!!
HUH?! OH, RIGHT...!!
YOU'RE INCORRIGIBLE!! FINE, DO WHAT YOU WANT! THIS WORLD WON'T BREAK SO EASILY!
GOOD LUCK...!!

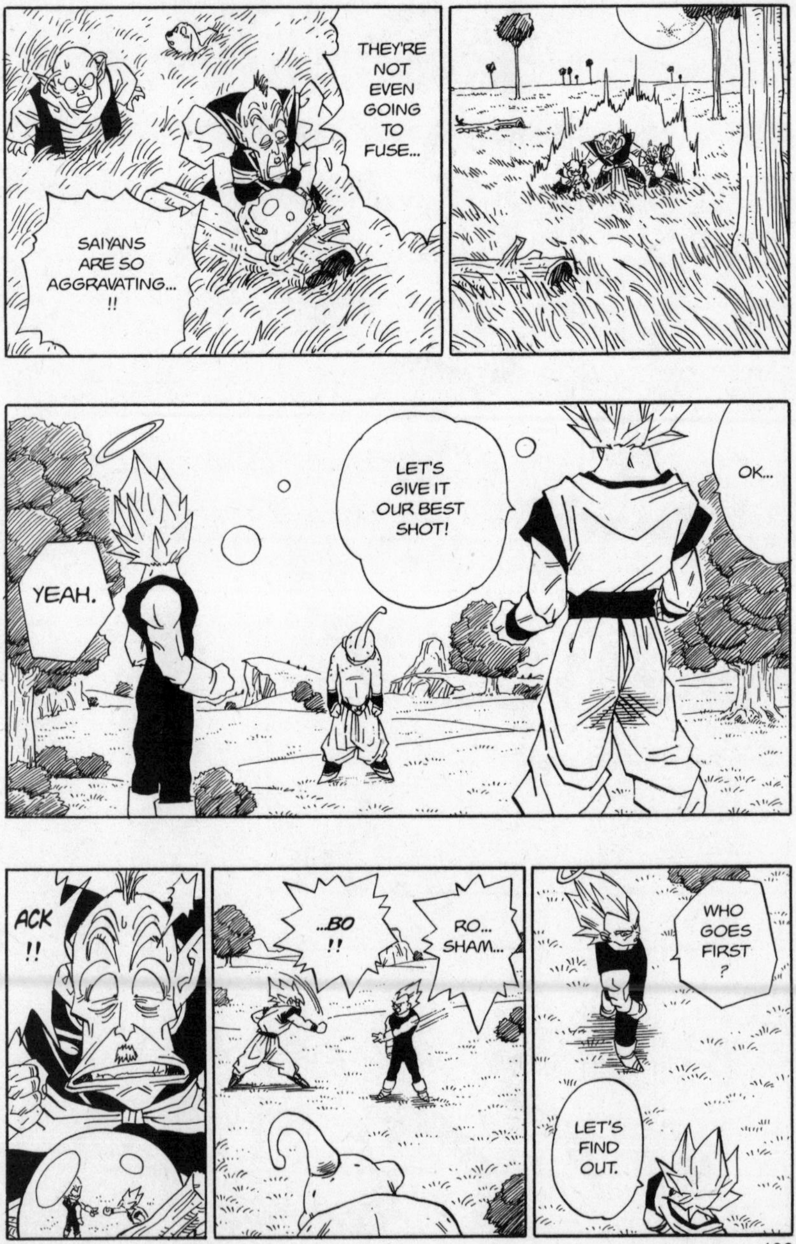
THEY'RE NOT EVEN GOING TO FUSE...
SAIYANS ARE SO AGGRAVATING... !!
OK...
LET'S GIVE IT OUR BEST SHOT!
YEAH.
WHO GOES FIRST ?
LET'S FIND OUT.
RO... SHAM...
...BO !!
ACK !!

READ THIS WAY

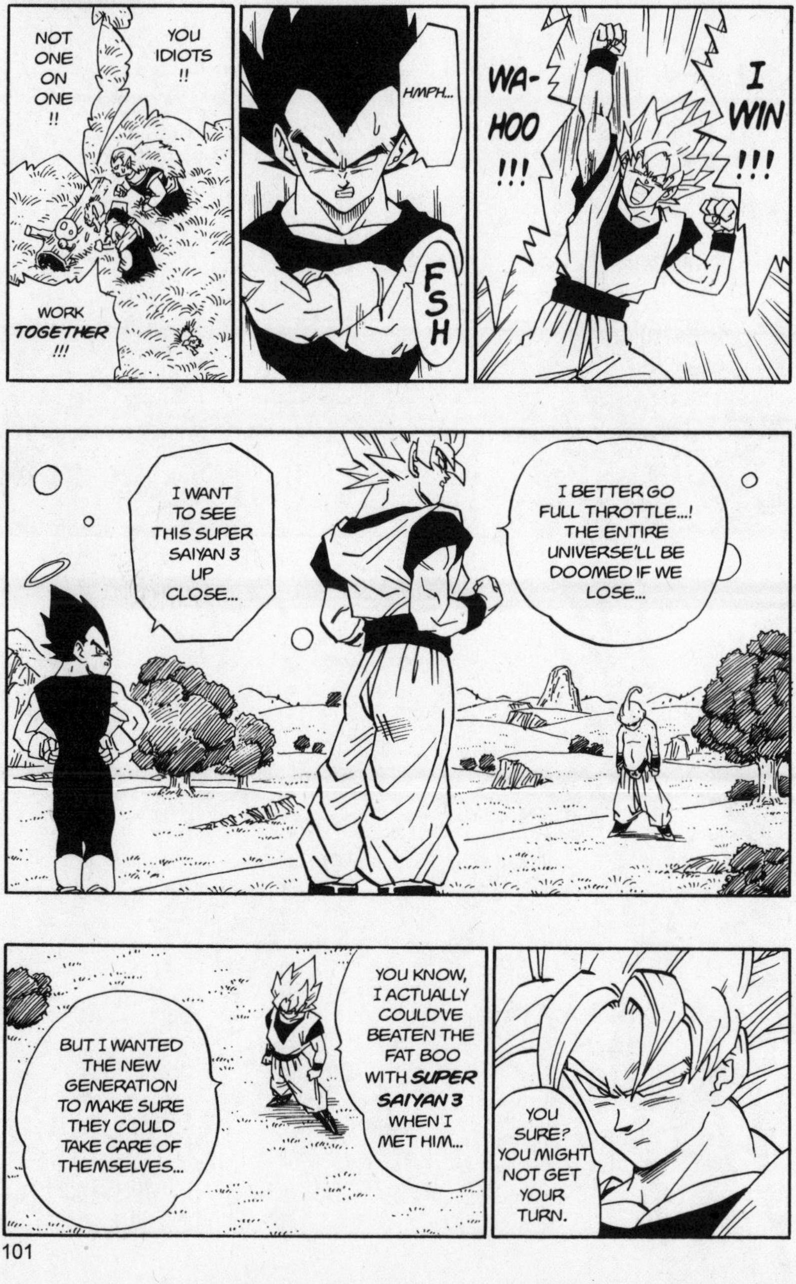
I WIN !!!
WA-HOO !!!
HMPH...
FSH
YOU IDIOTS !!
NOT ONE ON ONE !!
WORK ***TOGETHER*** !!!
I BETTER GO FULL THROTTLE...! THE ENTIRE UNIVERSE'LL BE DOOMED IF WE LOSE...
I WANT TO SEE THIS SUPER SAIYAN 3 UP CLOSE...
YOU SURE? YOU MIGHT NOT GET YOUR TURN.
YOU KNOW, I ACTUALLY COULD'VE BEATEN THE FAT BOO WITH ***SUPER SAIYAN 3*** WHEN I MET HIM...
BUT I WANTED THE NEW GENERATION TO MAKE SURE THEY COULD TAKE CARE OF THEMSELVES...

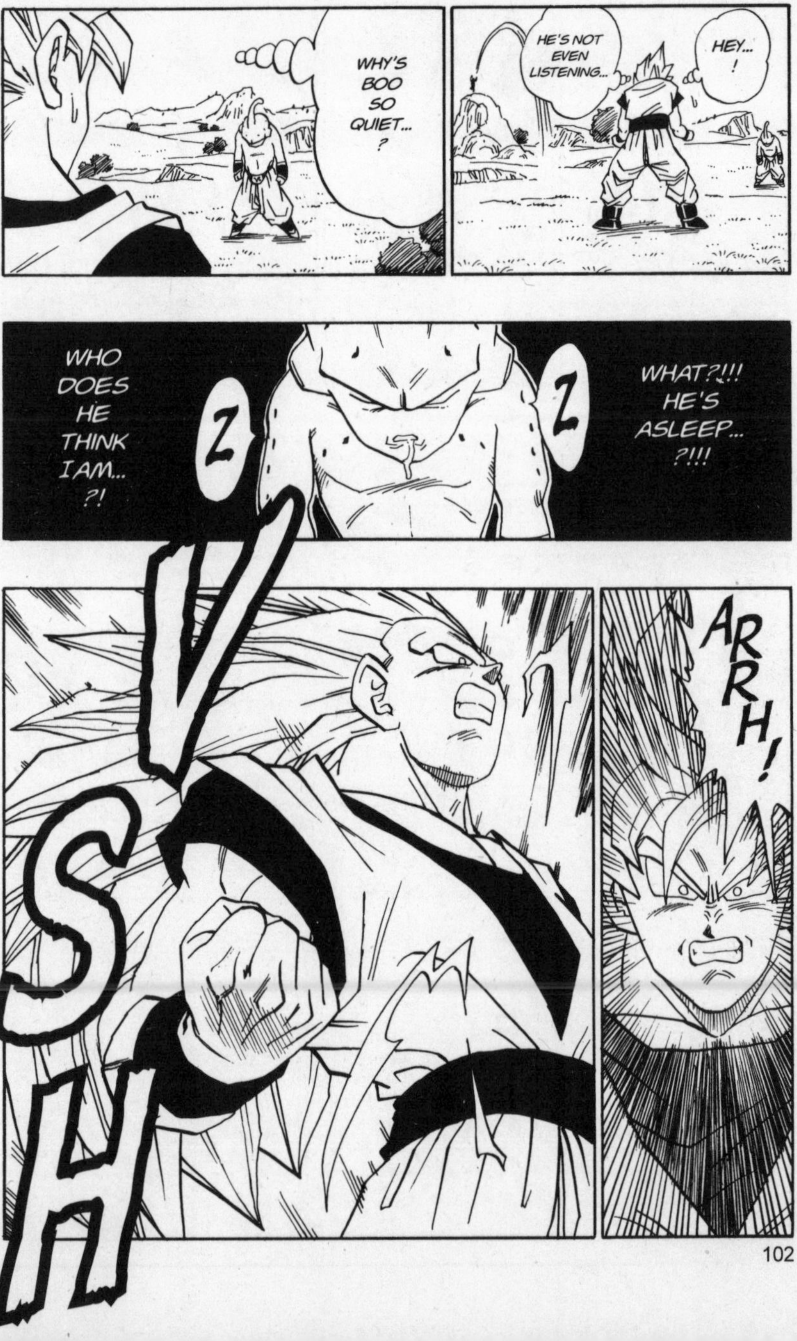
HEY... !
HE'S NOT EVEN LISTENING...
WHY'S BOO SO QUIET... ?
WHAT?!!! HE'S ASLEEP... ?!!!
Z
Z
WHO DOES HE THINK I AM... ?!
ARRH!

READ THIS WAY

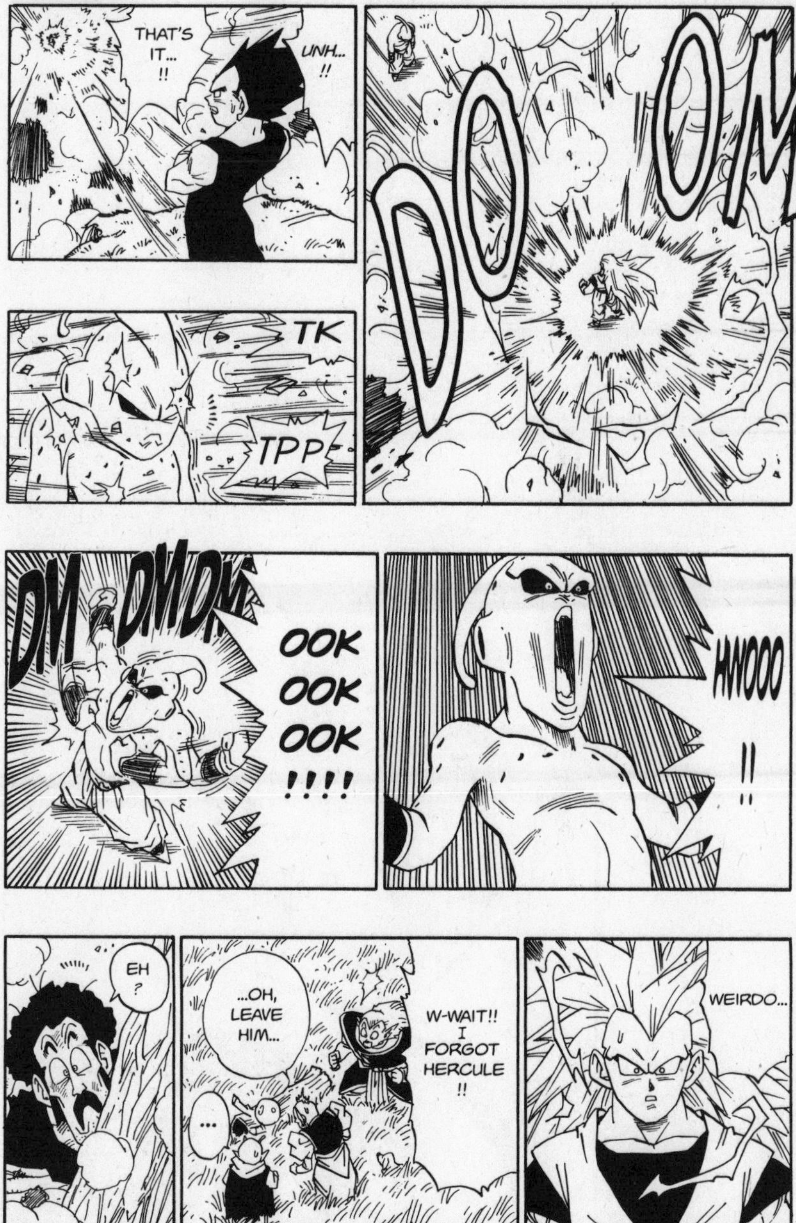

DO OM
UNH... !!
THAT'S IT... !!
TK
TPP
HWOOO !!
DM DMDM
OOK OOK OOK !!!!
WEIRDO...
W-WAIT!! I FORGOT HERCULE !!
...OH, LEAVE HIM...
...
EH ?

DBZ:316 · Vegeta and Kakarrot

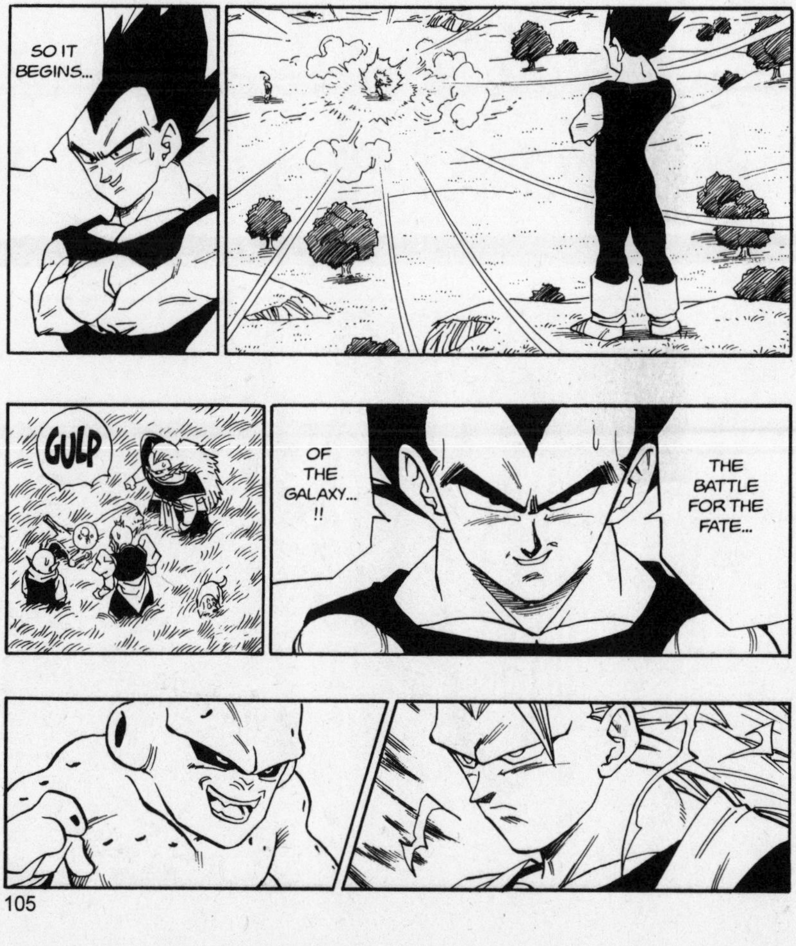
SO IT BEGINS...
THE BATTLE FOR THE FATE...
OF THE GALAXY... !!
GULP

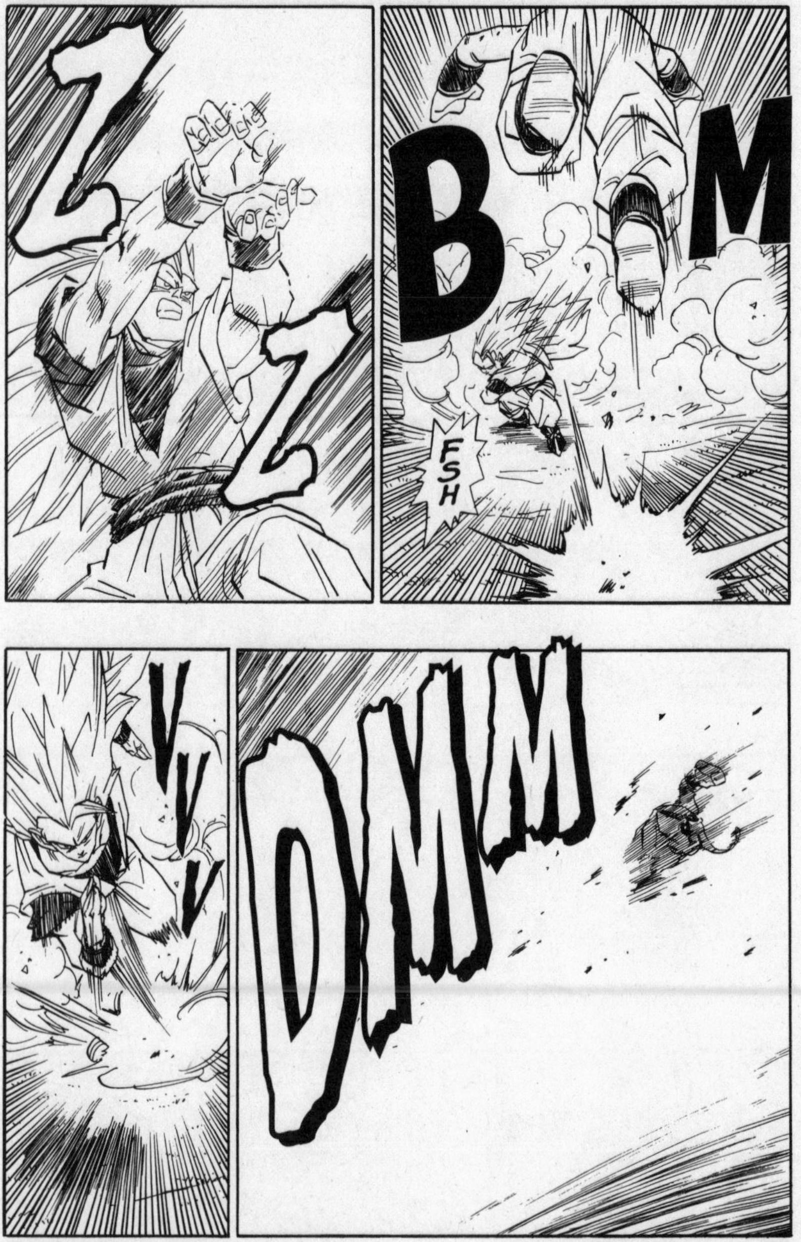
BM
FSH
ZZ
DMM
VVV

READ THIS WAY

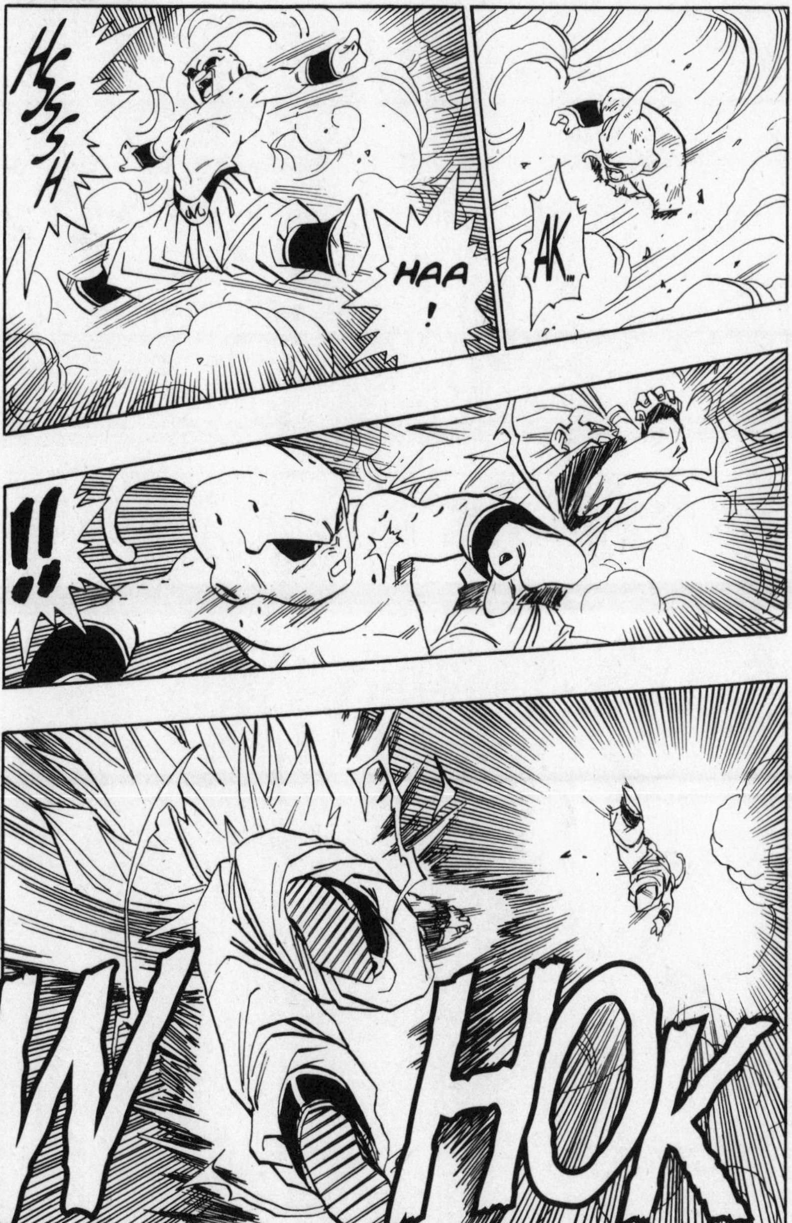
AK...
HSSSH
HAA!
!!
WHOK

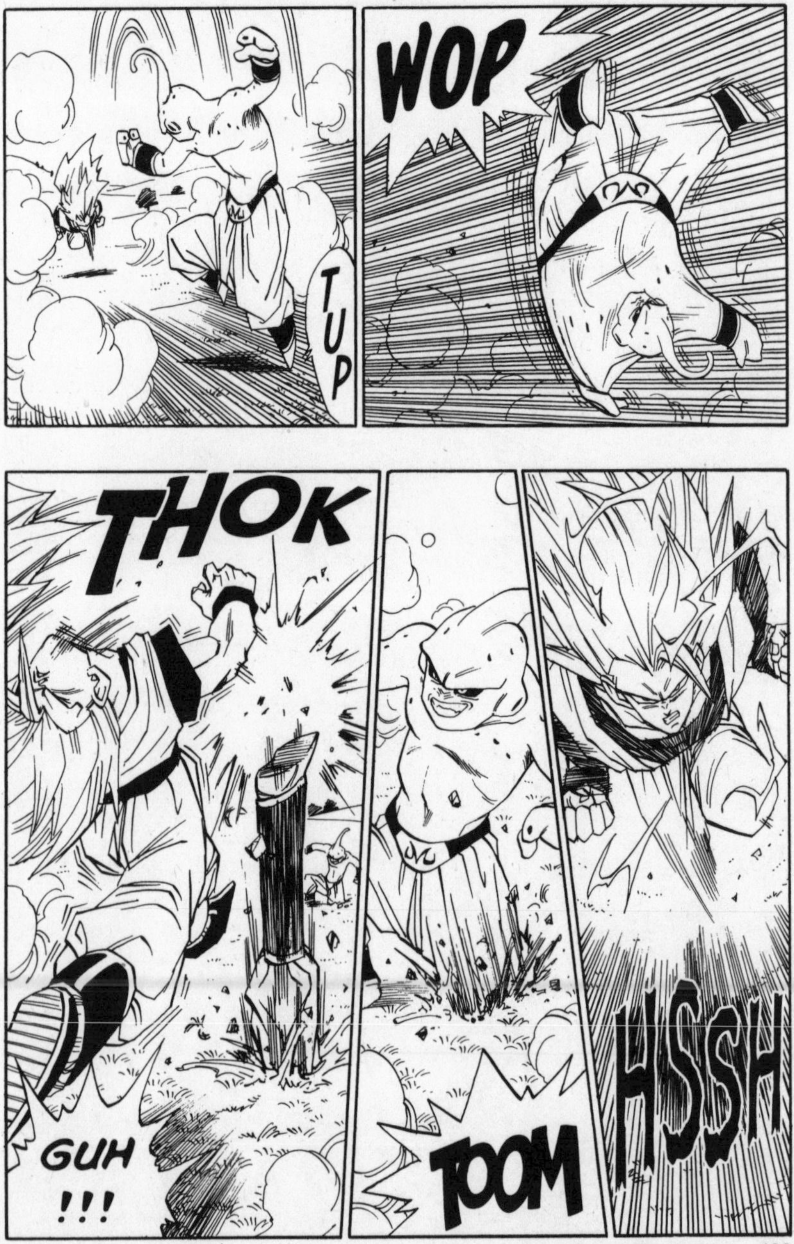
WOP
TUP
HSSH
TOOM
THOK
GUH !!!

READ THIS WAY

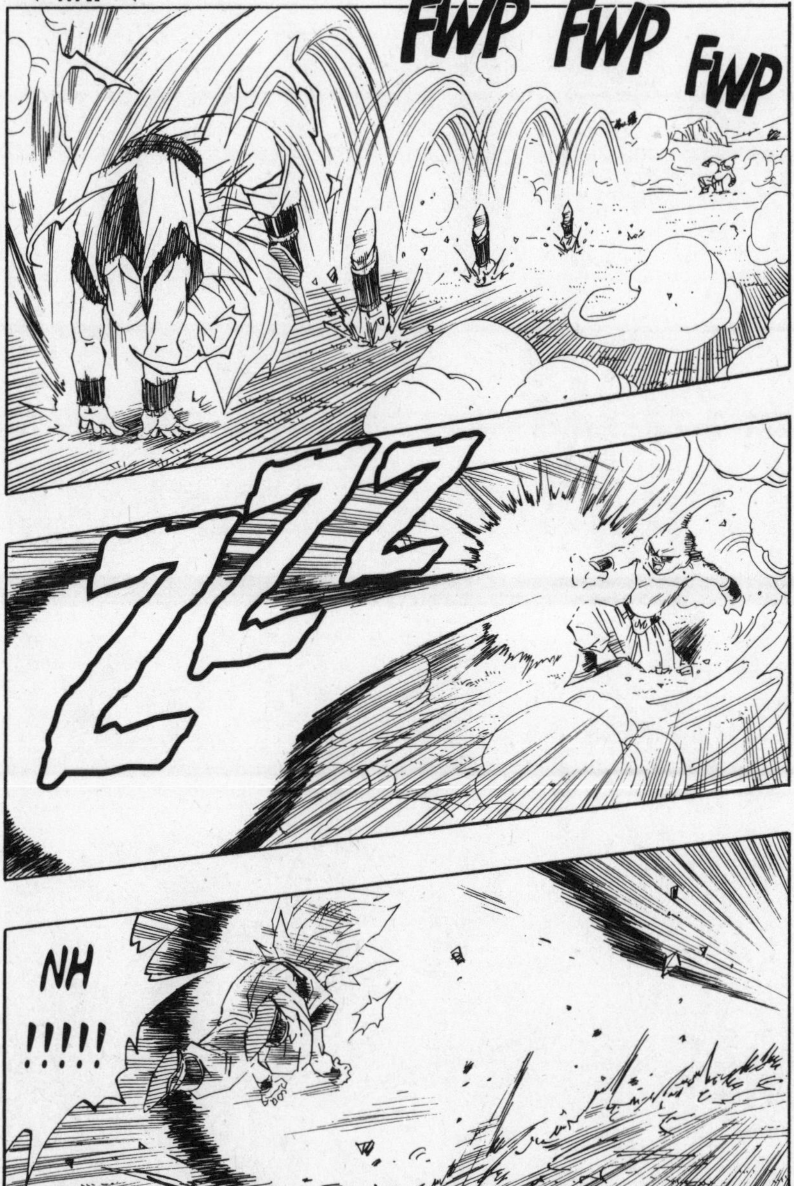
FWP FWP FWP
ZZ
NH
!!!!!

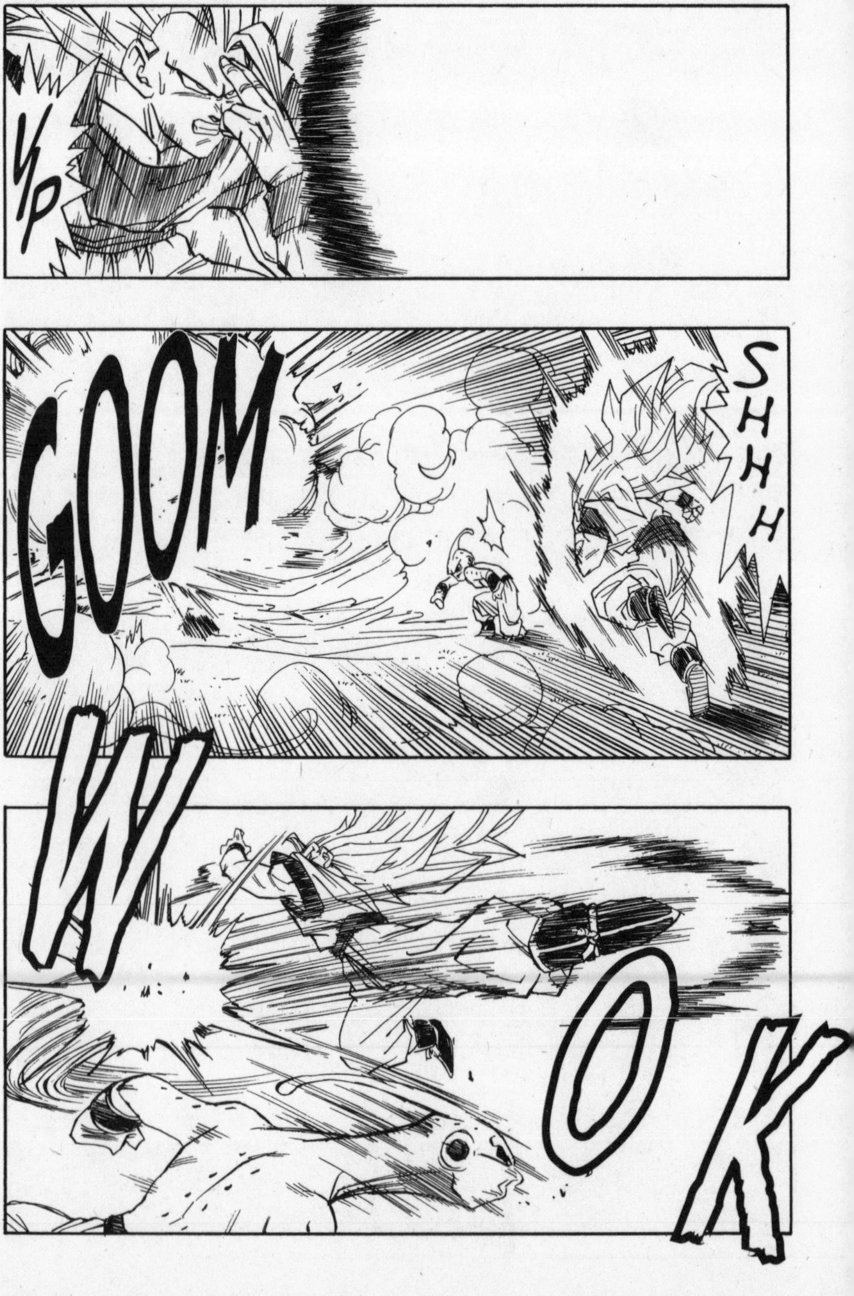
YIP
SHHH
GOOM
WOK

READ THIS WAY

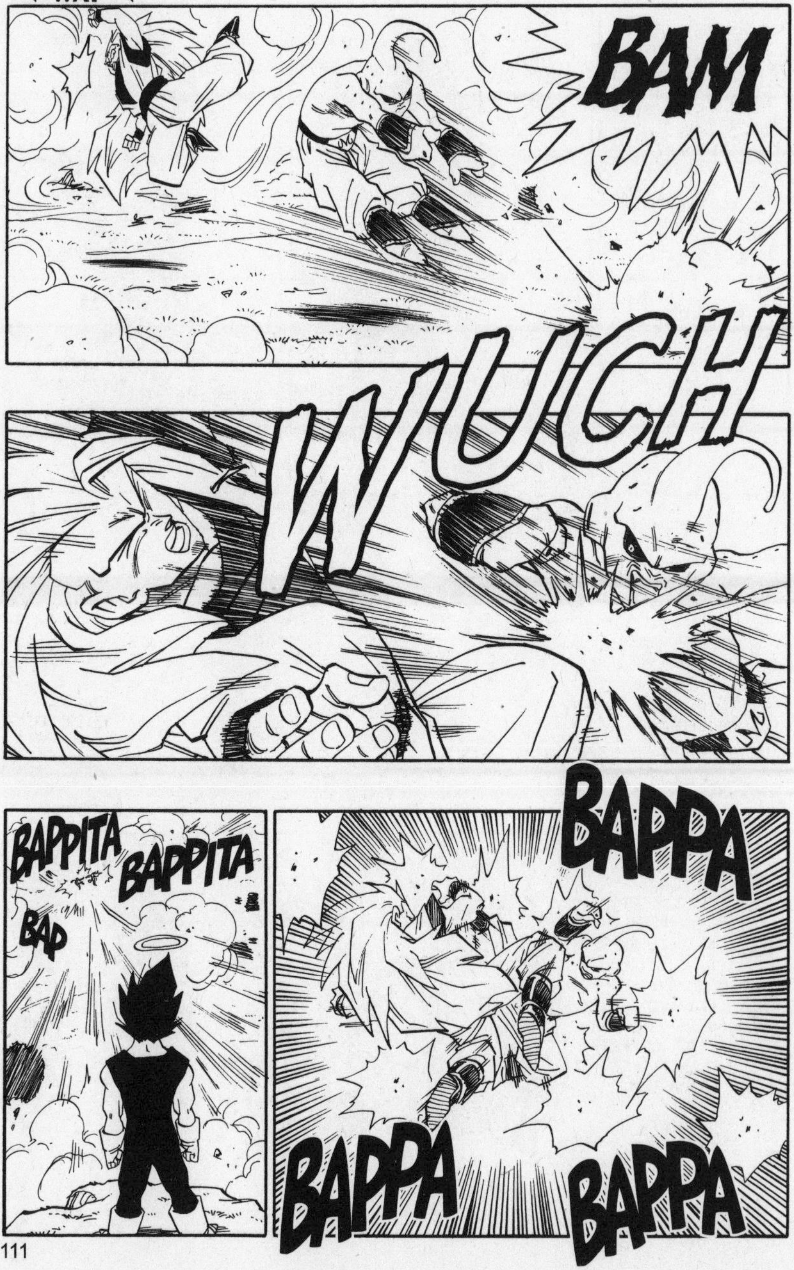
BAM
WUCH
BAPPA
BAPPA
BAPPA
BAPPITA
BAPPITA
BAP

READ THIS WAY

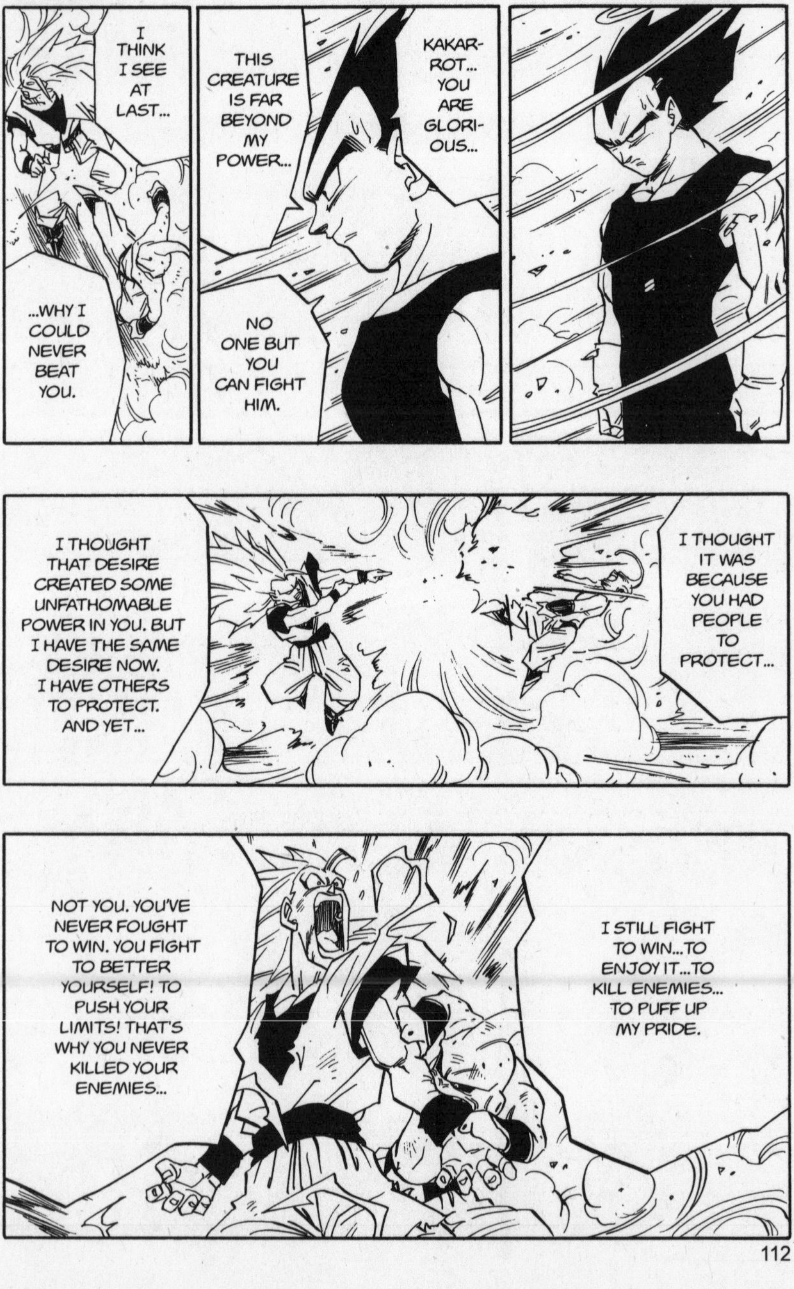

KAKARROT... YOU ARE GLORIOUS...
THIS CREATURE IS FAR BEYOND MY POWER...
NO ONE BUT YOU CAN FIGHT HIM.
I THINK I SEE AT LAST...
...WHY I COULD NEVER BEAT YOU.
I THOUGHT IT WAS BECAUSE YOU HAD PEOPLE TO PROTECT...
I THOUGHT THAT DESIRE CREATED SOME UNFATHOMABLE POWER IN YOU. BUT I HAVE THE SAME DESIRE NOW. I HAVE OTHERS TO PROTECT. AND YET...
I STILL FIGHT TO WIN...TO ENJOY IT...TO KILL ENEMIES... TO PUFF UP MY PRIDE.
NOT YOU. YOU'VE NEVER FOUGHT TO WIN. YOU FIGHT TO BETTER YOURSELF! TO PUSH YOUR LIMITS! THAT'S WHY YOU NEVER KILLED YOUR ENEMIES...

READ THIS WAY

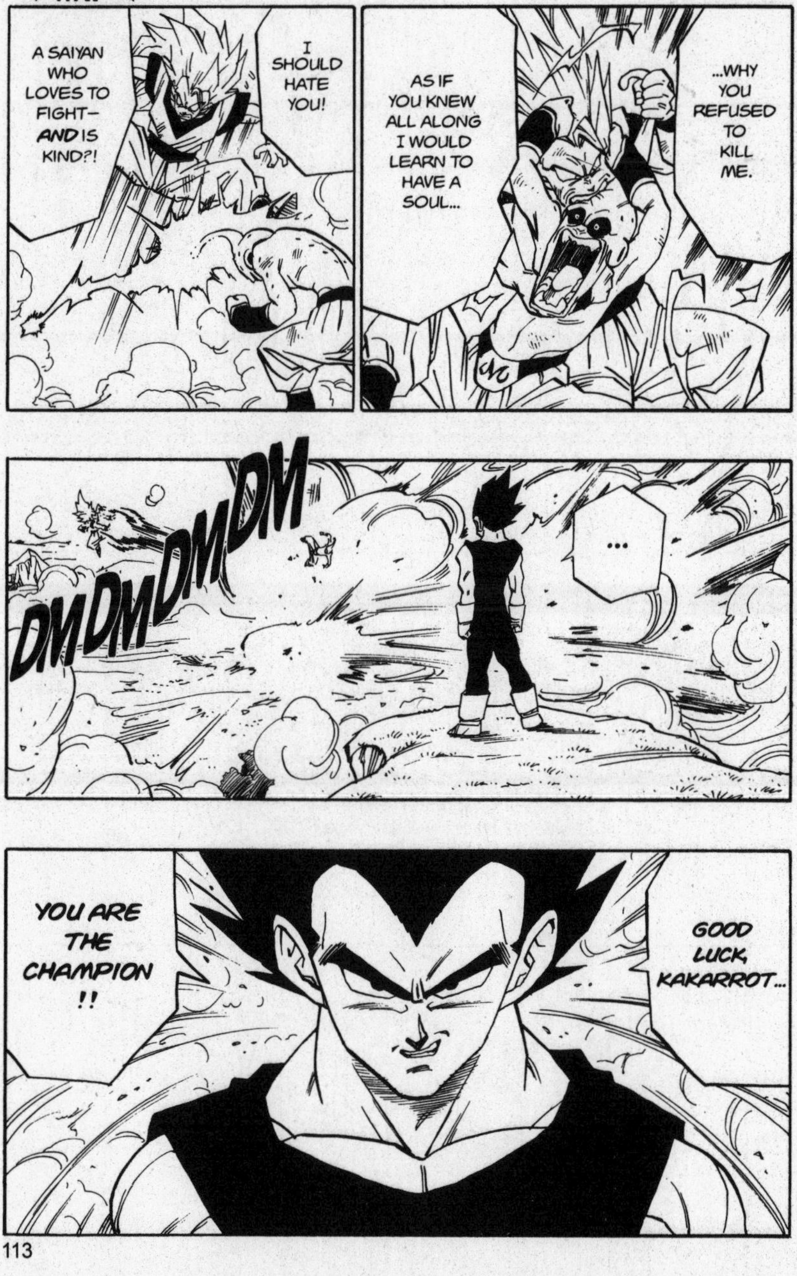
...WHY YOU REFUSED TO KILL ME.
AS IF YOU KNEW ALL ALONG I WOULD LEARN TO HAVE A SOUL...
I SHOULD HATE YOU!
A SAIYAN WHO LOVES TO FIGHT— AND IS KIND?!
...
DMDMDMDM
GOOD LUCK, KAKARROT...
YOU ARE THE CHAMPION !!

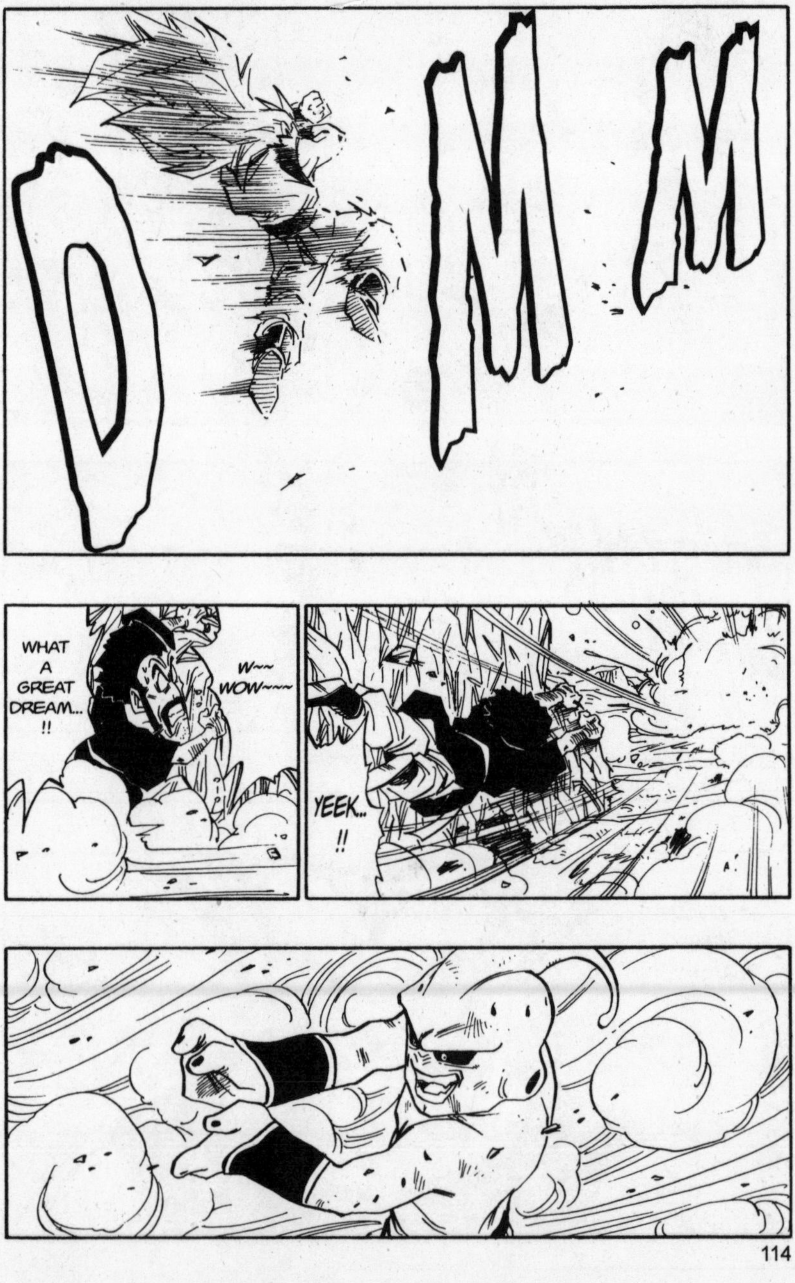
DMM
YEEK.. !!
W~~ WOW~~~
WHAT A GREAT DREAM... !!

READ THIS WAY

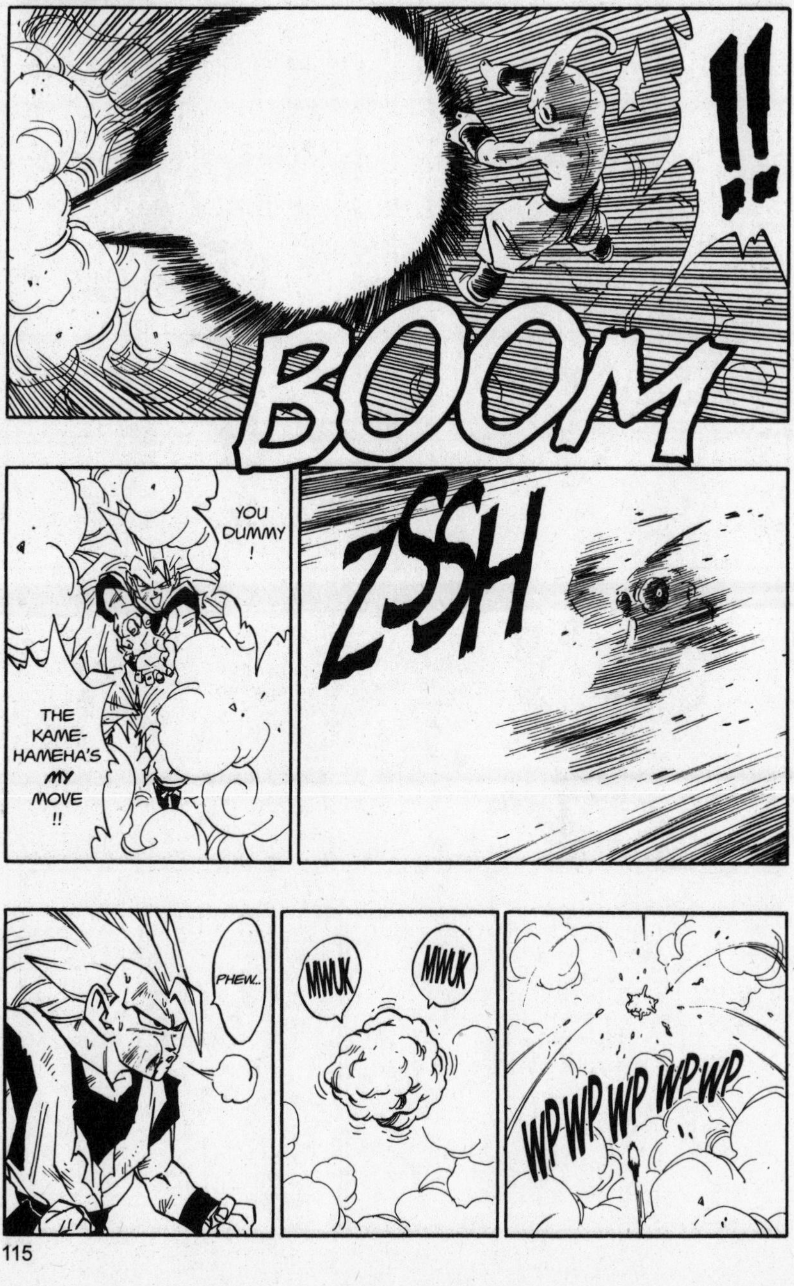
!!
BOOM
ZSSH
YOU DUMMY!
THE KAME-HAMEHA'S ***MY*** MOVE!!
WP WP WP WP WP WP
MWUK
MWUK
PHEW...

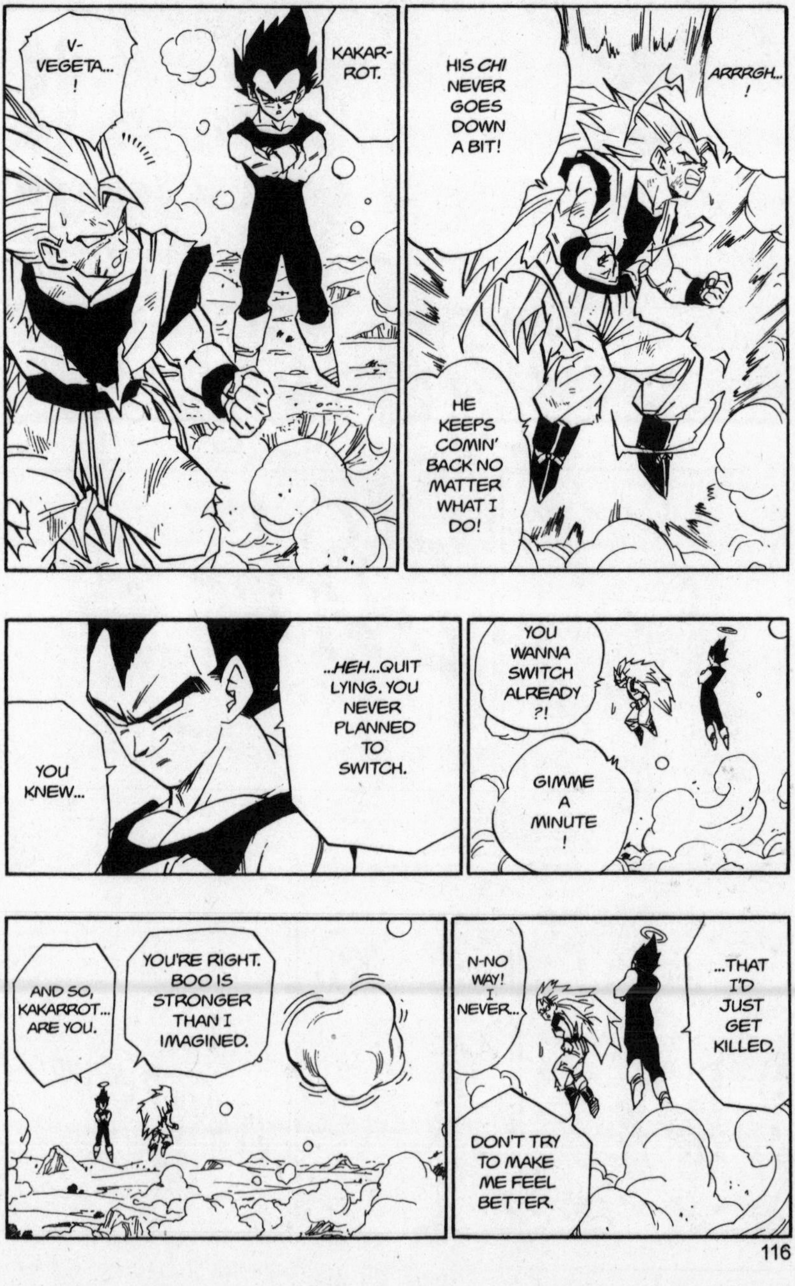
ARRRGH... !
HIS *CHI* NEVER GOES DOWN A BIT!
HE KEEPS COMIN' BACK NO MATTER WHAT I DO!
KAKAR-ROT.
V-VEGETA... !
YOU WANNA SWITCH ALREADY ?!
GIMME A MINUTE !
...*HEH*...QUIT LYING. YOU NEVER PLANNED TO SWITCH.
YOU KNEW...
...THAT I'D JUST GET KILLED.
N-NO WAY! I NEVER...
DON'T TRY TO MAKE ME FEEL BETTER.
YOU'RE RIGHT. BOO IS STRONGER THAN I IMAGINED.
AND SO, KAKARROT... ARE YOU.

READ THIS WAY

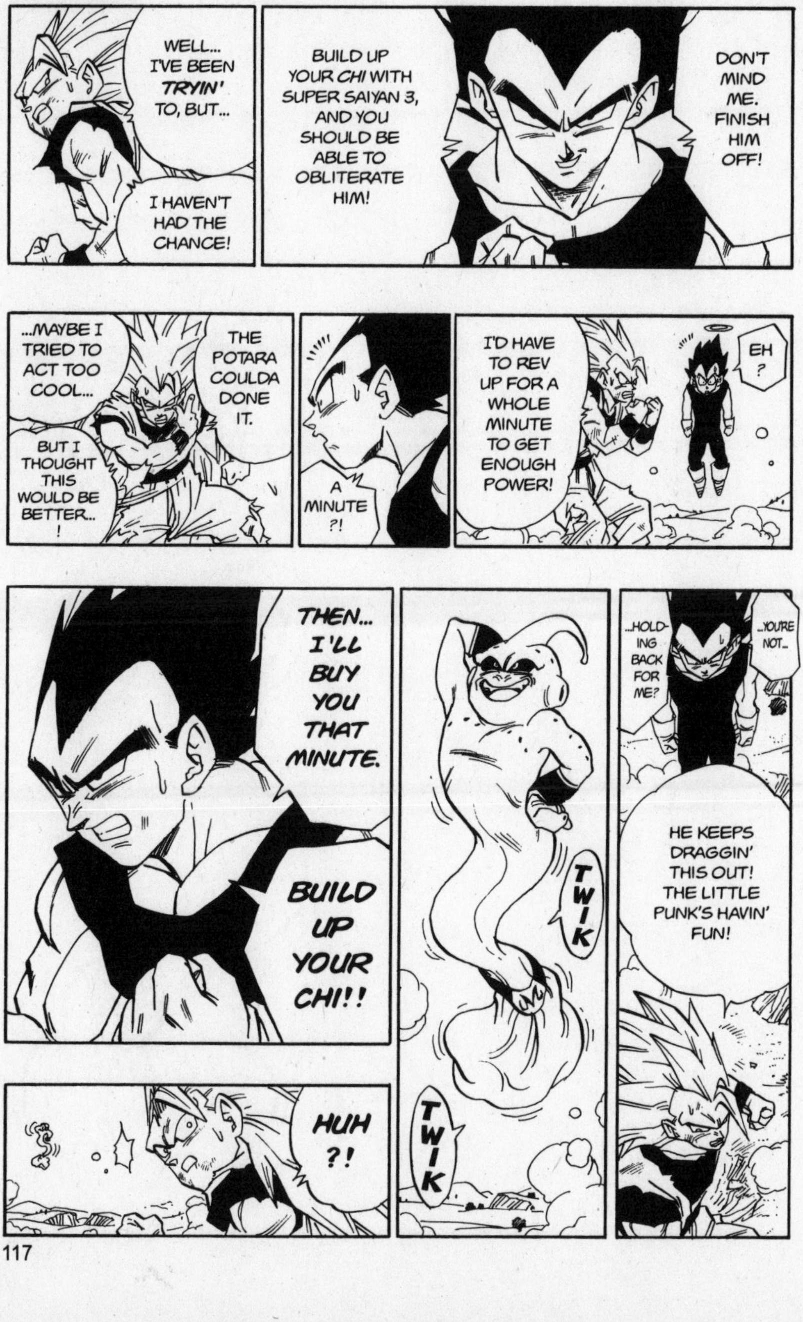

DON'T MIND ME. FINISH HIM OFF!
BUILD UP YOUR *CHI* WITH SUPER SAIYAN 3, AND YOU SHOULD BE ABLE TO OBLITERATE HIM!
WELL... I'VE BEEN *TRYIN'* TO, BUT...
I HAVEN'T HAD THE CHANCE!
EH?
I'D HAVE TO REV UP FOR A WHOLE MINUTE TO GET ENOUGH POWER!
A MINUTE?!
THE POTARA COULDA DONE IT.
...MAYBE I TRIED TO ACT TOO COOL...
BUT I THOUGHT THIS WOULD BE BETTER..!
...YOU'RE NOT...
...HOLDING BACK FOR ME?
HE KEEPS DRAGGIN' THIS OUT! THE LITTLE PUNK'S HAVIN' FUN!
TWIK
TWIK
THEN... I'LL BUY YOU THAT MINUTE.
BUILD UP YOUR CHI!!
HUH?!

DBZ:317
Vegeta Puts His Life on the Line!

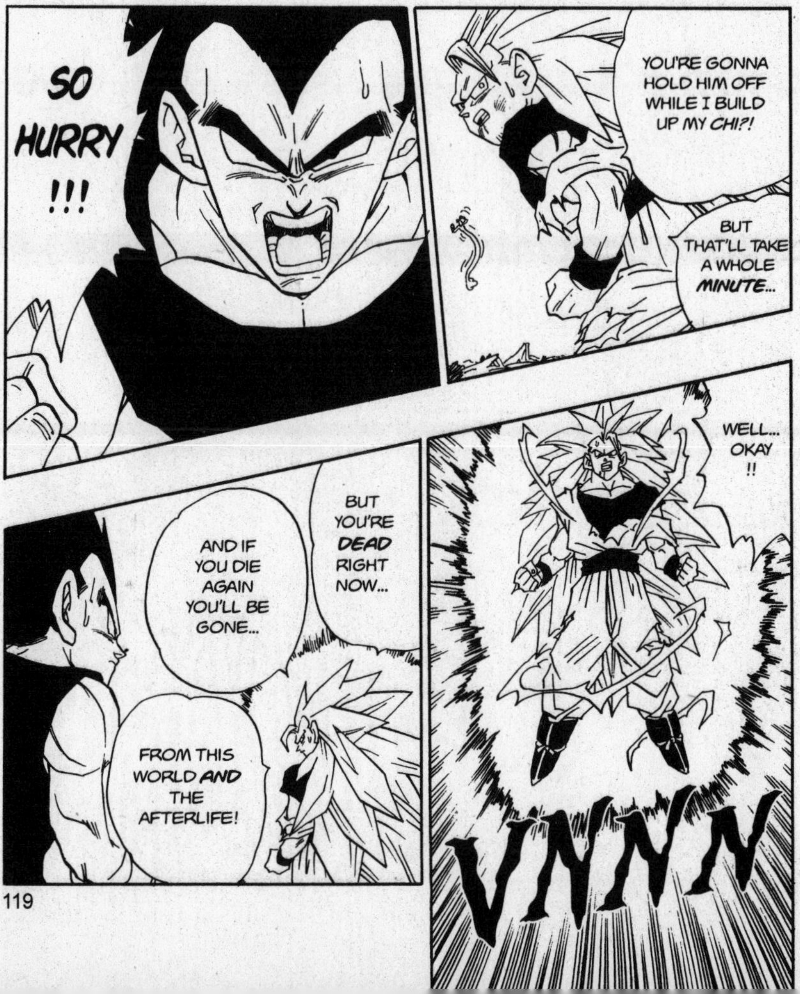
YOU'RE GONNA HOLD HIM OFF WHILE I BUILD UP MY *CHI*?!
BUT THAT'LL TAKE A WHOLE *MINUTE*...
SO HURRY !!!
WELL... OKAY !!
VNNN
BUT YOU'RE *DEAD* RIGHT NOW...
AND IF YOU DIE AGAIN YOU'LL BE GONE...
FROM THIS WORLD *AND* THE AFTERLIFE!

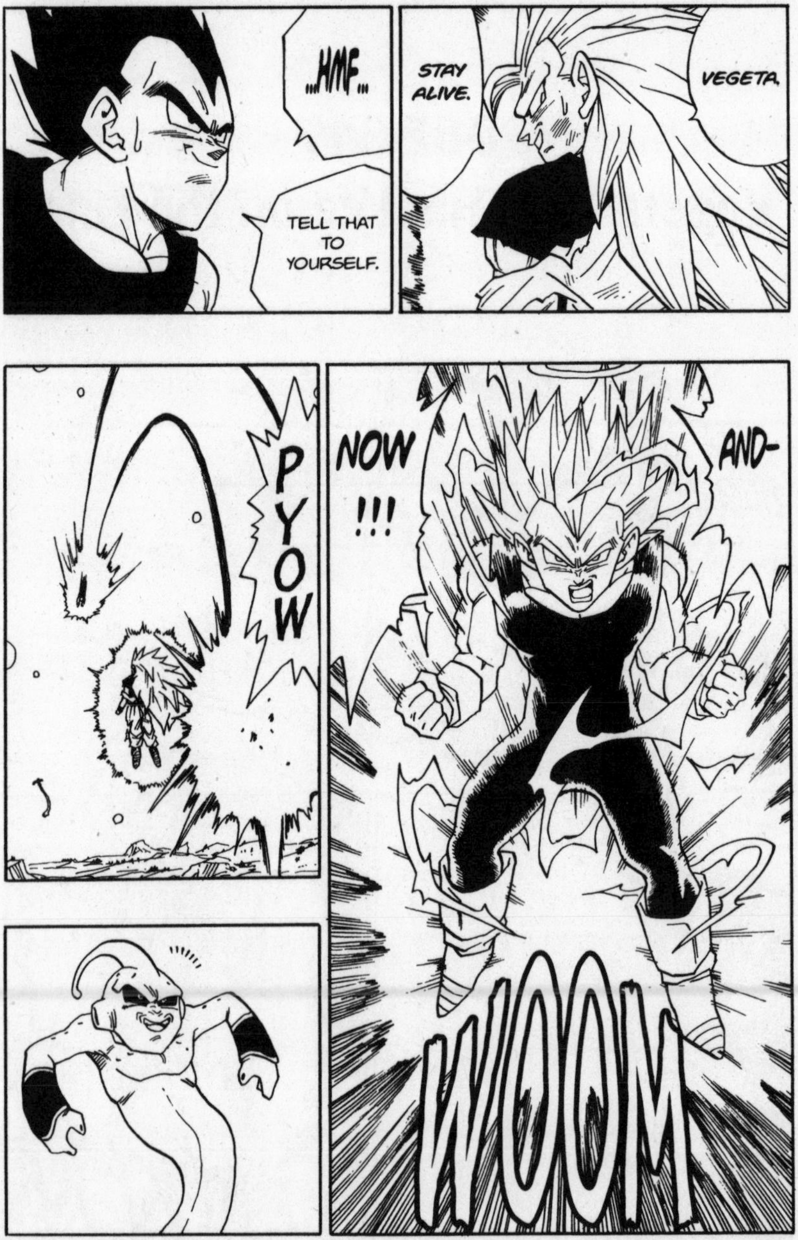

VEGETA.
STAY ALIVE.
...HMF...
TELL THAT TO YOURSELF.
AND-
NOW!!!
WOOM
PYOW

READ THIS WAY

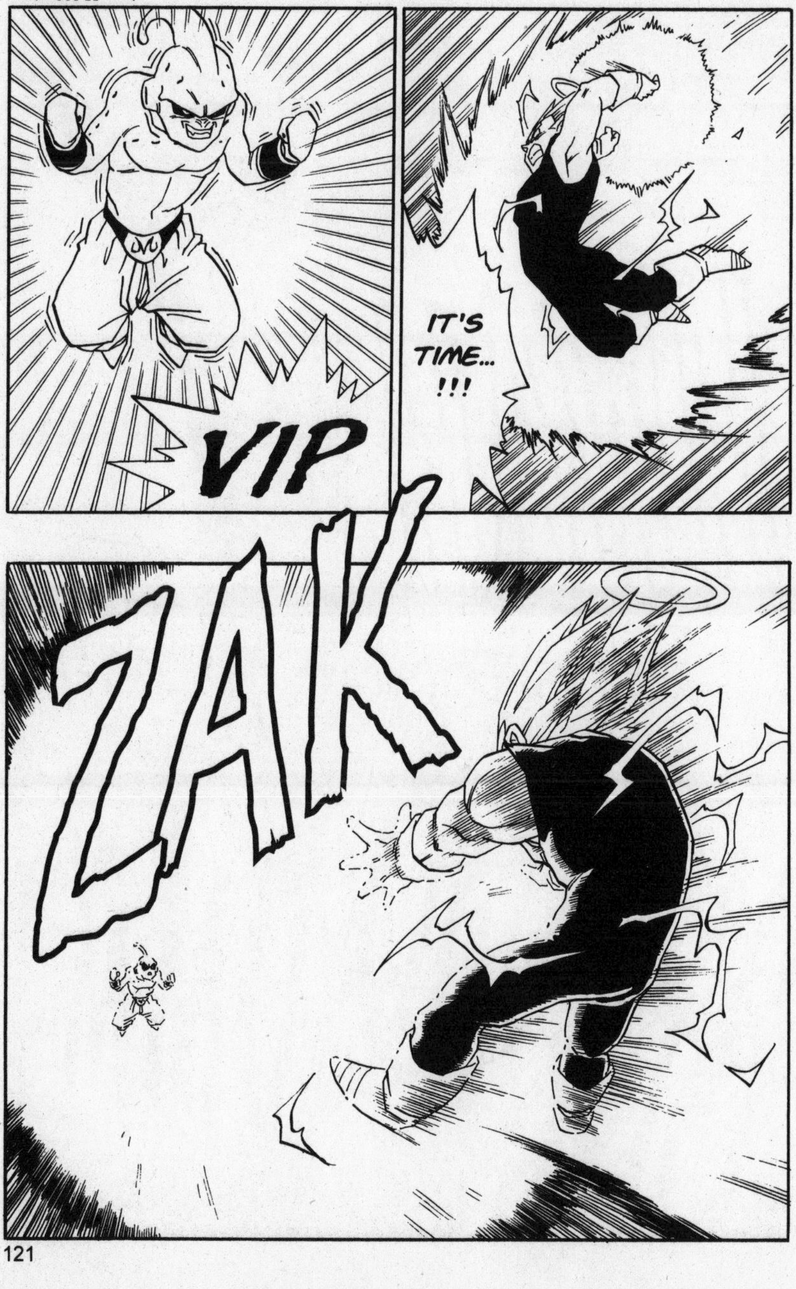
IT'S TIME... !!!
VIP
ZAK

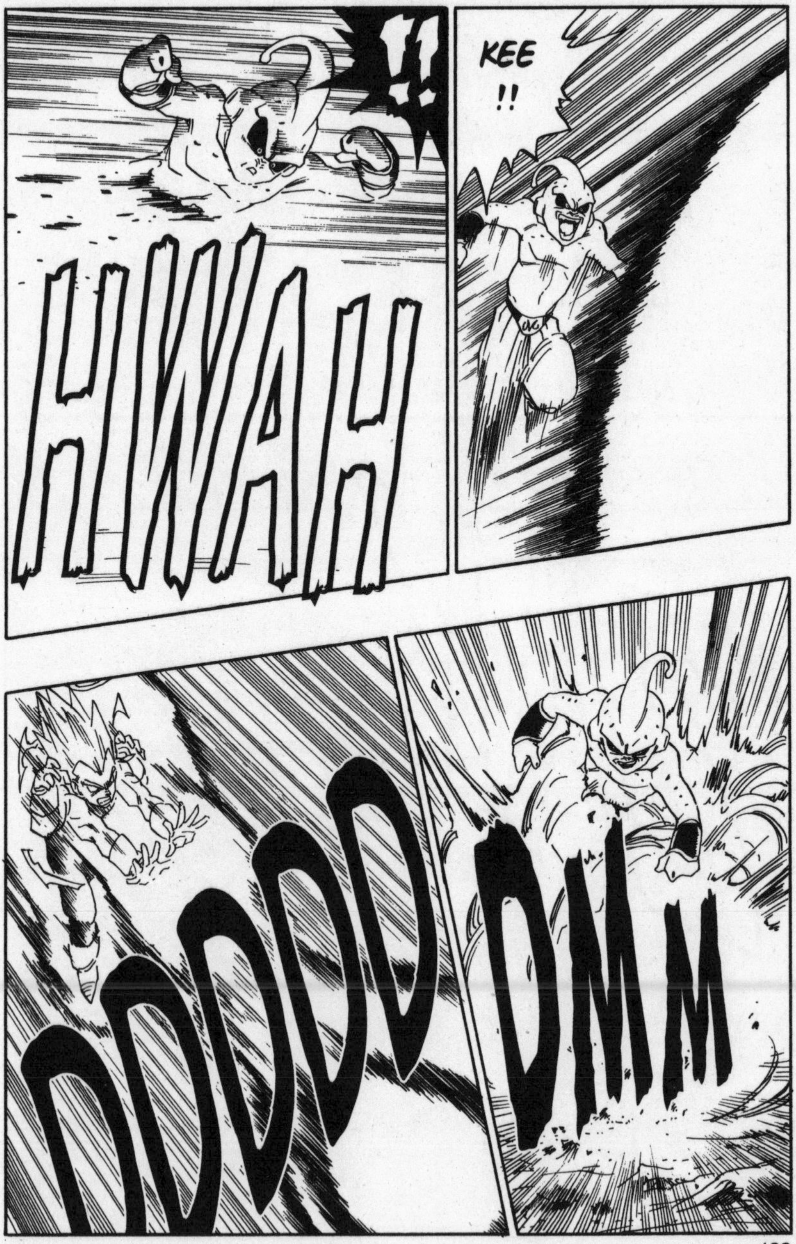
KEE !!
!!
HWAH
DDDDDDMM

READ THIS WAY

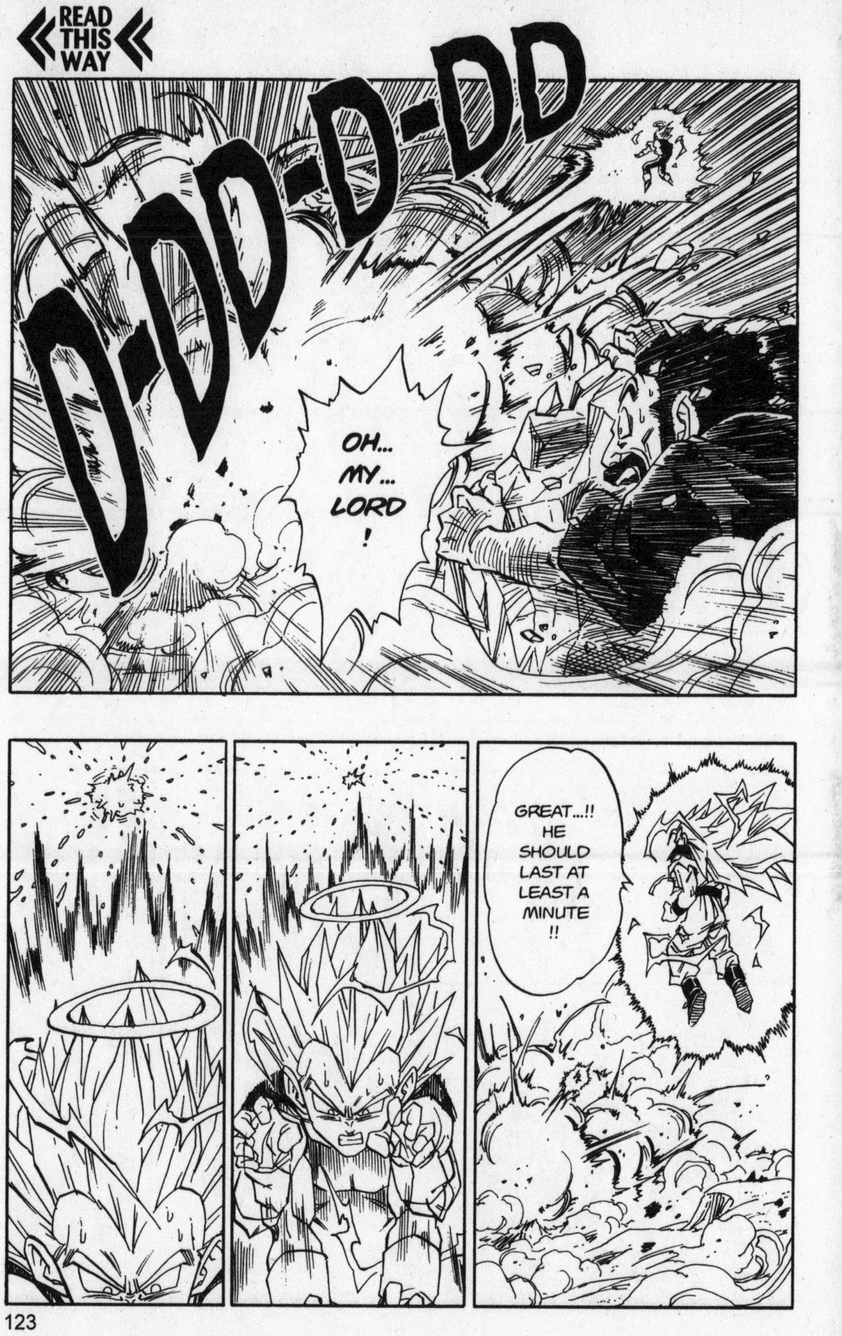
D-DD-D-DD
OH... MY... LORD!
GREAT...!! HE SHOULD LAST AT LEAST A MINUTE!!

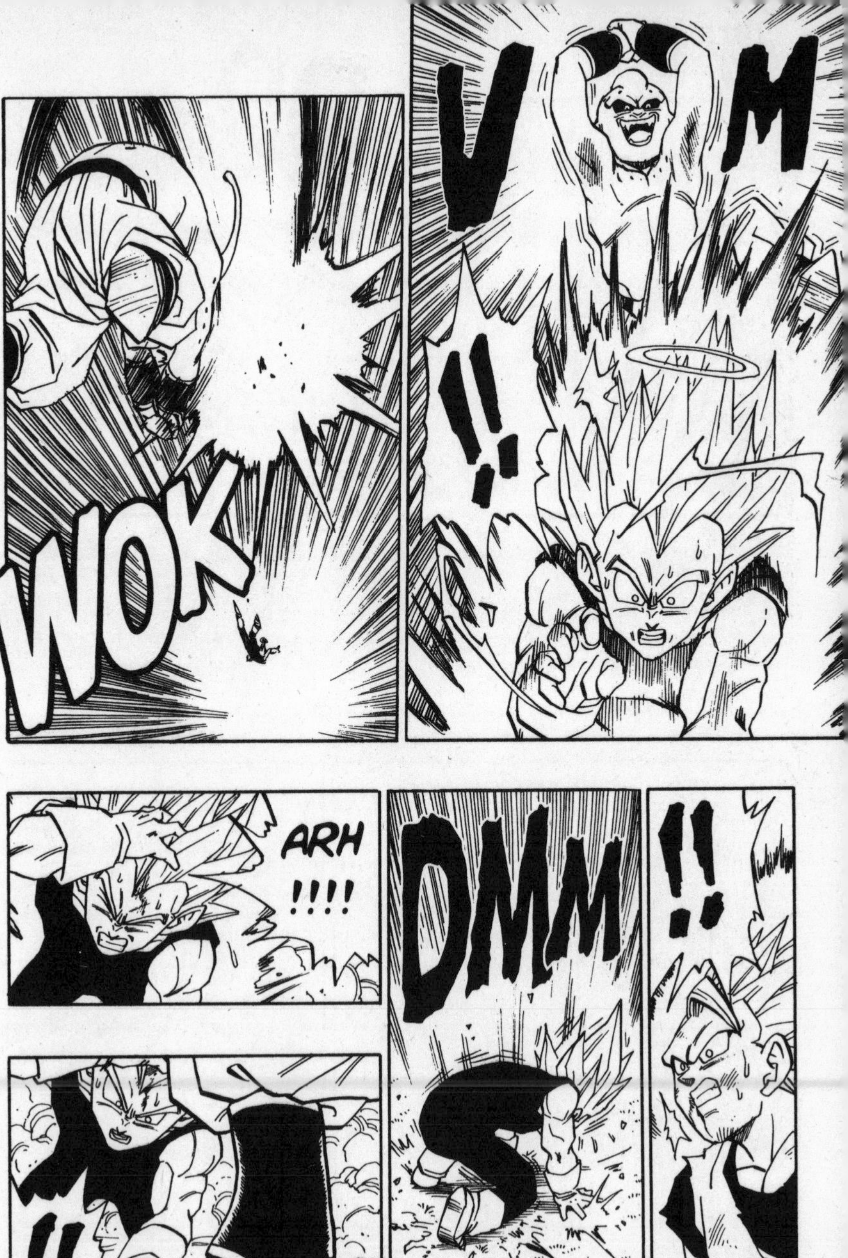
VM
!!
WOK
!!
DMM
ARH !!!!
!!

READ THIS WAY

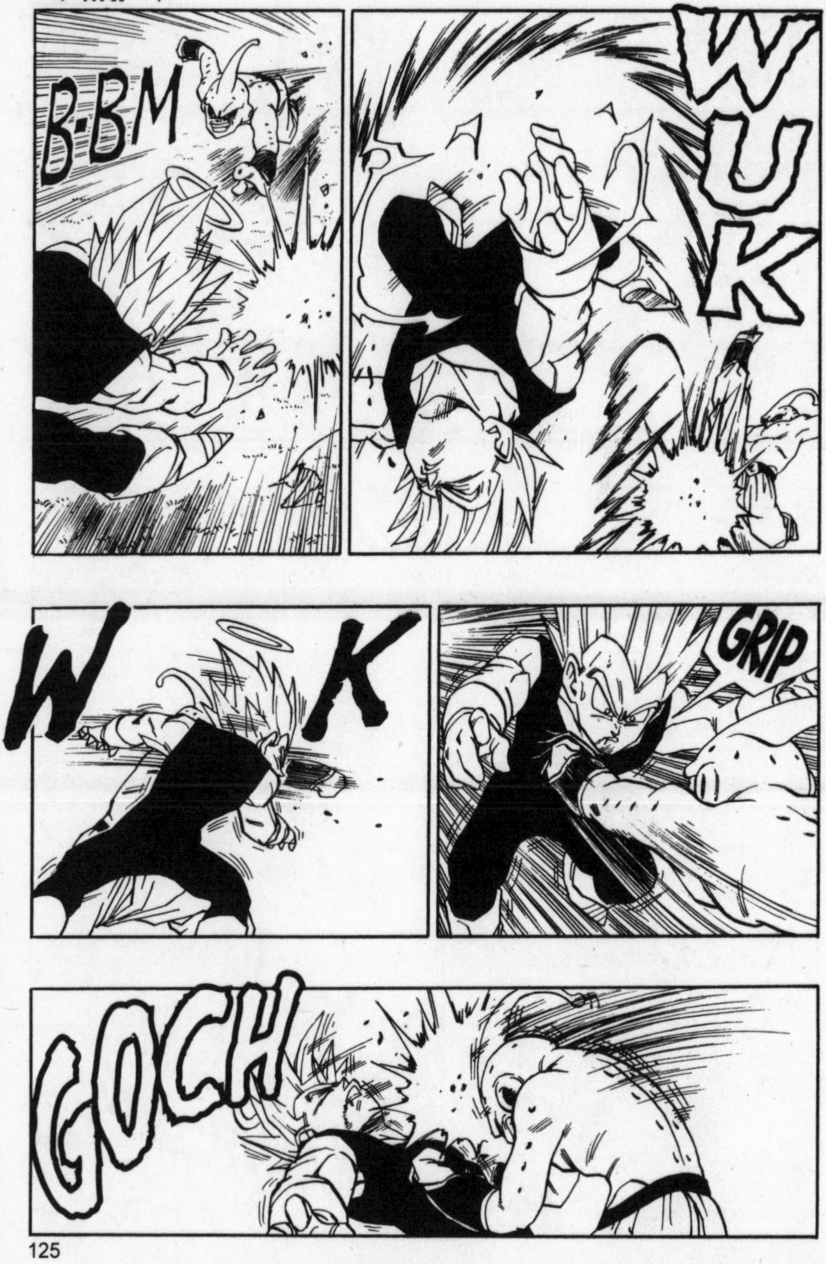
WUK
B-BM
GRIP
W
K
GOCH

READ THIS WAY

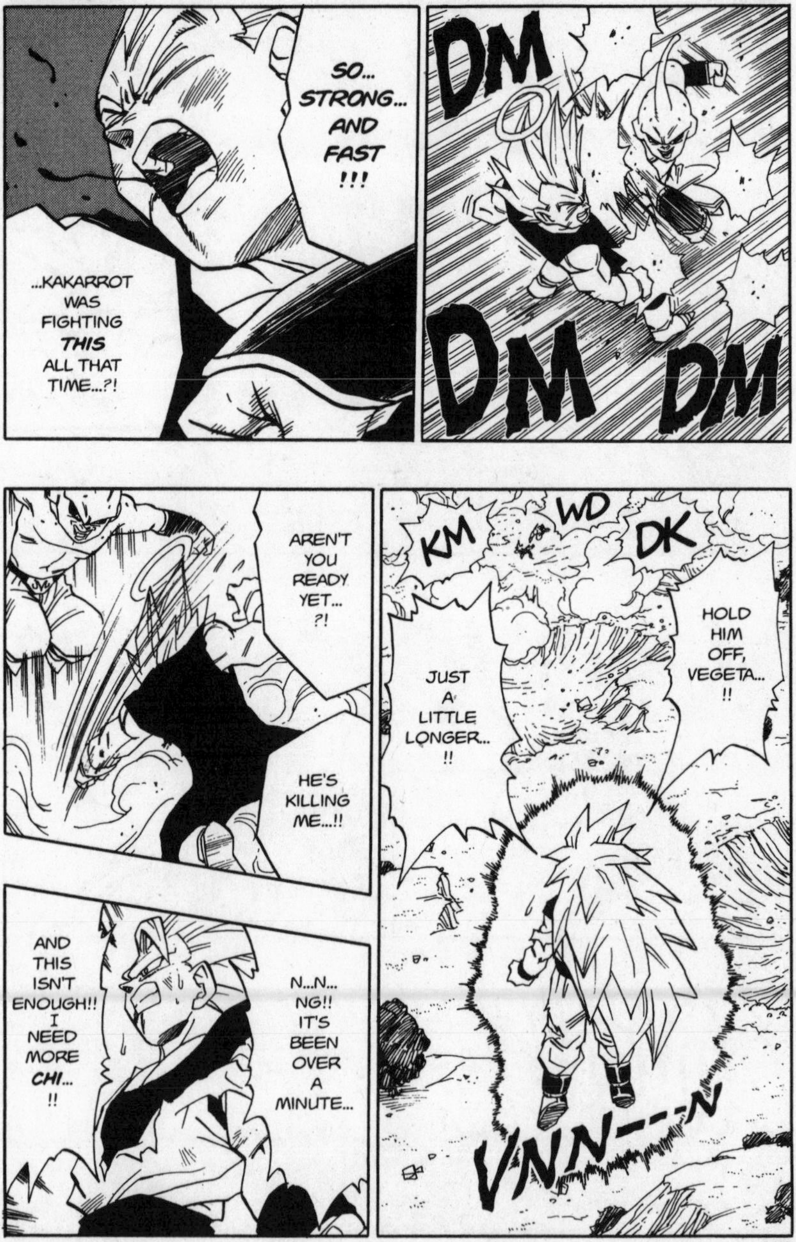
DM
DM DM
SO... STRONG... AND FAST!!!
...KAKARROT WAS FIGHTING THIS ALL THAT TIME...?!
KM
WD
DK
HOLD HIM OFF, VEGETA...!!
JUST A LITTLE LONGER...!!
VNN---N
AREN'T YOU READY YET...?!
HE'S KILLING ME...!!
N...N... NG!! IT'S BEEN OVER A MINUTE...
AND THIS ISN'T ENOUGH!! I NEED MORE CHI...!!

READ THIS WAY

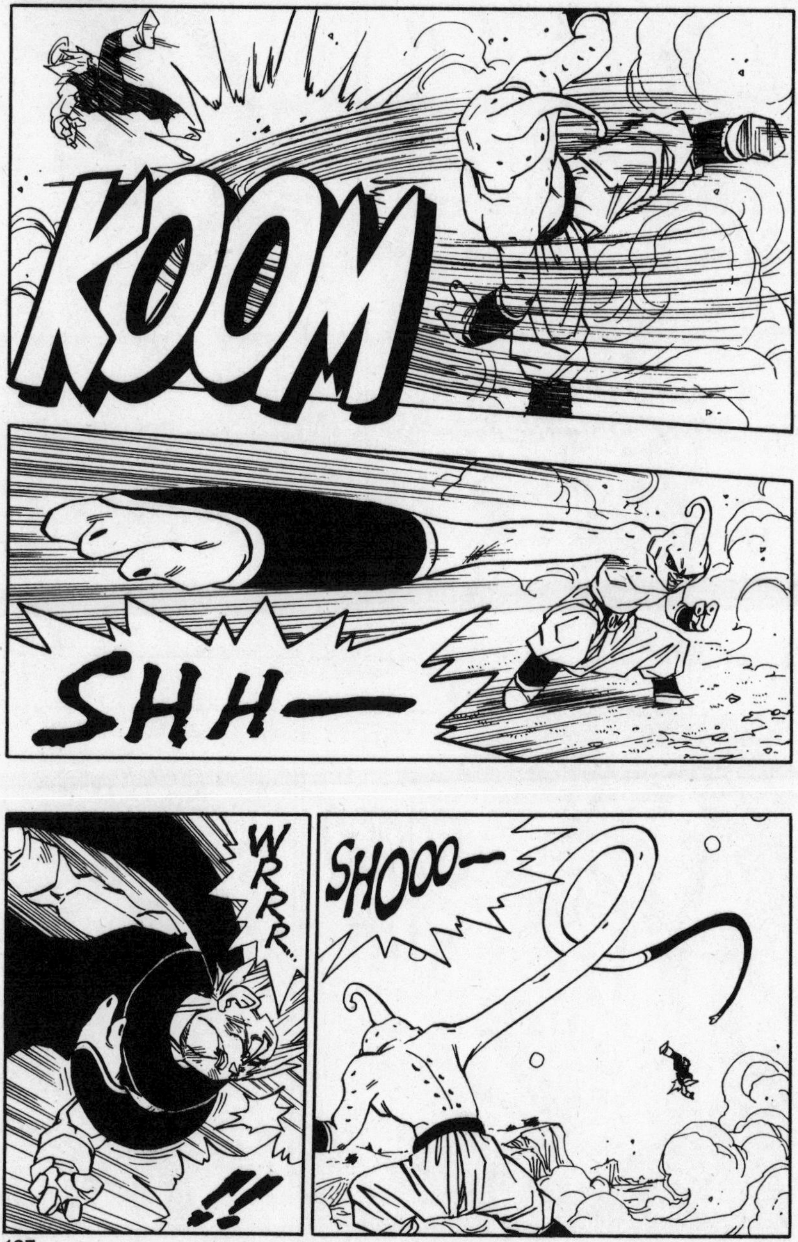
KOOM
SHH—
SHOOO—
WRRR...
!!

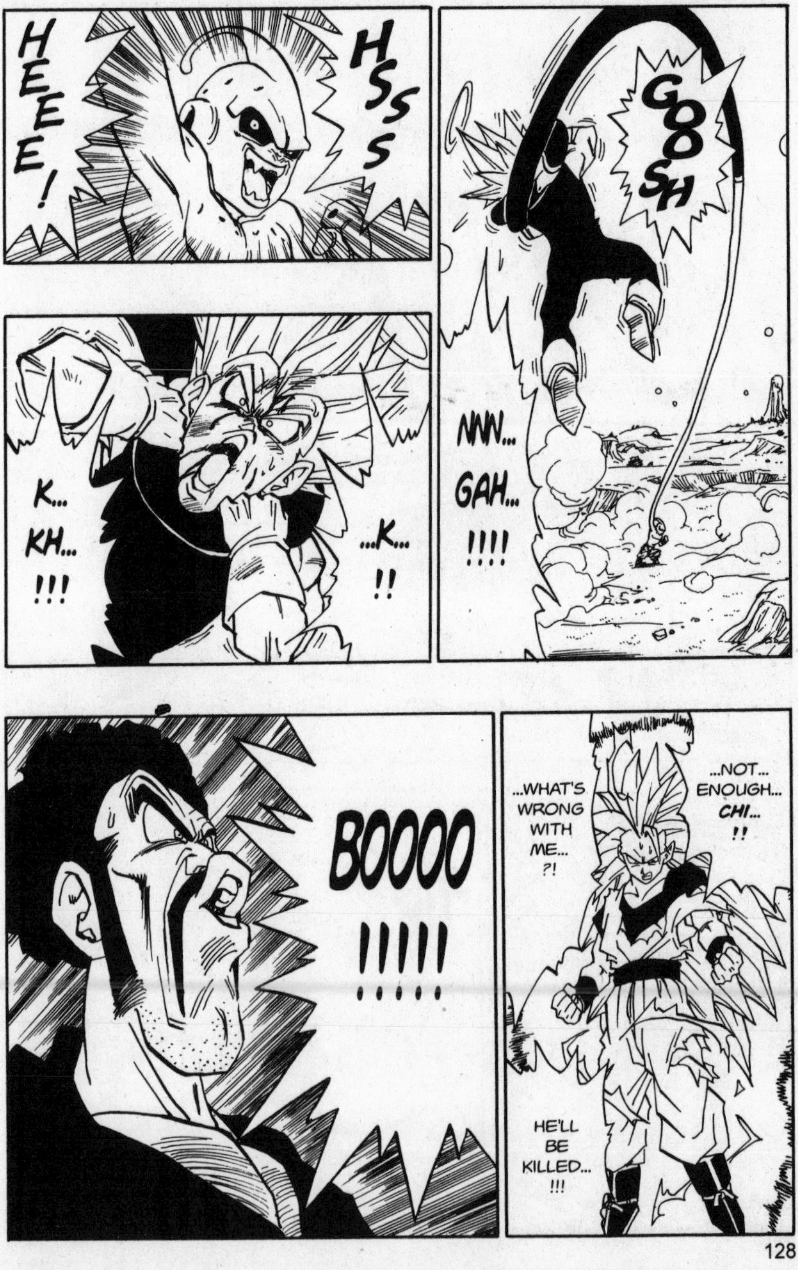
GOOSH
NNN... GAH... !!!!
HSSSS
HEEEE!
...K... !!
K... KH... !!!
...NOT... ENOUGH... CHI... !!
...WHAT'S WRONG WITH ME... ?!
HE'LL BE KILLED... !!!
BOOOO !!!!! !!!!!

READ THIS WAY

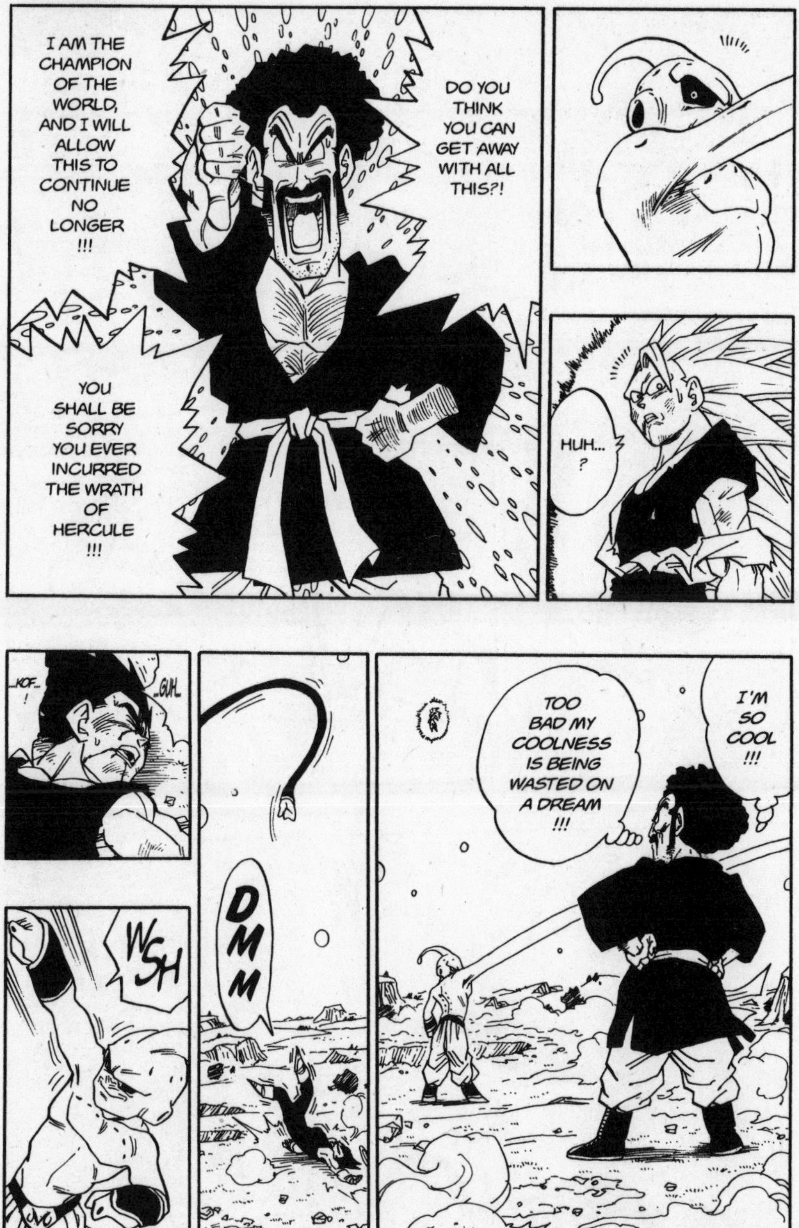

HUH... ?
DO YOU THINK YOU CAN GET AWAY WITH ALL THIS?!
I AM THE CHAMPION OF THE WORLD, AND I WILL ALLOW THIS TO CONTINUE NO LONGER !!!
YOU SHALL BE SORRY YOU EVER INCURRED THE WRATH OF HERCULE !!!
I'M SO COOL !!!
TOO BAD MY COOLNESS IS BEING WASTED ON A DREAM !!!
DMM
GUH...
...KOF... !
WSH

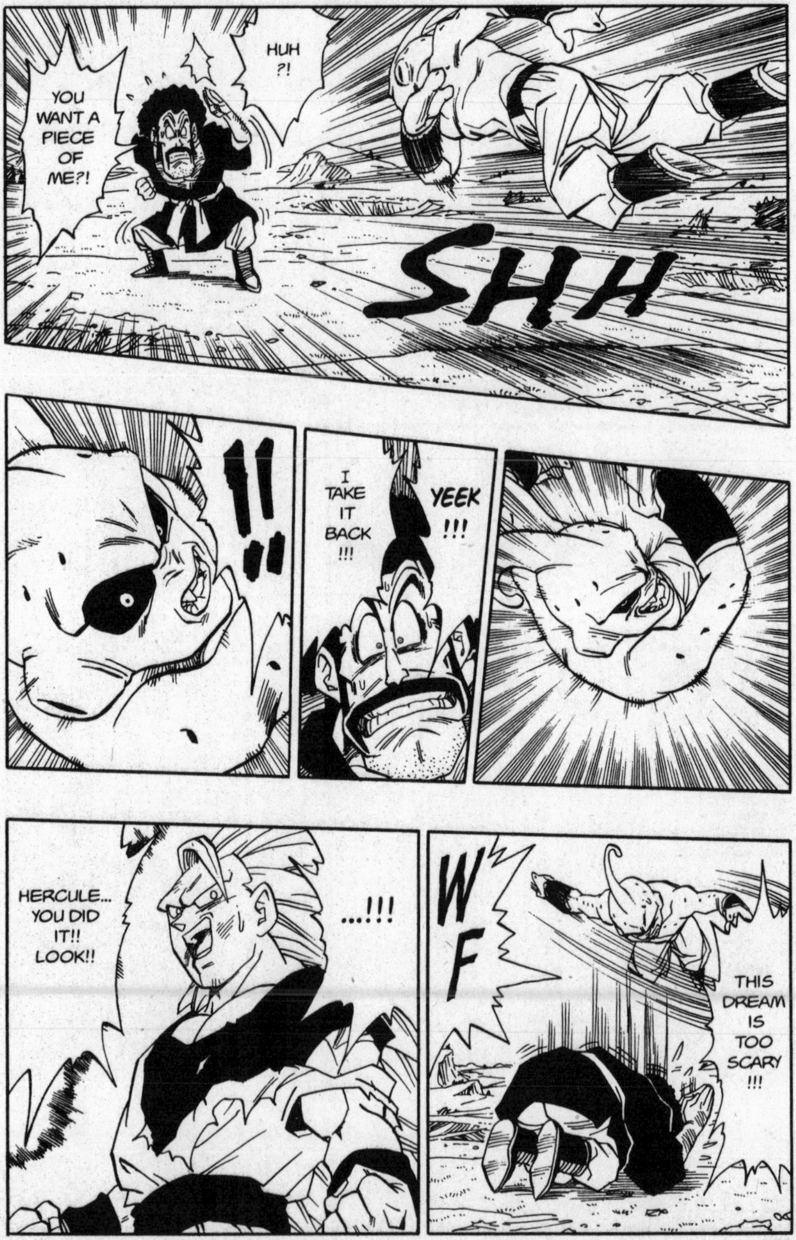
HUH ?!
YOU WANT A PIECE OF ME?!
SHH
YEEK !!!
I TAKE IT BACK !!!
!!
WF
THIS DREAM IS TOO SCARY !!!
...!!!
HERCULE... YOU DID IT!! LOOK!!

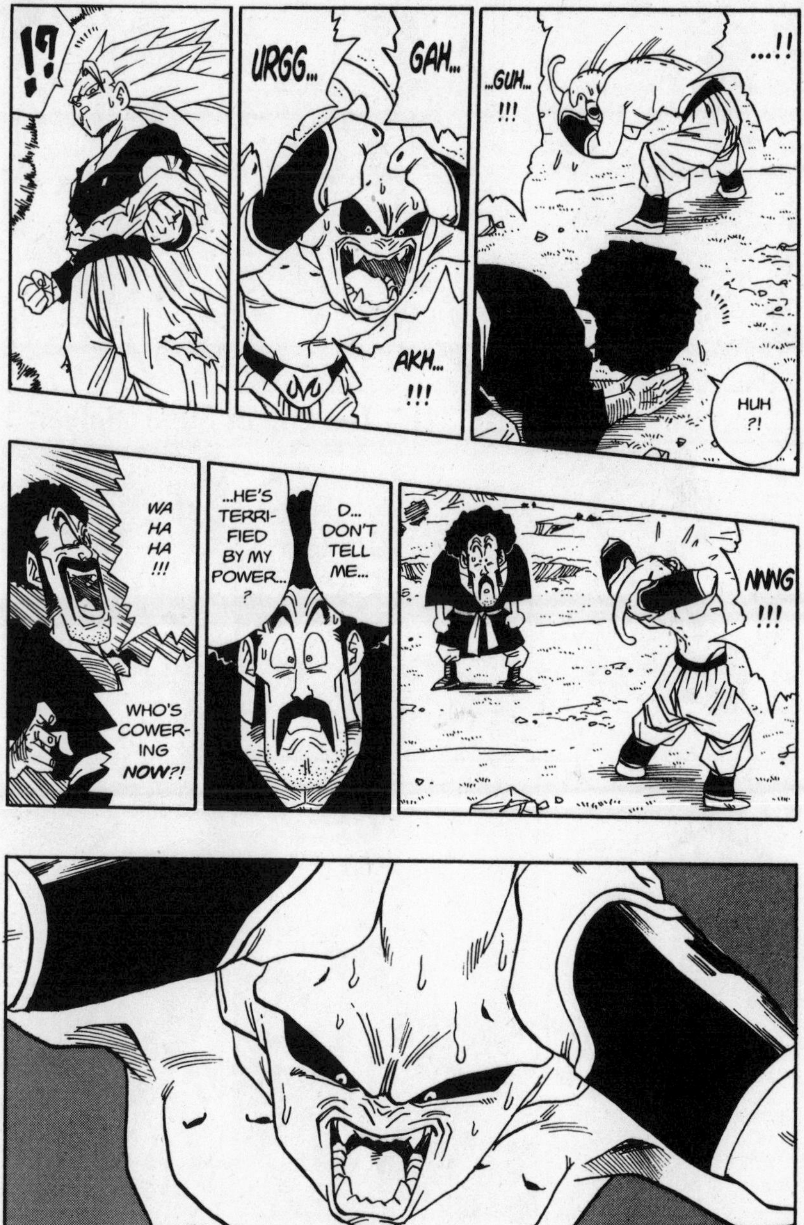
...!!
...GUH... !!!
HUH ?!
GAH...
URGG...
AKH... !!!
!?
NNNG !!!
D... DON'T TELL ME...
...HE'S TERRIFIED BY MY POWER... ?
WA HA HA !!!
WHO'S COWERING NOW?!

NEXT: Boo vs. Boo!

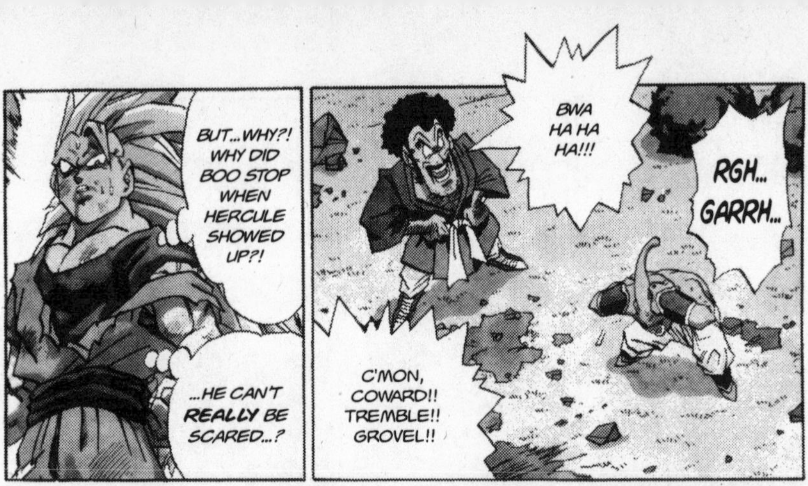
BWA HA HA HA!!!
RGH... GARRH...
C'MON, COWARD!! TREMBLE!! GROVEL!!
BUT...WHY?! WHY DID BOO STOP WHEN HERCULE SHOWED UP?!
...HE CAN'T REALLY BE SCARED...?

DBZ:318 • The End of Super Saiyan 3

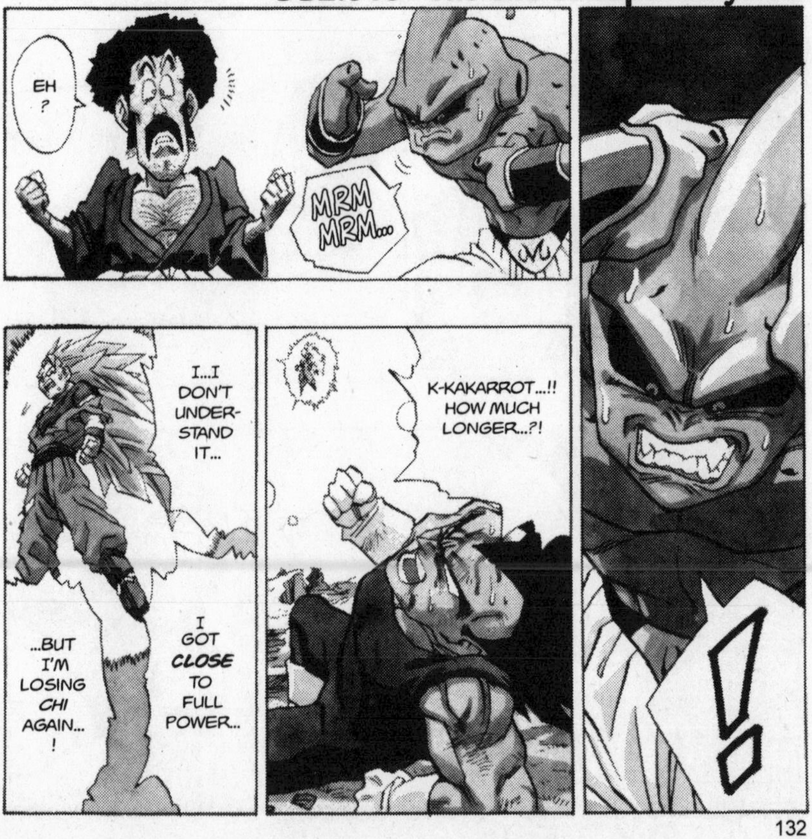
!
MRM MRM...
EH ?
K-KAKARROT...!! HOW MUCH LONGER...?!
I...I DON'T UNDER-STAND IT...
I GOT CLOSE TO FULL POWER...
...BUT I'M LOSING CHI AGAIN... !

READ THIS WAY

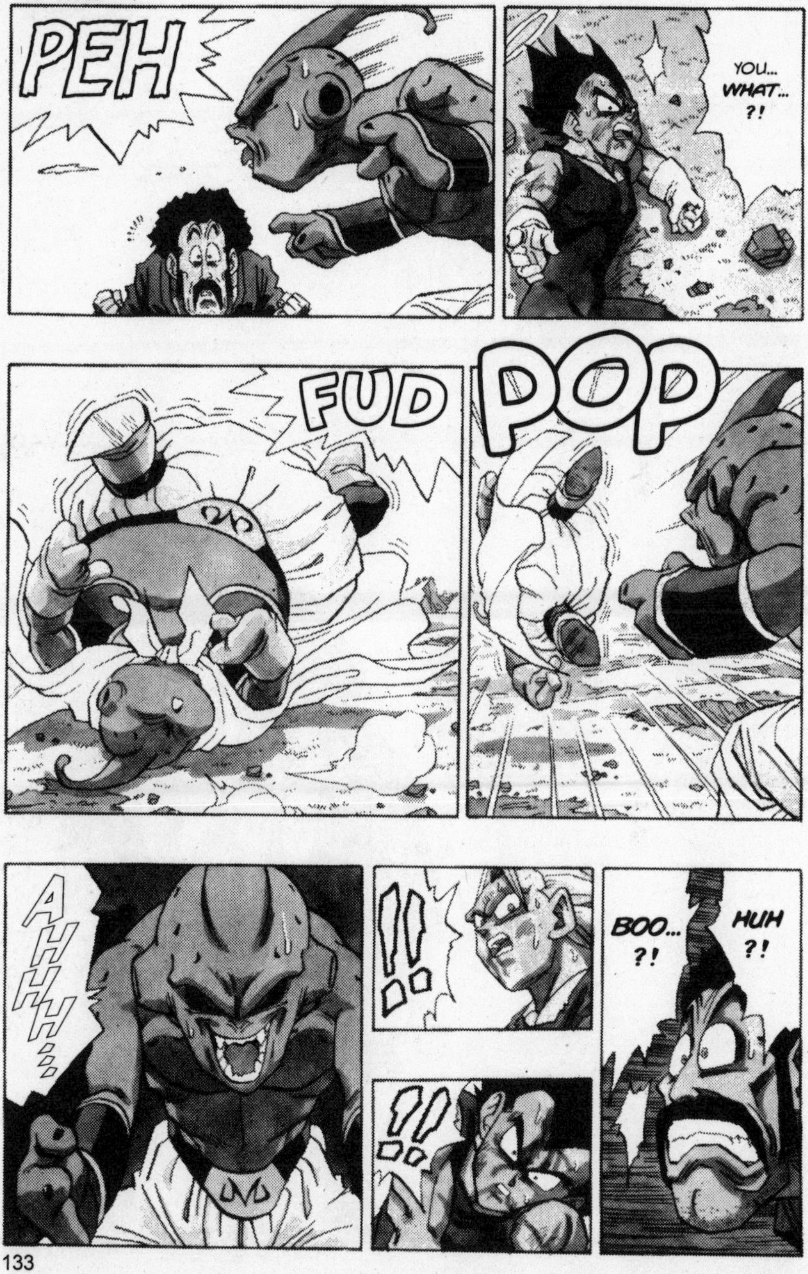
YOU... WHAT... ?!
PEH
POP
FUD
HUH ?!
BOO... ?!
!!
!!
AHHHH...

READ THIS WAY

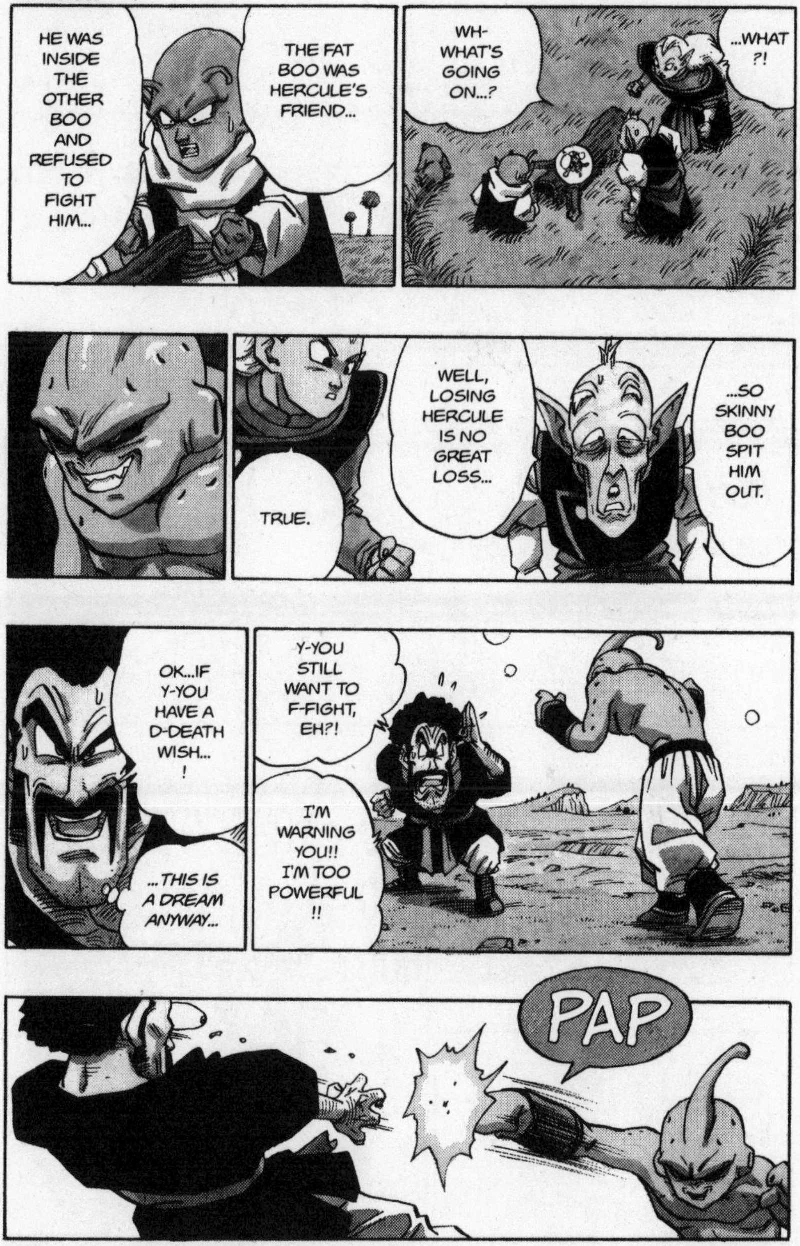
...WHAT ?!
WH- WHAT'S GOING ON...?
THE FAT BOO WAS HERCULE'S FRIEND...
HE WAS INSIDE THE OTHER BOO AND REFUSED TO FIGHT HIM...
...SO SKINNY BOO SPIT HIM OUT.
WELL, LOSING HERCULE IS NO GREAT LOSS...
TRUE.
Y-YOU STILL WANT TO F-FIGHT, EH?!
I'M WARNING YOU!! I'M TOO POWERFUL !!
OK...IF Y-YOU HAVE A D-DEATH WISH... !
...THIS IS A DREAM ANYWAY...
PAP

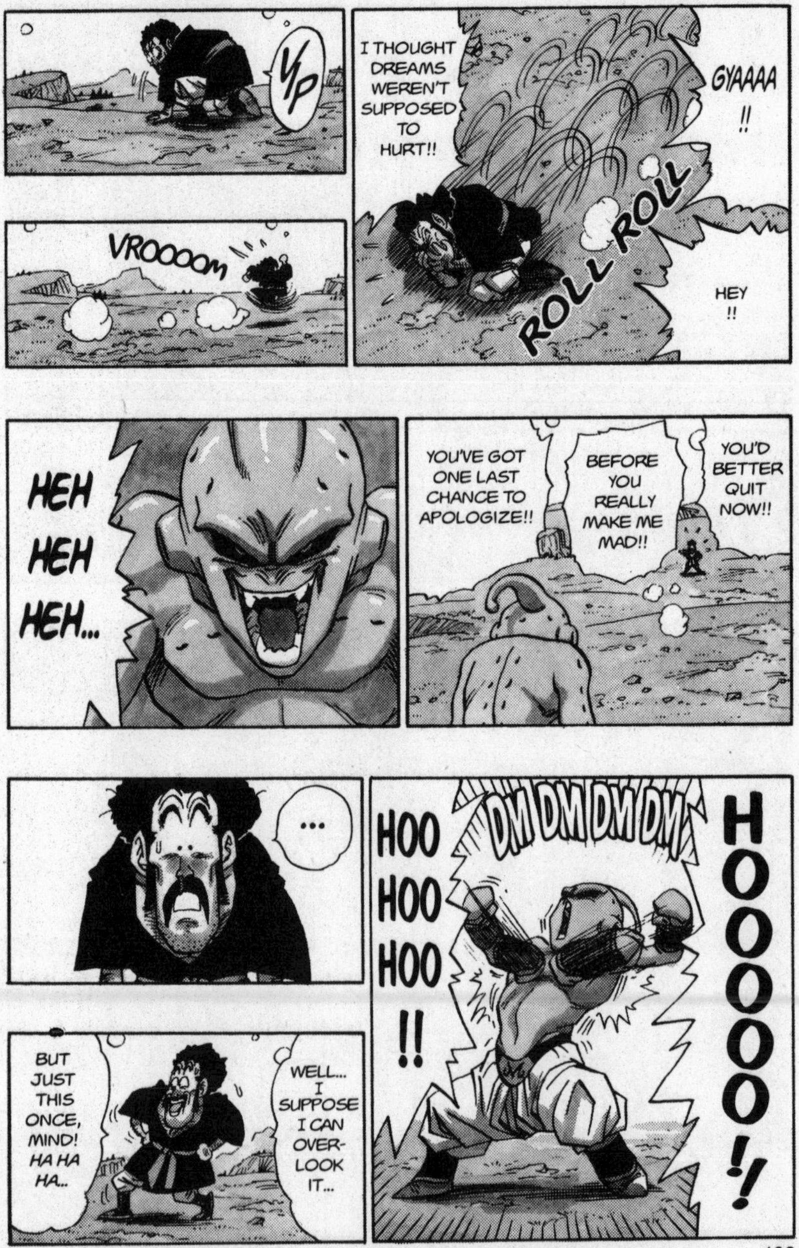
GYAAAA!!
I THOUGHT DREAMS WEREN'T SUPPOSED TO HURT!!
ROLL ROLL
HEY!!
YIP
VROOOOM
YOU'D BETTER QUIT NOW!!
BEFORE YOU REALLY MAKE ME MAD!!
YOU'VE GOT ONE LAST CHANCE TO APOLOGIZE!!
HEH HEH HEH...
HOOOOOO!!
DM DM DM DM
HOO HOO HOO!!
...
WELL... I SUPPOSE I CAN OVER-LOOK IT...
BUT JUST THIS ONCE, MIND! HA HA HA...

READ THIS WAY

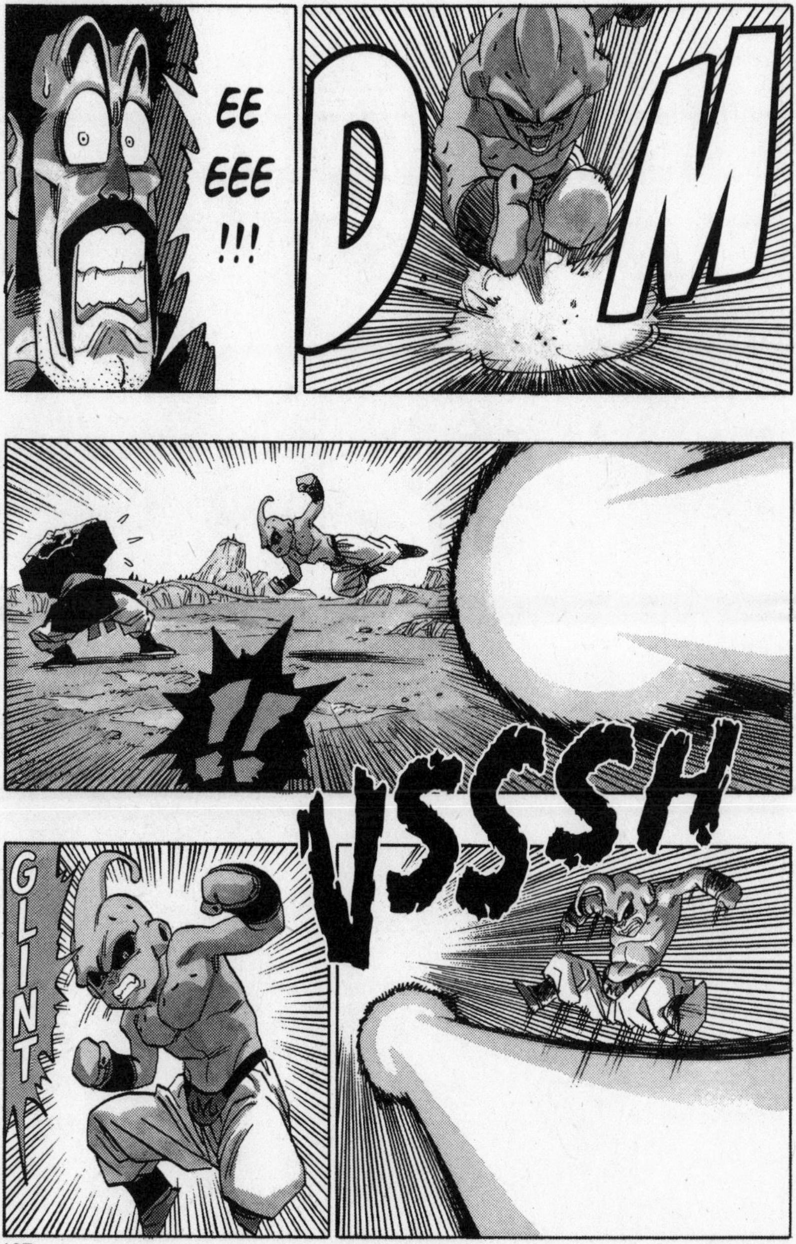
DM
EE EEE !!!
!!
VSSSH
GLINT

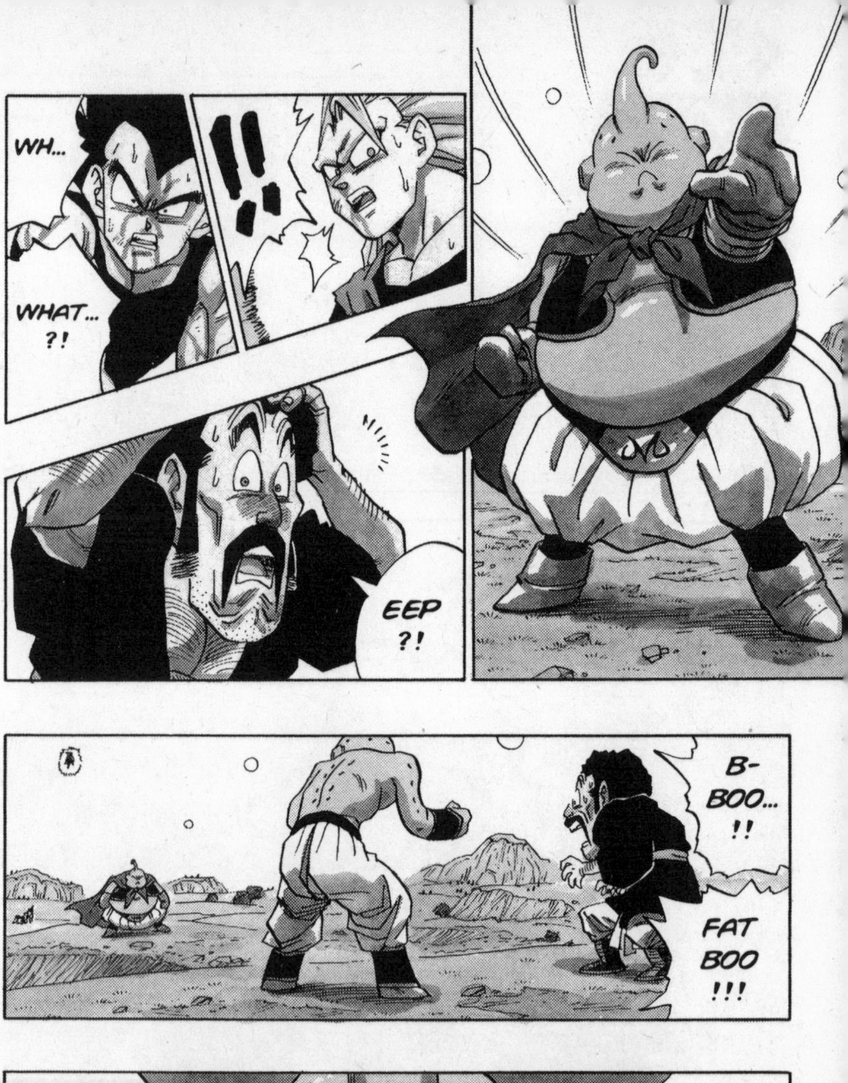
!!
WH... WHAT... ?!
EEP ?!
B-BOO... !!
FAT BOO !!!
I DON'T LIKE YOU.
STOP HURTING HERCULE.

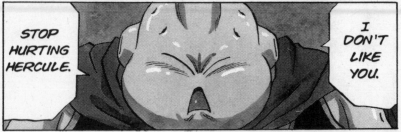

READ THIS WAY

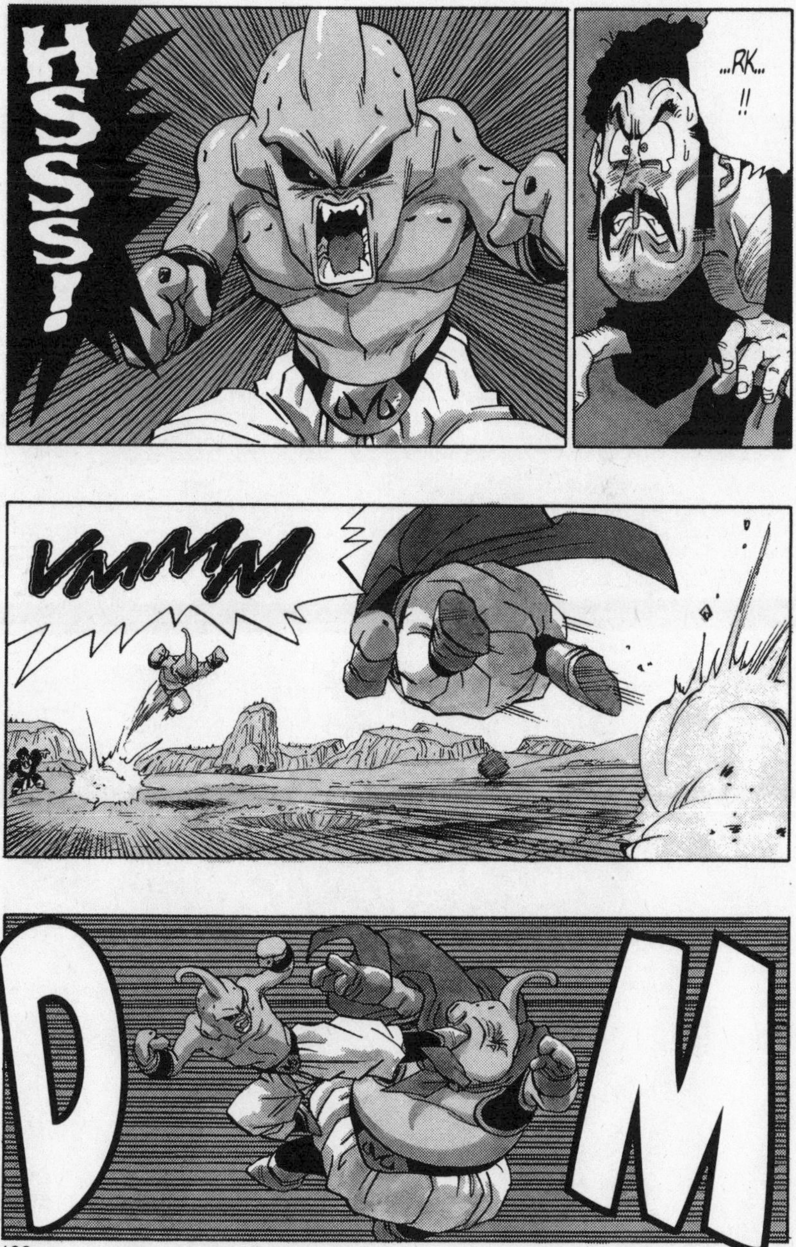

...RK...
!!
HSSS!
VMMM
D M

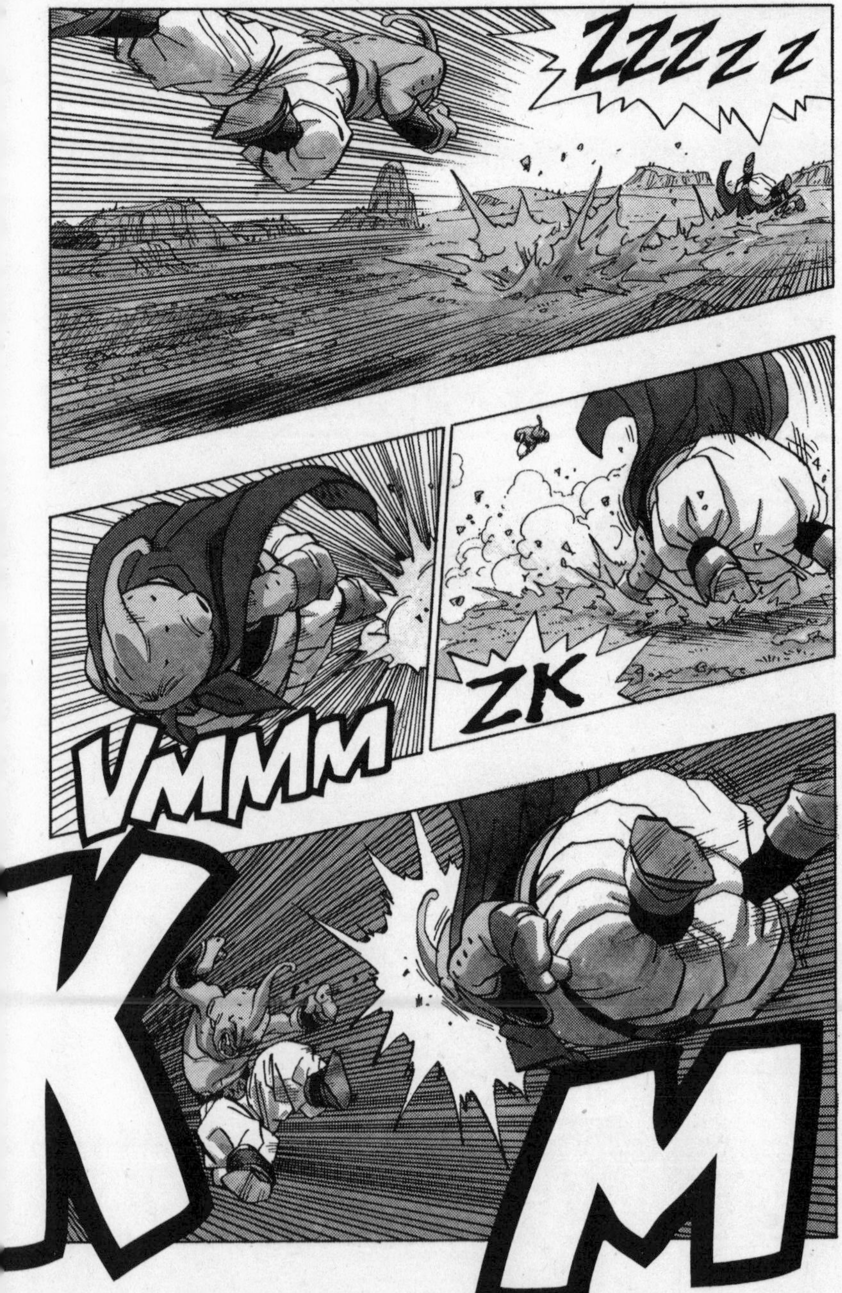
ZZZZZ
ZK
VMMMM
KM

READ THIS WAY

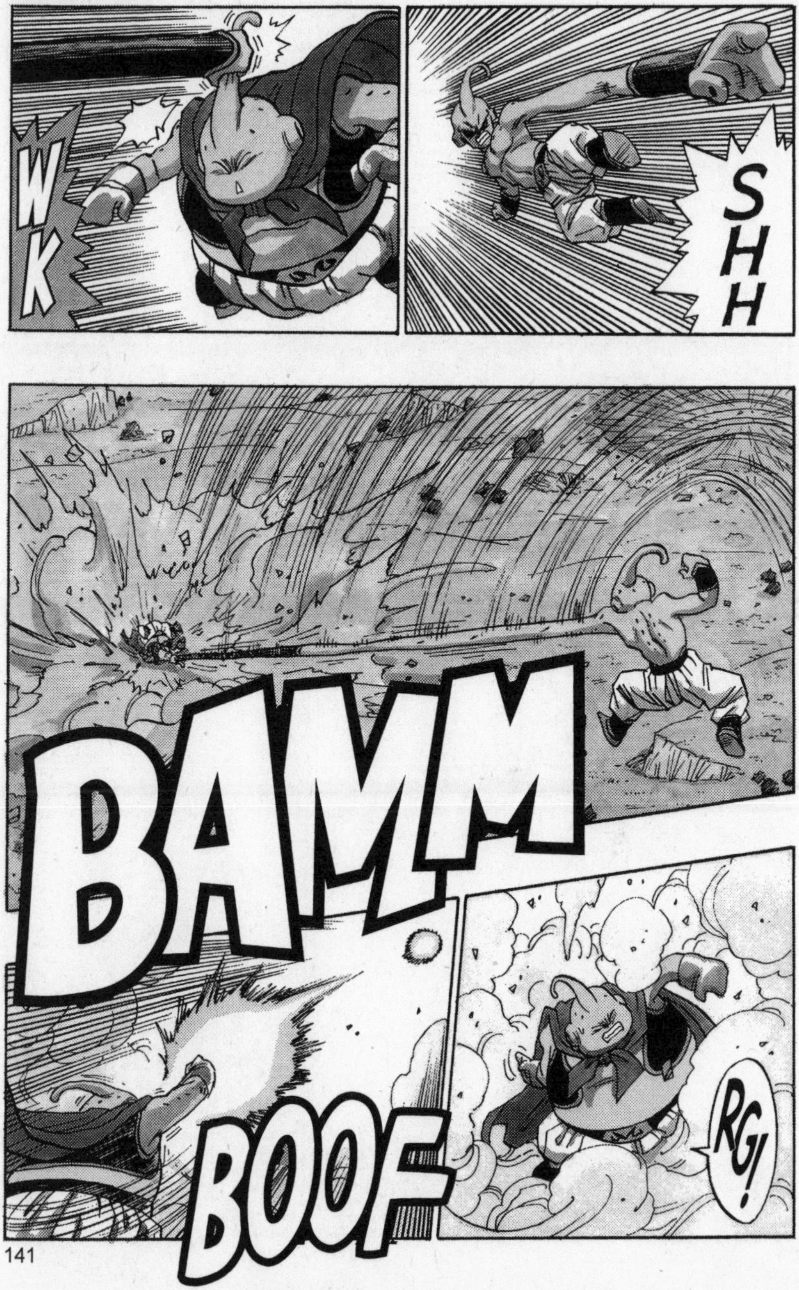
SHH
WK
BAMM
RG!
BOOF

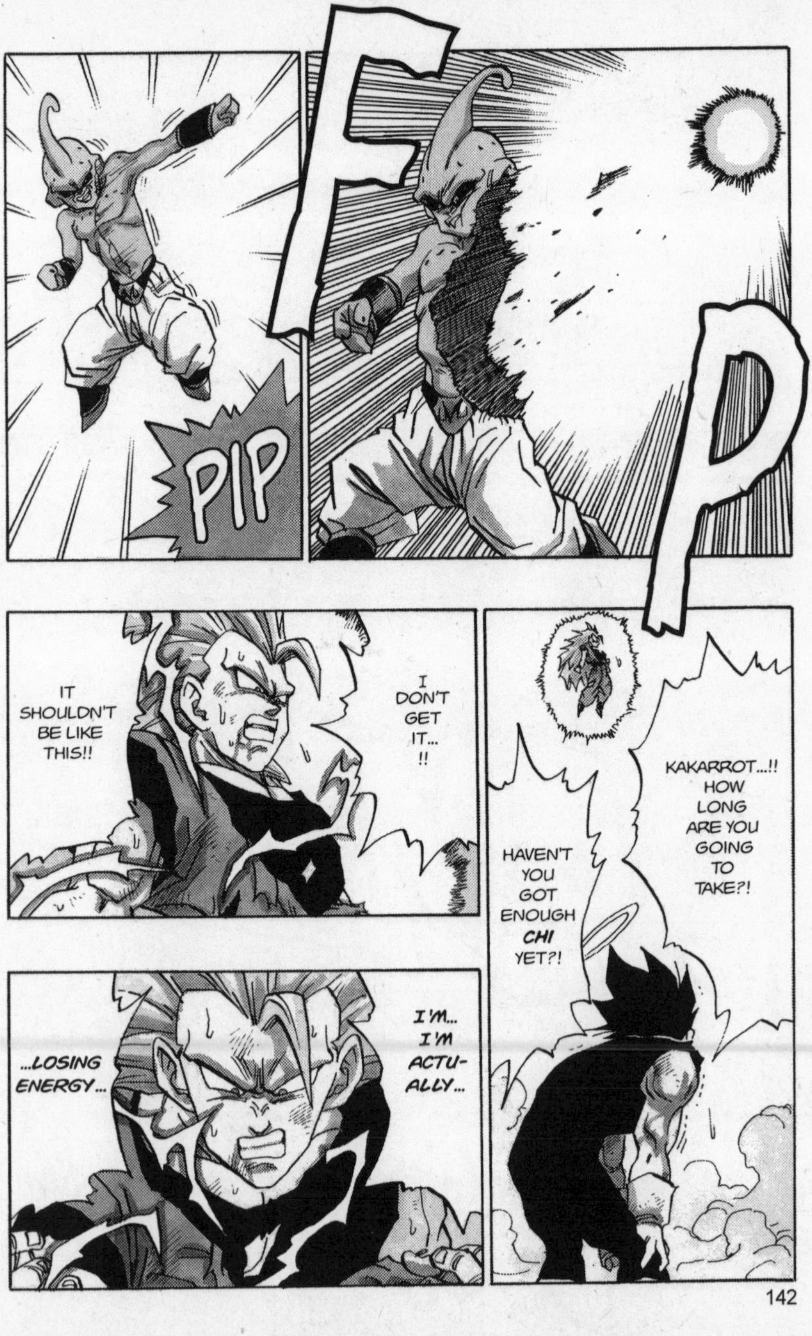
F
P
PIP
KAKARROT...!! HOW LONG ARE YOU GOING TO TAKE?!
HAVEN'T YOU GOT ENOUGH CHI YET?!
I DON'T GET IT... !!
IT SHOULDN'T BE LIKE THIS!!
I'M... I'M ACTU-ALLY...
...LOSING ENERGY...

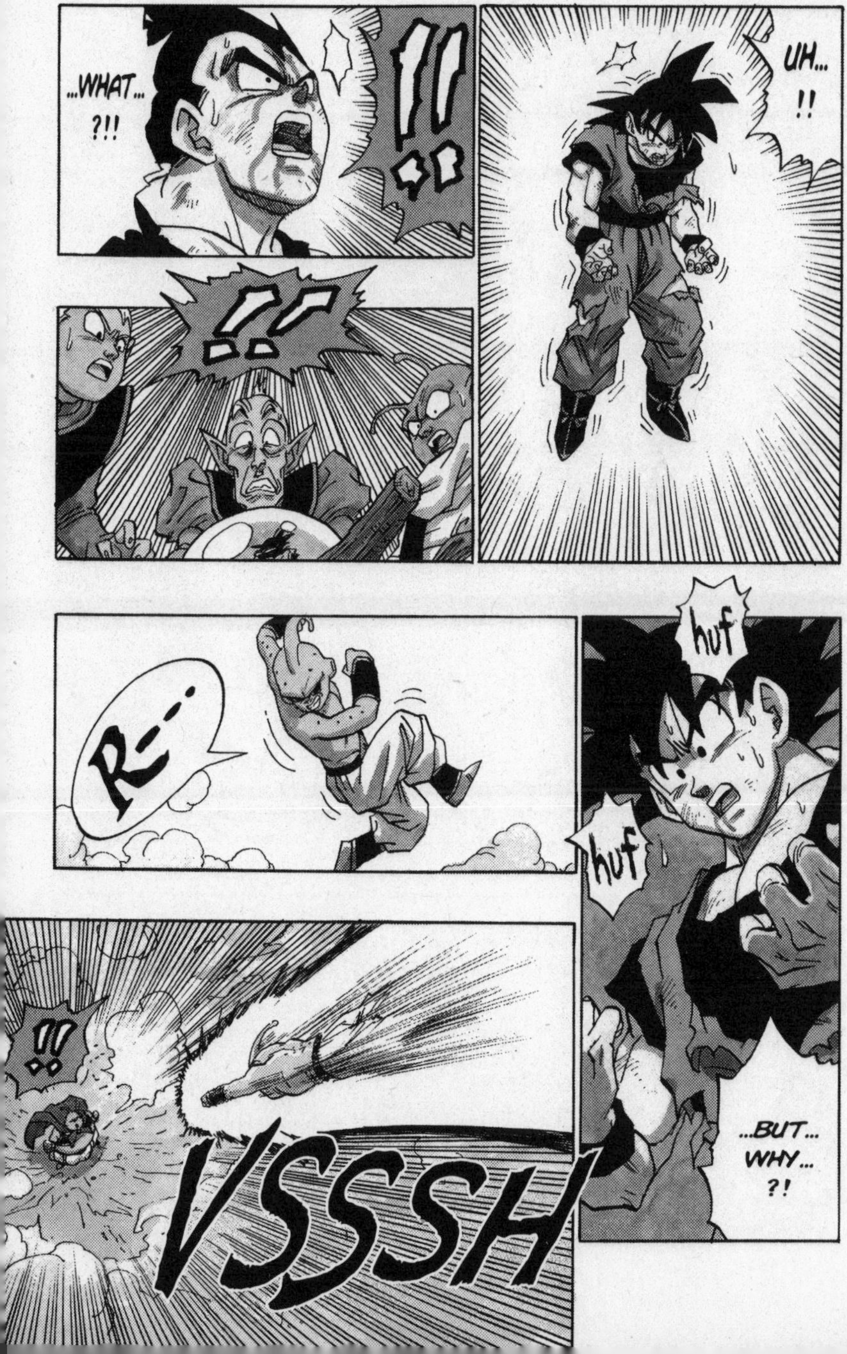
UH...
!!
...WHAT...
?!!
!!
!!
huf
huf
...BUT...
WHY...
?!
R-...
!!
VSSSH

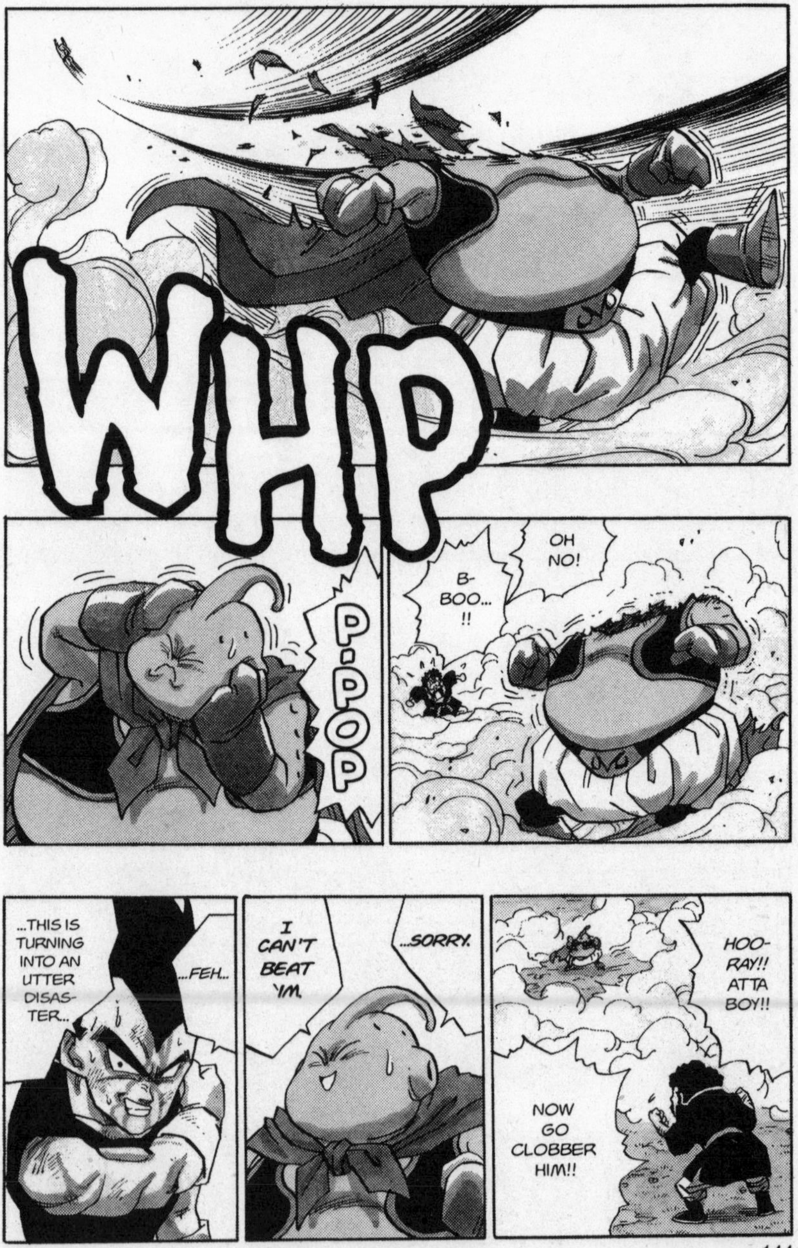
WHP
OH NO!
B-BOO...!!
P-POP
HOO-RAY!! ATTA BOY!!
NOW GO CLOBBER HIM!!
...SORRY.
I CAN'T BEAT 'IM.
...FEH...
...THIS IS TURNING INTO AN UTTER DISAS-TER...

DBZ:319 • Vegeta's Plan

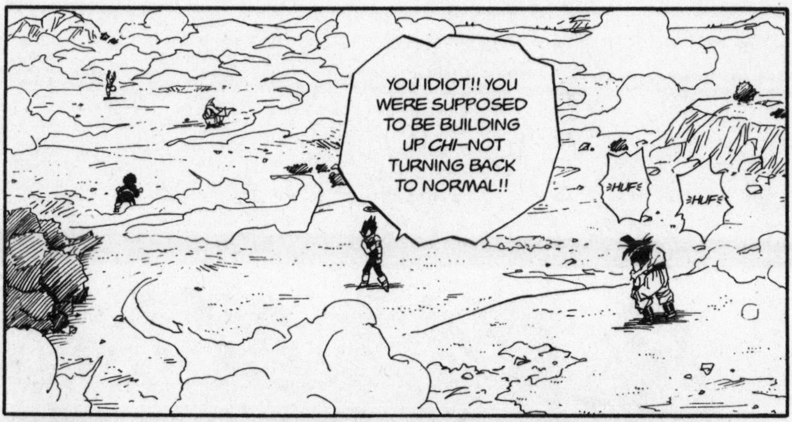
YOU IDIOT!! YOU WERE SUPPOSED TO BE BUILDING UP *CHI*—NOT TURNING BACK TO NORMAL!!
HUF
HUF

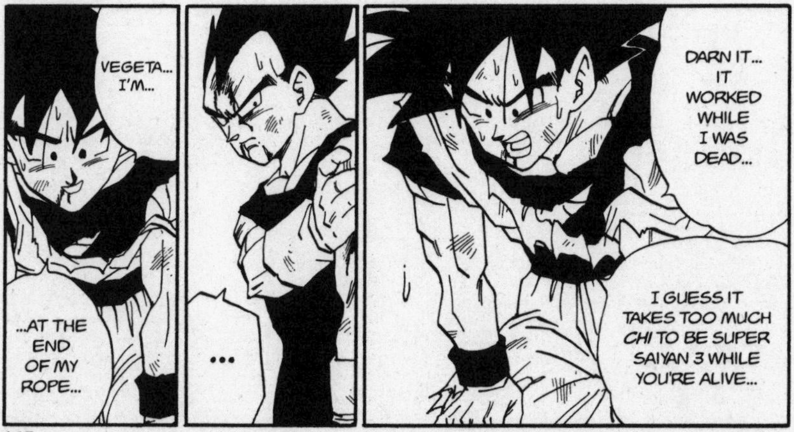
DARN IT... IT WORKED WHILE I WAS DEAD...
I GUESS IT TAKES TOO MUCH *CHI* TO BE SUPER SAIYAN 3 WHILE YOU'RE ALIVE...
...
VEGETA... I'M...
...AT THE END OF MY ROPE...

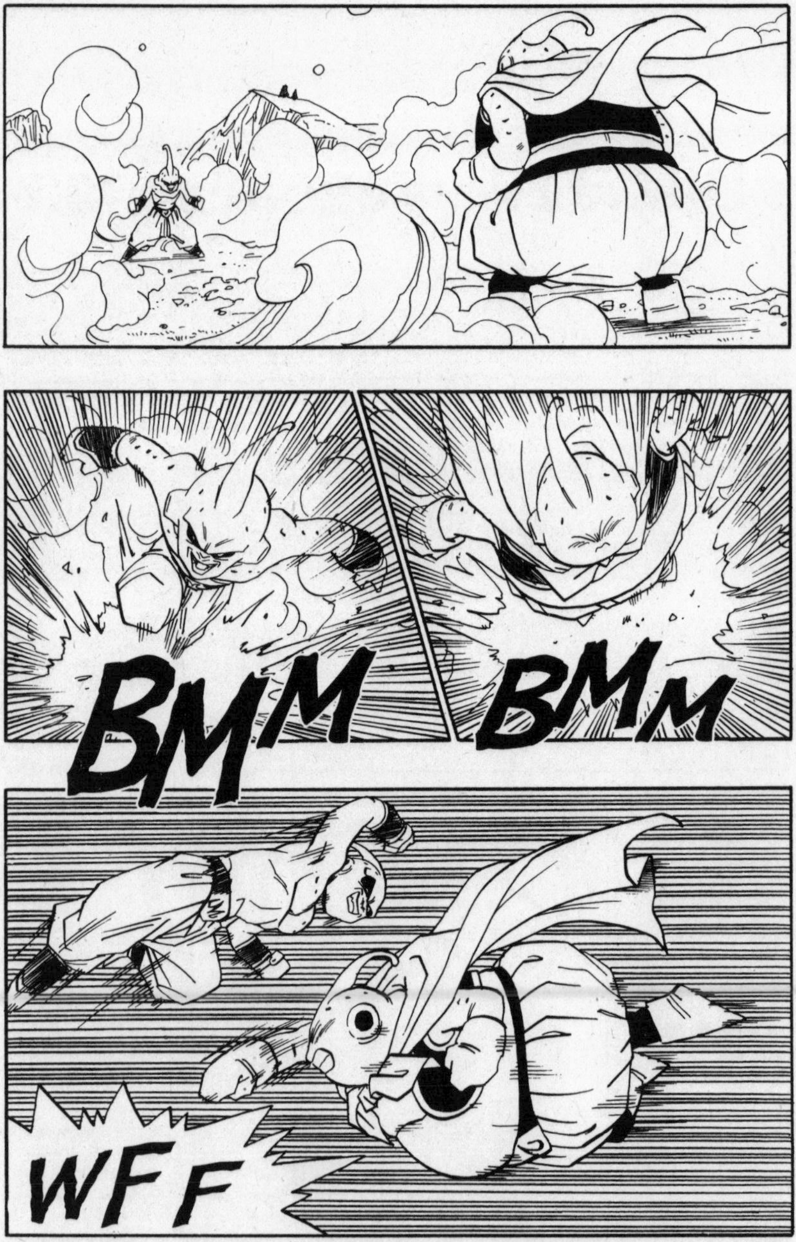
BMM
BMM
WFF

READ THIS WAY

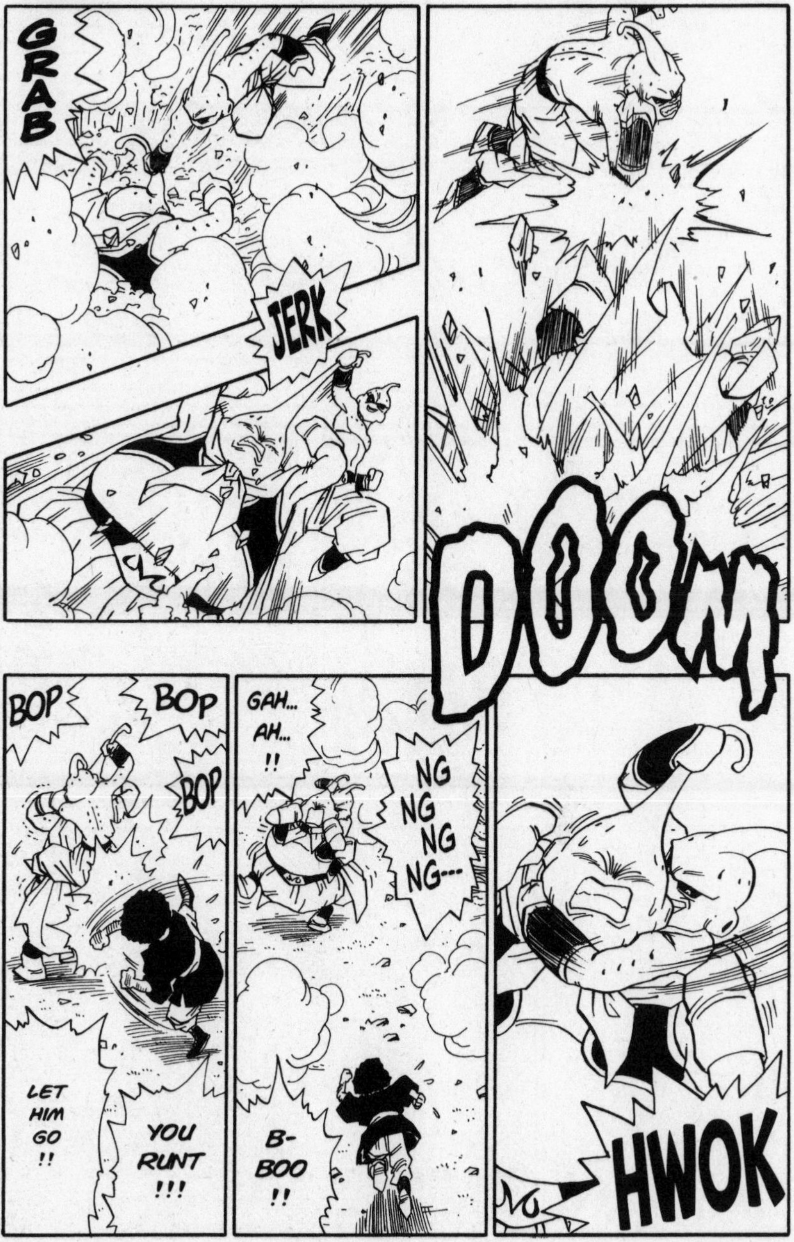

DOOM
GRAB
JERK
HWOK
GAH... AH... !!
NG NG NG NG---
B-BOO !!
BOP
BOP
BOP
LET HIM GO !!
YOU RUNT !!!

READ THIS WAY

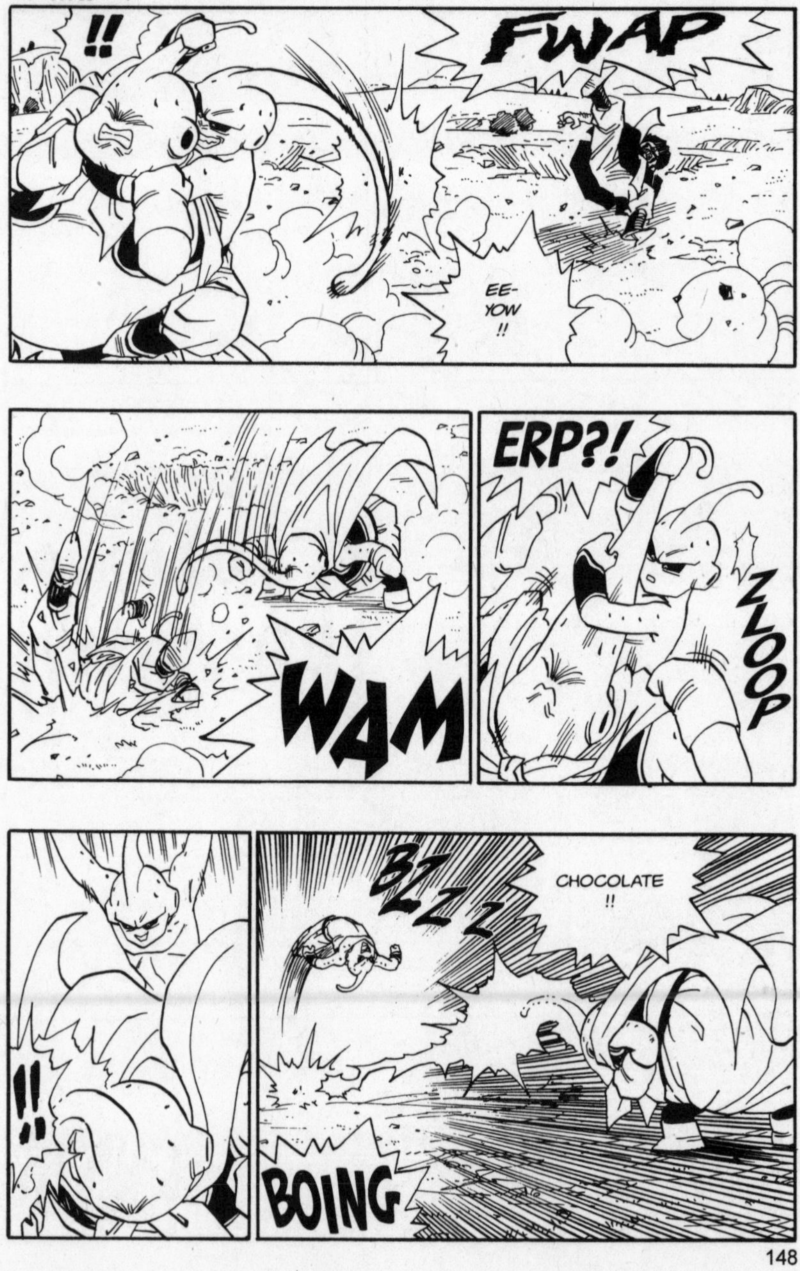
FWAP
!!
EE-YOW !!
ERP?!
ZLOOP
WAM
BZZZZ
CHOCOLATE !!
BOING
!!

READ THIS WAY

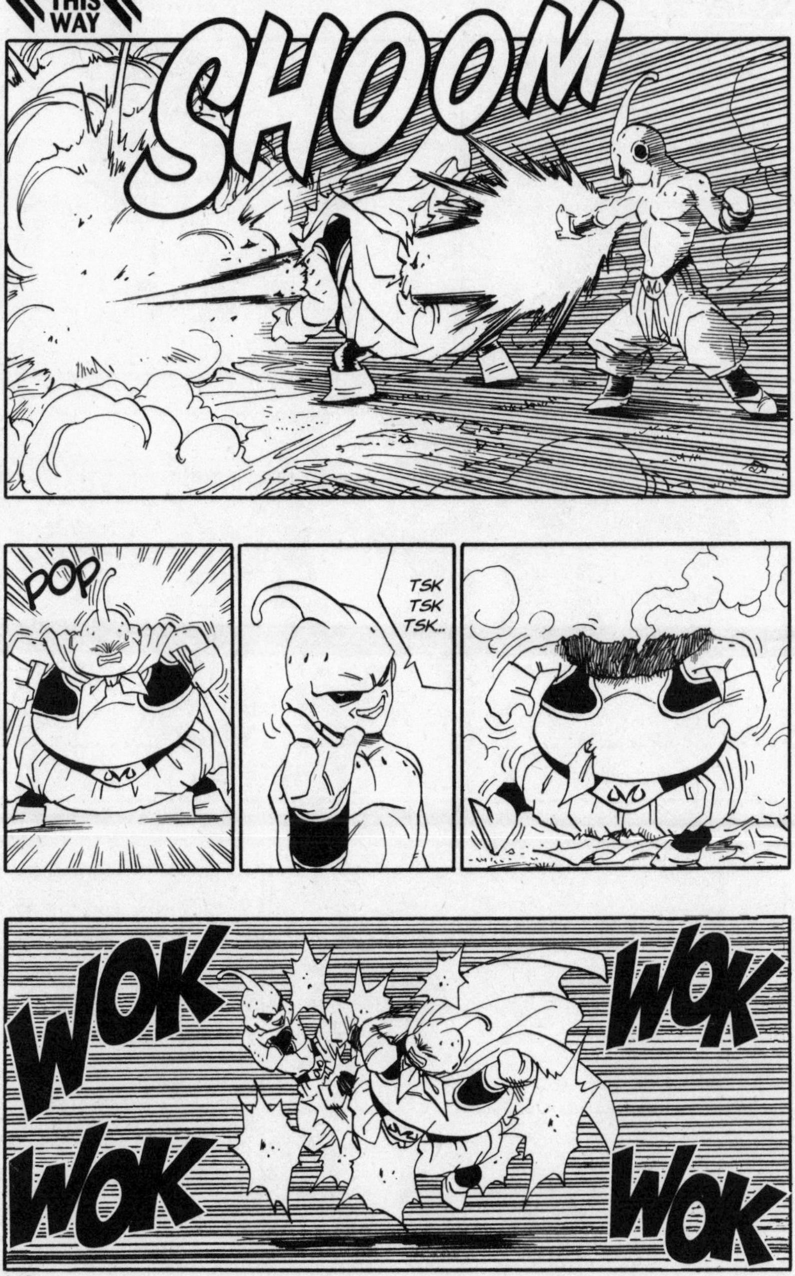
SHOOM
TSK TSK TSK...
POP
WOK
WOK
WOK
WOK

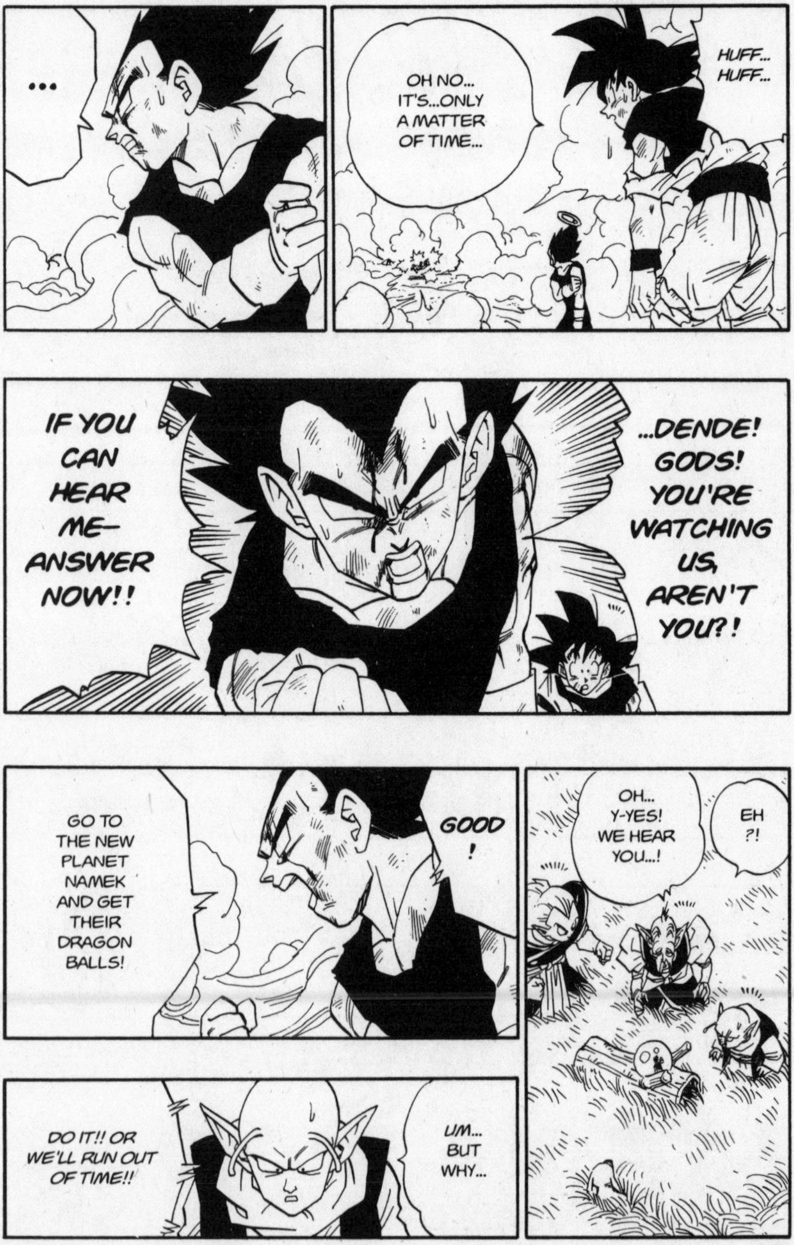
HUFF... HUFF...
OH NO... IT'S...ONLY A MATTER OF TIME...
...
...DENDE! GODS! YOU'RE WATCHING US, AREN'T YOU?!
IF YOU CAN HEAR ME— ANSWER NOW!!
EH ?!
OH... Y-YES! WE HEAR YOU...!
GOOD!
GO TO THE NEW PLANET NAMEK AND GET THEIR DRAGON BALLS!
UM... BUT WHY...
DO IT!! OR WE'LL RUN OUT OF TIME!!

READ THIS WAY

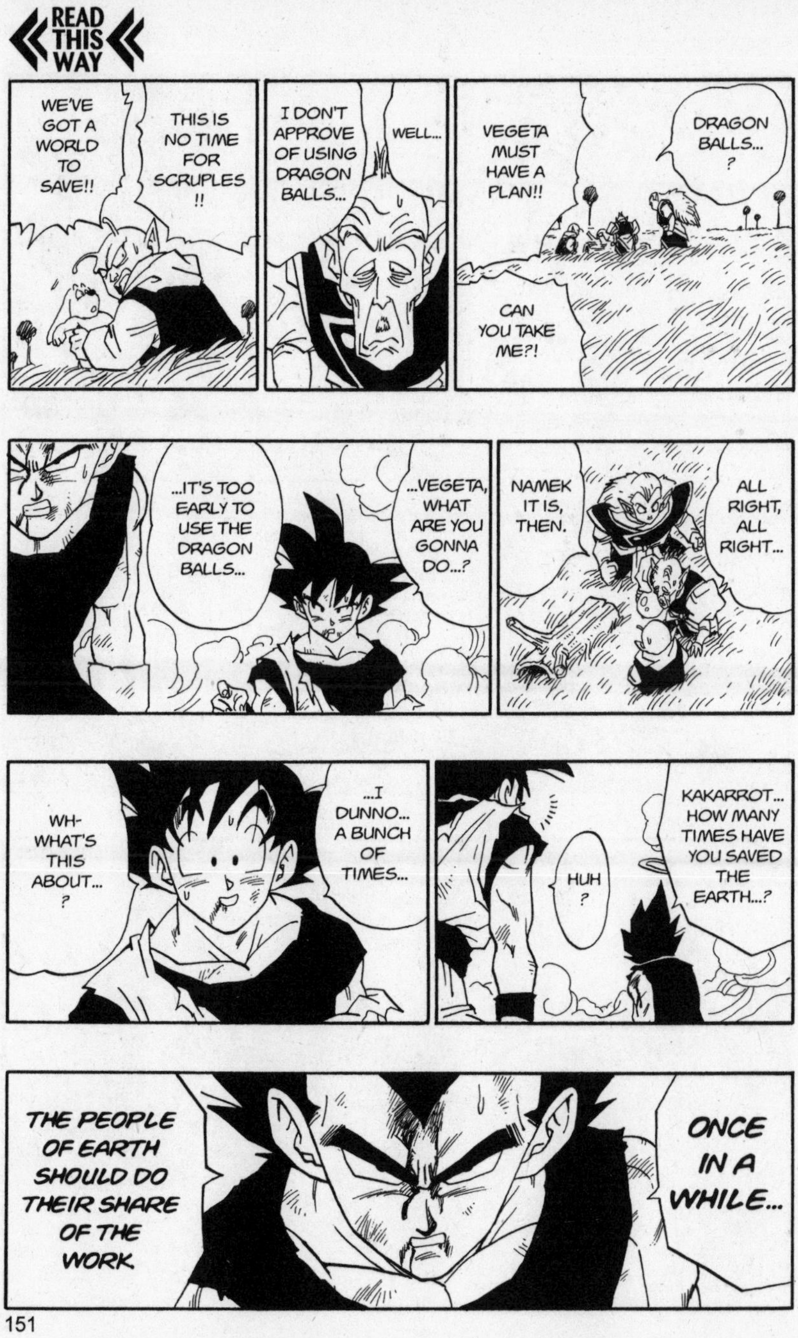
DRAGON BALLS...?
VEGETA MUST HAVE A PLAN!!
CAN YOU TAKE ME?!
WELL...
I DON'T APPROVE OF USING DRAGON BALLS...
THIS IS NO TIME FOR SCRUPLES!!
WE'VE GOT A WORLD TO SAVE!!
ALL RIGHT, ALL RIGHT...
NAMEK IT IS, THEN.
...VEGETA, WHAT ARE YOU GONNA DO...?
...IT'S TOO EARLY TO USE THE DRAGON BALLS...
KAKARROT... HOW MANY TIMES HAVE YOU SAVED THE EARTH...?
HUH?
...I DUNNO... A BUNCH OF TIMES...
WH-WHAT'S THIS ABOUT...?
ONCE IN A WHILE...
THE PEOPLE OF EARTH SHOULD DO THEIR SHARE OF THE WORK.

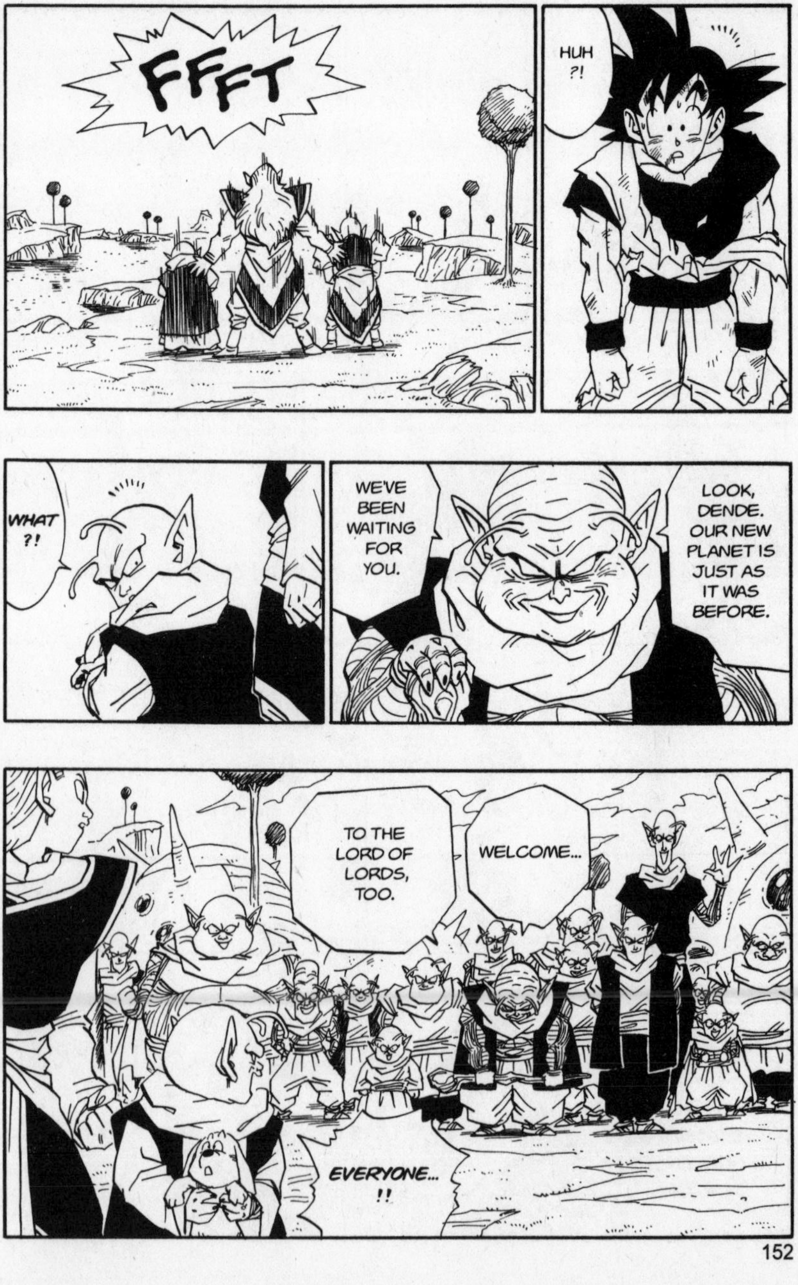
HUH ?!
FFFT
LOOK, DENDE. OUR NEW PLANET IS JUST AS IT WAS BEFORE.
WE'VE BEEN WAITING FOR YOU.
WHAT ?!
WELCOME...
TO THE LORD OF LORDS, TOO.
EVERYONE... !!

READ THIS WAY

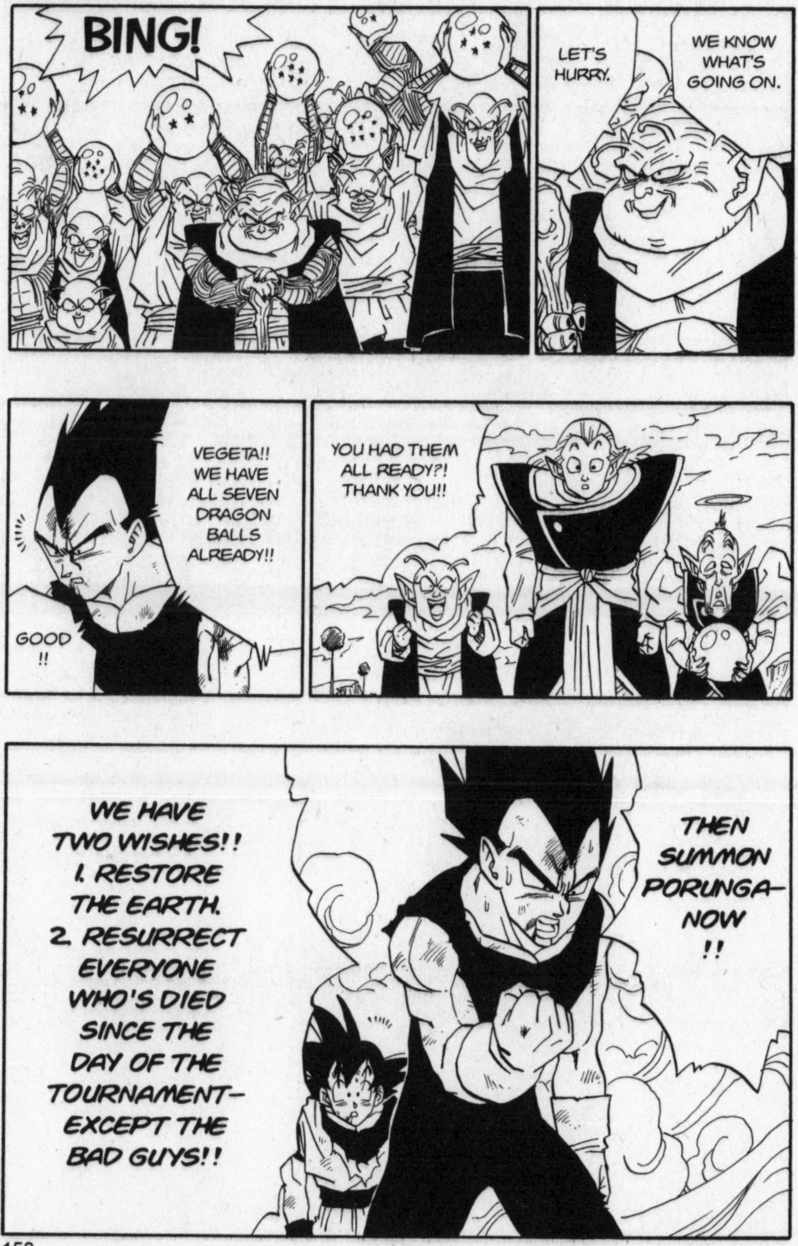
WE KNOW WHAT'S GOING ON.
LET'S HURRY.
BING!
YOU HAD THEM ALL READY?! THANK YOU!!
VEGETA!! WE HAVE ALL SEVEN DRAGON BALLS ALREADY!!
GOOD !!
THEN SUMMON PORUNGA-NOW !!
WE HAVE TWO WISHES!! 1. RESTORE THE EARTH. 2. RESURRECT EVERYONE WHO'S DIED SINCE THE DAY OF THE TOURNAMENT-EXCEPT THE BAD GUYS!!

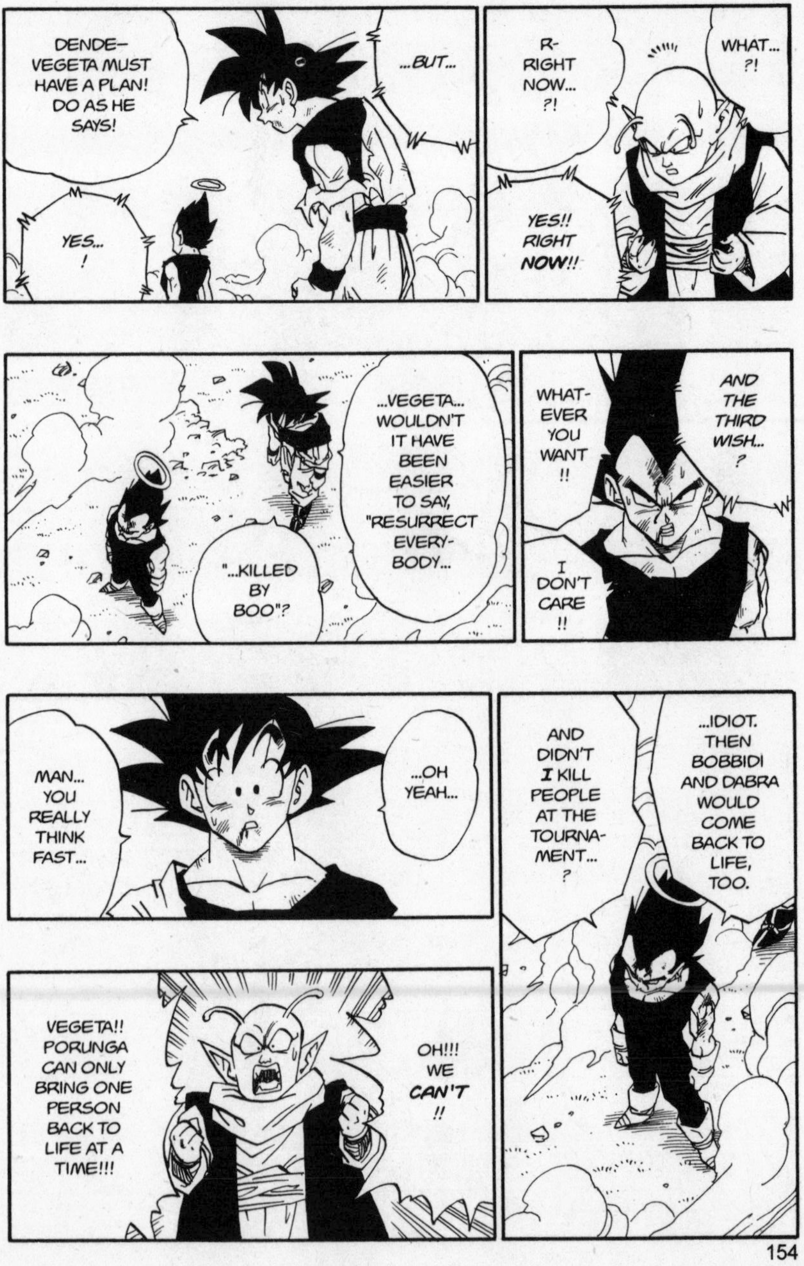
WHAT... ?!
R- RIGHT NOW... ?!
YES!! RIGHT **NOW**!!
...BUT...
DENDE— VEGETA MUST HAVE A PLAN! DO AS HE SAYS!
YES... !
AND THE THIRD WISH... ?
WHATEVER YOU WANT !!
I DON'T CARE !!
...VEGETA... WOULDN'T IT HAVE BEEN EASIER TO SAY, "RESURRECT EVERYBODY...
"...KILLED BY BOO"?
...IDIOT. THEN BOBBIDI AND DABRA WOULD COME BACK TO LIFE, TOO.
AND DIDN'T **I** KILL PEOPLE AT THE TOURNAMENT... ?
...OH YEAH...
MAN... YOU REALLY THINK FAST...
OH!!! WE **CAN'T** !!
VEGETA!! PORUNGA CAN ONLY BRING ONE PERSON BACK TO LIFE AT A TIME!!!

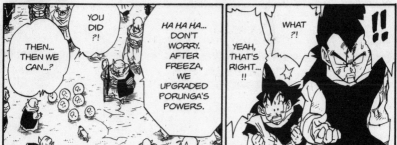

READ THIS WAY

!!
WHAT ?!
YEAH, THAT'S RIGHT... !!
HA HA HA... DON'T WORRY. AFTER FREEZA, WE UPGRADED PORUNGA'S POWERS.
YOU DID ?!
THEN... THEN WE CAN...?
OH, ARROGANCE... VANITY... !
TRIFLING WITH NATURE'S LAWS!!
THIS MAY WORK !!
...GOOD.
THEN DO IT!!
!?
KRAK

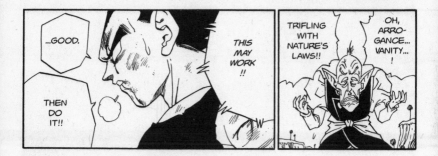

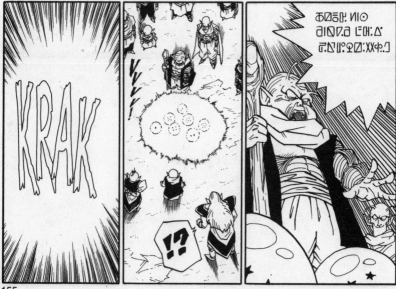

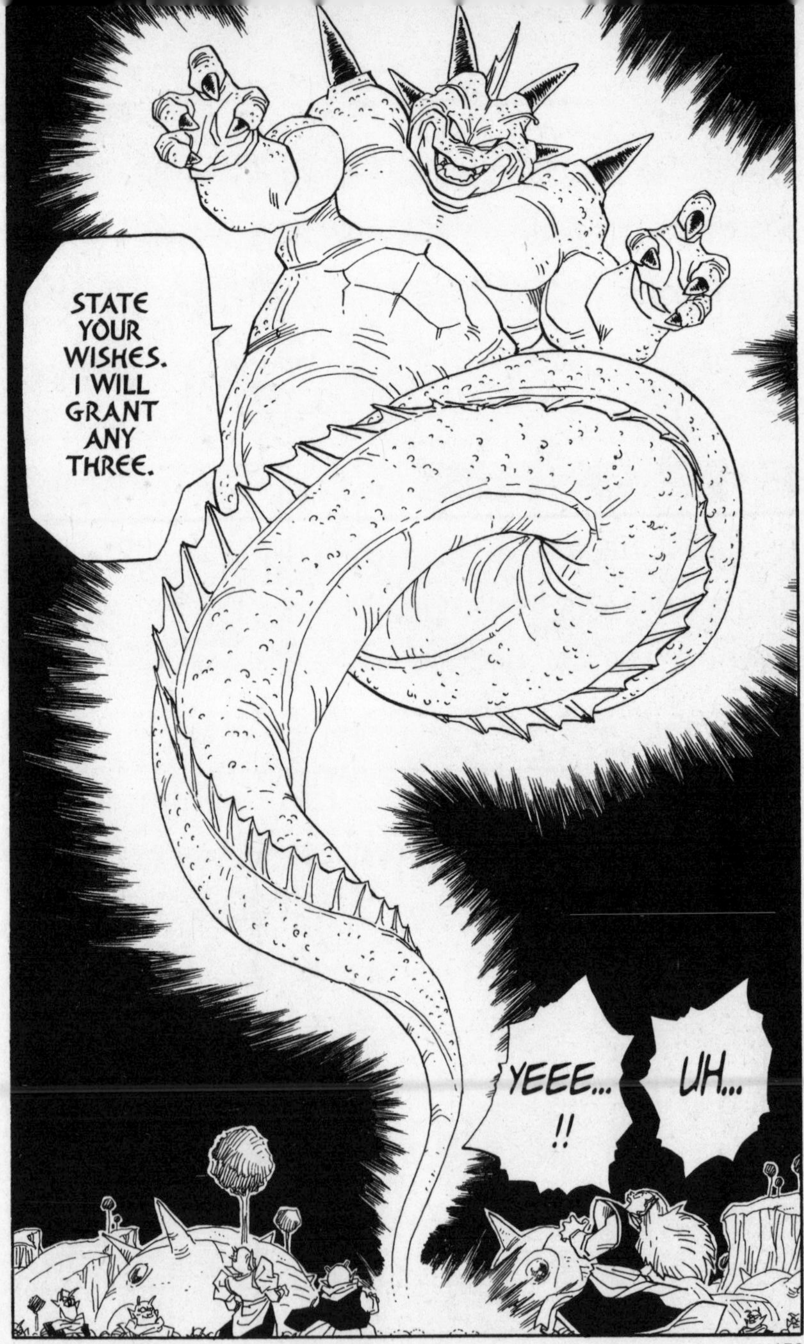
STATE YOUR WISHES. I WILL GRANT ANY THREE.
UH...
YEEE... !!

READ THIS WAY

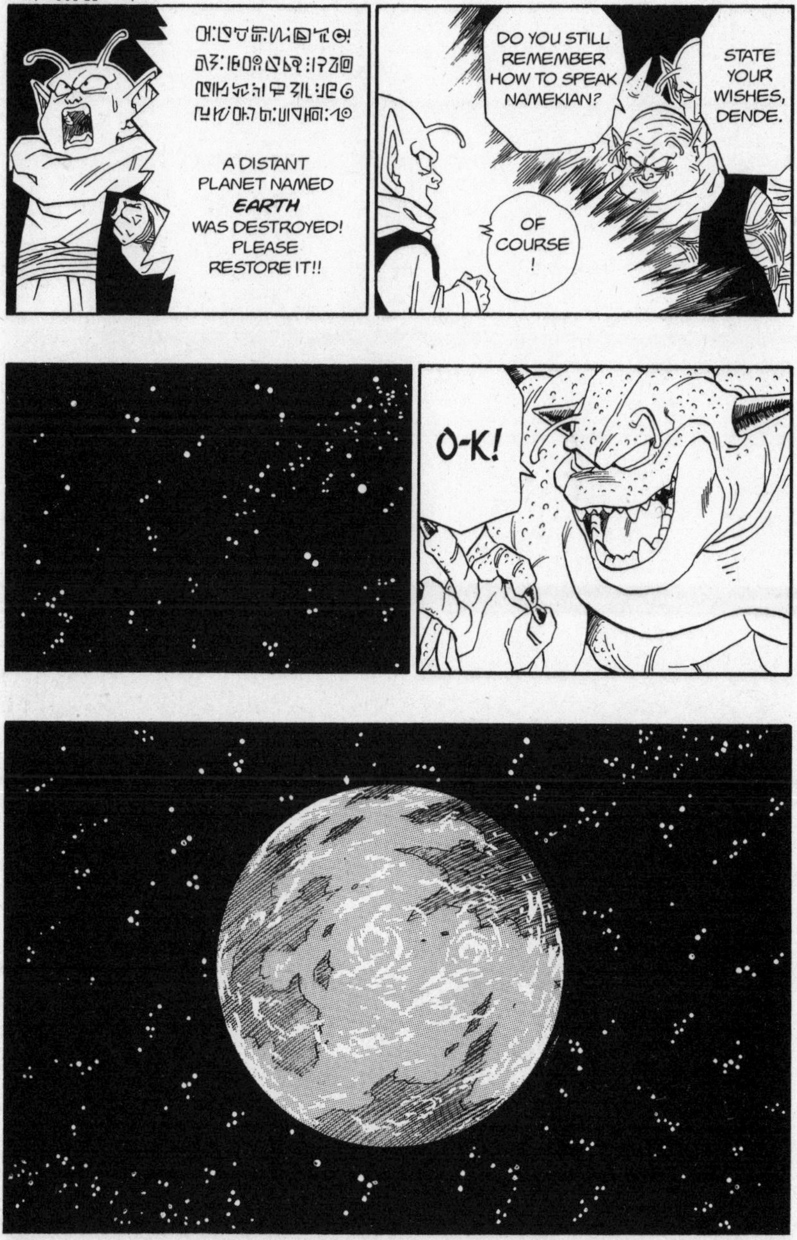

STATE YOUR WISHES, DENDE.
DO YOU STILL REMEMBER HOW TO SPEAK NAMEKIAN?
OF COURSE!
A DISTANT PLANET NAMED *EARTH* WAS DESTROYED! PLEASE RESTORE IT!!
O-K!

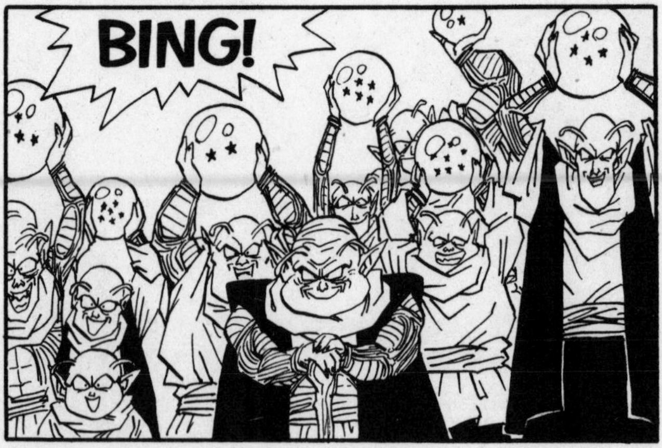
BING!

DBZ:320 • A Message to Earth

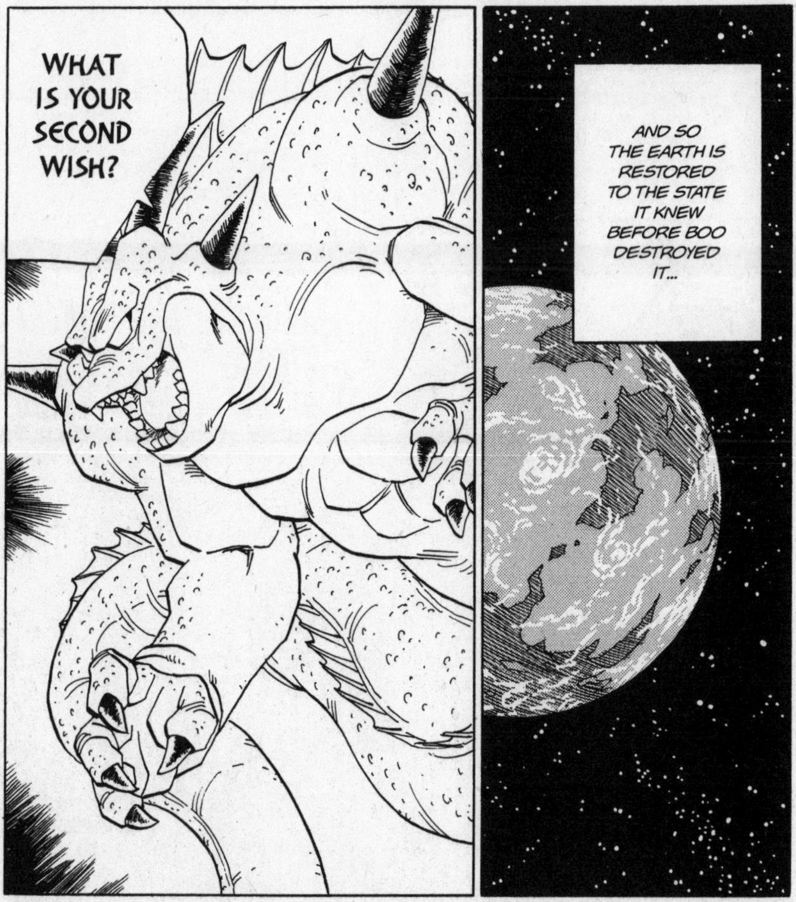
AND SO THE EARTH IS RESTORED TO THE STATE IT KNEW BEFORE BOO DESTROYED IT...
WHAT IS YOUR SECOND WISH?

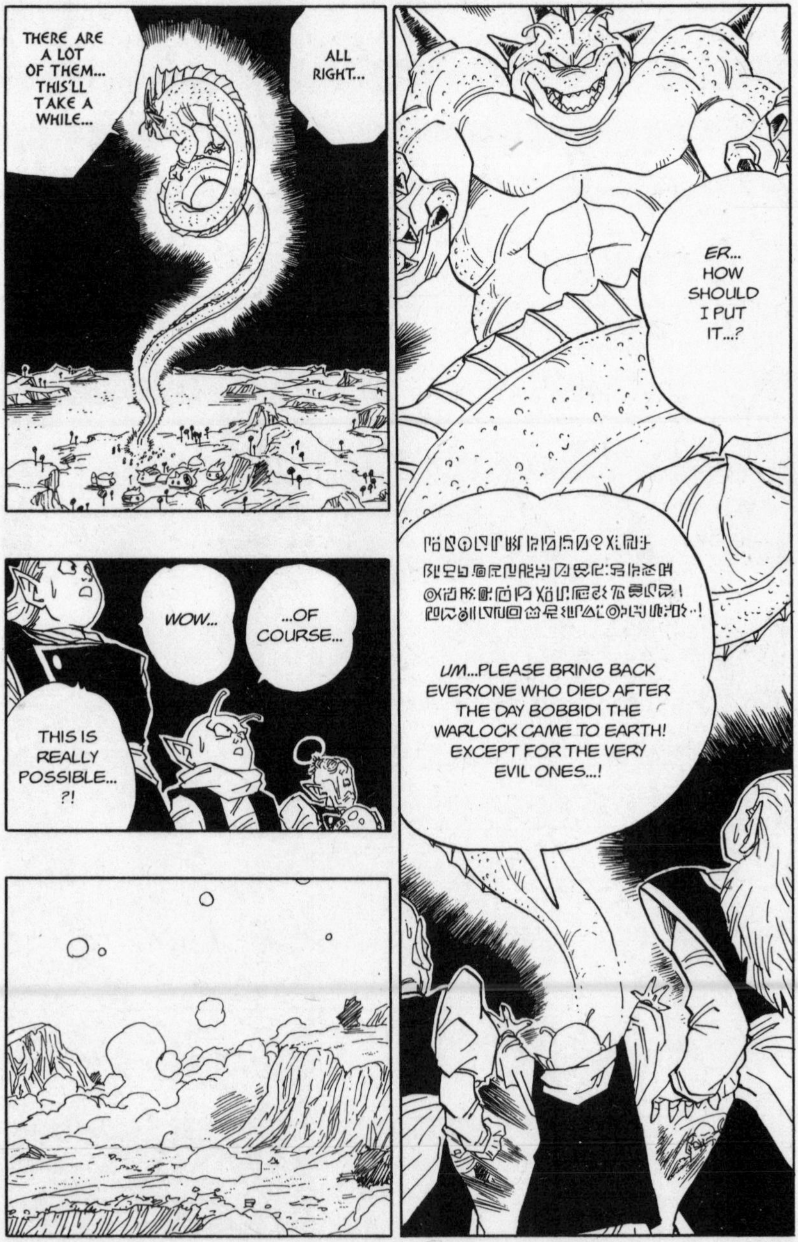
ER... HOW SHOULD I PUT IT...?
UM...PLEASE BRING BACK EVERYONE WHO DIED AFTER THE DAY BOBBIDI THE WARLOCK CAME TO EARTH! EXCEPT FOR THE VERY EVIL ONES...!
ALL RIGHT...
THERE ARE A LOT OF THEM... THIS'LL TAKE A WHILE...
...OF COURSE...
WOW...
THIS IS REALLY POSSIBLE...?!

READ THIS WAY

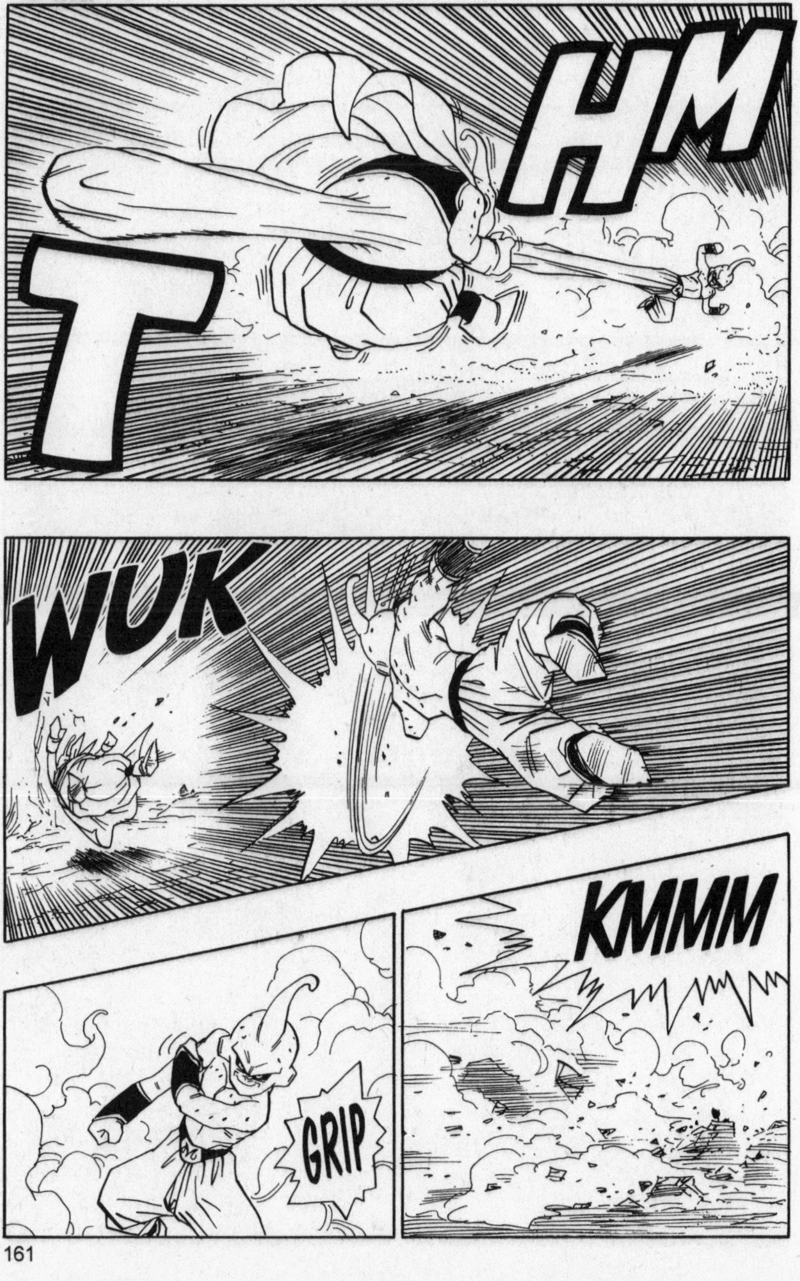
T
HM
WUK
KMMM
GRIP

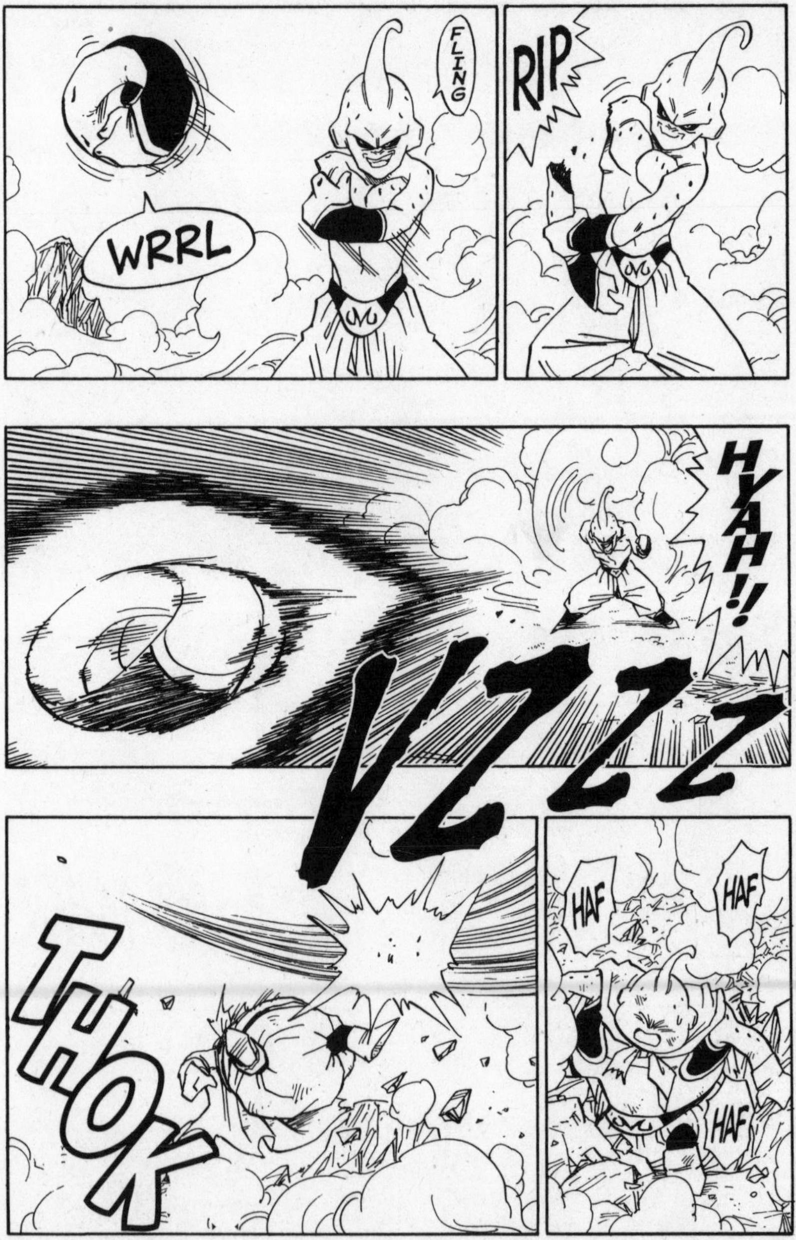
RIP
FLING
WRRL
HYAH!!
VZZZ
HAF
HAF
HAF
THOK

READ THIS WAY

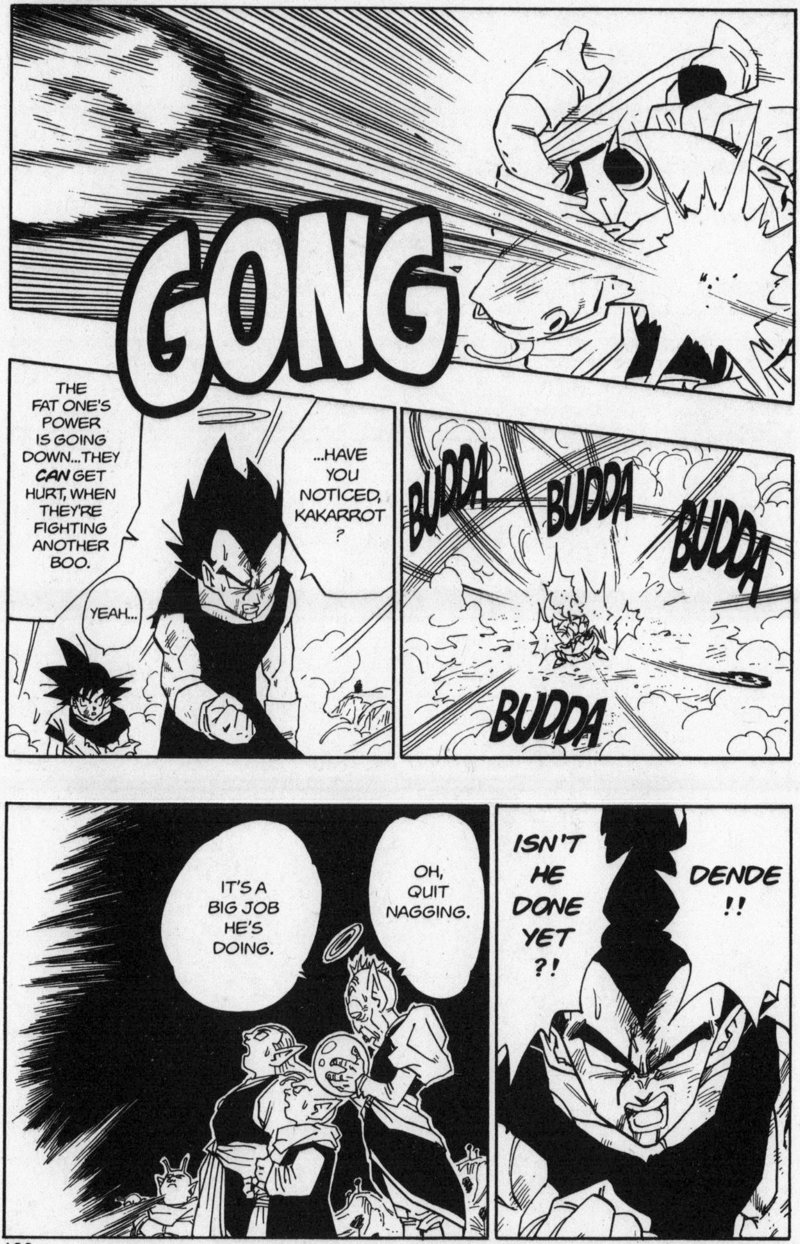
GONG
BUDDA
BUDDA
BUDDA
BUDDA
...HAVE YOU NOTICED, KAKARROT?
THE FAT ONE'S POWER IS GOING DOWN...THEY *CAN* GET HURT, WHEN THEY'RE FIGHTING ANOTHER BOO.
YEAH...
DENDE!!
ISN'T HE DONE YET?!
OH, QUIT NAGGING.
IT'S A BIG JOB HE'S DOING.

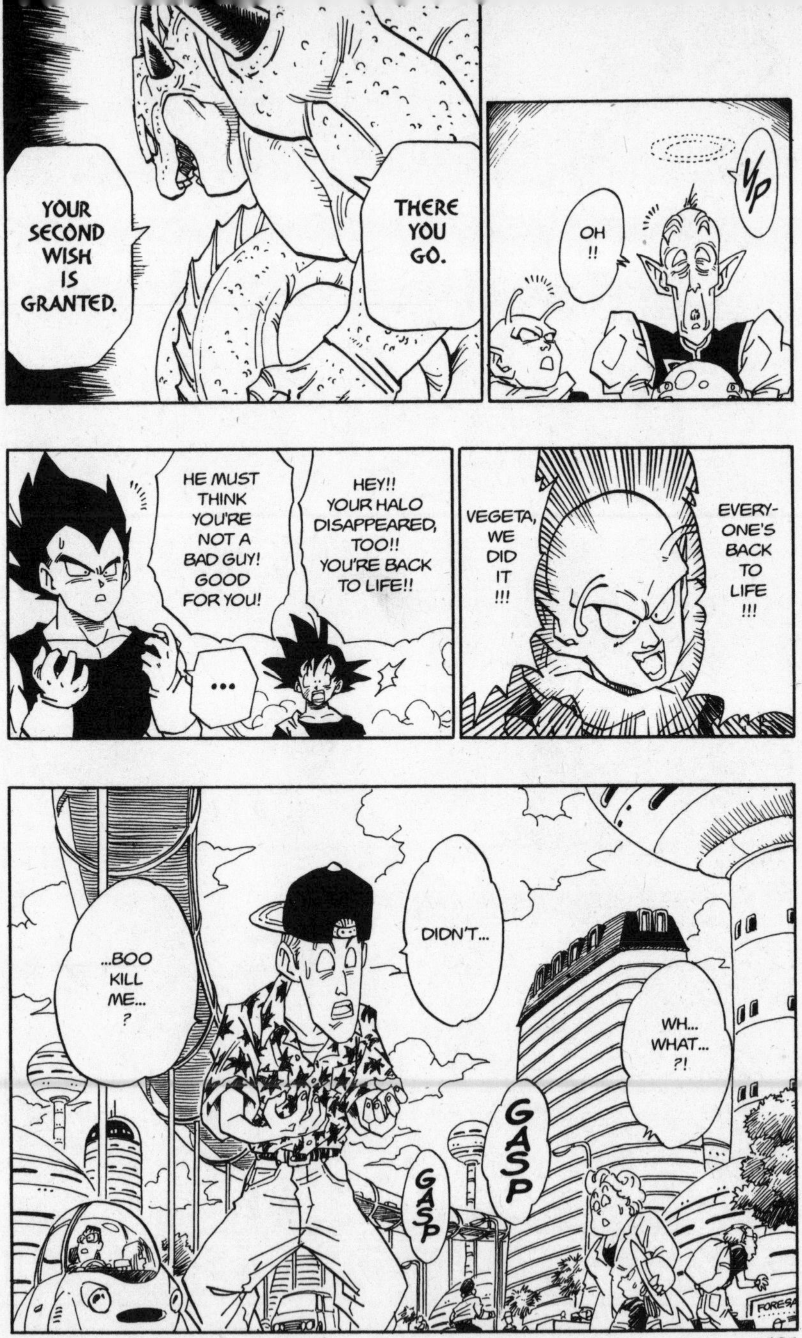
VIP
OH !!
THERE YOU GO.
YOUR SECOND WISH IS GRANTED.
EVERY-ONE'S BACK TO LIFE !!!
VEGETA, WE DID IT !!!
HEY!! YOUR HALO DISAPPEARED, TOO!! YOU'RE BACK TO LIFE!!
HE MUST THINK YOU'RE NOT A BAD GUY! GOOD FOR YOU!
...
WH... WHAT... ?!
GASP
GASP
DIDN'T...
...BOO KILL ME... ?

READ THIS WAY

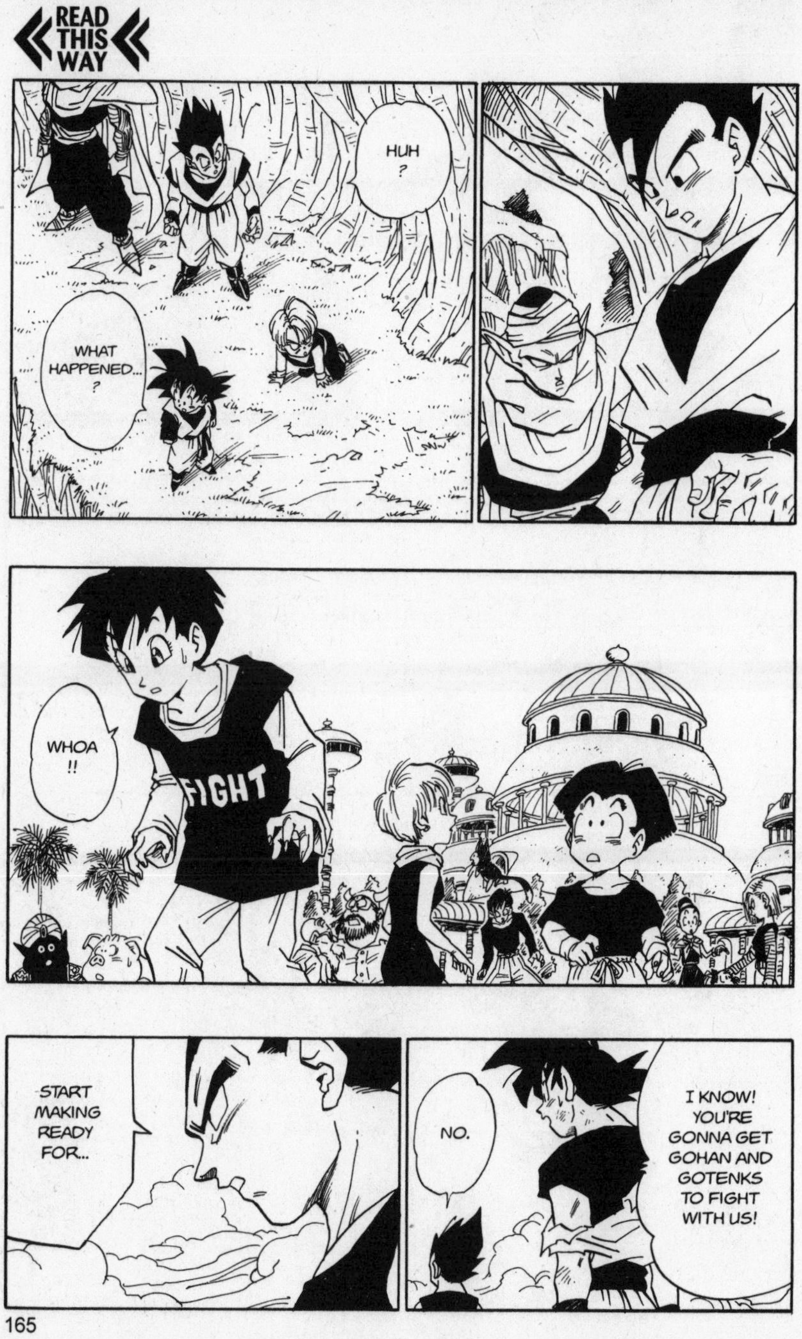
HUH ?
WHAT HAPPENED... ?
WHOA !!
FIGHT
I KNOW! YOU'RE GONNA GET GOHAN AND GOTENKS TO FIGHT WITH US!
NO.
START MAKING READY FOR...

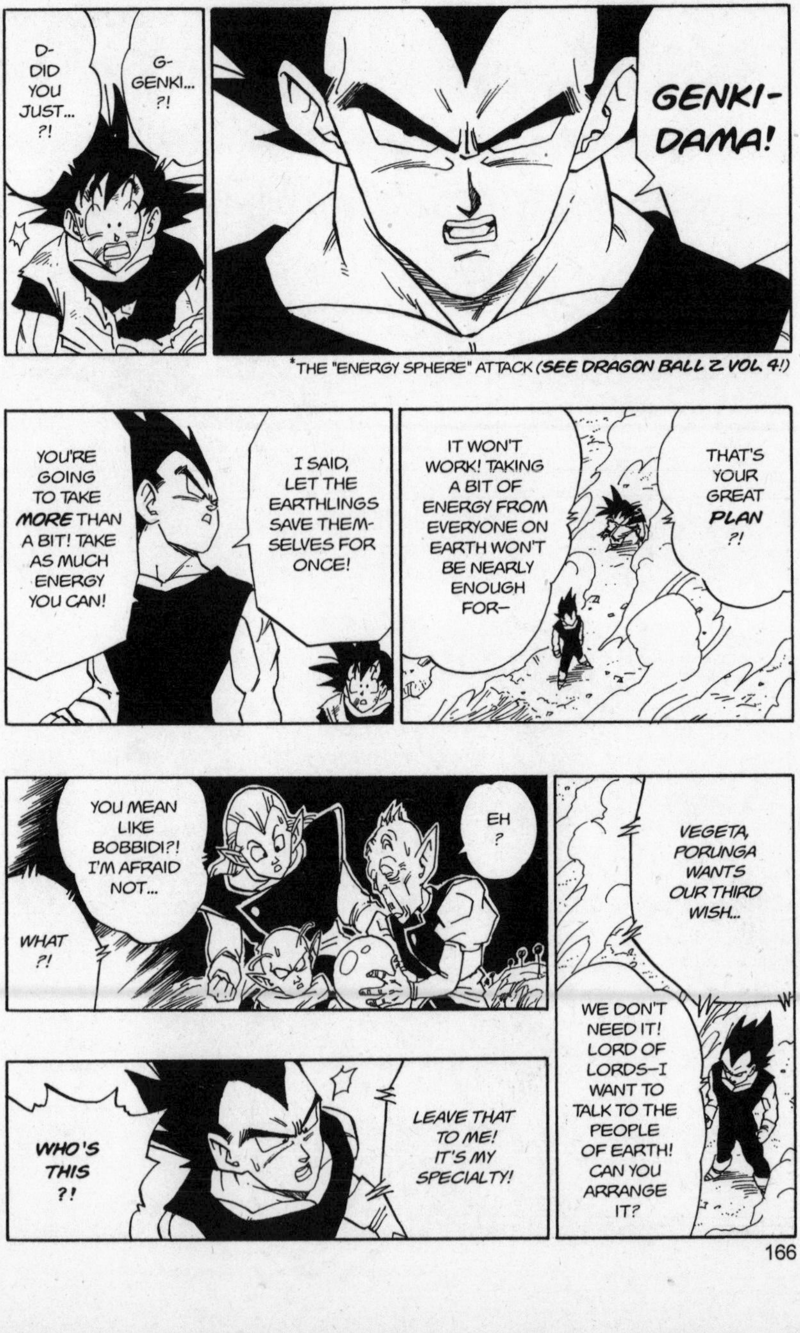
GENKI-DAMA!
G-GENKI...?!
D-DID YOU JUST...?!
THAT'S YOUR GREAT PLAN?!
IT WON'T WORK! TAKING A BIT OF ENERGY FROM EVERYONE ON EARTH WON'T BE NEARLY ENOUGH FOR–
I SAID, LET THE EARTHLINGS SAVE THEMSELVES FOR ONCE!
YOU'RE GOING TO TAKE MORE THAN A BIT! TAKE AS MUCH ENERGY YOU CAN!
VEGETA, PORUNGA WANTS OUR THIRD WISH...
WE DON'T NEED IT! LORD OF LORDS–I WANT TO TALK TO THE PEOPLE OF EARTH! CAN YOU ARRANGE IT?
EH?
YOU MEAN LIKE BOBBIDI?! I'M AFRAID NOT...
WHAT?!
LEAVE THAT TO ME! IT'S MY SPECIALTY!
WHO'S THIS?!
*THE "ENERGY SPHERE" ATTACK (SEE DRAGON BALL Z VOL. 4!)

READ THIS WAY

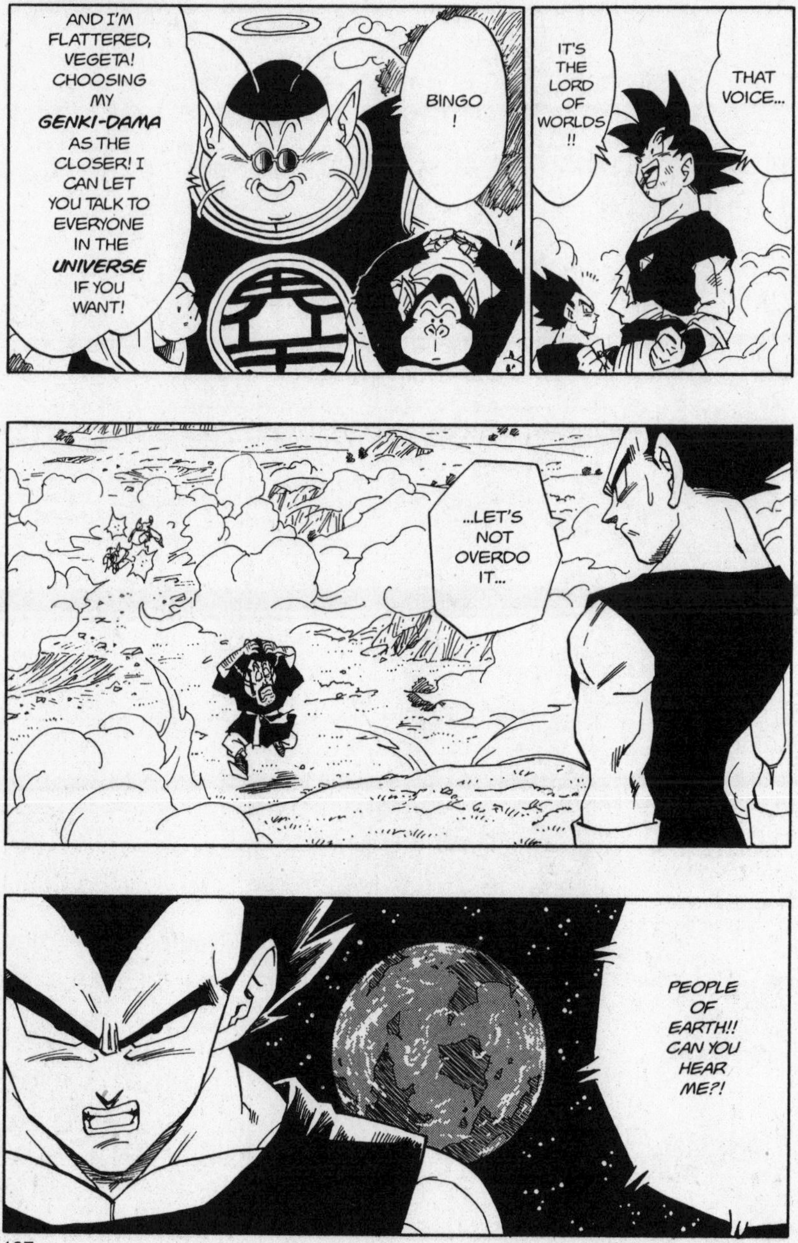

THAT VOICE...
IT'S THE LORD OF WORLDS!!
BINGO!
AND I'M FLATTERED, VEGETA! CHOOSING MY **GENKI-DAMA** AS THE CLOSER! I CAN LET YOU TALK TO EVERYONE IN THE **UNIVERSE** IF YOU WANT!
...LET'S NOT OVERDO IT...
PEOPLE OF EARTH!! CAN YOU HEAR ME?!

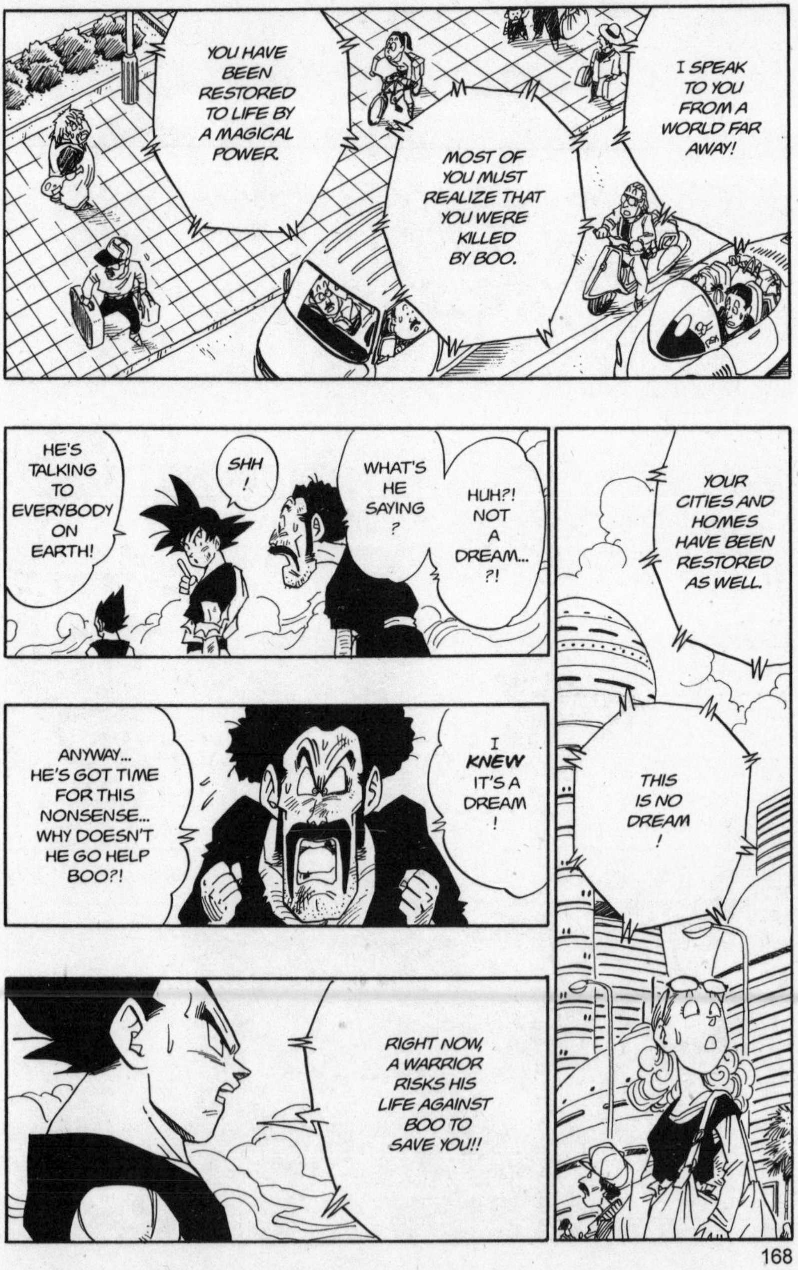
I SPEAK TO YOU FROM A WORLD FAR AWAY!
MOST OF YOU MUST REALIZE THAT YOU WERE KILLED BY BOO.
YOU HAVE BEEN RESTORED TO LIFE BY A MAGICAL POWER.
YOUR CITIES AND HOMES HAVE BEEN RESTORED AS WELL.
THIS IS NO DREAM!
HUH?! NOT A DREAM...?!
WHAT'S HE SAYING?
SHH!
HE'S TALKING TO EVERYBODY ON EARTH!
I **KNEW** IT'S A DREAM!
ANYWAY... HE'S GOT TIME FOR THIS NONSENSE... WHY DOESN'T HE GO HELP BOO?!
RIGHT NOW, A WARRIOR RISKS HIS LIFE AGAINST BOO TO SAVE YOU!!

READ THIS WAY

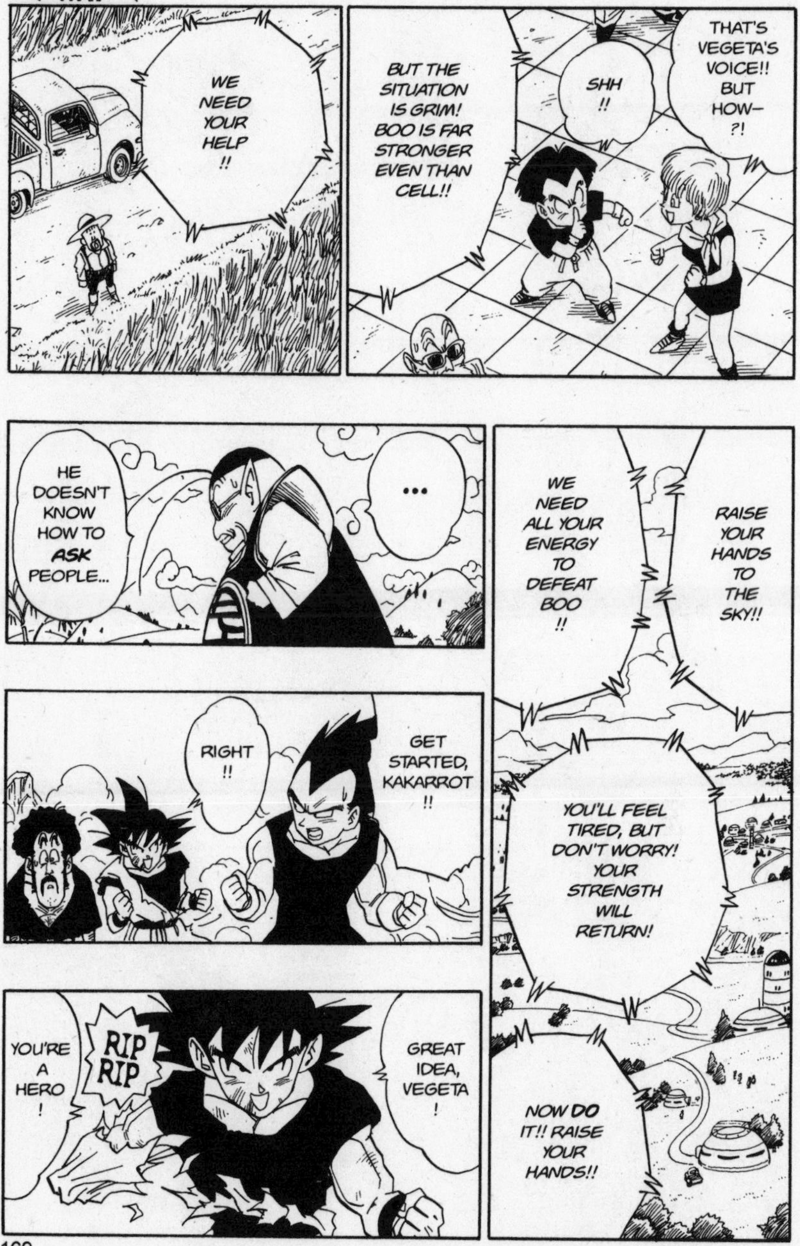
THAT'S VEGETA'S VOICE!! BUT HOW—?!
SHH !!
BUT THE SITUATION IS GRIM! BOO IS FAR STRONGER EVEN THAN CELL!!
WE NEED YOUR HELP !!
RAISE YOUR HANDS TO THE SKY!!
WE NEED ALL YOUR ENERGY TO DEFEAT BOO !!
YOU'LL FEEL TIRED, BUT DON'T WORRY! YOUR STRENGTH WILL RETURN!
NOW DO IT!! RAISE YOUR HANDS!!
...
HE DOESN'T KNOW HOW TO ASK PEOPLE...
GET STARTED, KAKARROT !!
RIGHT !!
GREAT IDEA, VEGETA !
RIP RIP
YOU'RE A HERO !

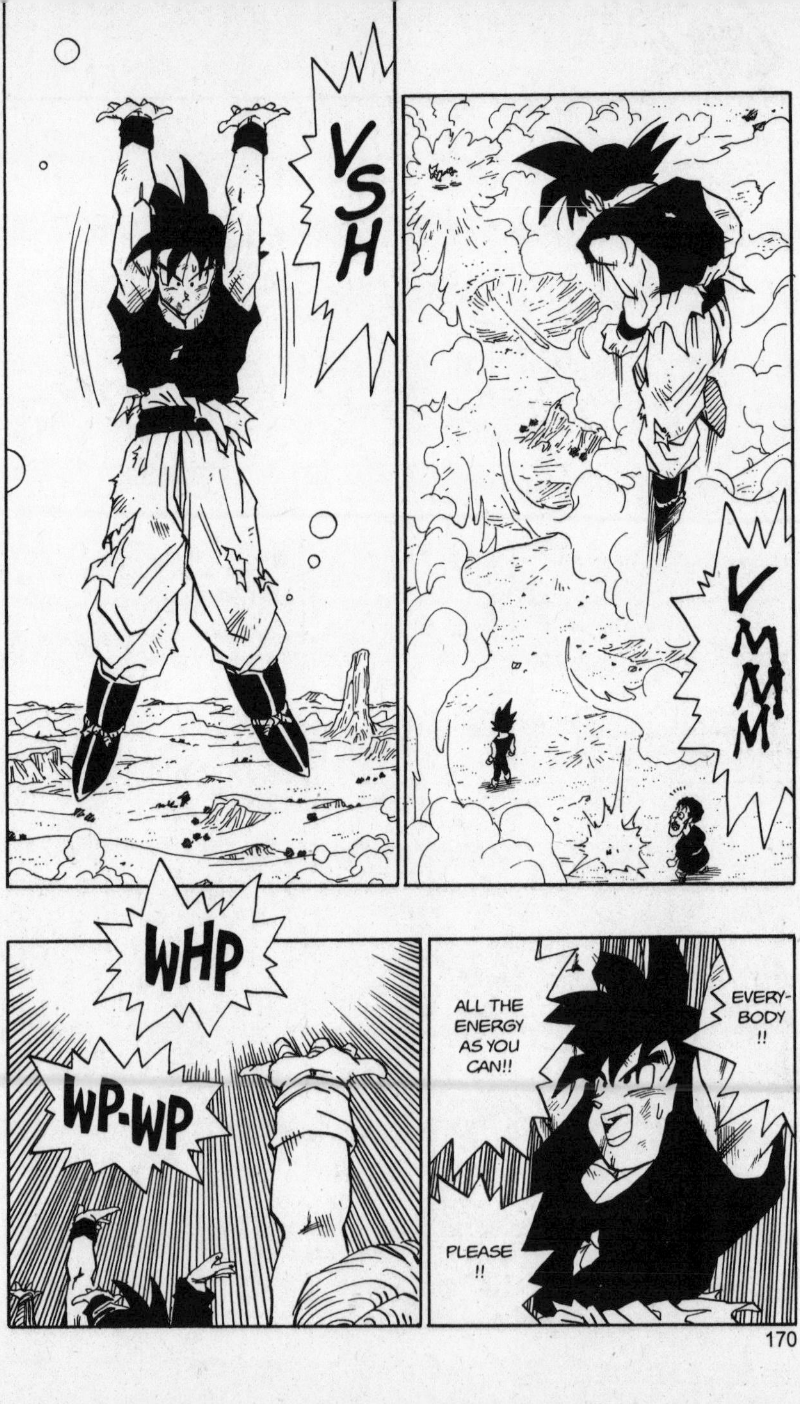
VMMM
VSH
EVERY-BODY!!
ALL THE ENERGY AS YOU CAN!!
PLEASE!!
WHP
WP-WP

READ THIS WAY

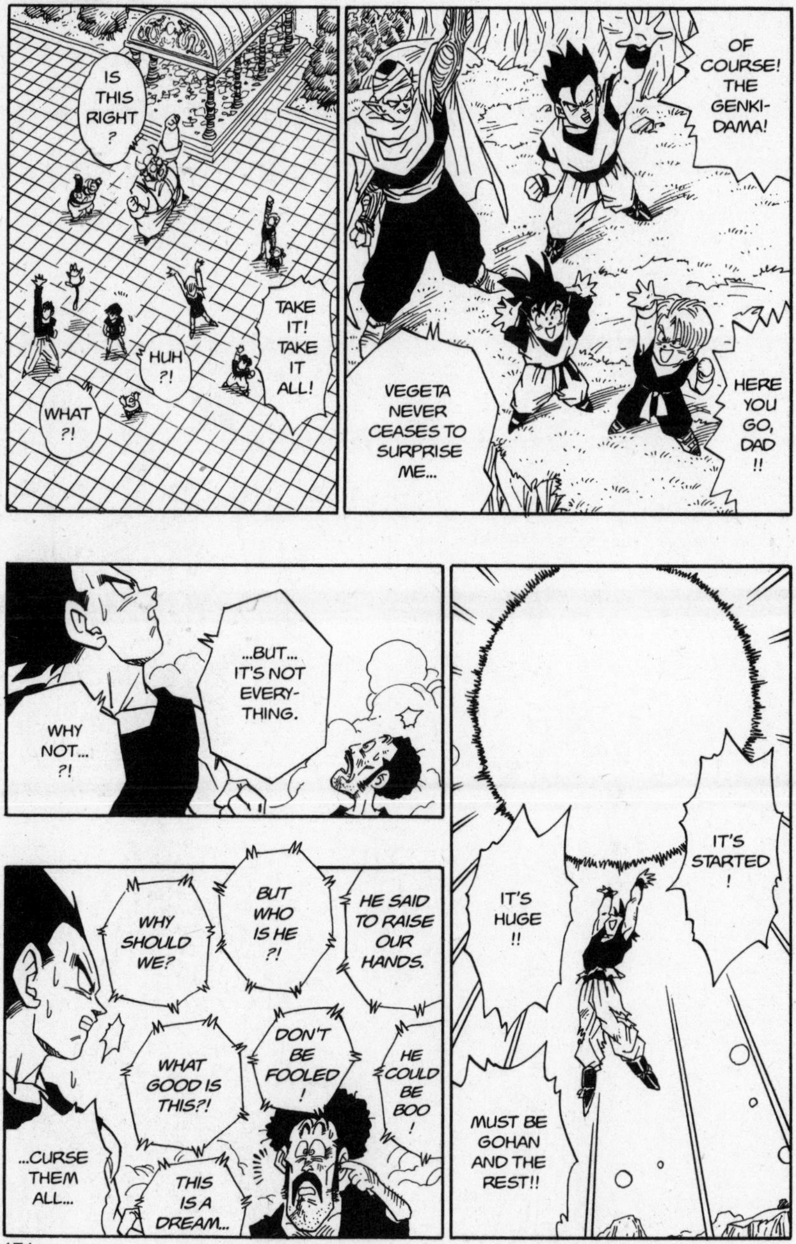
OF COURSE! THE GENKI-DAMA!
HERE YOU GO, DAD!!
VEGETA NEVER CEASES TO SURPRISE ME...
IS THIS RIGHT?
TAKE IT! TAKE IT ALL!
HUH?!
WHAT?!
IT'S STARTED!
IT'S HUGE!!
MUST BE GOHAN AND THE REST!!
...BUT... IT'S NOT EVERYTHING.
WHY NOT...?!
HE SAID TO RAISE OUR HANDS.
BUT WHO IS HE?!
WHY SHOULD WE?
HE COULD BE BOO!
DON'T BE FOOLED!
WHAT GOOD IS THIS?!
THIS IS A DREAM...
...CURSE THEM ALL...

DBZ:321 · Just Not Enough

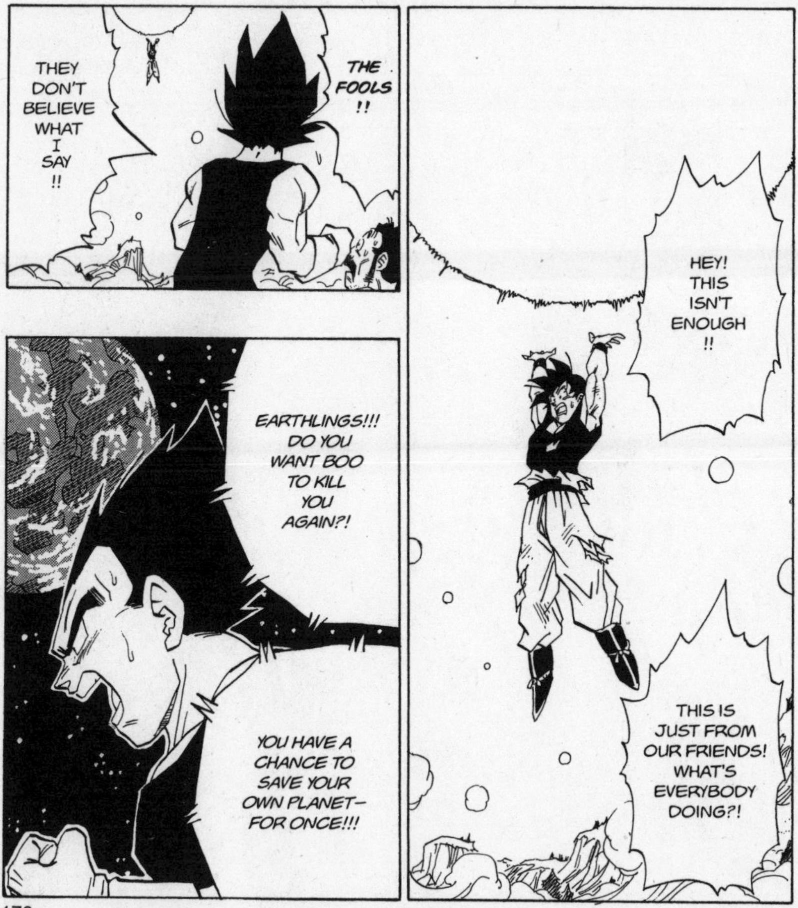
HEY! THIS ISN'T ENOUGH!!
THIS IS JUST FROM OUR FRIENDS! WHAT'S EVERYBODY DOING?!
THE FOOLS!!
THEY DON'T BELIEVE WHAT I SAY!!
EARTHLINGS!!! DO YOU WANT BOO TO KILL YOU AGAIN?!
YOU HAVE A CHANCE TO SAVE YOUR OWN PLANET—FOR ONCE!!!

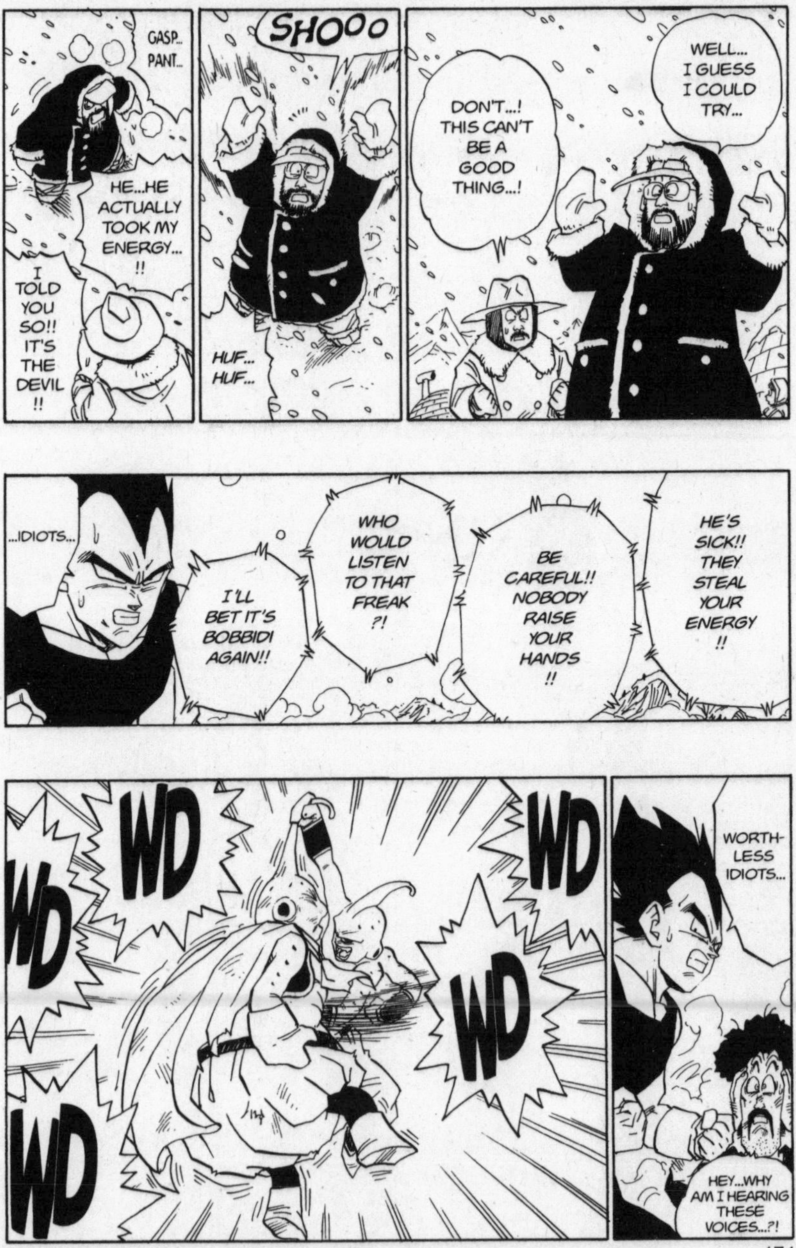
WELL... I GUESS I COULD TRY...
DON'T...! THIS CAN'T BE A GOOD THING...!
SHOOO
HUF... HUF...
GASP... PANT...
HE...HE ACTUALLY TOOK MY ENERGY...!!
I TOLD YOU SO!! IT'S THE DEVIL!!
HE'S SICK!! THEY STEAL YOUR ENERGY!!
BE CAREFUL!! NOBODY RAISE YOUR HANDS!!
WHO WOULD LISTEN TO THAT FREAK?!
I'LL BET IT'S BOBBIDI AGAIN!!
...IDIOTS...
WORTH-LESS IDIOTS...
HEY...WHY AM I HEARING THESE VOICES...?!
WD
WD
WD
WD
WD

READ THIS WAY

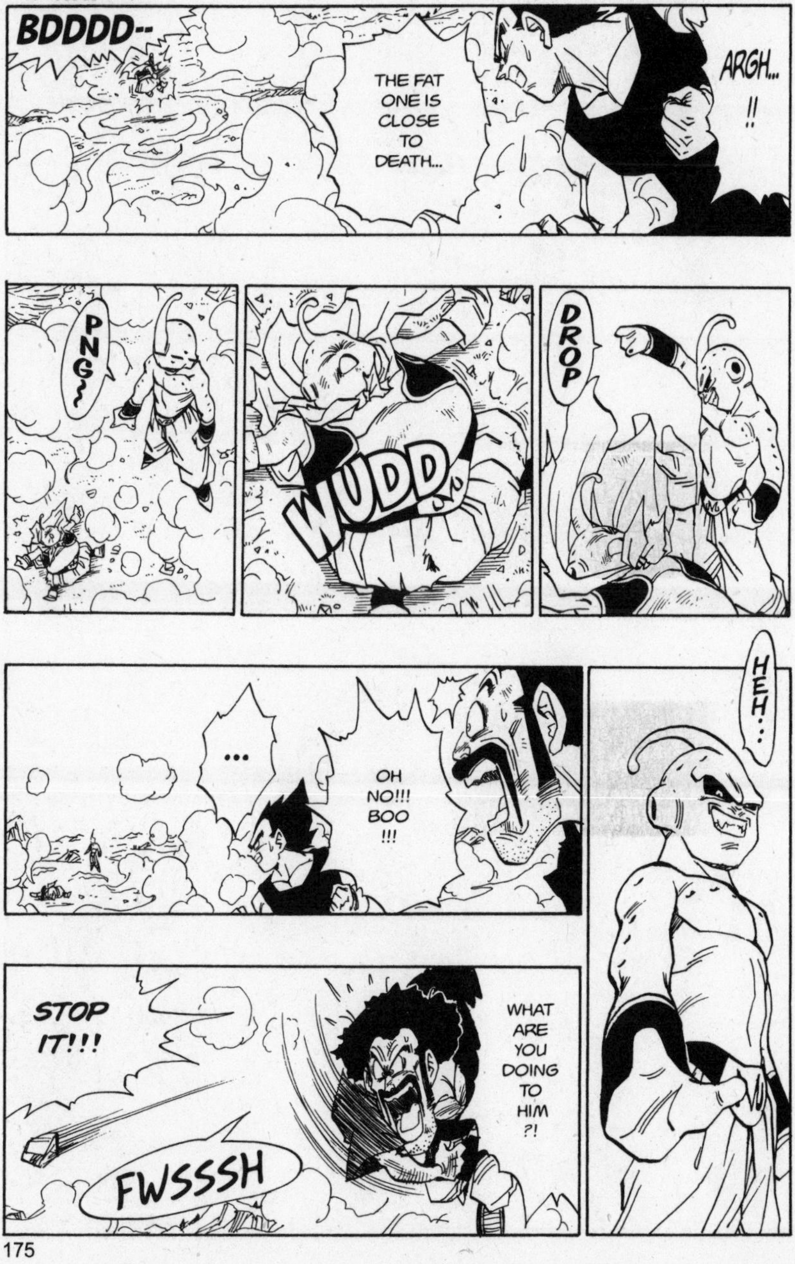
ARGH... !!
THE FAT ONE IS CLOSE TO DEATH...
BDDDD--
DROP
WUDD
PNG~
HEH...
OH NO!!! BOO !!!
...
WHAT ARE YOU DOING TO HIM ?!
STOP IT!!!
FWSSSH

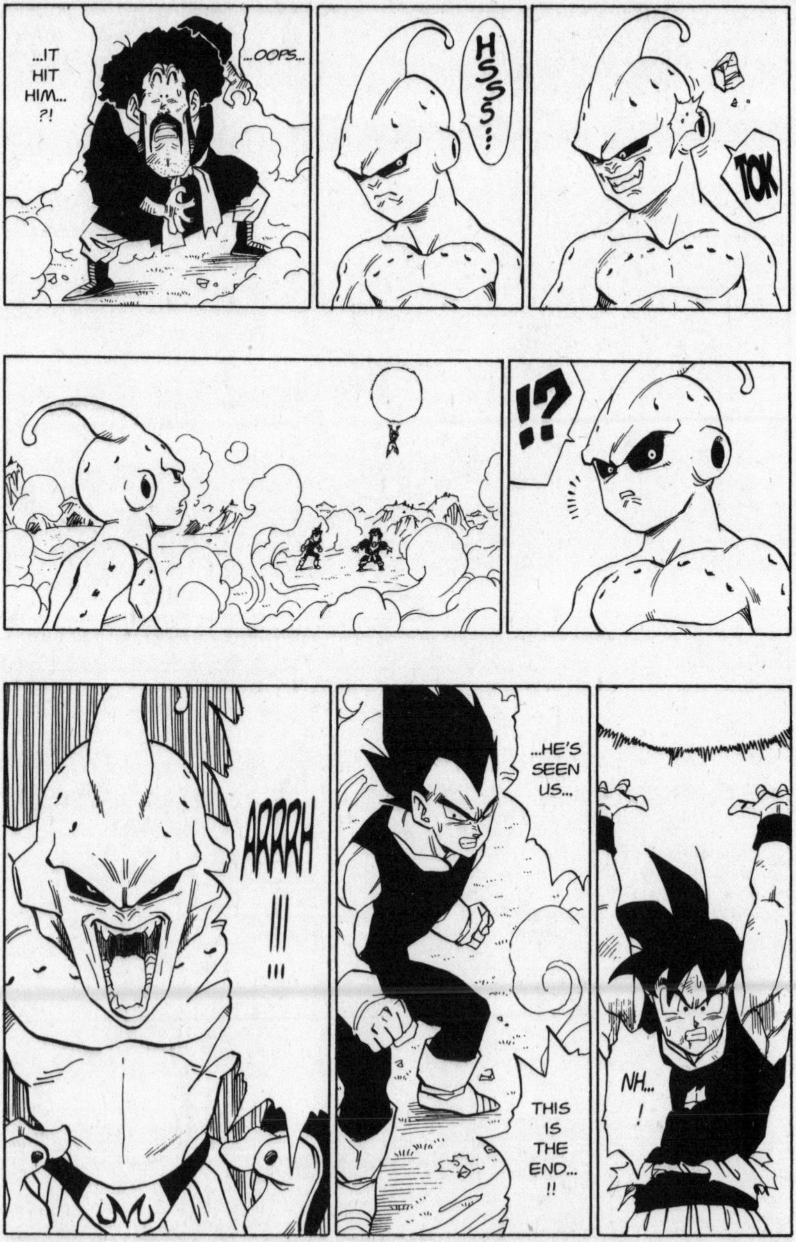
TOK
HSSS...
...OOPS...
...IT HIT HIM... ?!
!?
NH... !
...HE'S SEEN US...
THIS IS THE END... !!
ARRRH !!!!!!

READ THIS WAY

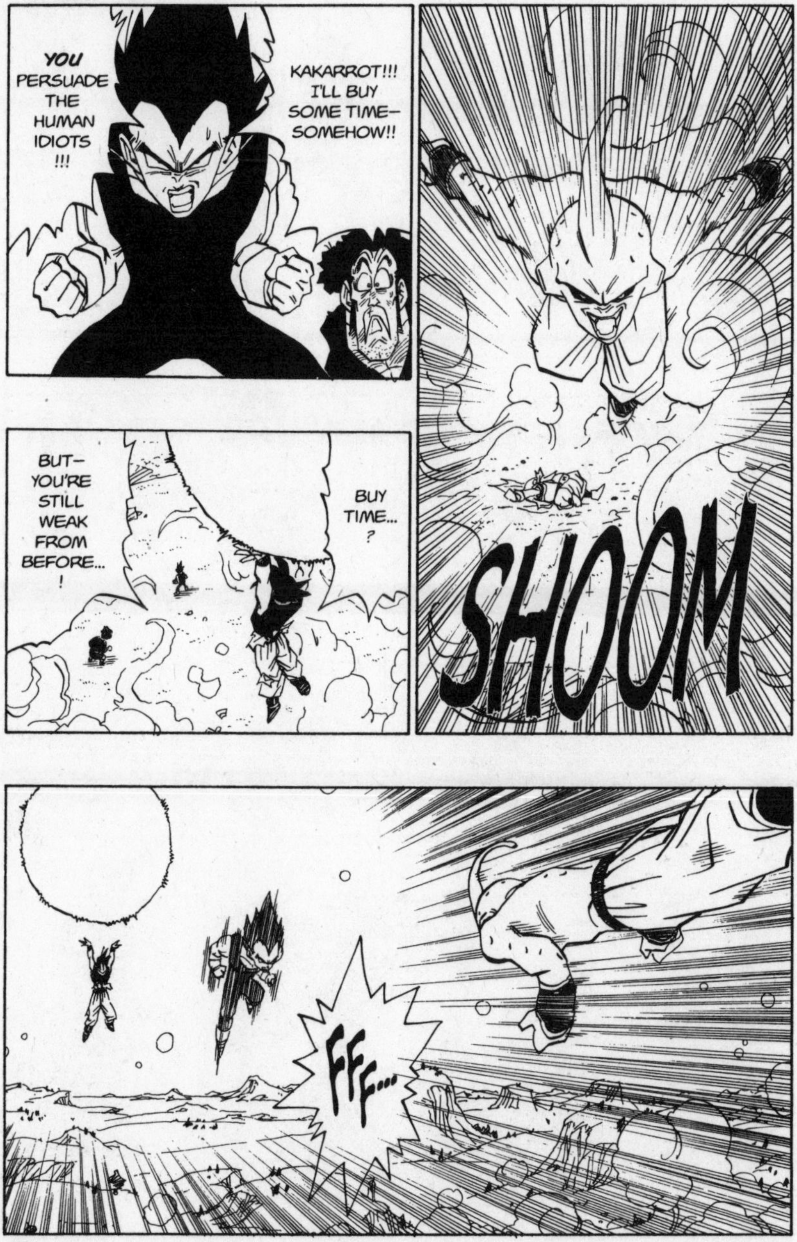

SHOOM
KAKARROT!!! I'LL BUY SOME TIME— SOMEHOW!!
YOU PERSUADE THE HUMAN IDIOTS !!!
BUY TIME... ?
BUT— YOU'RE STILL WEAK FROM BEFORE... !
FFF...

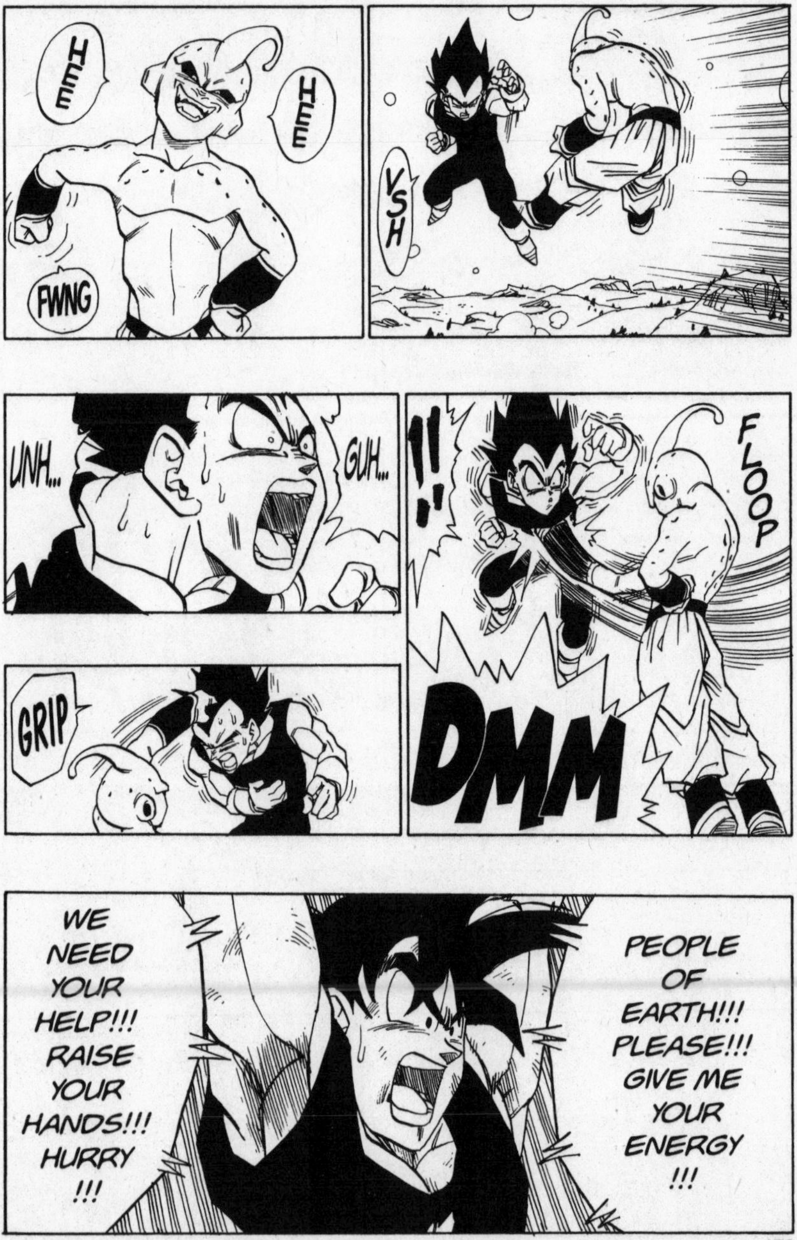

VSH
HEE
HEE
FWNG
FLOOP
!!
DMM
GUH...
UNH...
GRIP
PEOPLE OF EARTH!!! PLEASE!!! GIVE ME YOUR ENERGY !!!
WE NEED YOUR HELP!!! RAISE YOUR HANDS!!! HURRY !!!

READ THIS WAY

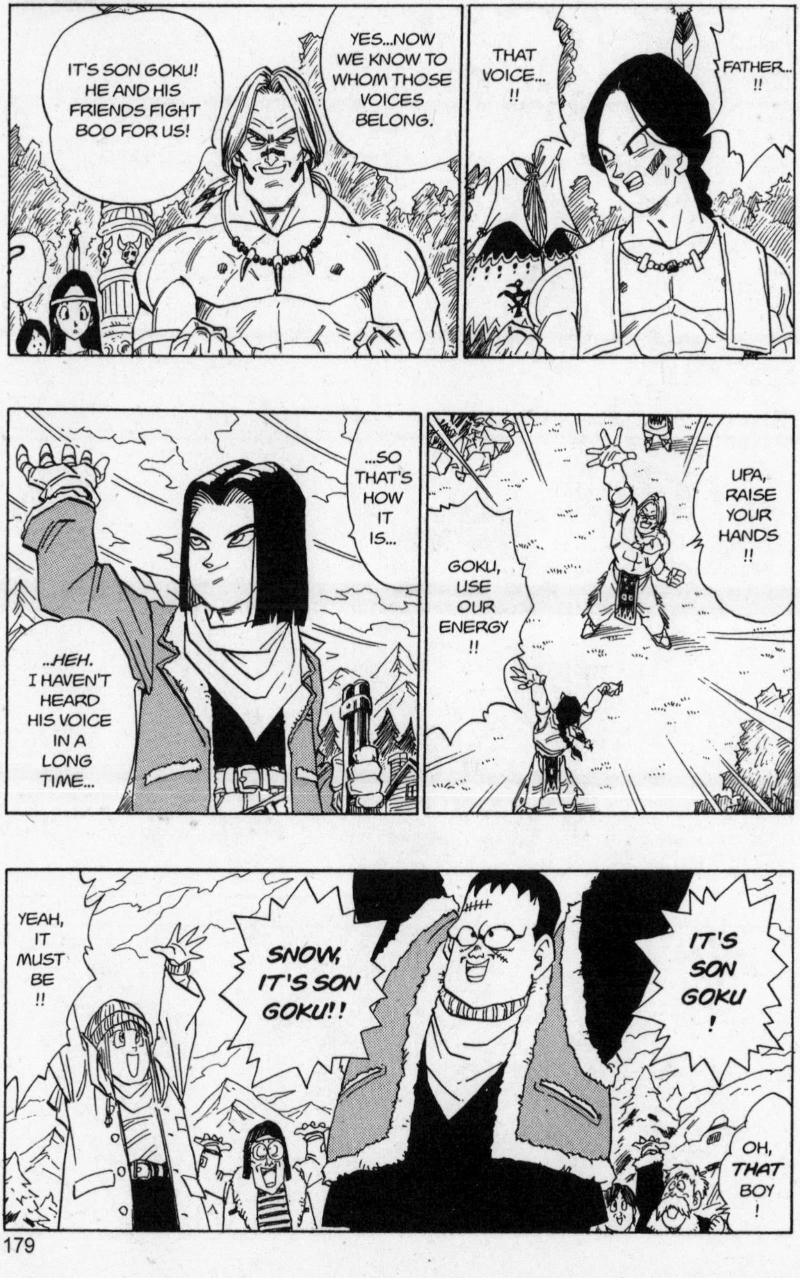
FATHER.. !!
THAT VOICE... !!
YES...NOW WE KNOW TO WHOM THOSE VOICES BELONG.
IT'S SON GOKU! HE AND HIS FRIENDS FIGHT BOO FOR US!
UPA, RAISE YOUR HANDS !!
GOKU, USE OUR ENERGY !!
...SO THAT'S HOW IT IS...
...HEH. I HAVEN'T HEARD HIS VOICE IN A LONG TIME...
OH, THAT BOY !
IT'S SON GOKU !
SNOW, IT'S SON GOKU!!
YEAH, IT MUST BE !!

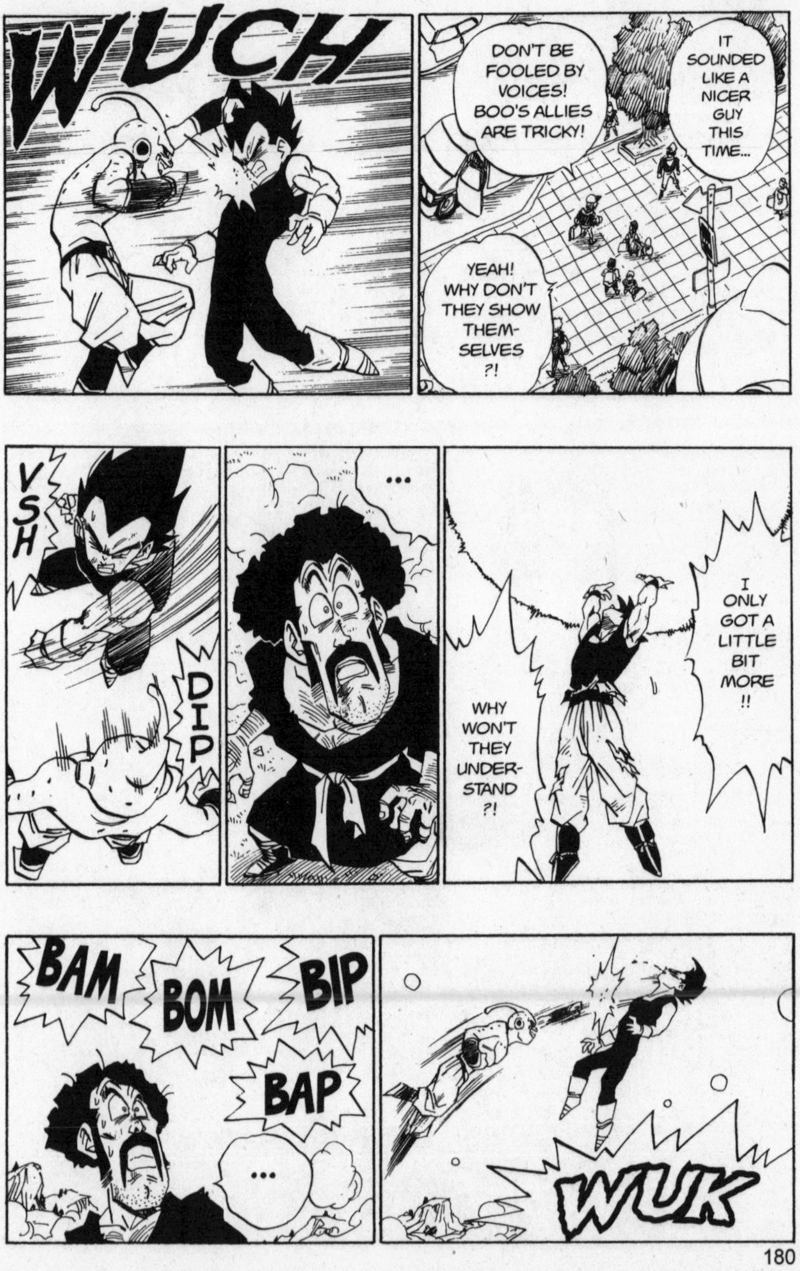
IT SOUNDED LIKE A NICER GUY THIS TIME...
DON'T BE FOOLED BY VOICES! BOO'S ALLIES ARE TRICKY!
YEAH! WHY DON'T THEY SHOW THEM-SELVES ?!
WUCH
I ONLY GOT A LITTLE BIT MORE !!
WHY WON'T THEY UNDER-STAND ?!
...
VSH
DIP
WUK
BIP
BOM
BAM
BAP
...

READ THIS WAY

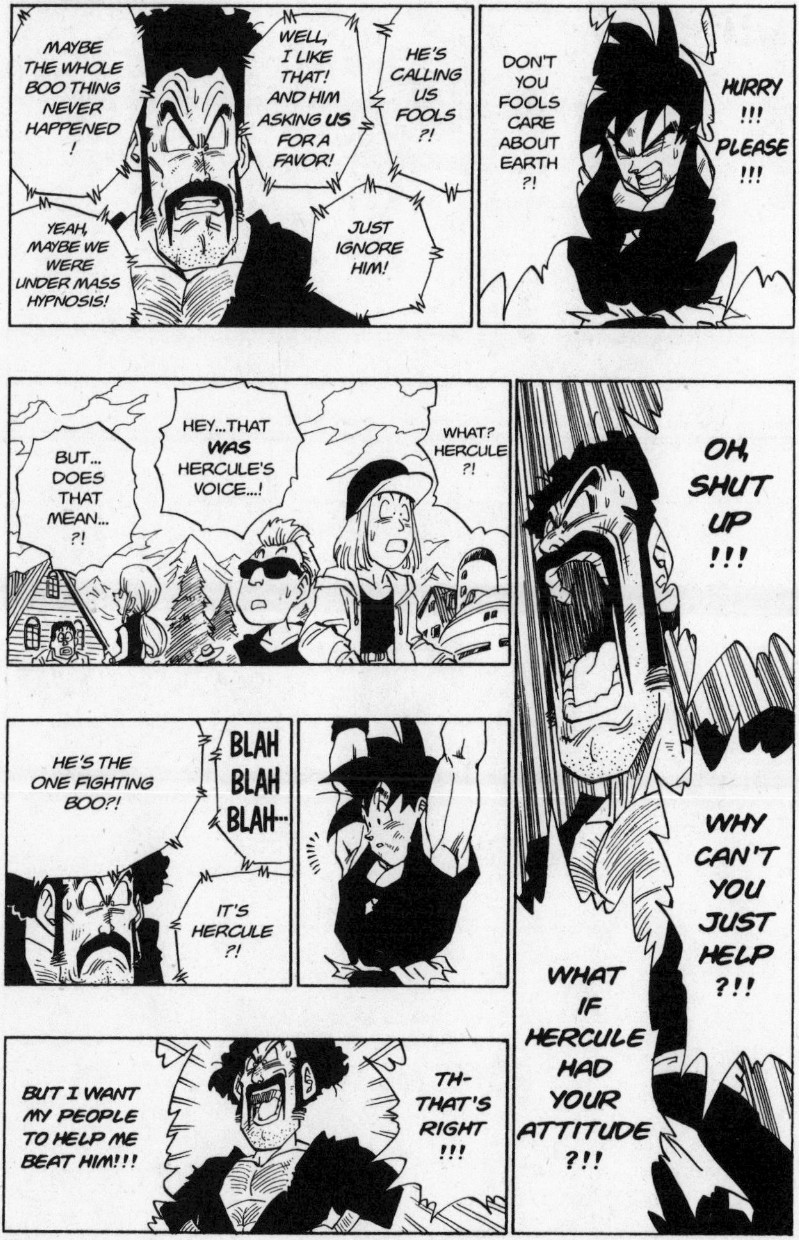
HURRY!!! PLEASE!!!
DON'T YOU FOOLS CARE ABOUT EARTH?!
HE'S CALLING US FOOLS?!
WELL, I LIKE THAT! AND HIM ASKING US FOR A FAVOR!
MAYBE THE WHOLE BOO THING NEVER HAPPENED!
JUST IGNORE HIM!
YEAH, MAYBE WE WERE UNDER MASS HYPNOSIS!
OH, SHUT UP!!!
WHY CAN'T YOU JUST HELP?!!
WHAT IF HERCULE HAD YOUR ATTITUDE?!!
WHAT? HERCULE?!
HEY...THAT WAS HERCULE'S VOICE...!
BUT... DOES THAT MEAN...?!
BLAH BLAH BLAH...
HE'S THE ONE FIGHTING BOO?!
IT'S HERCULE?!
TH-THAT'S RIGHT!!!
BUT I WANT MY PEOPLE TO HELP ME BEAT HIM!!!

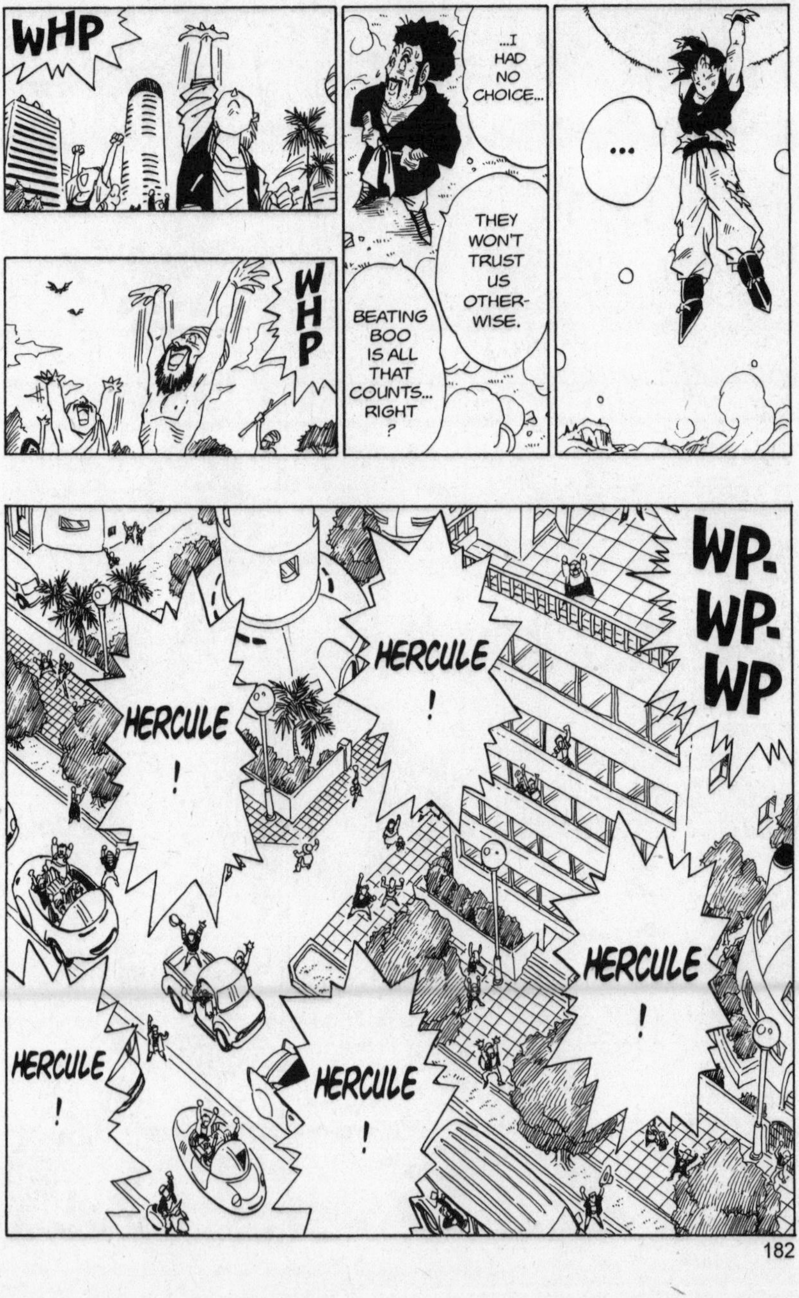
...
...I HAD NO CHOICE...
THEY WON'T TRUST US OTHERWISE.
BEATING BOO IS ALL THAT COUNTS... RIGHT?
WHP
WHP
WP-WP-WP
HERCULE!
HERCULE!
HERCULE!
HERCULE!
HERCULE!

READ THIS WAY

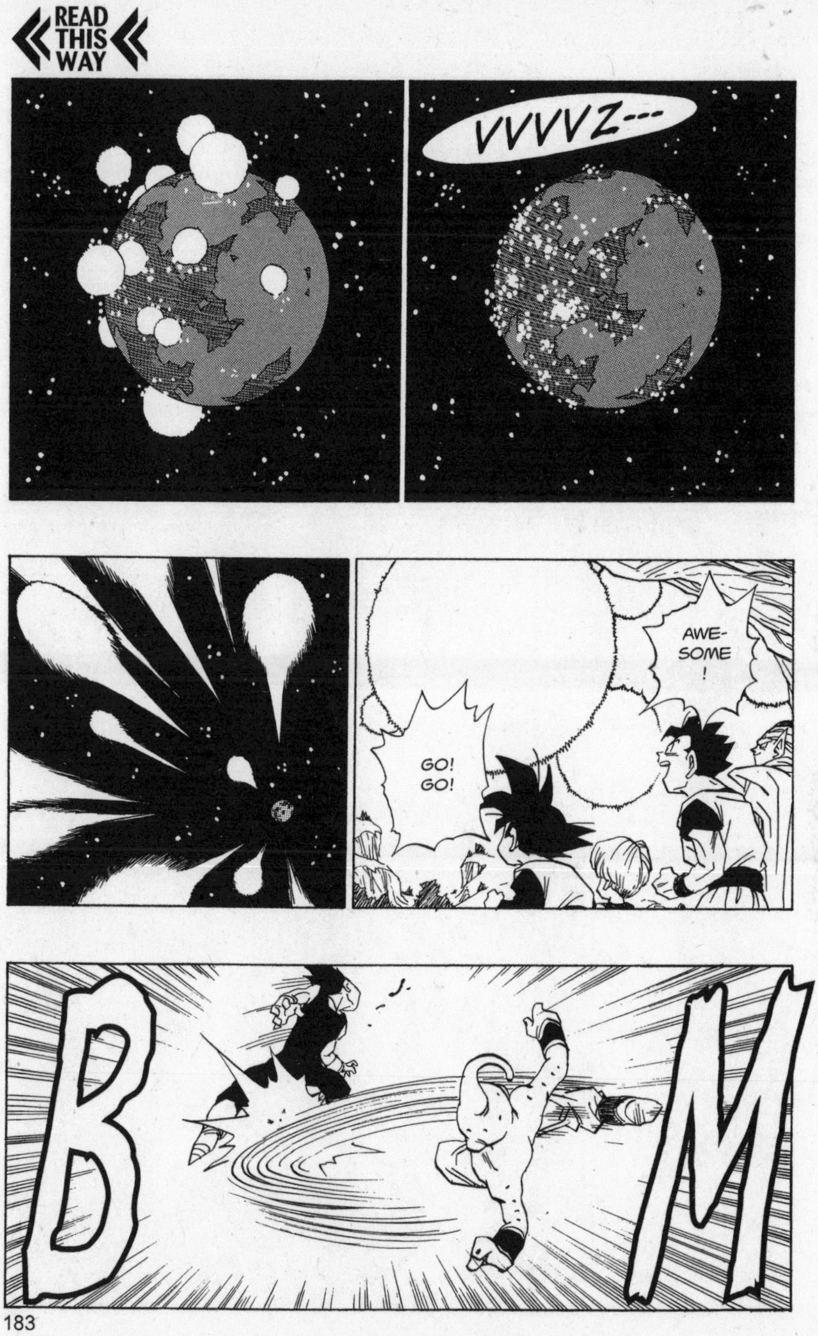
VVVVZ---
AWE-SOME!
GO! GO!
B M

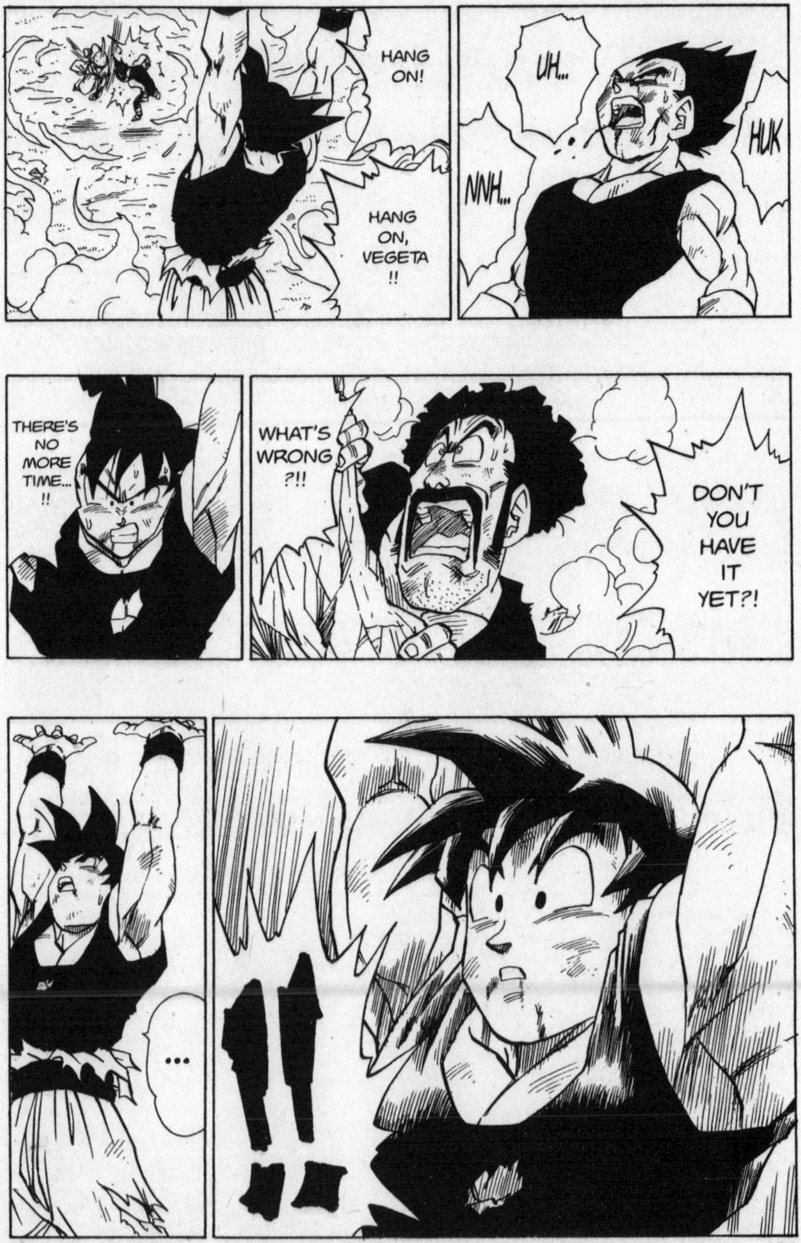
UH...
HUK
NNH...
HANG ON!
HANG ON, VEGETA !!
DON'T YOU HAVE IT YET?!
WHAT'S WRONG ?!!
THERE'S NO MORE TIME... !!
!!
...

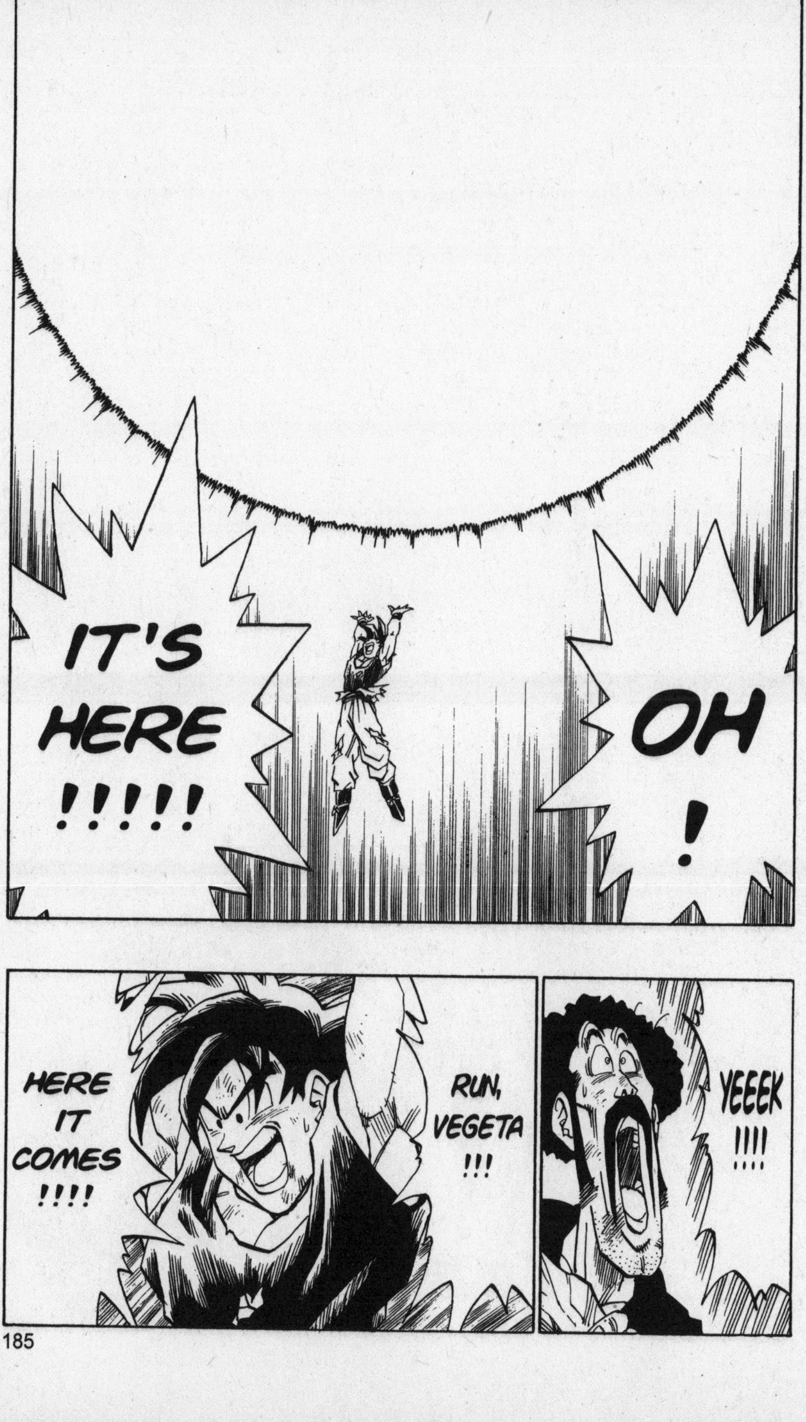
OH!
IT'S HERE!!!!!
YEEEK!!!!
RUN, VEGETA!!!
HERE IT COMES!!!!

DBZ:322 • Battle's End

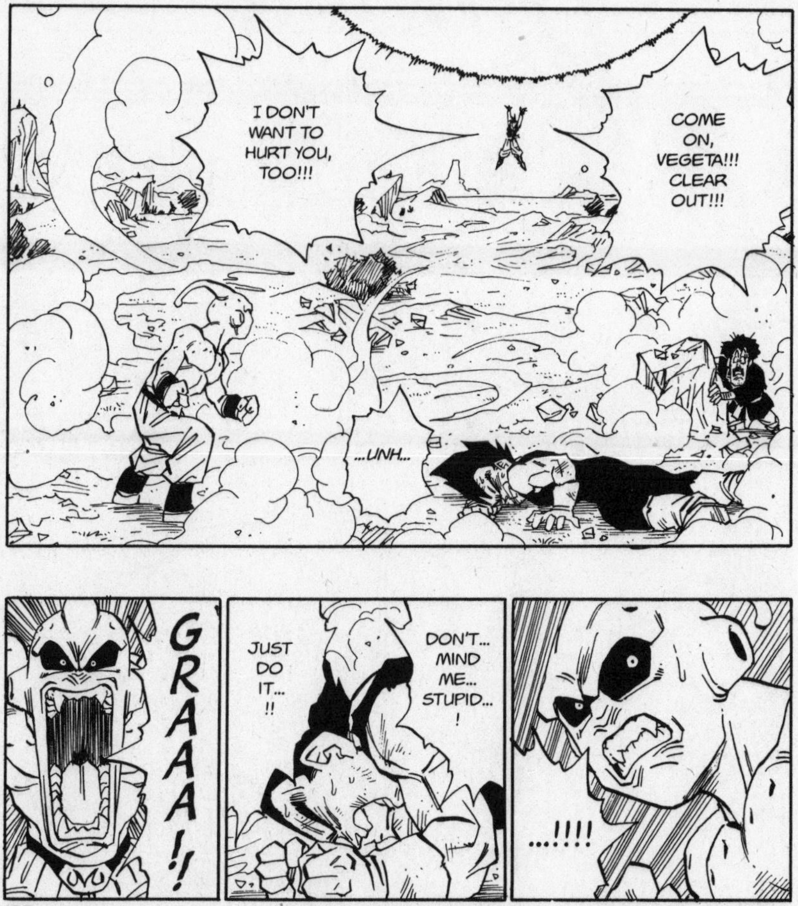
COME ON, VEGETA!!! CLEAR OUT!!!
I DON'T WANT TO HURT YOU, TOO!!!
...UNH...
...!!!!
DON'T... MIND ME... STUPID...!
JUST DO IT...!!
GRAAAA!!

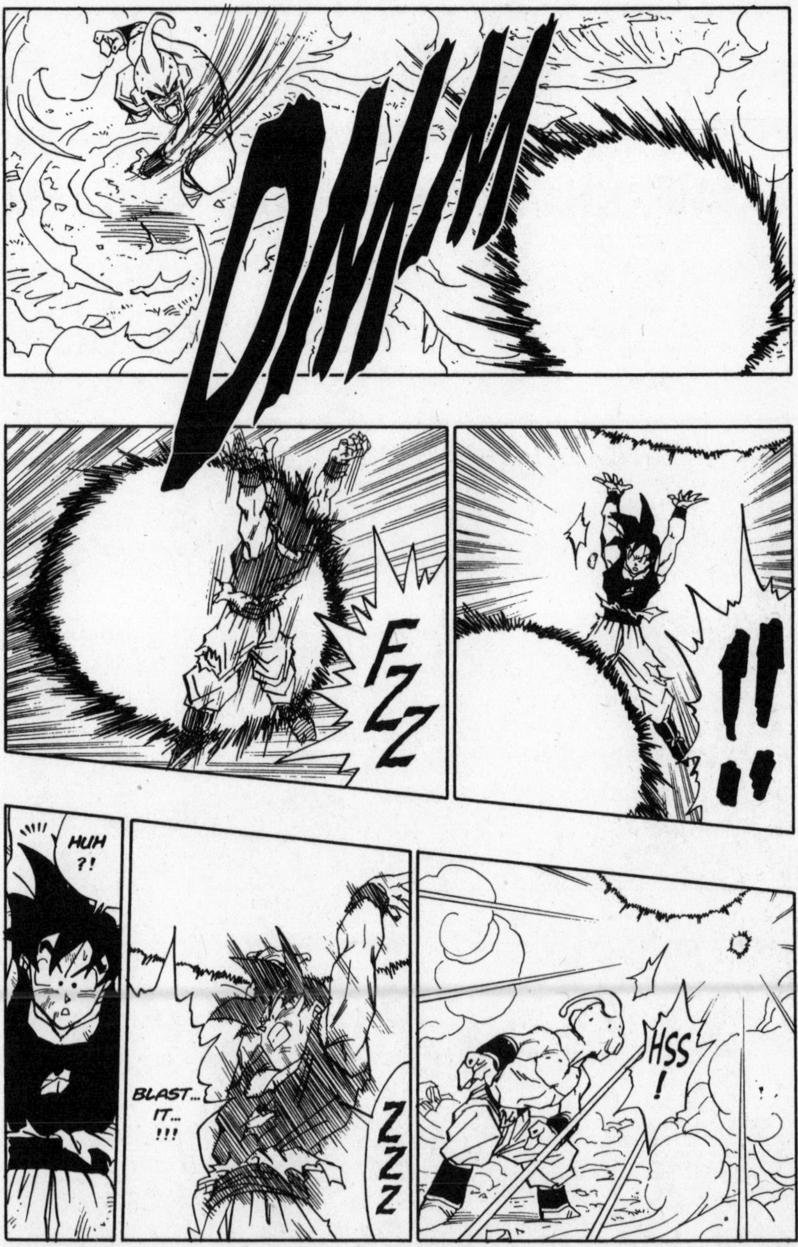
DMM
!!
!!
FZZ
HSS !
BLAST... IT... !!!
ZZZ
HUH ?!

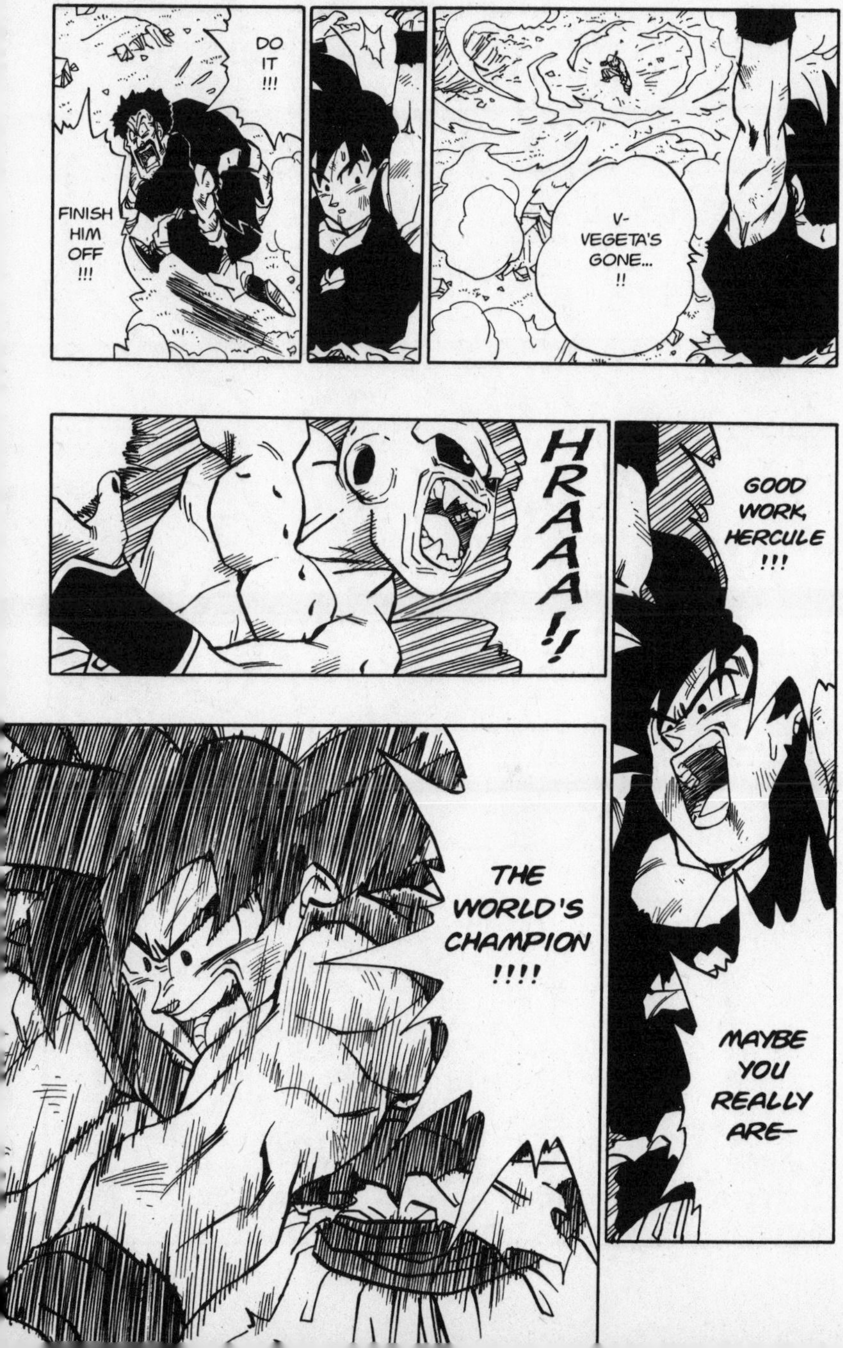
V- VEGETA'S GONE... !!
DO IT !!!
FINISH HIM OFF !!!
GOOD WORK, HERCULE !!!
MAYBE YOU REALLY ARE—
HRAAAA!!
THE WORLD'S CHAMPION !!!!

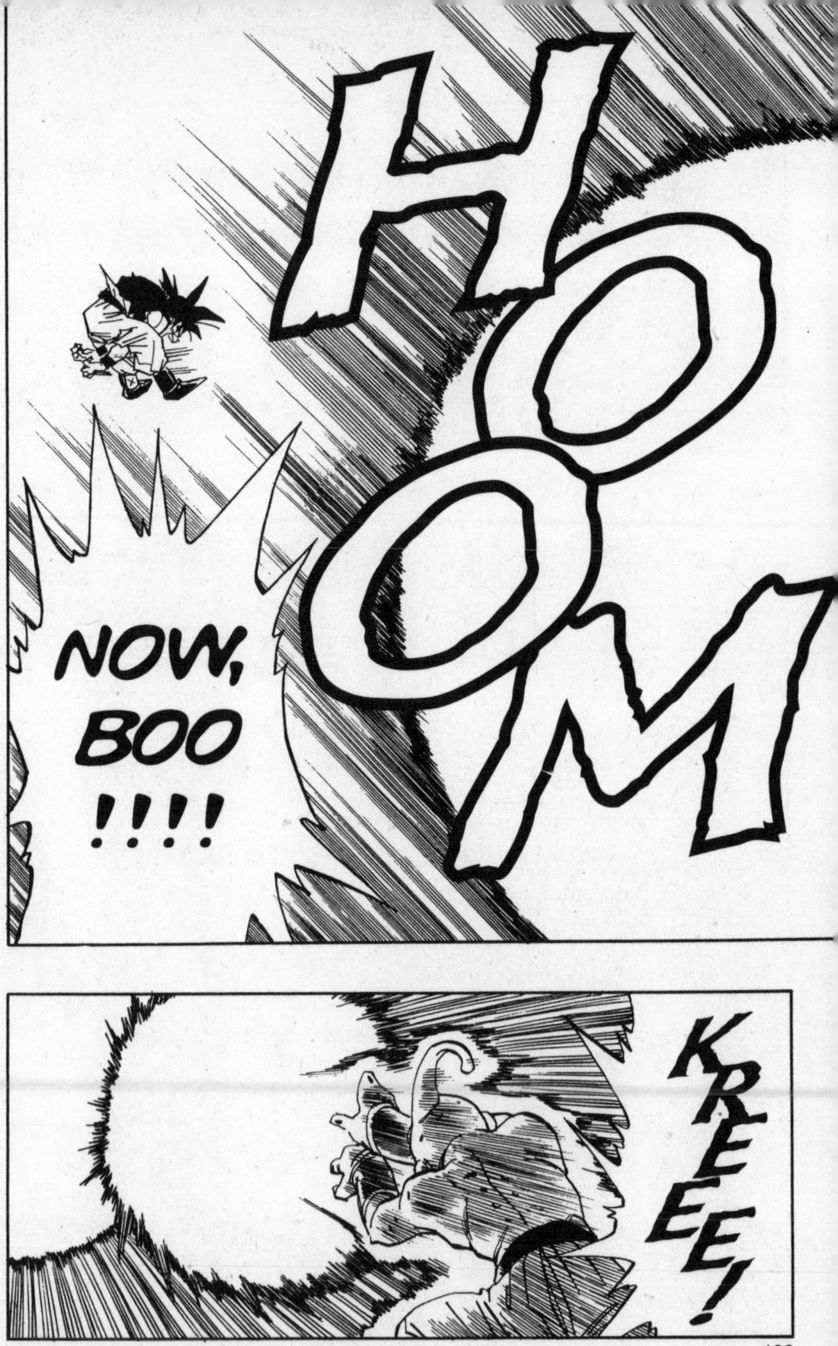
HOOOM
NOW, BOO !!!!
KREEE!

READ THIS WAY

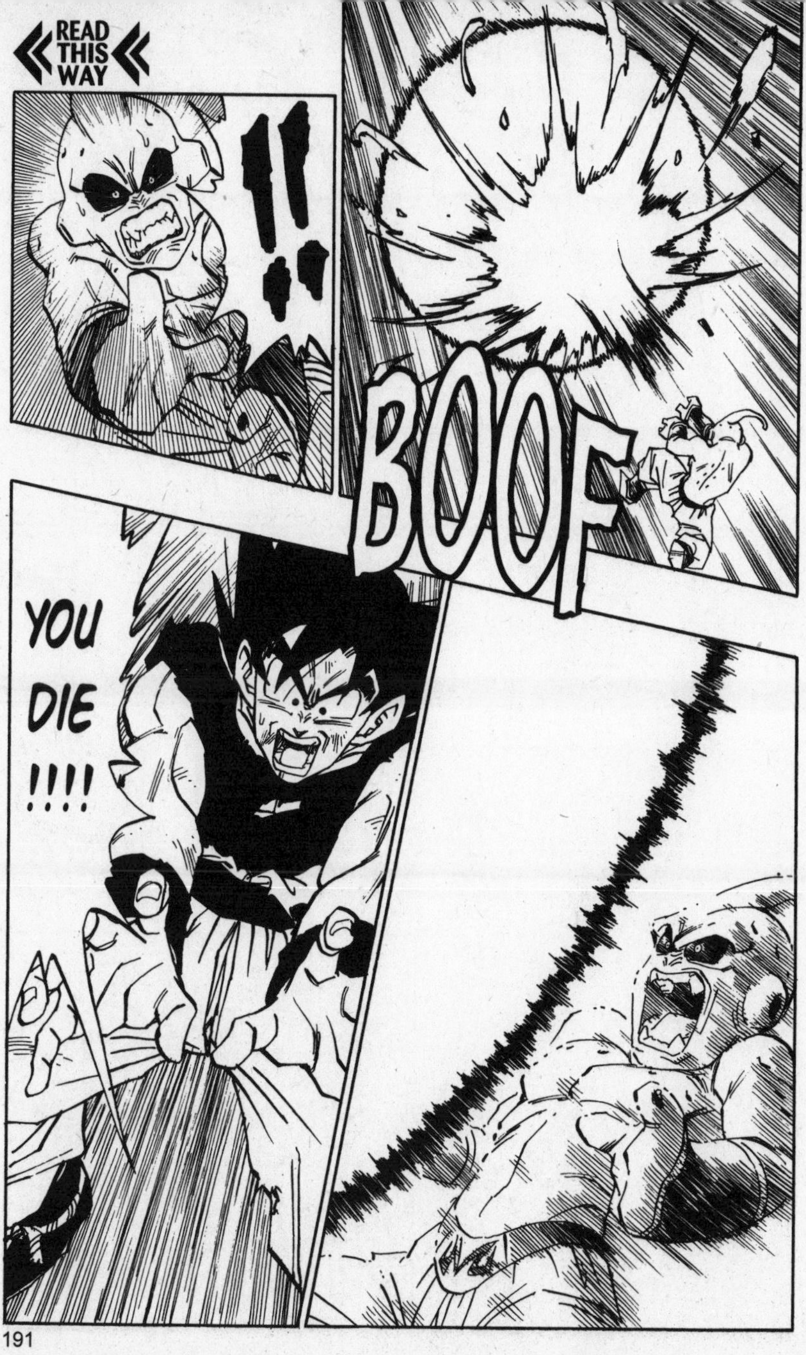

BOOF
!!
YOU DIE!!!!

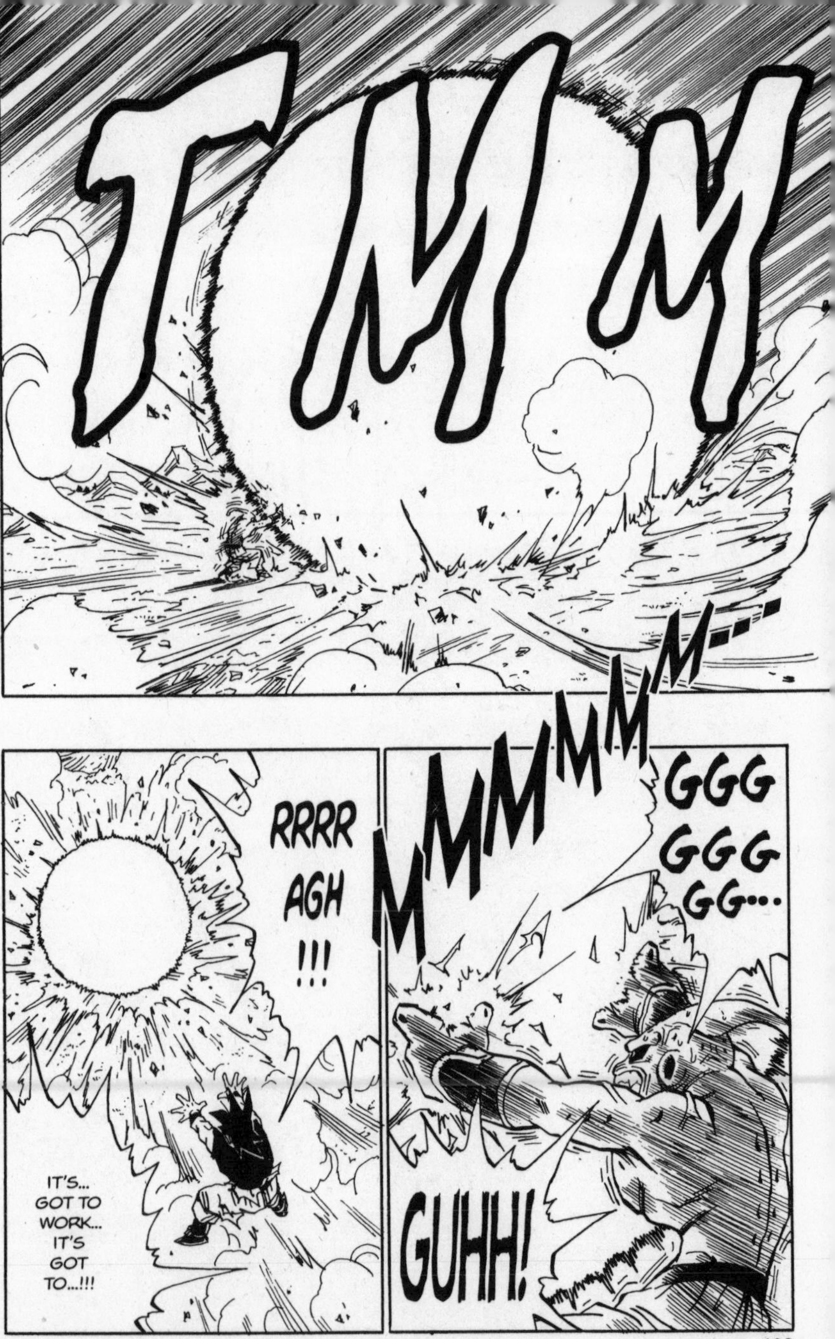
TMM
MMMMMMM...
GGG GGG GG...
GUHH!
RRRR AGH !!!
IT'S... GOT TO WORK... IT'S GOT TO...!!!

READ THIS WAY

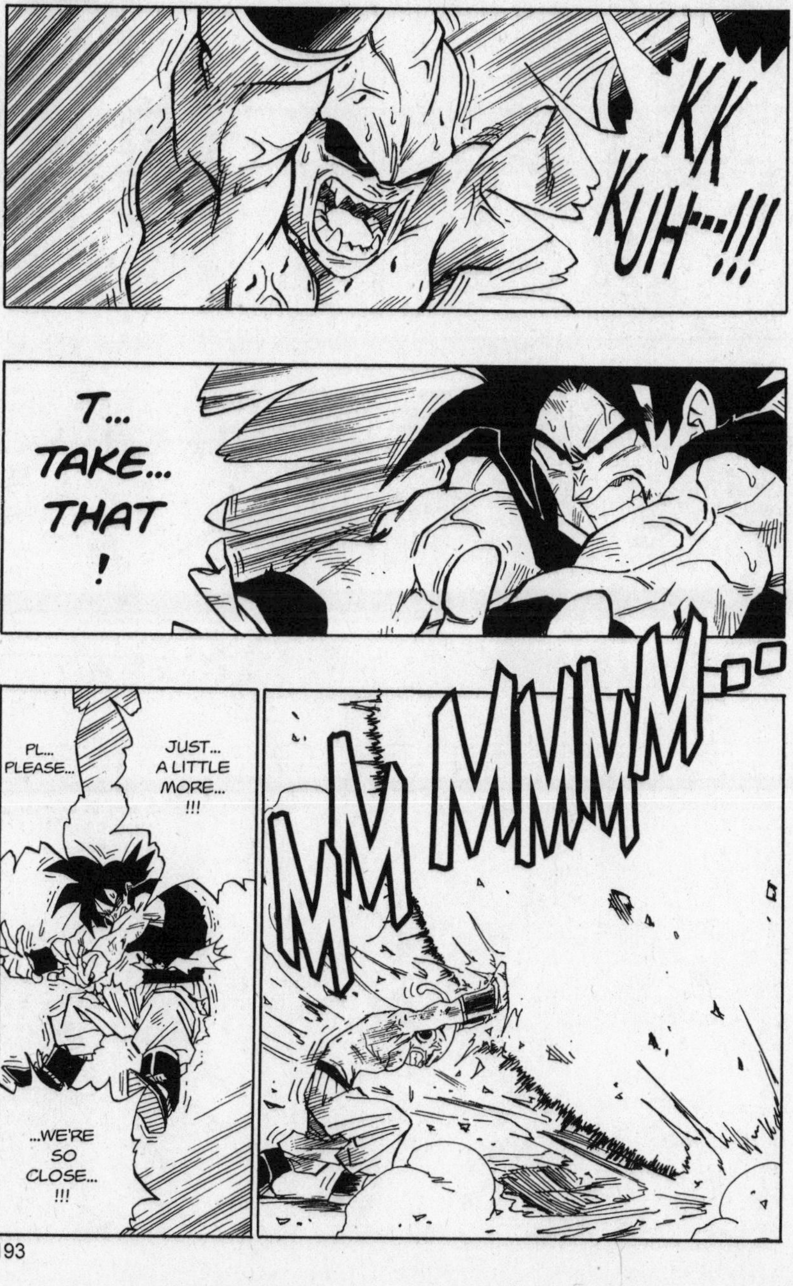

KKKUH...!!!
T... TAKE... THAT!
MMMMMMMM...
JUST... A LITTLE MORE... !!!
PL... PLEASE...
...WE'RE SO CLOSE... !!!

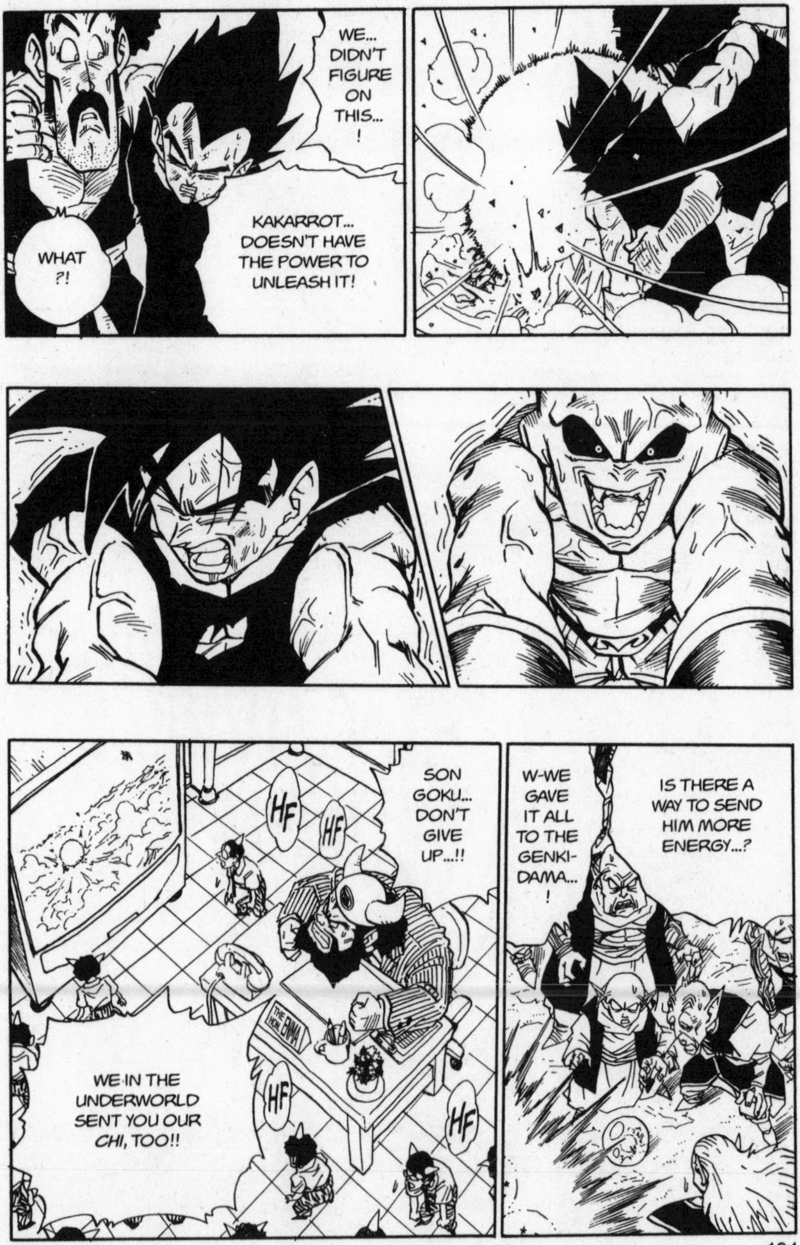
WE... DIDN'T FIGURE ON THIS... !
KAKARROT... DOESN'T HAVE THE POWER TO UNLEASH IT!
WHAT ?!
IS THERE A WAY TO SEND HIM MORE ENERGY...?
W-WE GAVE IT ALL TO THE GENKI-DAMA... !
SON GOKU... DON'T GIVE UP...!!
HF
HF
THE HON. ENMA
WE IN THE UNDERWORLD SENT YOU OUR *CHI*, TOO!!
HF
HF

READ THIS WAY

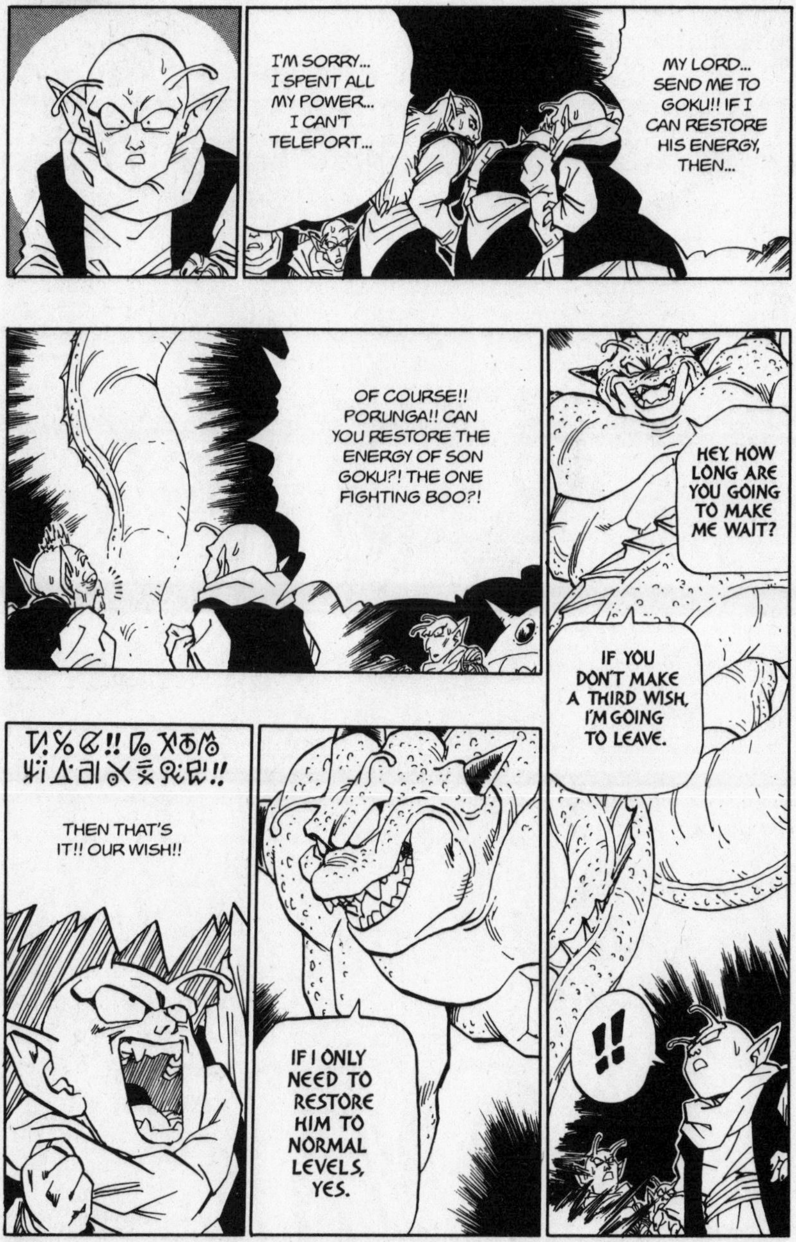

MY LORD... SEND ME TO GOKU!! IF I CAN RESTORE HIS ENERGY, THEN...
I'M SORRY... I SPENT ALL MY POWER... I CAN'T TELEPORT...
HEY, HOW LONG ARE YOU GOING TO MAKE ME WAIT?
IF YOU DON'T MAKE A THIRD WISH, I'M GOING TO LEAVE.
!!
OF COURSE!! PORUNGA!! CAN YOU RESTORE THE ENERGY OF SON GOKU?! THE ONE FIGHTING BOO?!
IF I ONLY NEED TO RESTORE HIM TO NORMAL LEVELS, YES.
THEN THAT'S IT!! OUR WISH!!

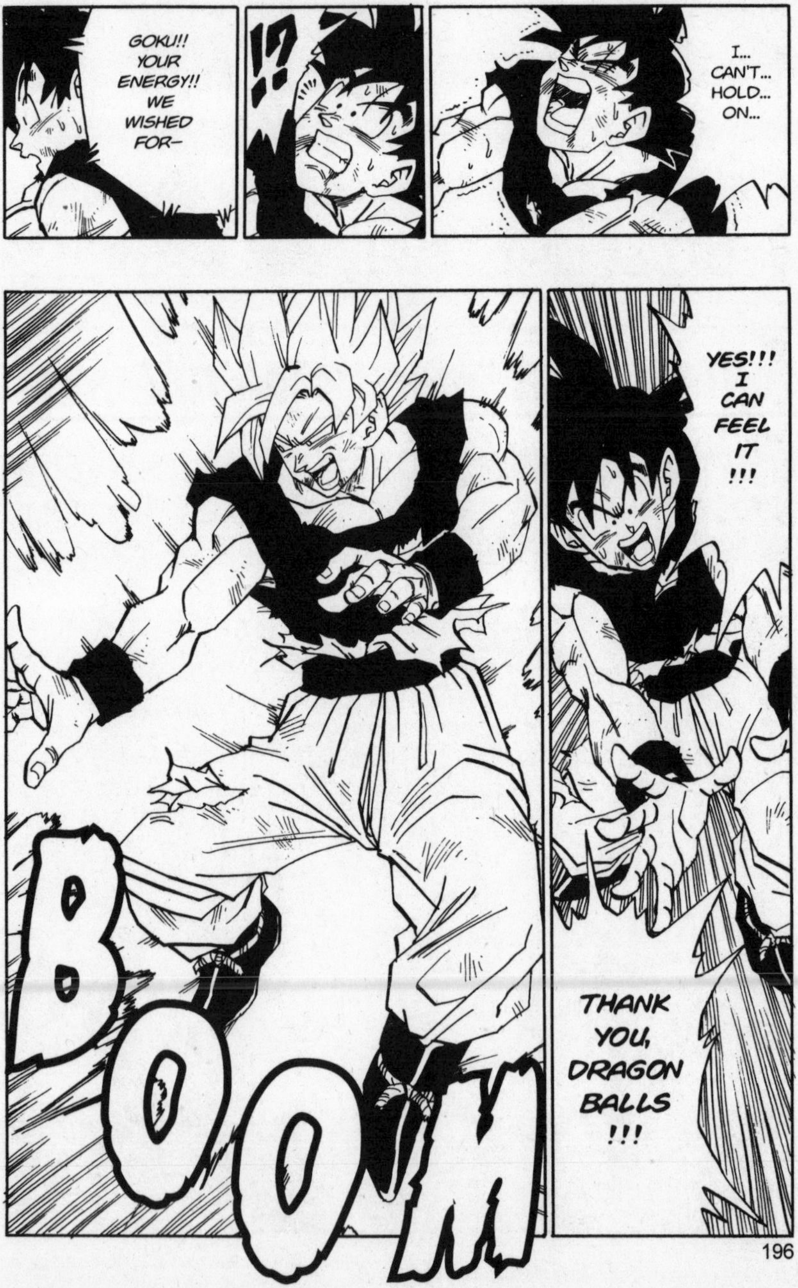
I... CAN'T... HOLD... ON...
!?
GOKU!! YOUR ENERGY!! WE WISHED FOR–
YES!!! I CAN FEEL IT !!!
THANK YOU, DRAGON BALLS !!!
BOOM

READ THIS WAY

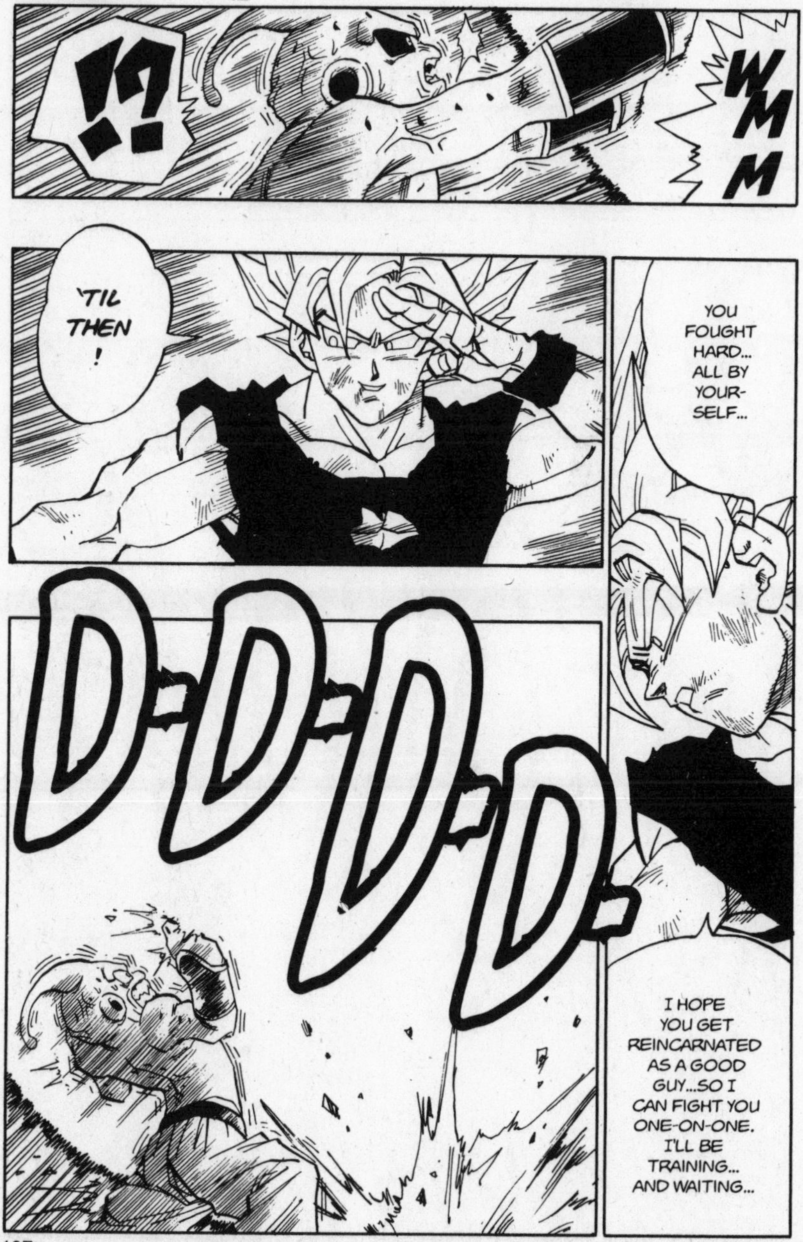
WMM
!?
YOU FOUGHT HARD... ALL BY YOURSELF...
I HOPE YOU GET REINCARNATED AS A GOOD GUY...SO I CAN FIGHT YOU ONE-ON-ONE. I'LL BE TRAINING... AND WAITING...
'TIL THEN!
D-D-D-D

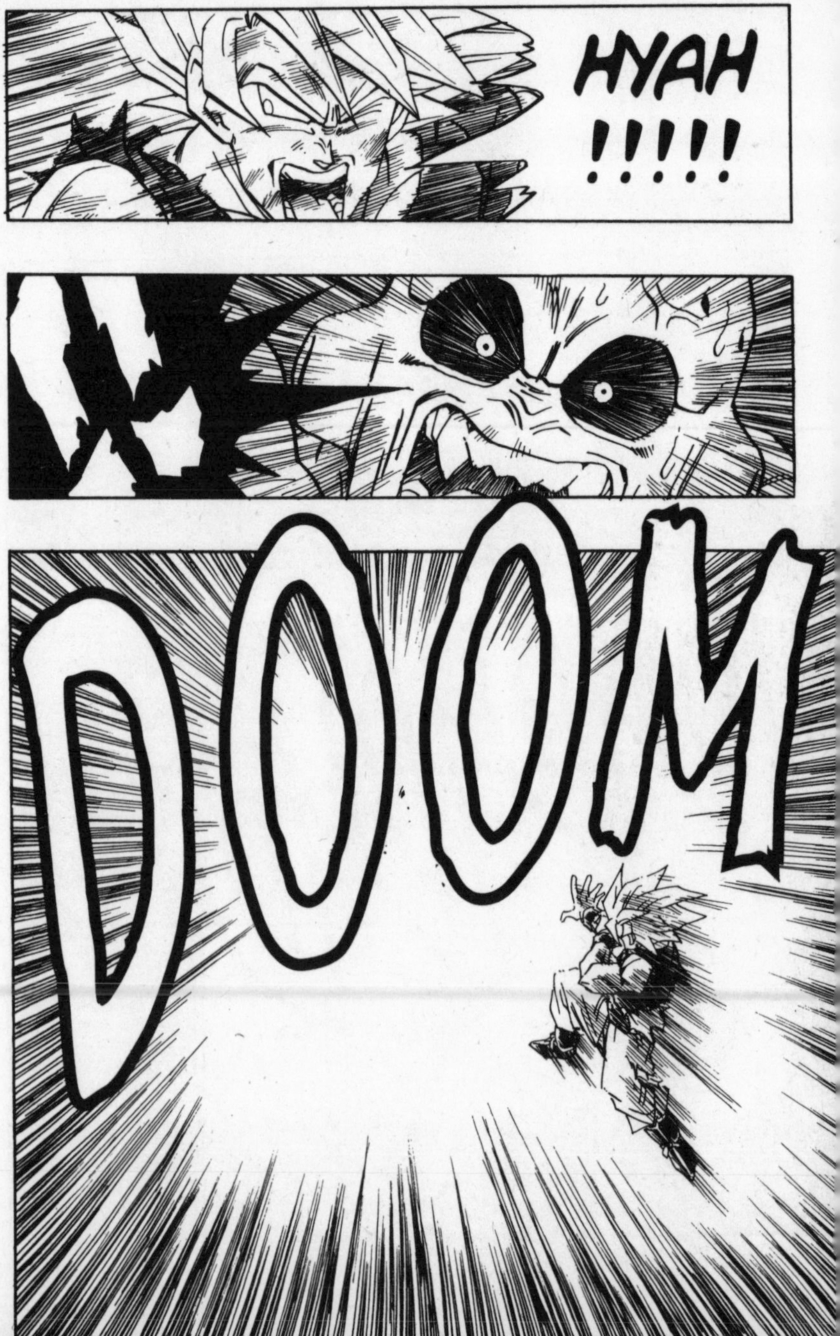
HYAH !!!!!
DOOM

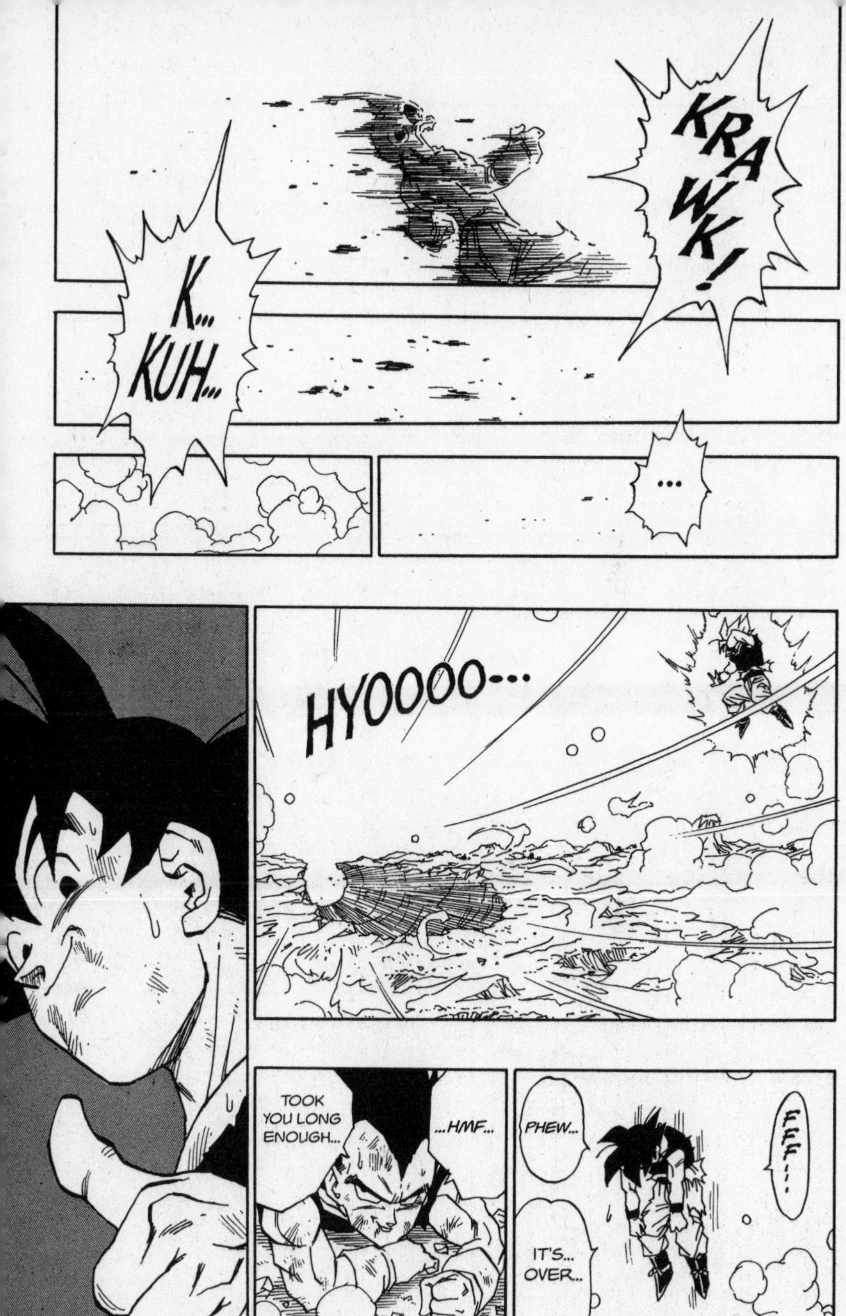
KRAWK!
K... KUH...
...
HYOOOO...
EEK...
PHEW...
IT'S... OVER...
...HMF...
TOOK YOU LONG ENOUGH...

NEXT: What Now?

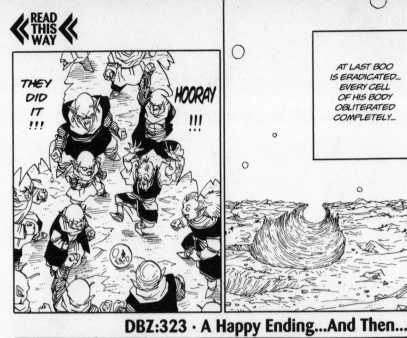

THEY DID IT!!!

HOORAY!!!

AT LAST BOO IS ERADICATED... EVERY CELL OF HIS BODY OBLITERATED COMPLETELY...

DBZ:323 · A Happy Ending...And Then...

YES!!!

...I DO BELIEVE...

BOO'S CHI... IS GONE.

WELL, PICCOLO?

D-DID YOU GET HIM?

HEH HEH...

I-I-IS IT OVER?

READ THIS WAY

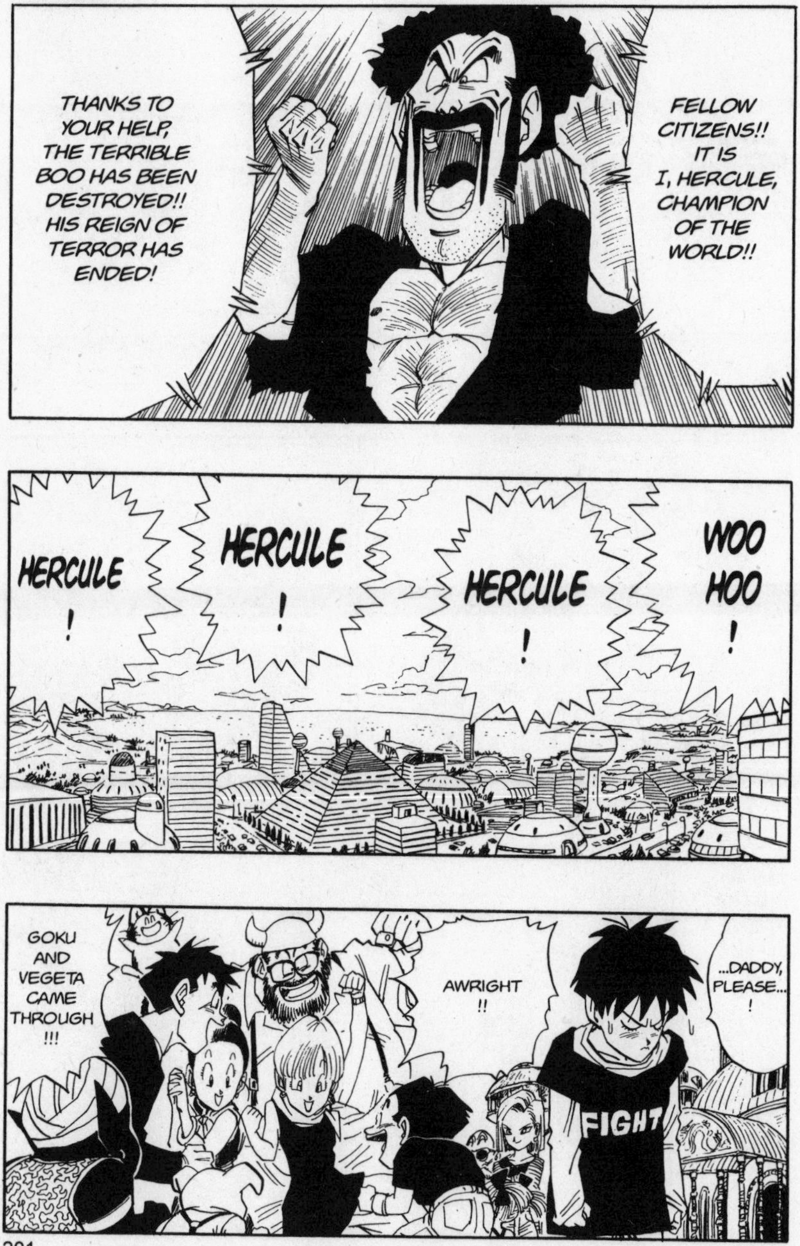

FELLOW CITIZENS!! IT IS I, HERCULE, CHAMPION OF THE WORLD!!
THANKS TO YOUR HELP, THE TERRIBLE BOO HAS BEEN DESTROYED!! HIS REIGN OF TERROR HAS ENDED!
WOO HOO!
HERCULE!
HERCULE!
HERCULE!
...DADDY, PLEASE...!
AWRIGHT!!
GOKU AND VEGETA CAME THROUGH!!!
FIGHT

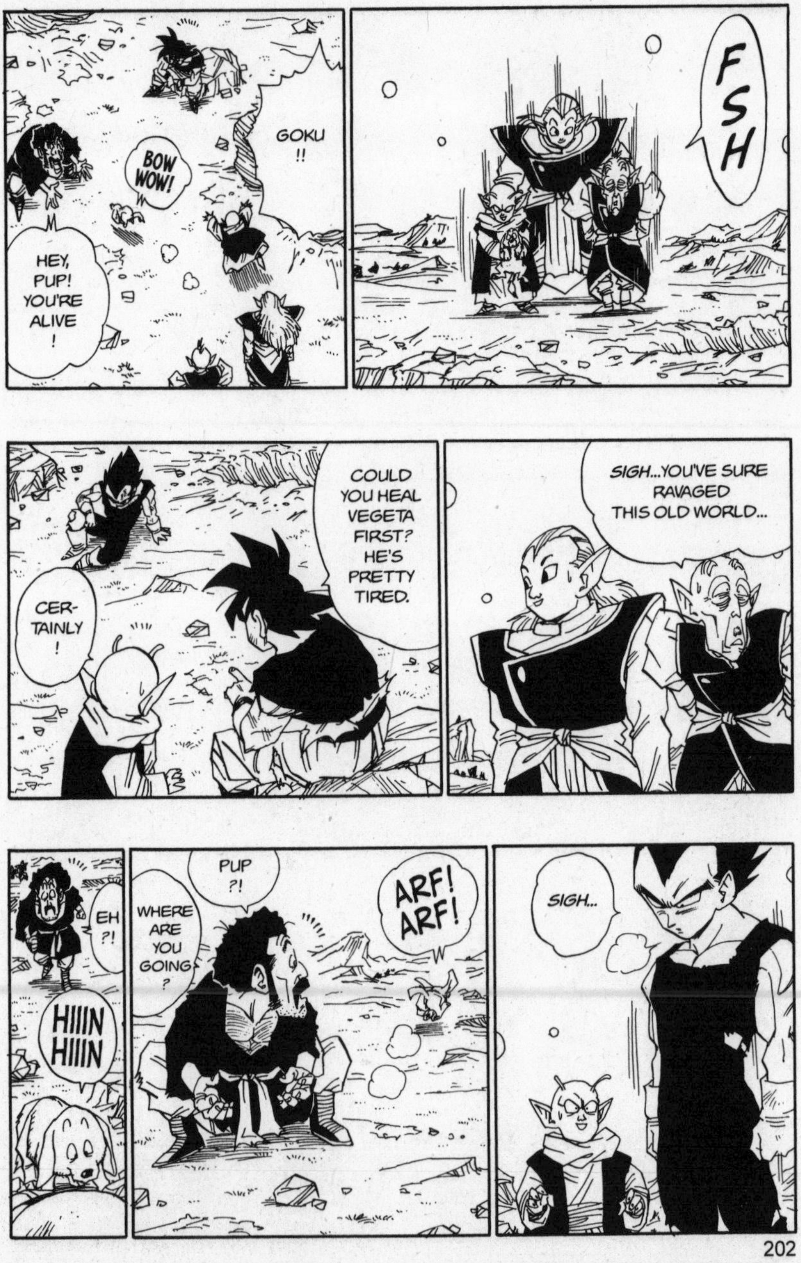
FSH
GOKU !!
BOW WOW!
HEY, PUP! YOU'RE ALIVE !
SIGH...YOU'VE SURE RAVAGED THIS OLD WORLD...
COULD YOU HEAL VEGETA FIRST? HE'S PRETTY TIRED.
CER-TAINLY !
SIGH...
ARF! ARF!
PUP ?!
WHERE ARE YOU GOING ?
EH ?!
HIIIN HIIIN

READ THIS WAY

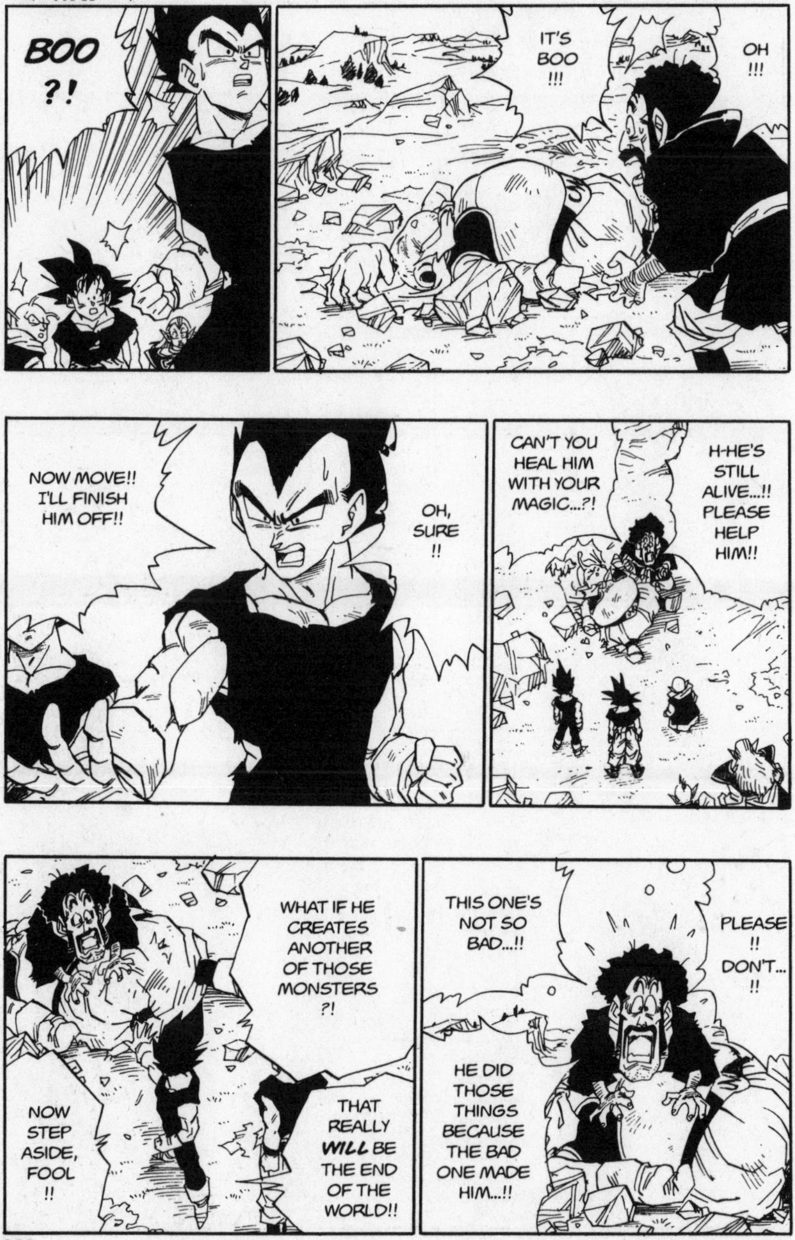

OH !!!
IT'S BOO !!!
BOO ?!
H-HE'S STILL ALIVE...!! PLEASE HELP HIM!!
CAN'T YOU HEAL HIM WITH YOUR MAGIC...?!
OH, SURE !!
NOW MOVE!! I'LL FINISH HIM OFF!!
PLEASE !! DON'T... !!
THIS ONE'S NOT SO BAD...!!
HE DID THOSE THINGS BECAUSE THE BAD ONE MADE HIM...!!
WHAT IF HE CREATES ANOTHER OF THOSE MONSTERS ?!
THAT REALLY WILL BE THE END OF THE WORLD!!
NOW STEP ASIDE, FOOL !!

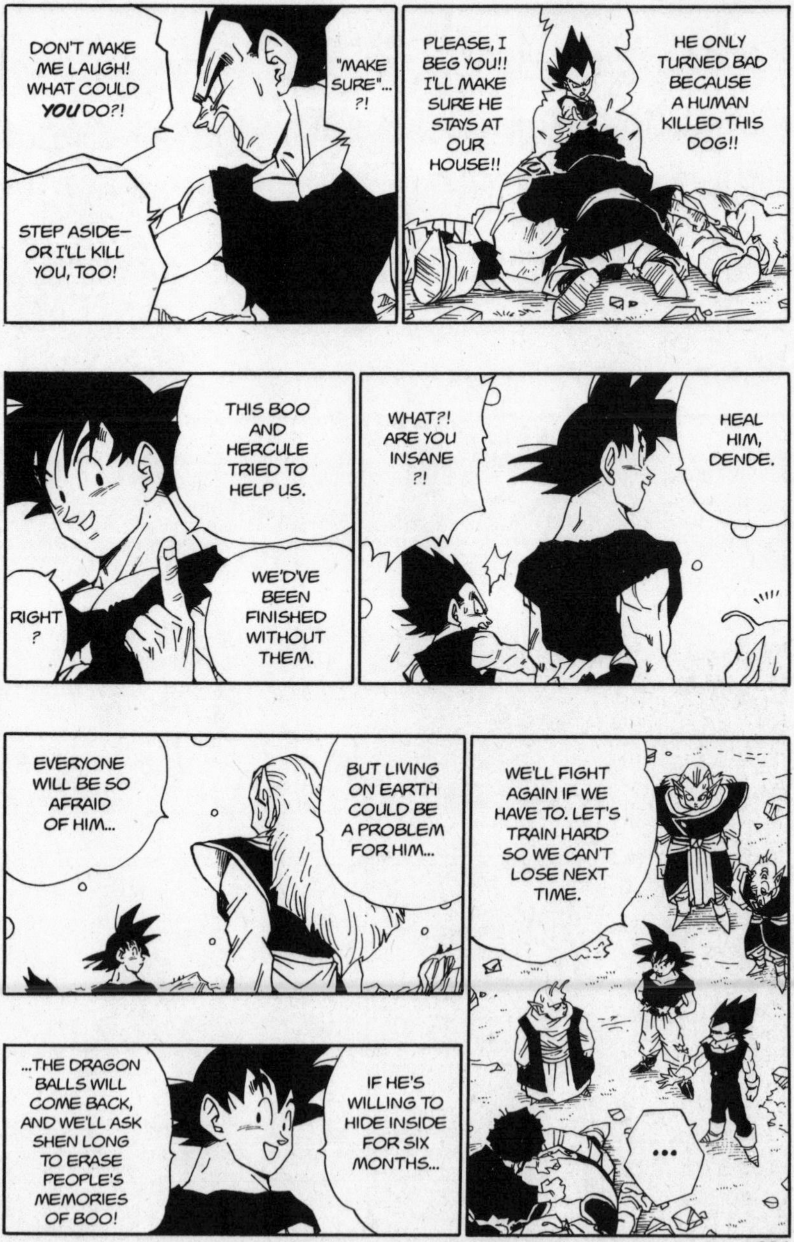
HE ONLY TURNED BAD BECAUSE A HUMAN KILLED THIS DOG!!
PLEASE, I BEG YOU!! I'LL MAKE SURE HE STAYS AT OUR HOUSE!!
"MAKE SURE"... ?!
DON'T MAKE ME LAUGH! WHAT COULD **YOU** DO?!
STEP ASIDE— OR I'LL KILL YOU, TOO!
HEAL HIM, DENDE.
WHAT?! ARE YOU INSANE ?!
THIS BOO AND HERCULE TRIED TO HELP US.
WE'D'VE BEEN FINISHED WITHOUT THEM.
RIGHT ?
WE'LL FIGHT AGAIN IF WE HAVE TO. LET'S TRAIN HARD SO WE CAN'T LOSE NEXT TIME.
...
BUT LIVING ON EARTH COULD BE A PROBLEM FOR HIM...
EVERYONE WILL BE SO AFRAID OF HIM...
IF HE'S WILLING TO HIDE INSIDE FOR SIX MONTHS...
...THE DRAGON BALLS WILL COME BACK, AND WE'LL ASK SHEN LONG TO ERASE PEOPLE'S MEMORIES OF BOO!

READ THIS WAY

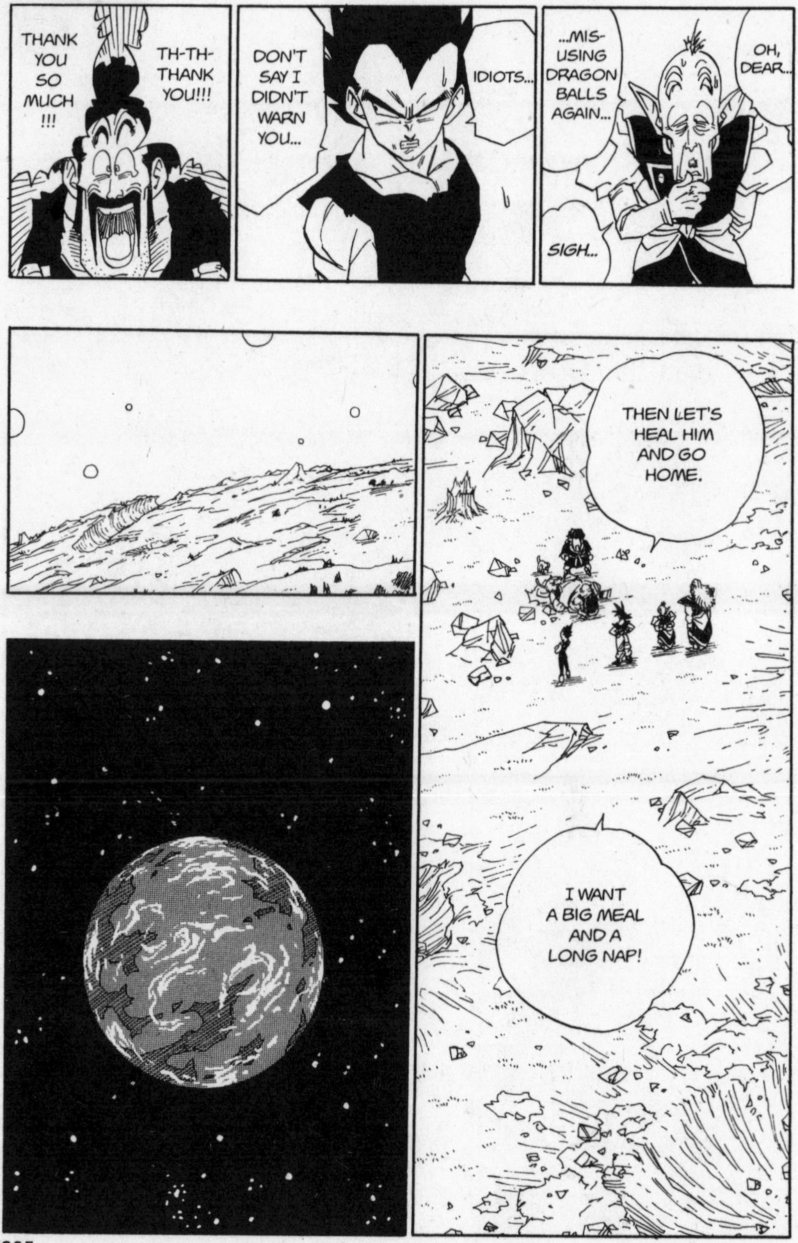
OH, DEAR...
...MIS-USING DRAGON BALLS AGAIN...
SIGH...
IDIOTS...
DON'T SAY I DIDN'T WARN YOU...
TH-TH-THANK YOU!!!
THANK YOU SO MUCH !!!
THEN LET'S HEAL HIM AND GO HOME.
I WANT A BIG MEAL AND A LONG NAP!

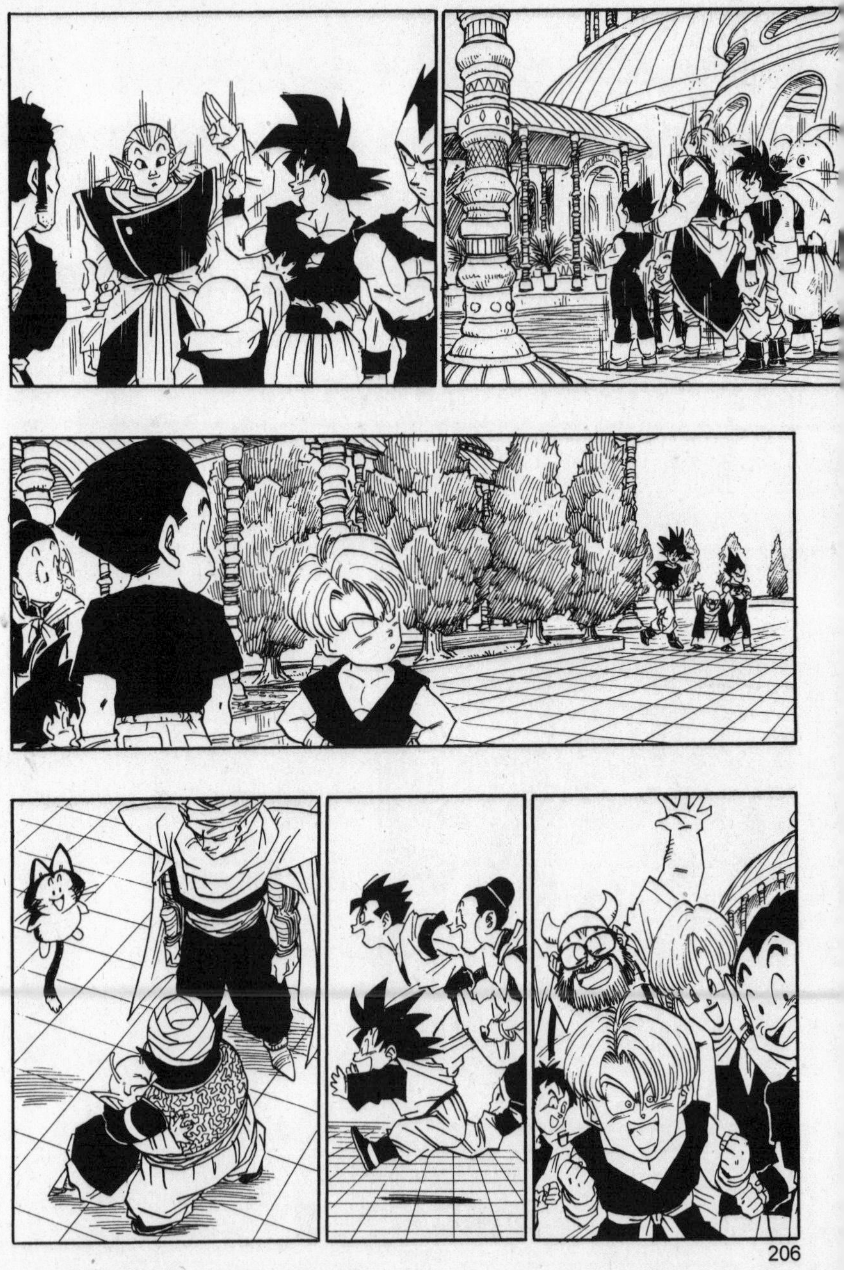

READ THIS WAY

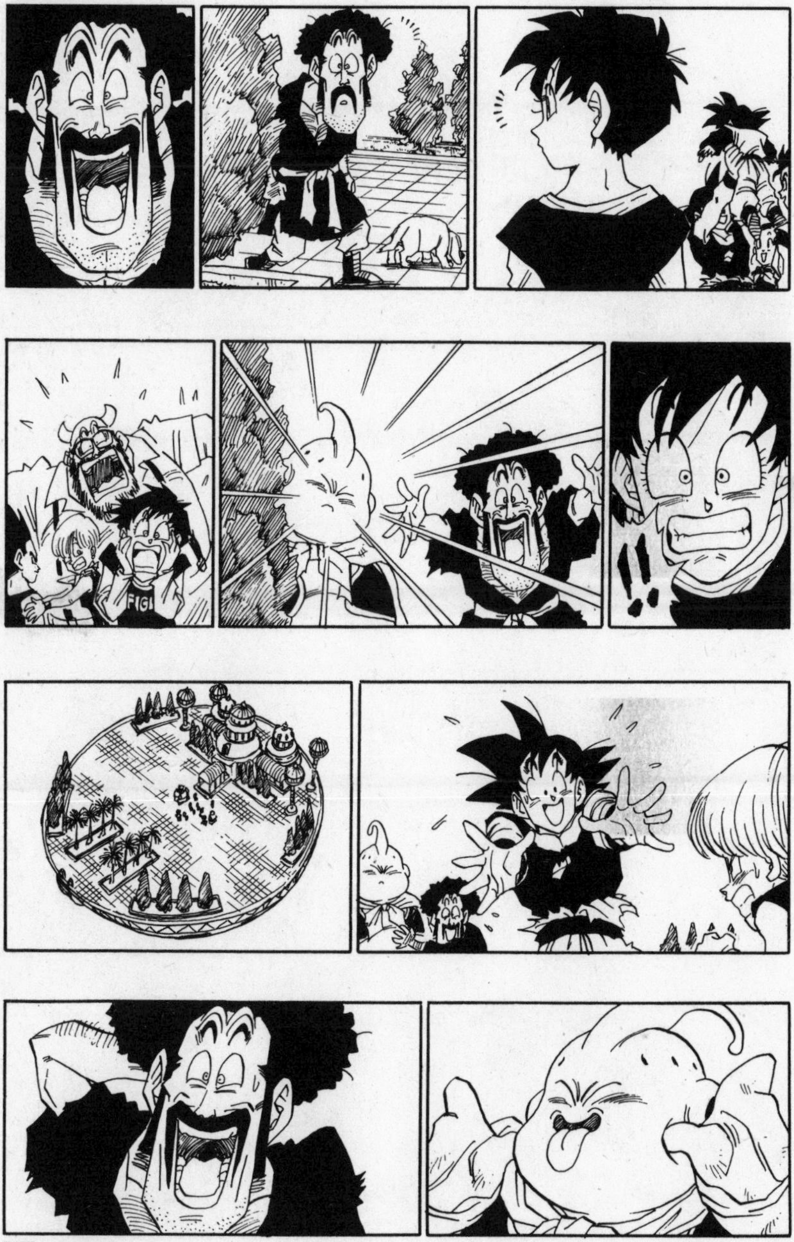
FIGI

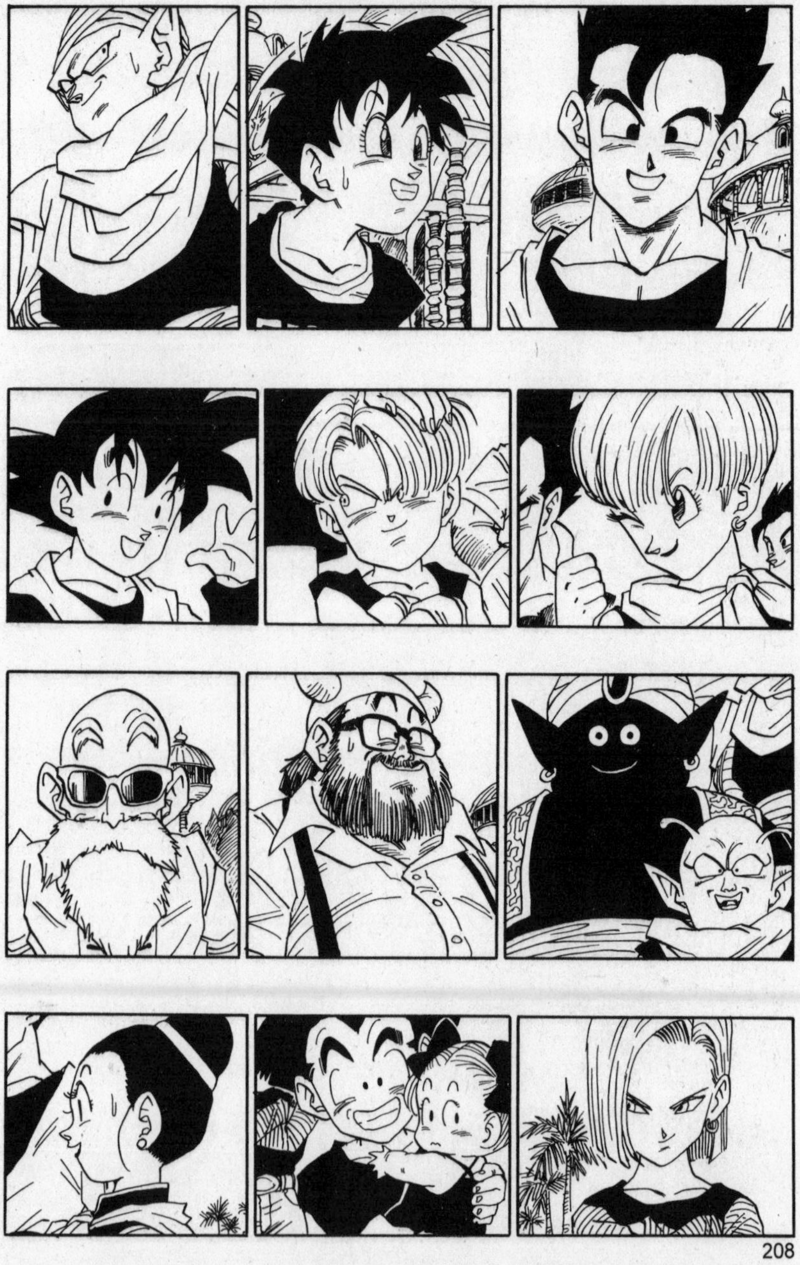

READ THIS WAY

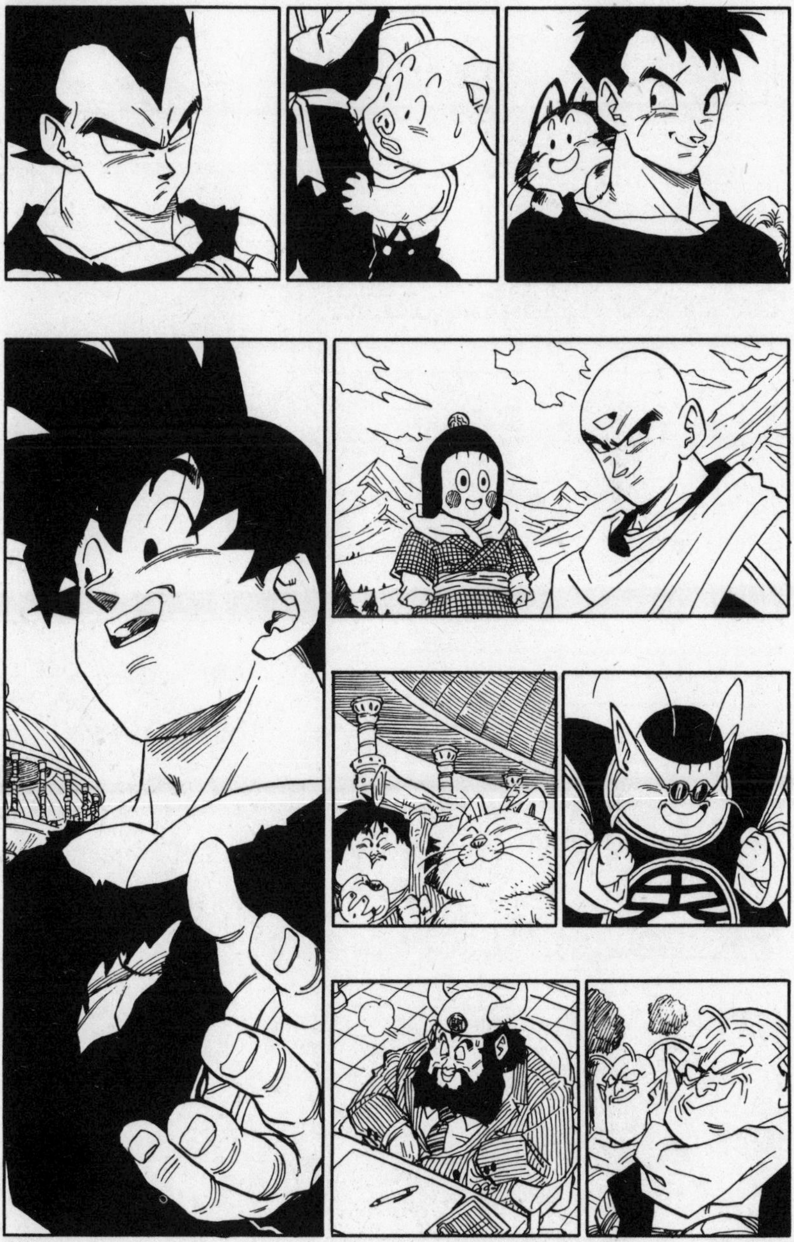

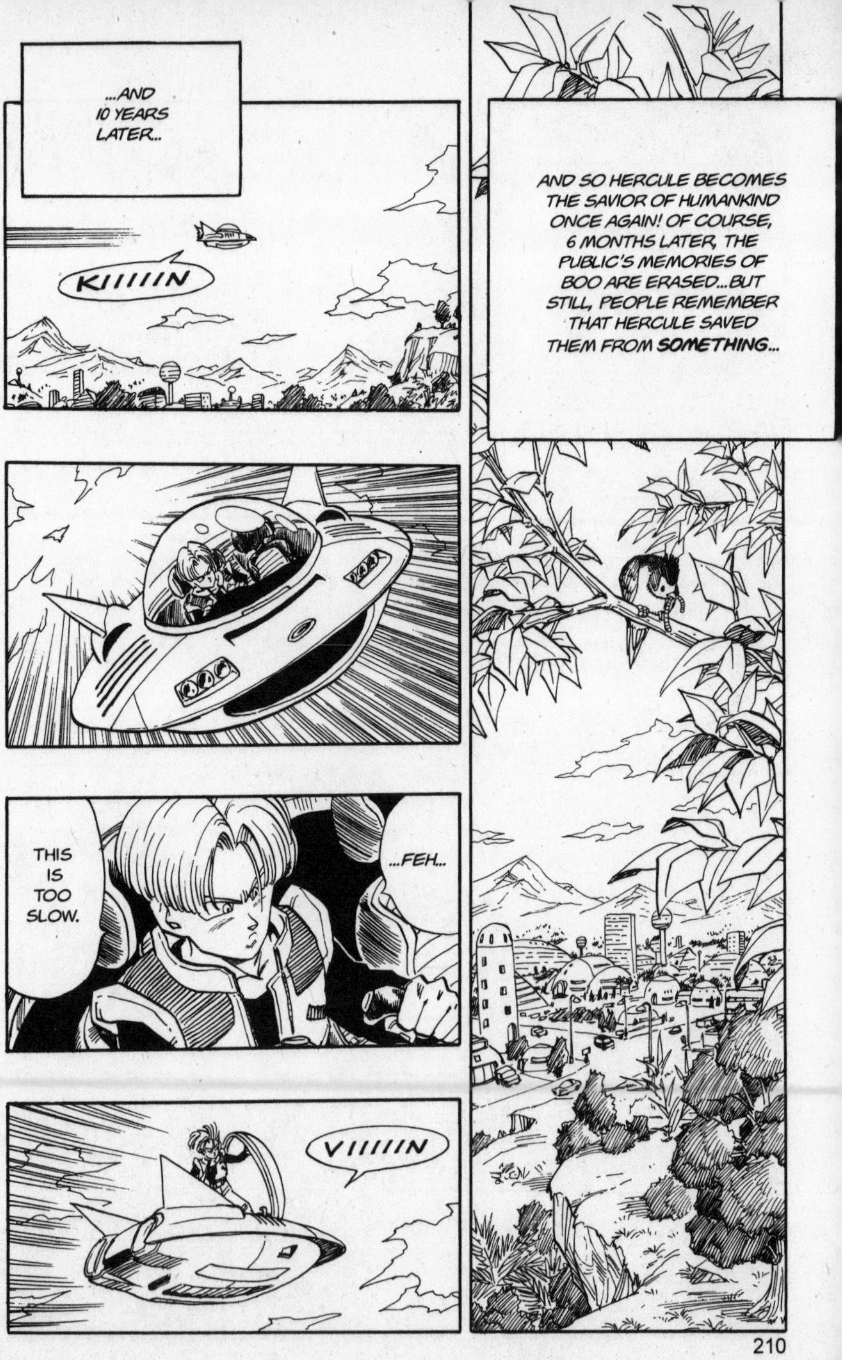
AND SO HERCULE BECOMES THE SAVIOR OF HUMANKIND ONCE AGAIN! OF COURSE, 6 MONTHS LATER, THE PUBLIC'S MEMORIES OF BOO ARE ERASED...BUT STILL, PEOPLE REMEMBER THAT HERCULE SAVED THEM FROM **SOMETHING**...
...AND 10 YEARS LATER...
KIIIIN
...FEH...
THIS IS TOO SLOW.
VIIIIN

READ THIS WAY

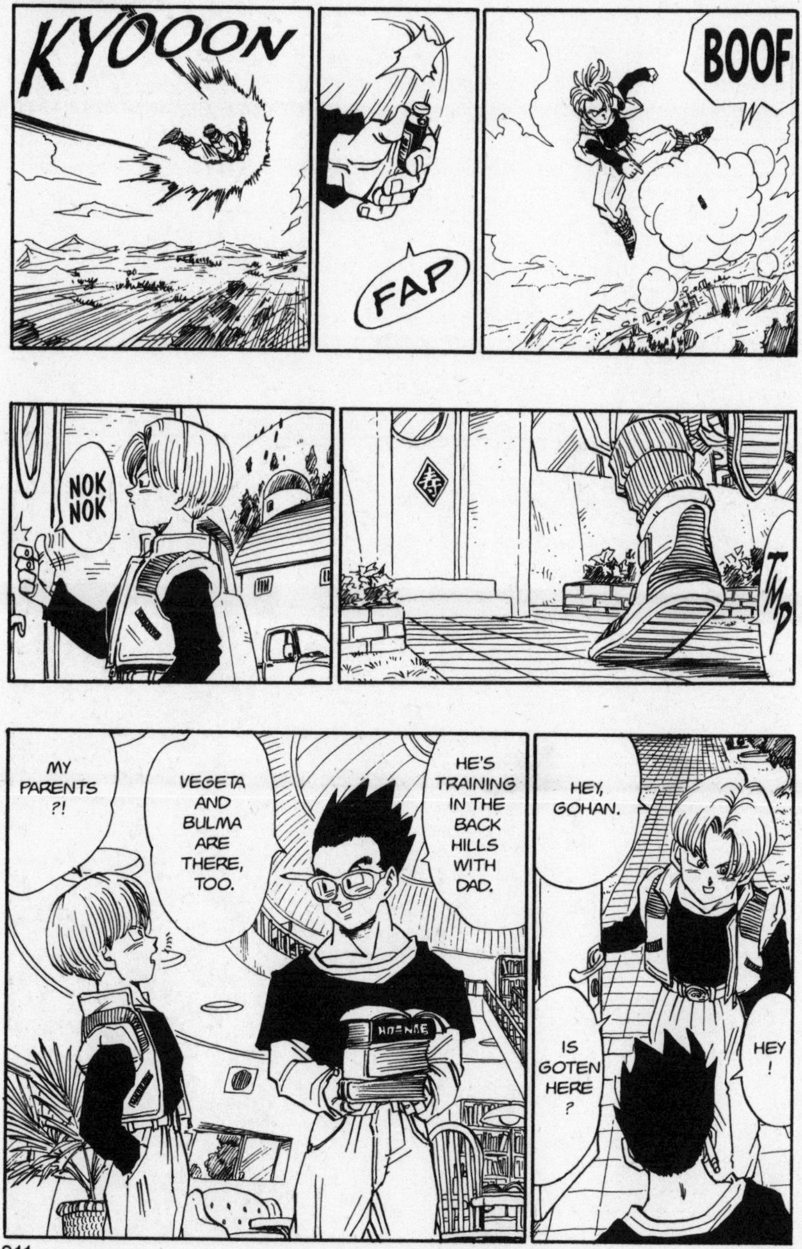

BOOF
FAP
KYOOON
TMP
NOK NOK
HEY, GOHAN.
HEY!
IS GOTEN HERE?
HE'S TRAINING IN THE BACK HILLS WITH DAD.
VEGETA AND BULMA ARE THERE, TOO.
MY PARENTS?!

DBZ:324 · 10 Years After

★ The Cast--10 Years Older ★

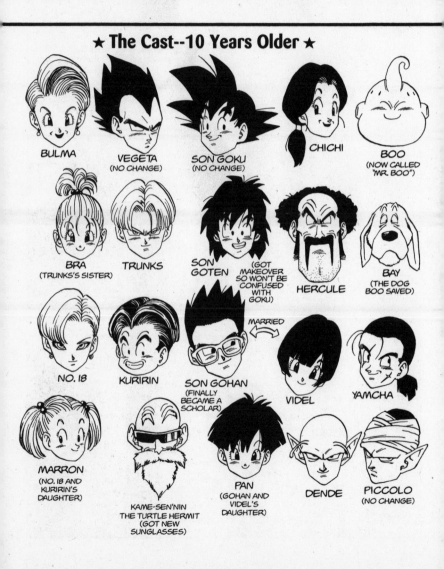

BULMA

VEGETA
(NO CHANGE)

SON GOKU
(NO CHANGE)

CHICHI

BOO
(NOW CALLED
"MR. BOO")

BRA
(TRUNKS'S SISTER)

TRUNKS

SON
GOTEN

(GOT
MAKEOVER
SO WON'T BE
CONFUSED
WITH
GOKU)

HERCULE

BAY
(THE DOG
BOO SAVED)

NO. 18

KURIRIN

SON GOHAN
(FINALLY
BECAME A
SCHOLAR)

MARRIED

VIDEL

YAMCHA

MARRON
(NO. 18 AND
KURIRIN'S
DAUGHTER)

KAME-SEN'NIN
THE TURTLE HERMIT
(GOT NEW
SUNGLASSES)

PAN
(GOHAN AND
VIDEL'S
DAUGHTER)

DENDE

PICCOLO
(NO CHANGE)

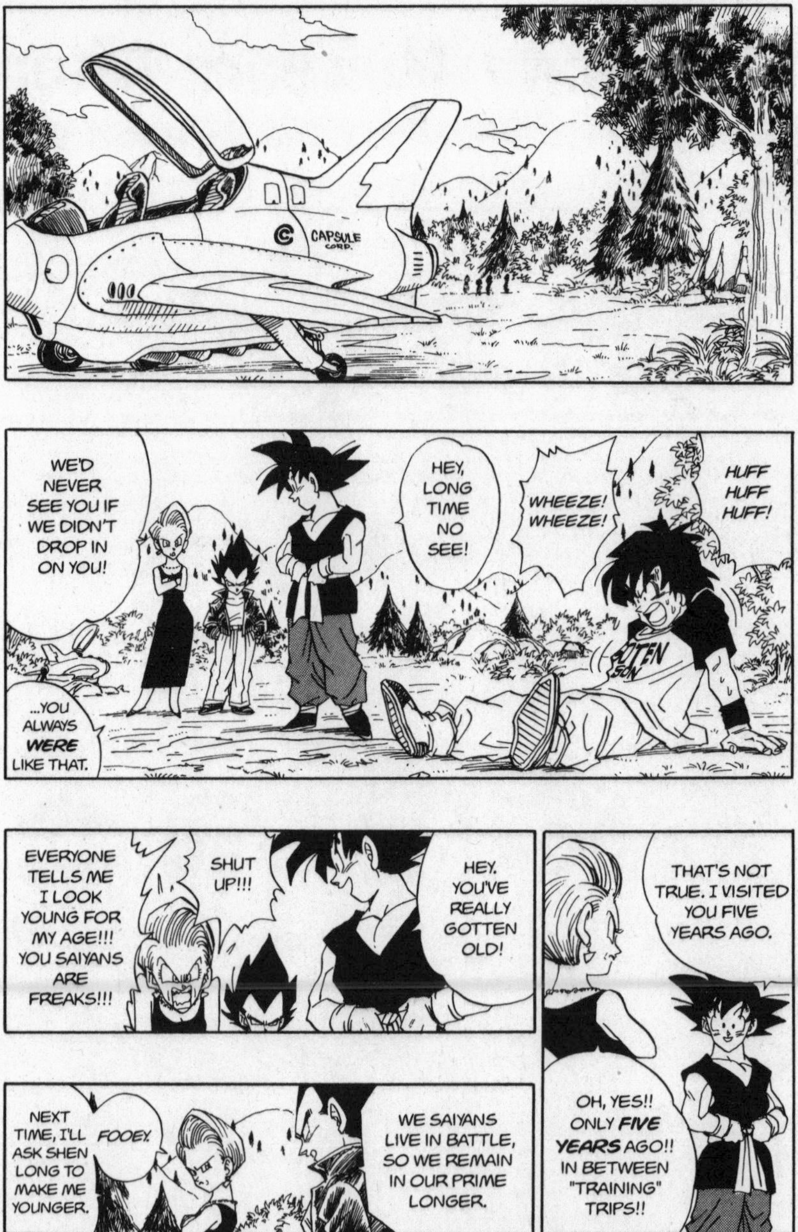
HUFF HUFF HUFF!
WHEEZE! WHEEZE!
HEY, LONG TIME NO SEE!
WE'D NEVER SEE YOU IF WE DIDN'T DROP IN ON YOU!
...YOU ALWAYS **WERE** LIKE THAT.
THAT'S NOT TRUE. I VISITED YOU FIVE YEARS AGO.
OH, YES!! ONLY **FIVE YEARS** AGO!! IN BETWEEN "TRAINING" TRIPS!!
HEY. YOU'VE REALLY GOTTEN OLD!
SHUT UP!!!
EVERYONE TELLS ME I LOOK YOUNG FOR MY AGE!!! YOU SAIYANS ARE FREAKS!!!
WE SAIYANS LIVE IN BATTLE, SO WE REMAIN IN OUR PRIME LONGER.
FOOEY.
NEXT TIME, I'LL ASK SHEN LONG TO MAKE ME YOUNGER.

READ THIS WAY

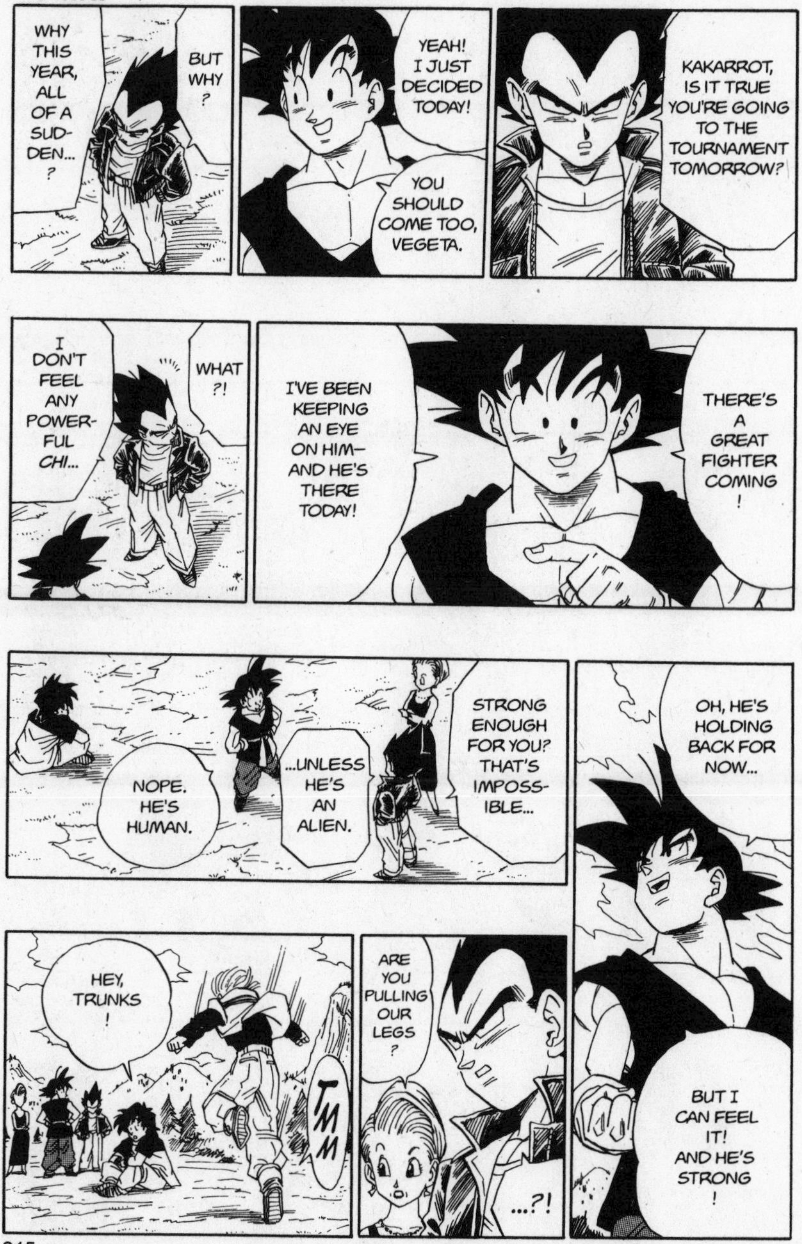

KAKARROT, IS IT TRUE YOU'RE GOING TO THE TOURNAMENT TOMORROW?
YEAH! I JUST DECIDED TODAY!
YOU SHOULD COME TOO, VEGETA.
BUT WHY?
WHY THIS YEAR, ALL OF A SUDDEN...?
THERE'S A GREAT FIGHTER COMING!
I'VE BEEN KEEPING AN EYE ON HIM—AND HE'S THERE TODAY!
WHAT?!
I DON'T FEEL ANY POWERFUL CHI...
OH, HE'S HOLDING BACK FOR NOW...
BUT I CAN FEEL IT! AND HE'S STRONG!
STRONG ENOUGH FOR YOU? THAT'S IMPOSSIBLE...
...UNLESS HE'S AN ALIEN.
NOPE. HE'S HUMAN.
ARE YOU PULLING OUR LEGS?
...?!
HEY, TRUNKS!
TMM

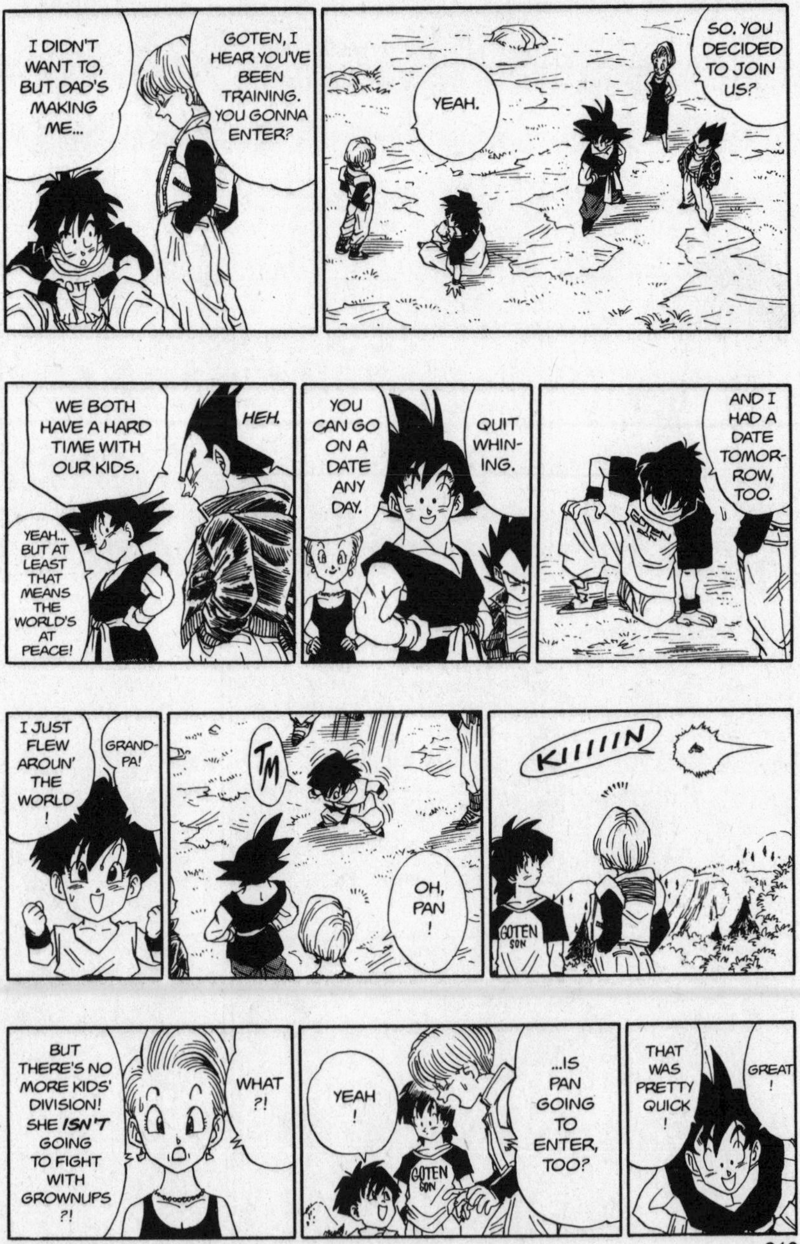
SO. YOU DECIDED TO JOIN US?
YEAH.
GOTEN, I HEAR YOU'VE BEEN TRAINING. YOU GONNA ENTER?
I DIDN'T WANT TO, BUT DAD'S MAKING ME...
AND I HAD A DATE TOMORROW, TOO.
QUIT WHINING.
YOU CAN GO ON A DATE ANY DAY.
HEH.
WE BOTH HAVE A HARD TIME WITH OUR KIDS.
YEAH... BUT AT LEAST THAT MEANS THE WORLD'S AT PEACE!
KIIIIIN
TM
OH, PAN!
GRANDPA!
I JUST FLEW AROUN' THE WORLD!
GREAT!
THAT WAS PRETTY QUICK!
...IS PAN GOING TO ENTER, TOO?
YEAH!
WHAT?!
BUT THERE'S NO MORE KIDS' DIVISION! SHE *ISN'T* GOING TO FIGHT WITH GROWNUPS?!

READ THIS WAY

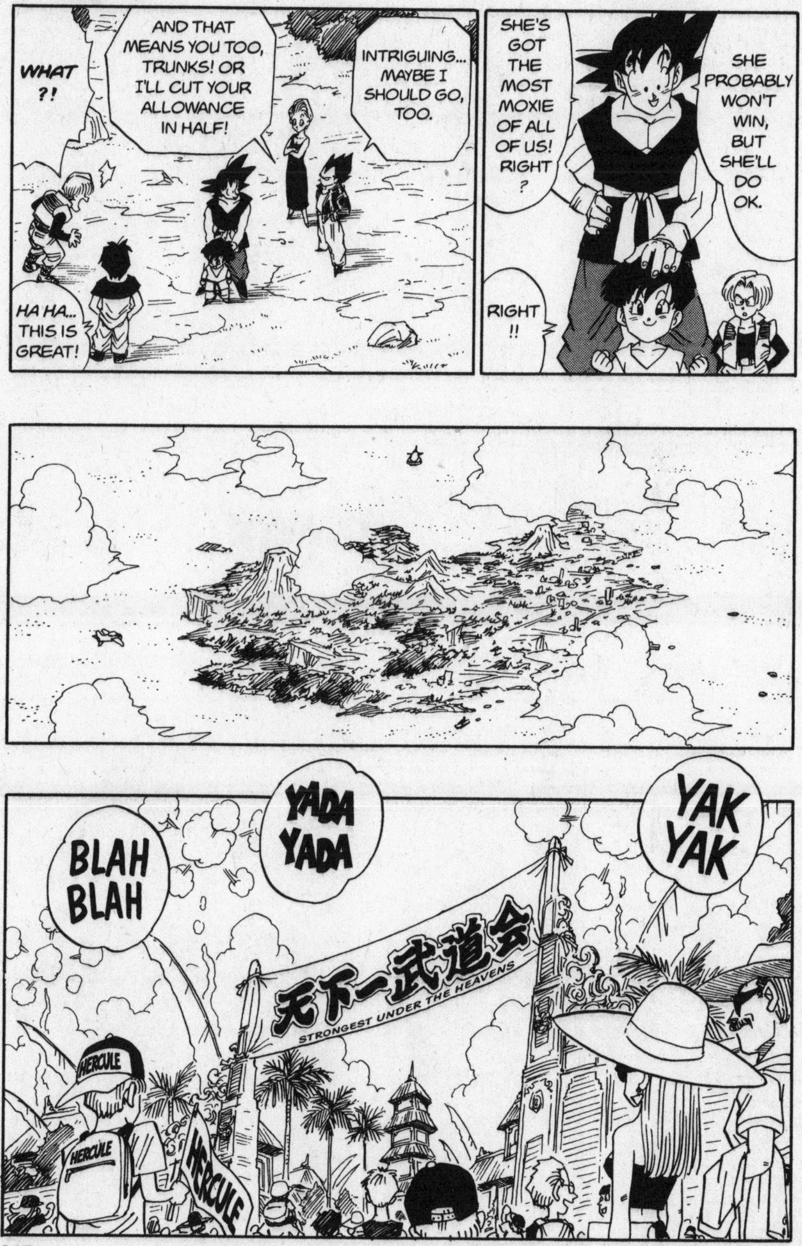
SHE PROBABLY WON'T WIN, BUT SHE'LL DO OK.
SHE'S GOT THE MOST MOXIE OF ALL OF US! RIGHT?
RIGHT!!
INTRIGUING... MAYBE I SHOULD GO, TOO.
AND THAT MEANS YOU TOO, TRUNKS! OR I'LL CUT YOUR ALLOWANCE IN HALF!
WHAT?!
HA HA... THIS IS GREAT!
YAK YAK
YADA YADA
BLAH BLAH
天下一武道会
STRONGEST UNDER THE HEAVENS
HERCULE
HERCULE
HERCULE

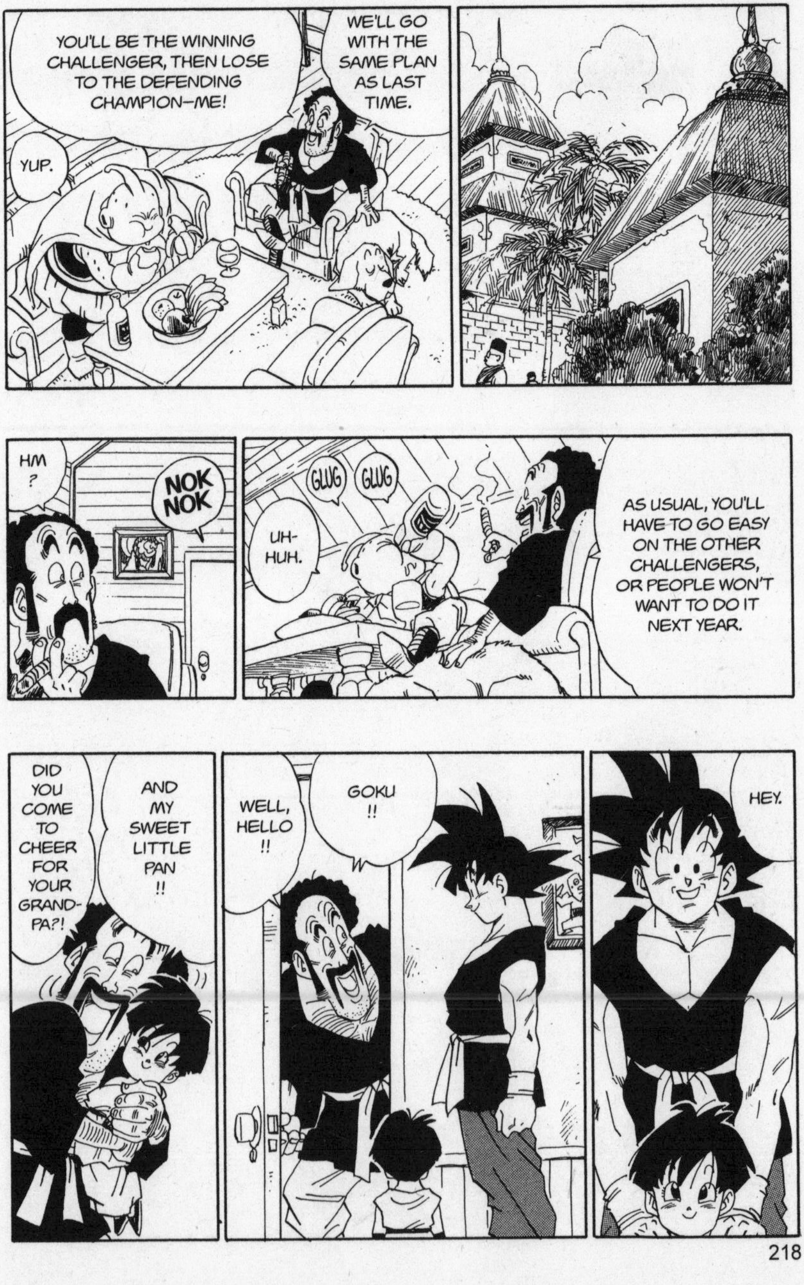
WE'LL GO WITH THE SAME PLAN AS LAST TIME.
YOU'LL BE THE WINNING CHALLENGER, THEN LOSE TO THE DEFENDING CHAMPION—ME!
YUP.
AS USUAL, YOU'LL HAVE TO GO EASY ON THE OTHER CHALLENGERS, OR PEOPLE WON'T WANT TO DO IT NEXT YEAR.
GLUG GLUG
UH-HUH.
NOK NOK
HM ?
HEY.
GOKU !!
WELL, HELLO !!
AND MY SWEET LITTLE PAN !!
DID YOU COME TO CHEER FOR YOUR GRAND-PA?!

READ THIS WAY

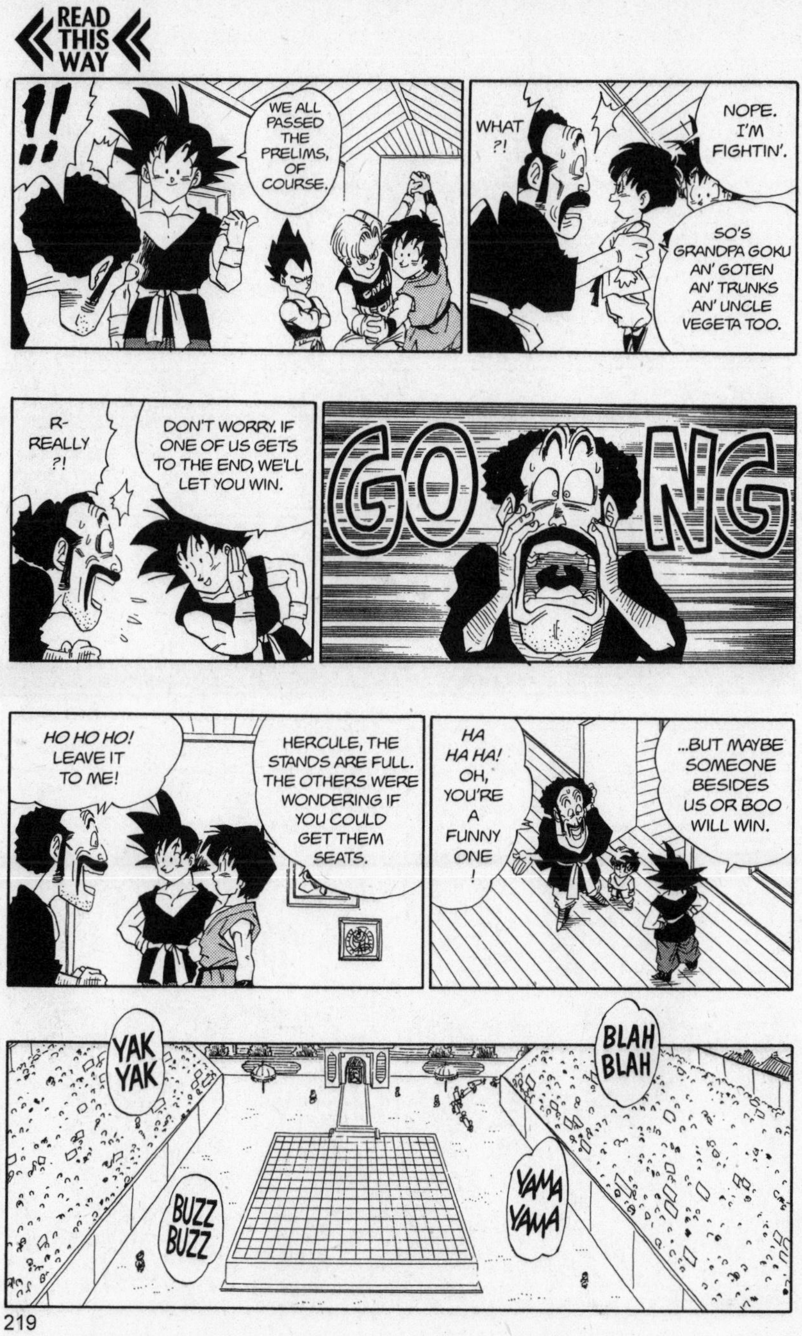
NOPE. I'M FIGHTIN'.
WHAT ?!
SO'S GRANDPA GOKU AN' GOTEN AN' TRUNKS AN' UNCLE VEGETA TOO.
!!
WE ALL PASSED THE PRELIMS, OF COURSE.
GONG
DON'T WORRY. IF ONE OF US GETS TO THE END, WE'LL LET YOU WIN.
R- REALLY ?!
...BUT MAYBE SOMEONE BESIDES US OR BOO WILL WIN.
HA HA HA! OH, YOU'RE A FUNNY ONE !
HERCULE, THE STANDS ARE FULL. THE OTHERS WERE WONDERING IF YOU COULD GET THEM SEATS.
HO HO HO! LEAVE IT TO ME!
BLAH BLAH
YAK YAK
YAMA YAMA
BUZZ BUZZ

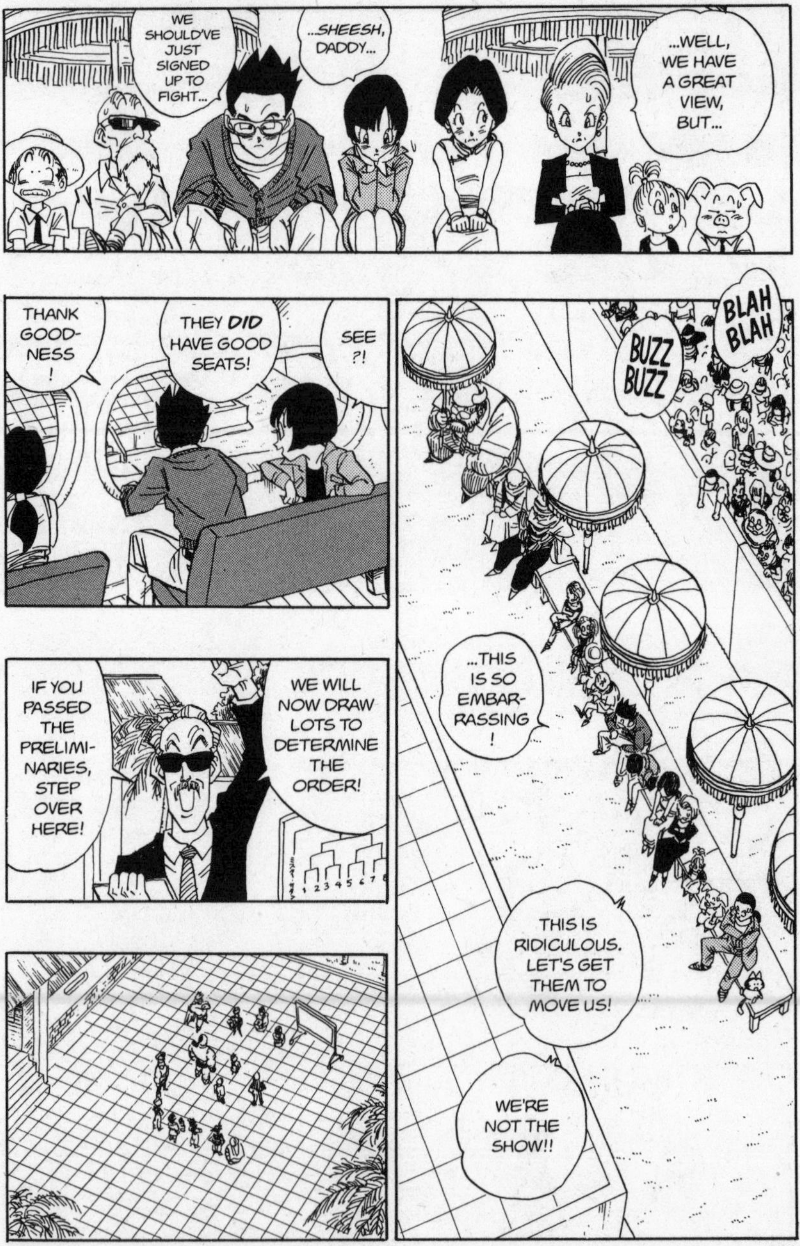
...WELL, WE HAVE A GREAT VIEW, BUT...
...SHEESH, DADDY...
WE SHOULD'VE JUST SIGNED UP TO FIGHT...
BLAH BLAH
BUZZ BUZZ
...THIS IS SO EMBARRASSING!
THIS IS RIDICULOUS. LET'S GET THEM TO MOVE US!
WE'RE NOT THE SHOW!!
SEE?!
THEY DID HAVE GOOD SEATS!
THANK GOODNESS!
WE WILL NOW DRAW LOTS TO DETERMINE THE ORDER!
IF YOU PASSED THE PRELIMINARIES, STEP OVER HERE!
1 2 3 4 5 6 7 8

READ THIS WAY

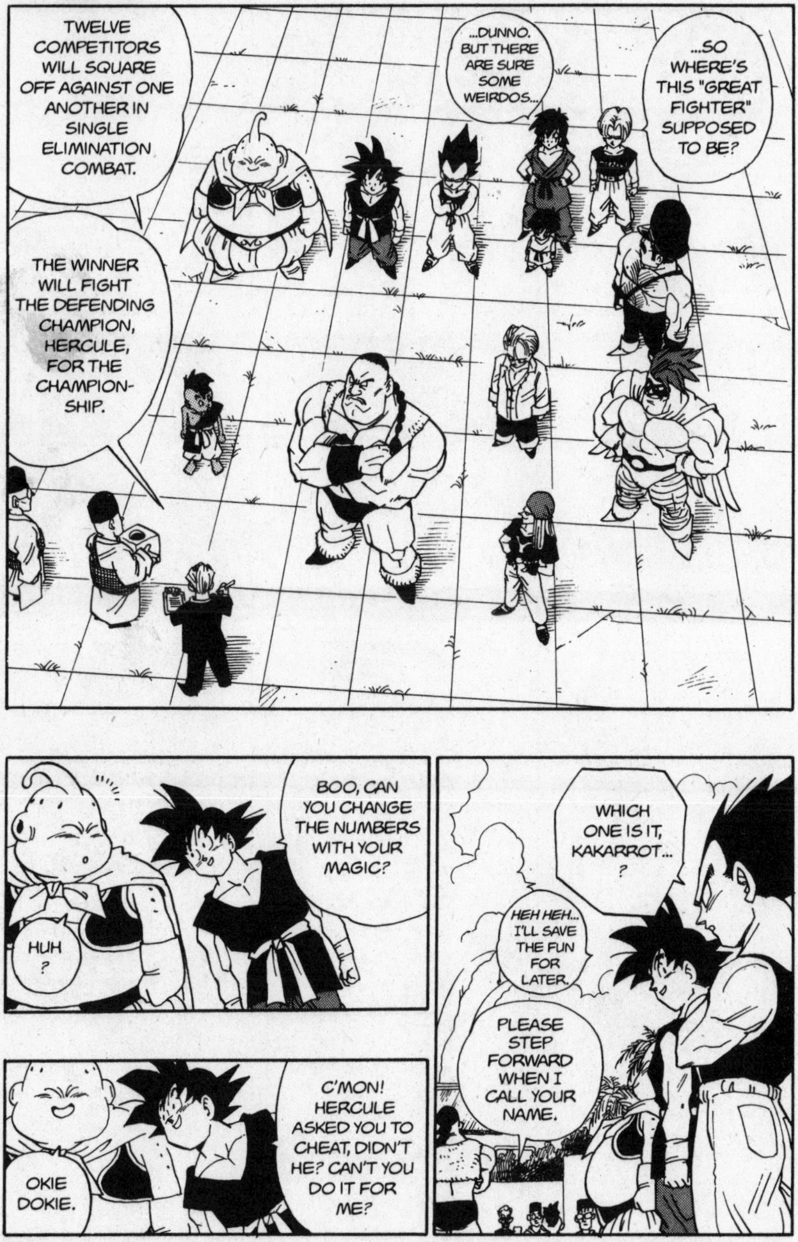

...SO WHERE'S THIS "GREAT FIGHTER" SUPPOSED TO BE?
...DUNNO. BUT THERE ARE SURE SOME WEIRDOS...
TWELVE COMPETITORS WILL SQUARE OFF AGAINST ONE ANOTHER IN SINGLE ELIMINATION COMBAT.
THE WINNER WILL FIGHT THE DEFENDING CHAMPION, HERCULE, FOR THE CHAMPION-SHIP.
WHICH ONE IS IT, KAKARROT... ?
HEH HEH... I'LL SAVE THE FUN FOR LATER.
PLEASE STEP FORWARD WHEN I CALL YOUR NAME.
BOO, CAN YOU CHANGE THE NUMBERS WITH YOUR MAGIC?
HUH ?
C'MON! HERCULE ASKED YOU TO CHEAT, DIDN'T HE? CAN'T YOU DO IT FOR ME?
OKIE DOKIE.

THE FINALISTS

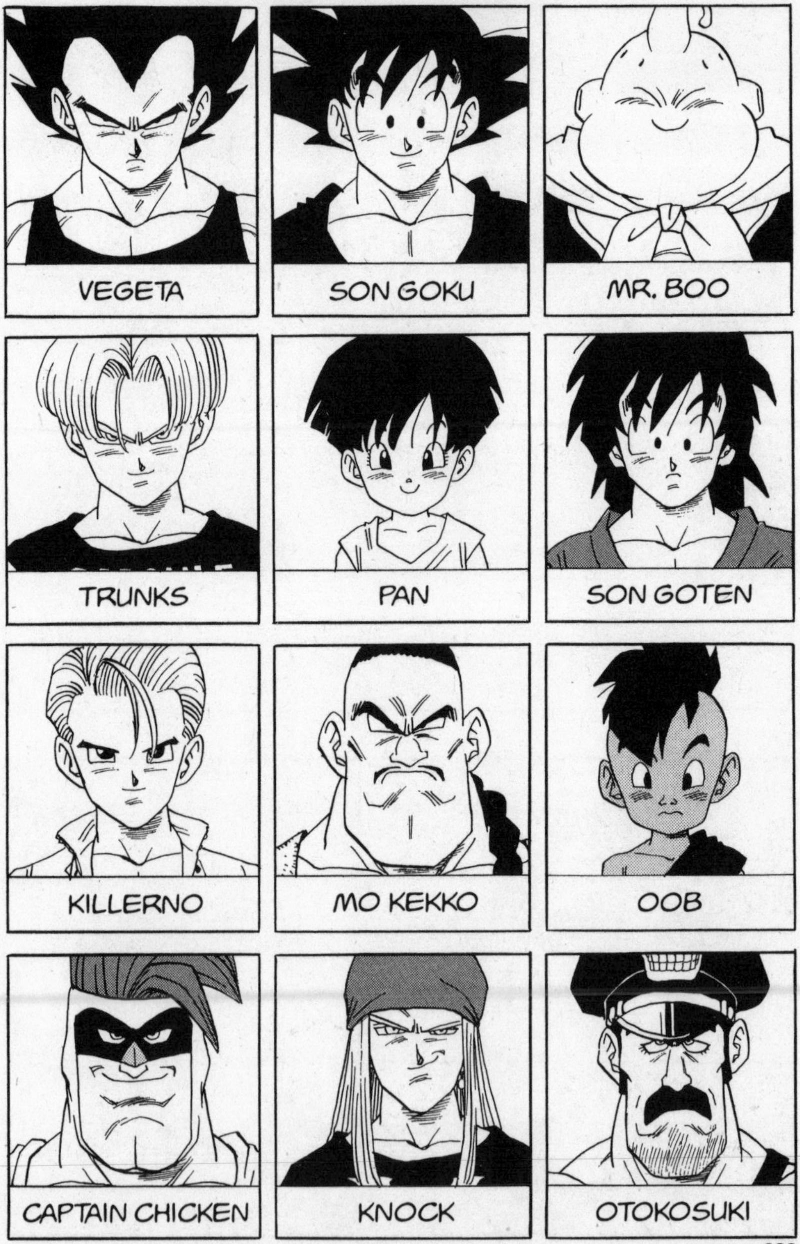
VEGETA
SON GOKU
MR. BOO
TRUNKS
PAN
SON GOTEN
KILLERNO
MO KEKKO
OOB
CAPTAIN CHICKEN
KNOCK
OTOKOSUKI

READ THIS WAY

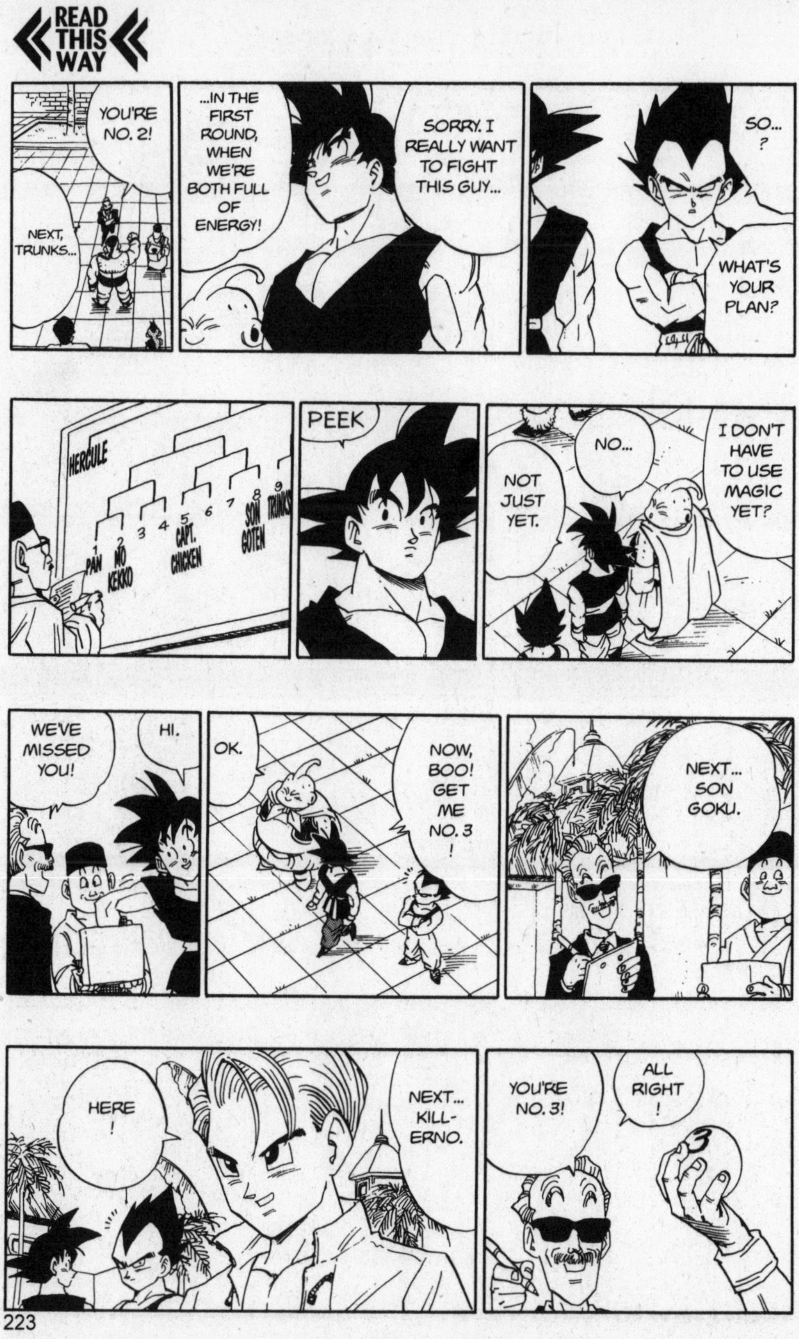
SO... ?
WHAT'S YOUR PLAN?
SORRY. I REALLY WANT TO FIGHT THIS GUY...
...IN THE FIRST ROUND, WHEN WE'RE BOTH FULL OF ENERGY!
YOU'RE NO. 2!
NEXT, TRUNKS...
I DON'T HAVE TO USE MAGIC YET?
NO...
NOT JUST YET.
PEEK
HERCULE
1 PAN
2 MO KEKKO
3
4
5 CAPT. CHICKEN
6
7
8 SON GOTEN
9 TRUNKS
NEXT... SON GOKU.
NOW, BOO! GET ME NO. 3!
OK.
HI.
WE'VE MISSED YOU!
ALL RIGHT!
YOU'RE NO. 3!
3
NEXT... KILL-ERNO.
HERE!

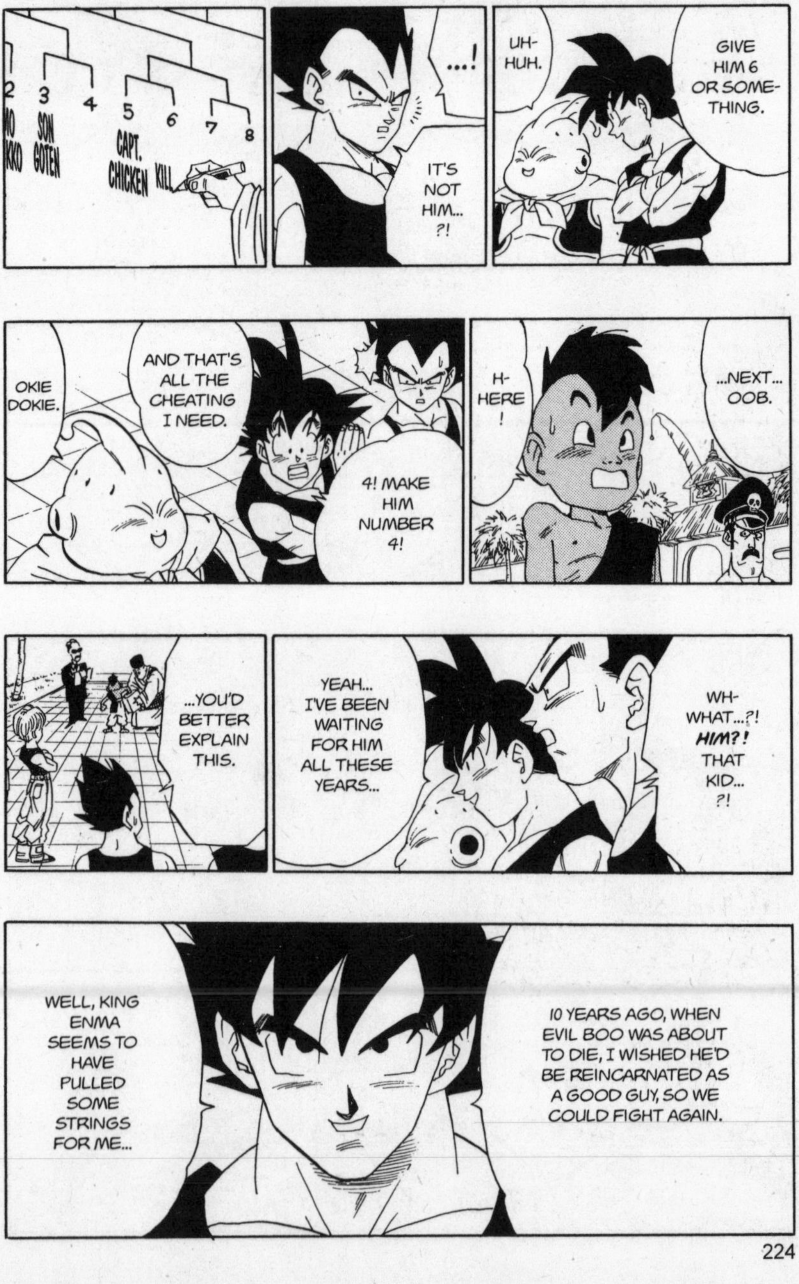
GIVE HIM 6 OR SOMETHING.
UH-HUH.
....!
IT'S NOT HIM...?!
2 3 4 5 6 7 8
SON GOTEN
CAPT. CHICKEN
KILL
...NEXT... OOB.
H-HERE!
AND THAT'S ALL THE CHEATING I NEED.
4! MAKE HIM NUMBER 4!
OKIE DOKIE.
WH-WHAT...?! ***HIM?!*** THAT KID...?!
YEAH... I'VE BEEN WAITING FOR HIM ALL THESE YEARS...
...YOU'D BETTER EXPLAIN THIS.
10 YEARS AGO, WHEN EVIL BOO WAS ABOUT TO DIE, I WISHED HE'D BE REINCARNATED AS A GOOD GUY, SO WE COULD FIGHT AGAIN.
WELL, KING ENMA SEEMS TO HAVE PULLED SOME STRINGS FOR ME...

READ THIS WAY

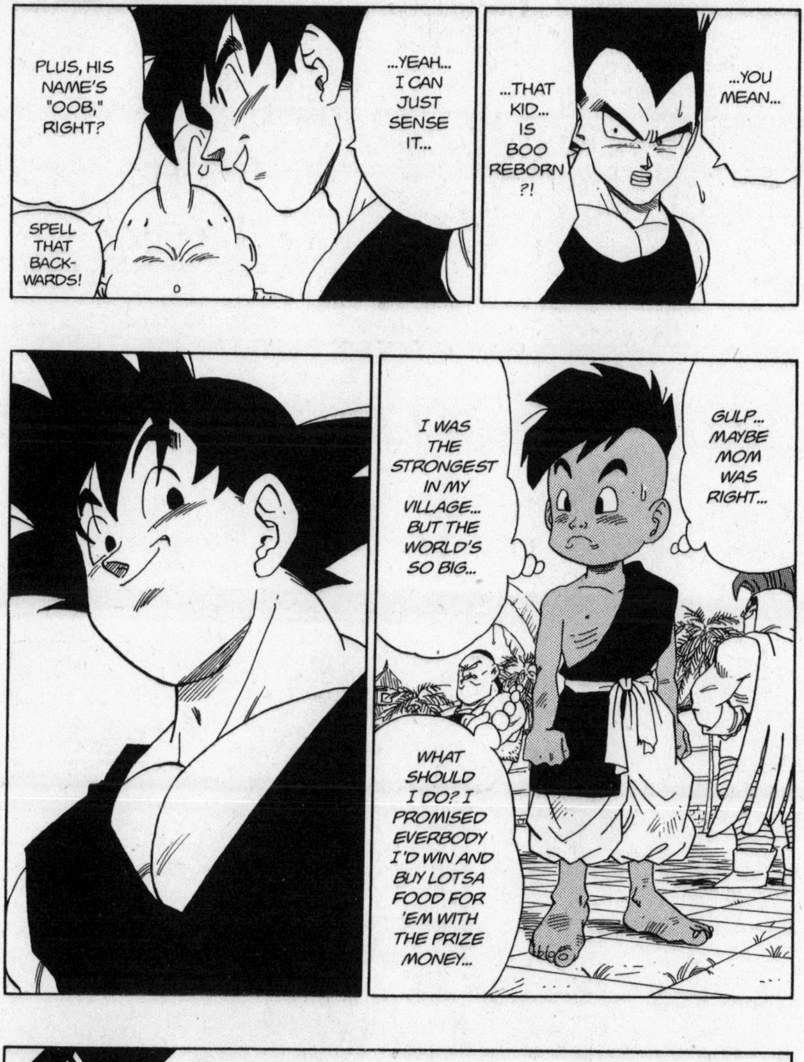
...YOU MEAN...
...THAT KID... IS BOO REBORN?!
...YEAH... I CAN JUST SENSE IT...
PLUS, HIS NAME'S "OOB," RIGHT?
SPELL THAT BACKWARDS!
GULP... MAYBE MOM WAS RIGHT...
I WAS THE STRONGEST IN MY VILLAGE... BUT THE WORLD'S SO BIG...
WHAT SHOULD I DO? I PROMISED EVERBODY I'D WIN AND BUY LOTSA FOOD FOR 'EM WITH THE PRIZE MONEY...

EXTRA!!

SOMETHING'S GOING TO HAPPEN IN THE NEXT EPISODE OF DRAGON BALL!!!!

WHAT WILL IT BE?!
DON'T EXPECT TOO MUCH!!

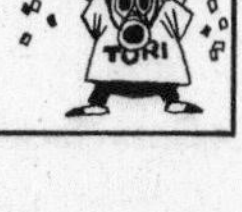
TORI

DBZ:325
Farewell, Dragon World!

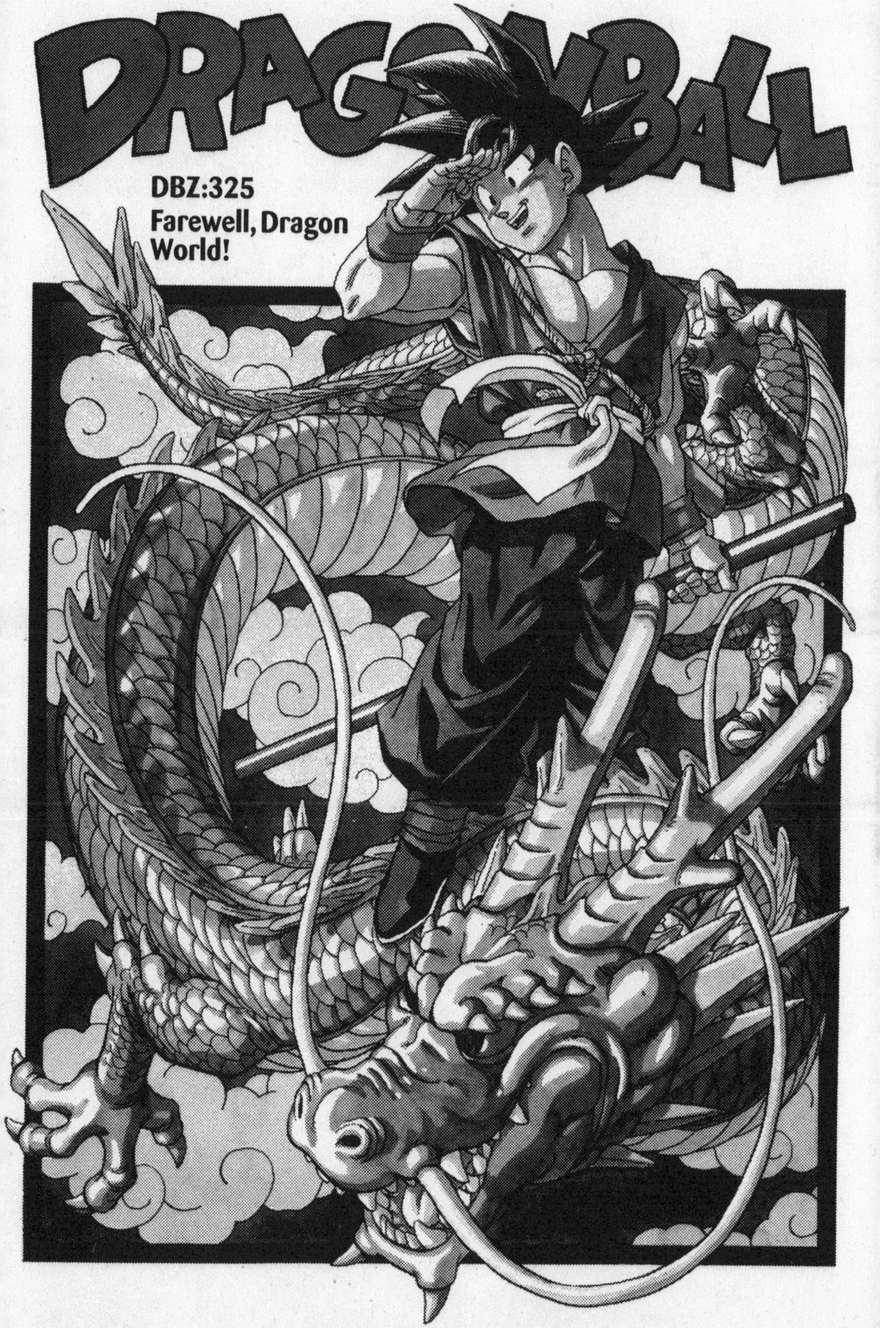
DRAGON BALL

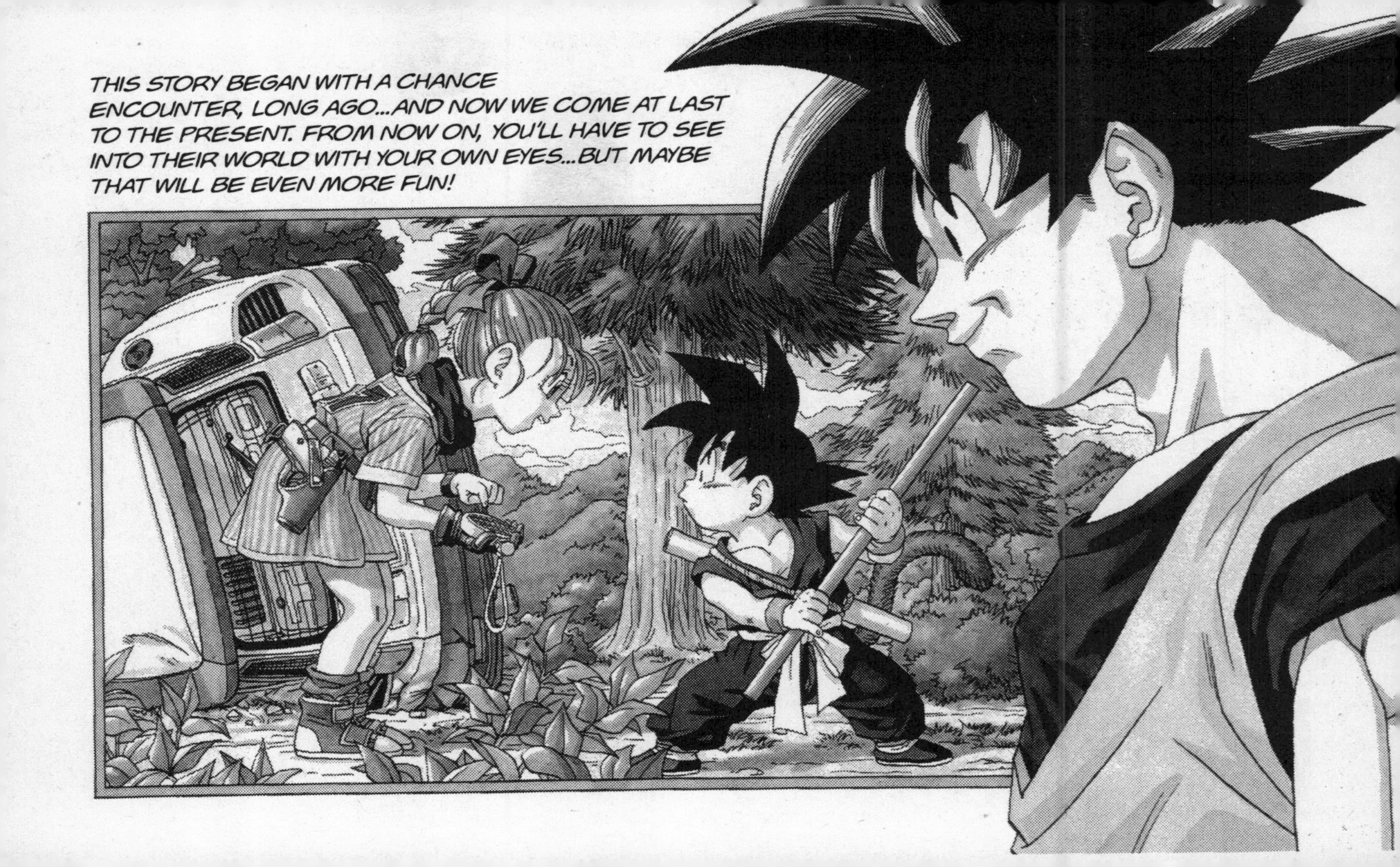
THIS STORY BEGAN WITH A CHANCE ENCOUNTER, LONG AGO...AND NOW WE COME AT LAST TO THE PRESENT. FROM NOW ON, YOU'LL HAVE TO SEE INTO THEIR WORLD WITH YOUR OWN EYES...BUT MAYBE THAT WILL BE EVEN MORE FUN!

READ THIS WAY

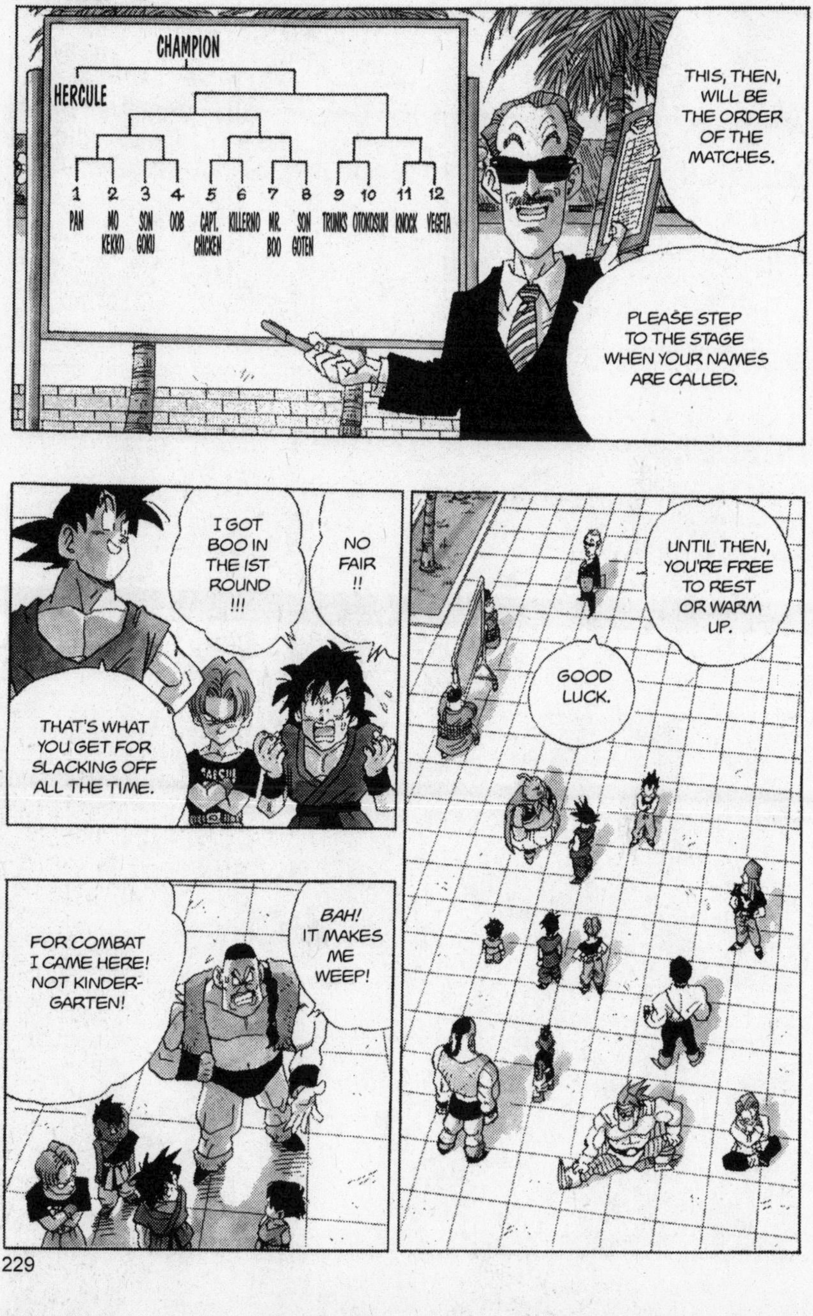
CHAMPION
HERCULE
1 PAN
2 MO KEKKO
3 SON GOKU
4 OOB
5 CAPT. CHICKEN
6 KILLERNO
7 MR. BOO
8 SON GOTEN
9 TRUNKS
10 OTOKOSUKI
11 KNOCK
12 VEGETA
THIS, THEN, WILL BE THE ORDER OF THE MATCHES.
PLEASE STEP TO THE STAGE WHEN YOUR NAMES ARE CALLED.
UNTIL THEN, YOU'RE FREE TO REST OR WARM UP.
GOOD LUCK.
NO FAIR !!
I GOT BOO IN THE 1ST ROUND !!!
THAT'S WHAT YOU GET FOR SLACKING OFF ALL THE TIME.
BAH! IT MAKES ME WEEP!
FOR COMBAT I CAME HERE! NOT KINDER-GARTEN!

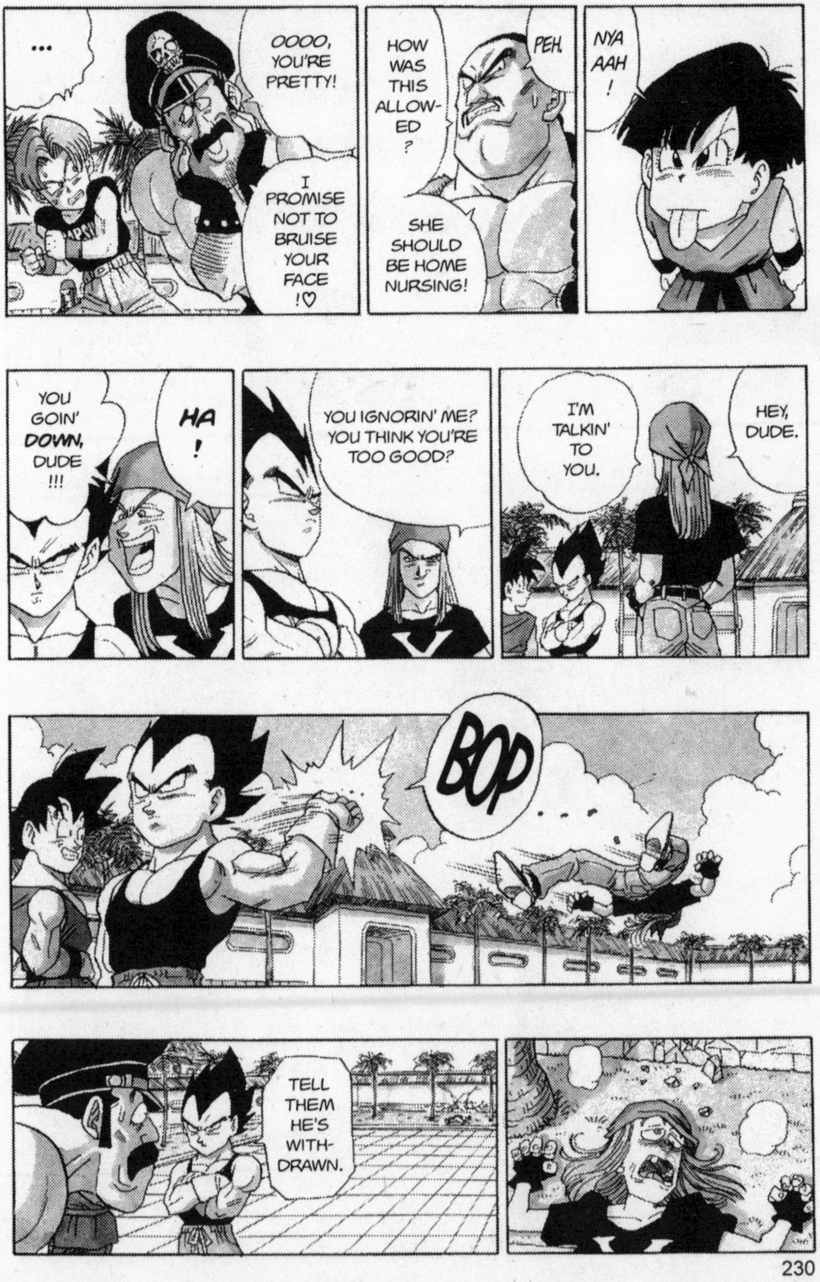
NYA AAH !
PEH.
HOW WAS THIS ALLOWED-ED ?
SHE SHOULD BE HOME NURSING!
OOOO, YOU'RE PRETTY!
I PROMISE NOT TO BRUISE YOUR FACE !♡
...
HEY, DUDE.
I'M TALKIN' TO YOU.
YOU IGNORIN' ME? YOU THINK YOU'RE TOO GOOD?
HA !
YOU GOIN' DOWN, DUDE !!!
BOP
TELL THEM HE'S WITH-DRAWN.

READ THIS WAY

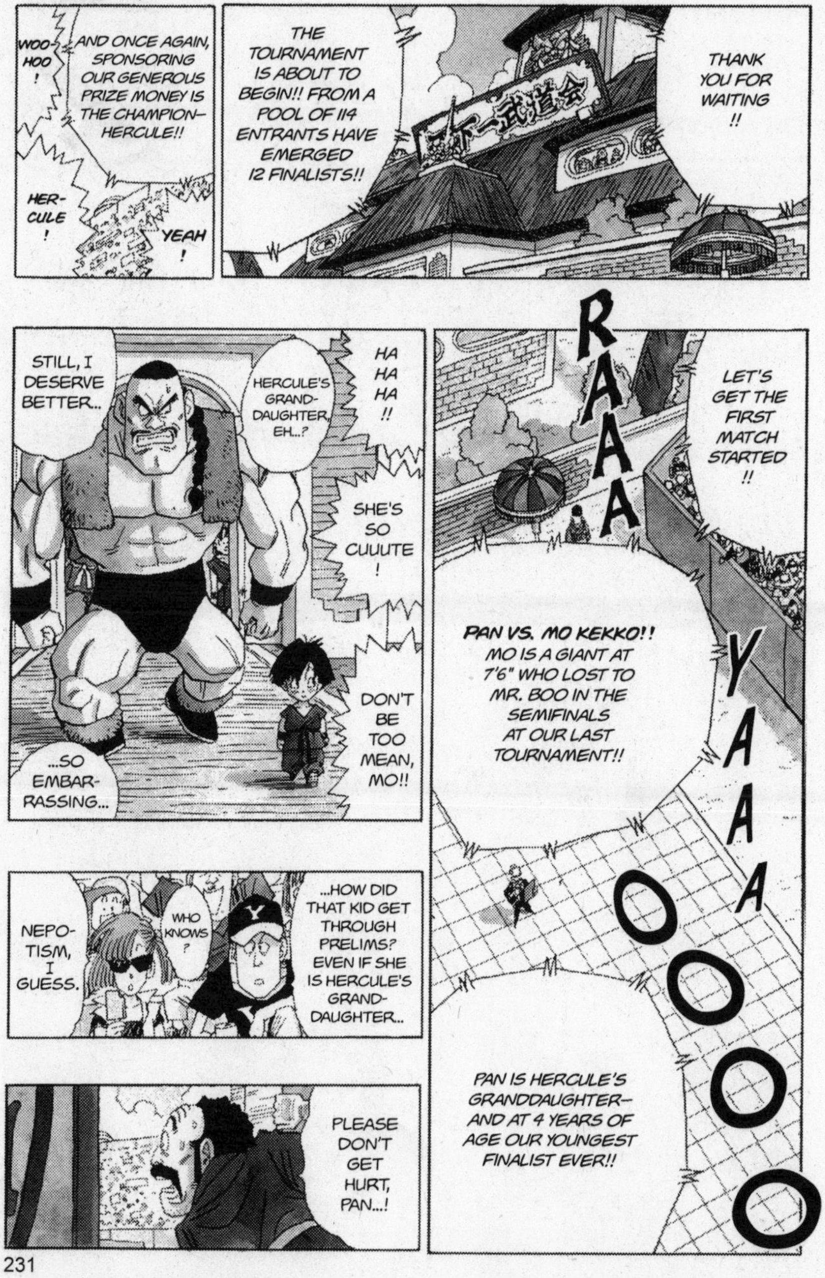

THANK YOU FOR WAITING!!
THE TOURNAMENT IS ABOUT TO BEGIN!! FROM A POOL OF 114 ENTRANTS HAVE EMERGED 12 FINALISTS!!
AND ONCE AGAIN, SPONSORING OUR GENEROUS PRIZE MONEY IS THE CHAMPION—HERCULE!!
WOO-HOO!
HERCULE!
YEAH!
LET'S GET THE FIRST MATCH STARTED!!
RAAAA
YAAAA
OOOOO
PAN VS. MO KEKKO!! MO IS A GIANT AT 7'6" WHO LOST TO MR. BOO IN THE SEMIFINALS AT OUR LAST TOURNAMENT!!
PAN IS HERCULE'S GRANDDAUGHTER—AND AT 4 YEARS OF AGE OUR YOUNGEST FINALIST EVER!!
HA HA HA!!
HERCULE'S GRANDDAUGHTER, EH...?
STILL, I DESERVE BETTER..
SHE'S SO CUUUTE!
DON'T BE TOO MEAN, MO!!
...SO EMBARRASSING...
...HOW DID THAT KID GET THROUGH PRELIMS? EVEN IF SHE IS HERCULE'S GRANDDAUGHTER..
WHO KNOWS?
NEPOTISM, I GUESS.
PLEASE DON'T GET HURT, PAN...!

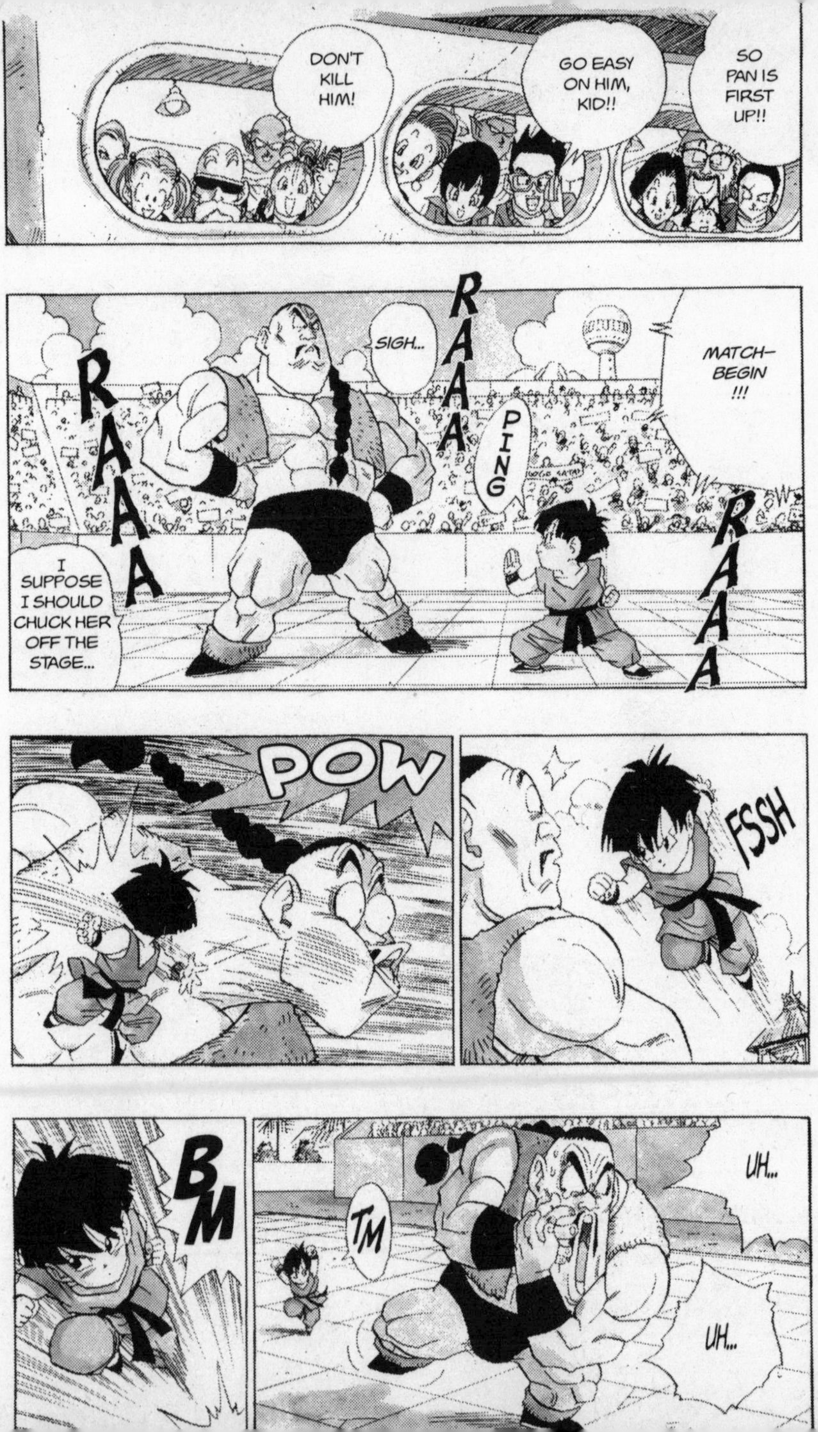
SO PAN IS FIRST UP!!
GO EASY ON HIM, KID!!
DON'T KILL HIM!
MATCH-BEGIN!!!
RAAAA
PING
RAAAA
SIGH...
RAAAA
I SUPPOSE I SHOULD CHUCK HER OFF THE STAGE...
FSSH
POW
UH...
UH...
TM
BM

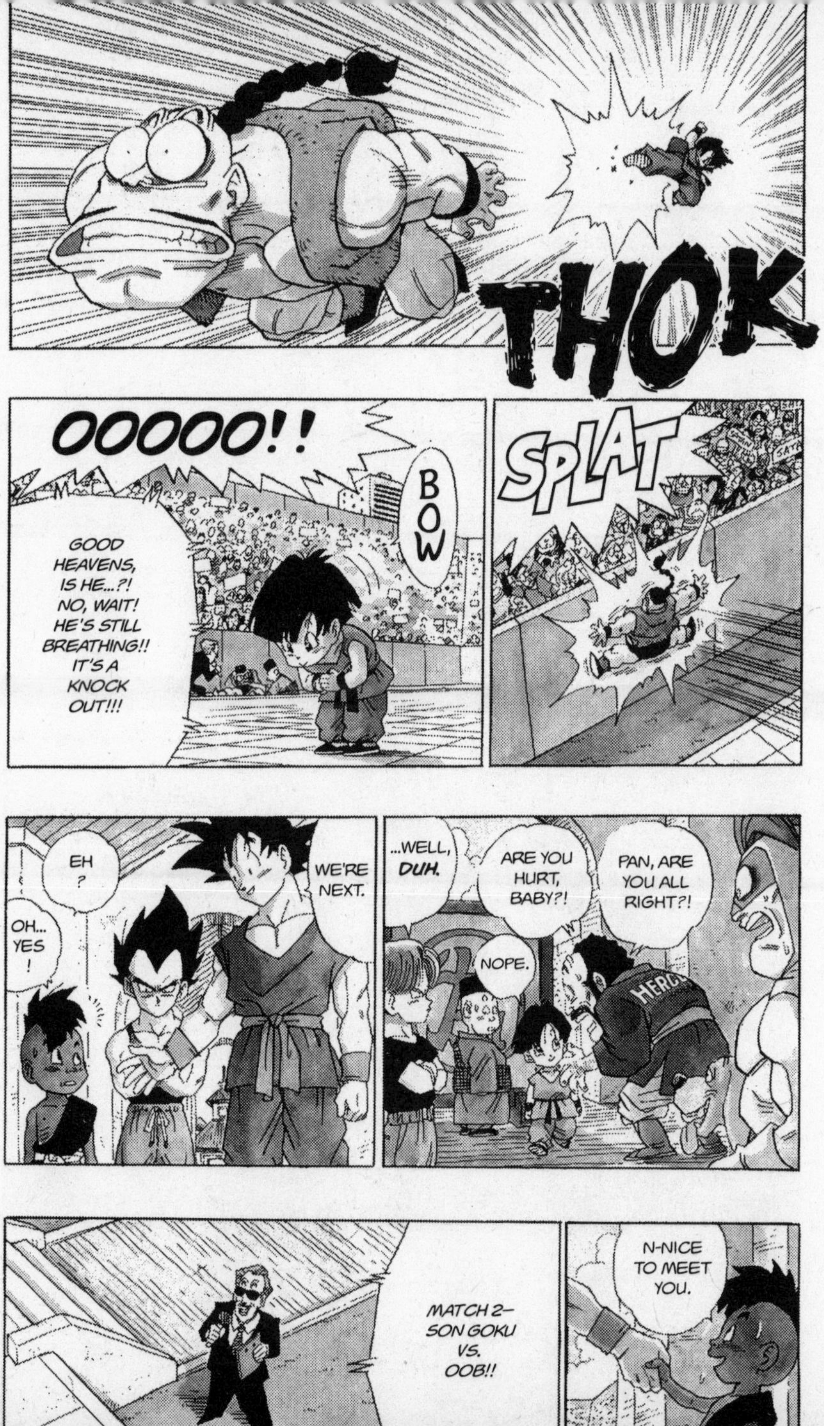
THOK
SPLAT
OOOOO!!
BOW
GOOD HEAVENS, IS HE...?! NO, WAIT! HE'S STILL BREATHING!! IT'S A KNOCK OUT!!!
PAN, ARE YOU ALL RIGHT?!
ARE YOU HURT, BABY?!
...WELL, DUH.
NOPE.
WE'RE NEXT.
EH ?
OH... YES !
N-NICE TO MEET YOU.
MATCH 2— SON GOKU VS. OOB!!

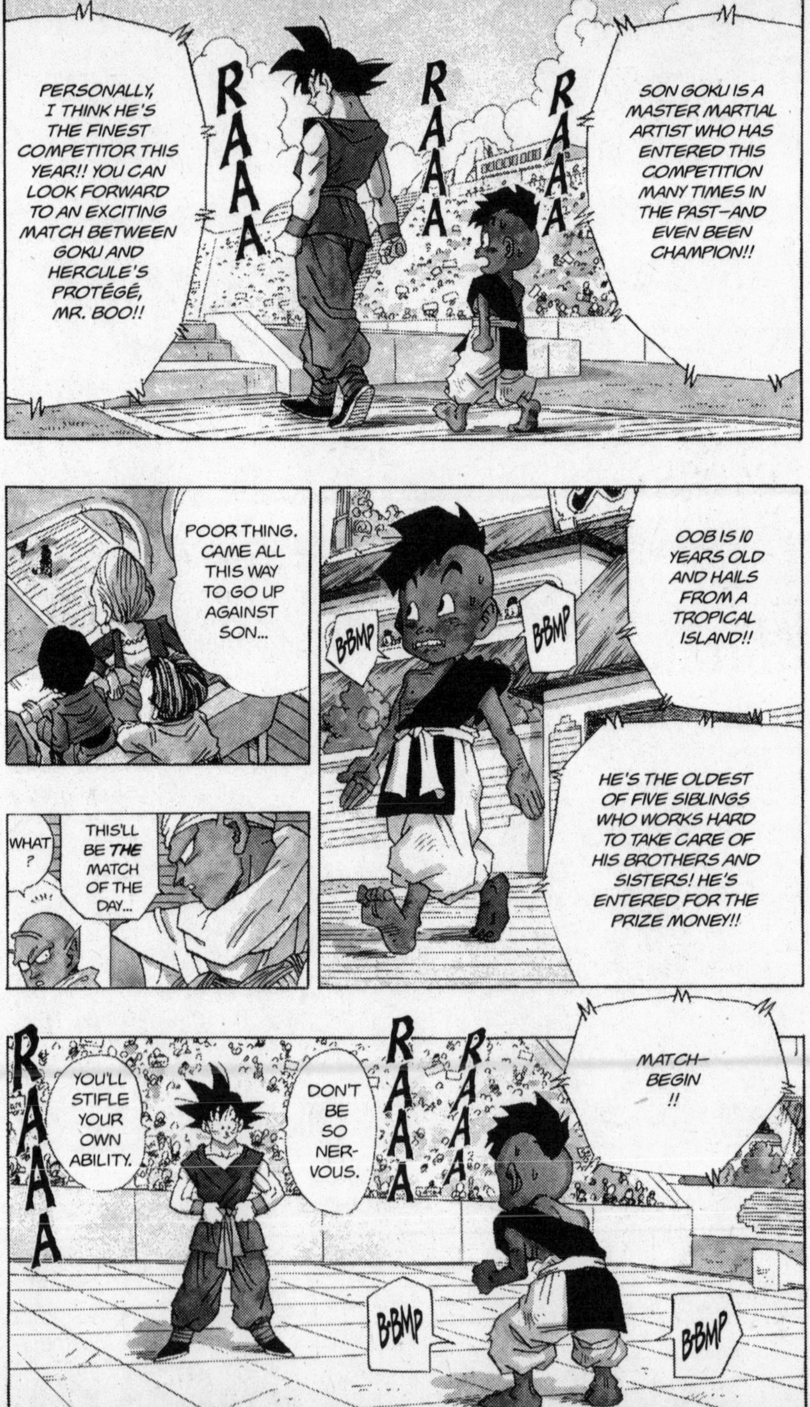
SON GOKU IS A MASTER MARTIAL ARTIST WHO HAS ENTERED THIS COMPETITION MANY TIMES IN THE PAST—AND EVEN BEEN CHAMPION!!
RAAAA
RAAAA
RAAAA
PERSONALLY, I THINK HE'S THE FINEST COMPETITOR THIS YEAR!! YOU CAN LOOK FORWARD TO AN EXCITING MATCH BETWEEN GOKU AND HERCULE'S PROTÉGÉ, MR. BOO!!
OOB IS 10 YEARS OLD AND HAILS FROM A TROPICAL ISLAND!!
B-BMP
B-BMP
HE'S THE OLDEST OF FIVE SIBLINGS WHO WORKS HARD TO TAKE CARE OF HIS BROTHERS AND SISTERS! HE'S ENTERED FOR THE PRIZE MONEY!!
POOR THING. CAME ALL THIS WAY TO GO UP AGAINST SON...
THIS'LL BE *THE* MATCH OF THE DAY...
WHAT ?
MATCH— BEGIN !!
RAAAA
RAAAA
DON'T BE SO NER-VOUS.
YOU'LL STIFLE YOUR OWN ABILITY.
RAAAA
B-BMP
B-BMP

READ THIS WAY

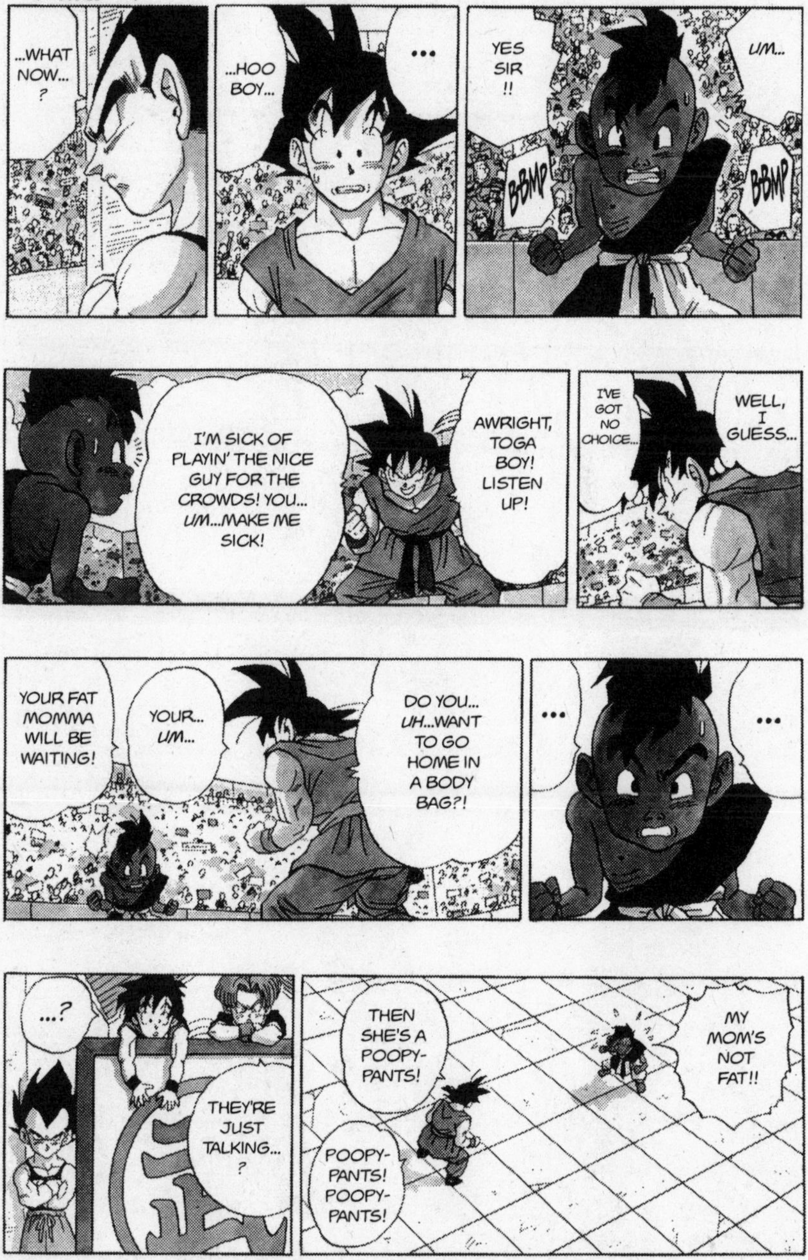
UM...
YES SIR !!
BBMP
BBMP
...
...HOO BOY...
...WHAT NOW... ?
WELL, I GUESS...
I'VE GOT NO CHOICE...
AWRIGHT, TOGA BOY! LISTEN UP!
I'M SICK OF PLAYIN' THE NICE GUY FOR THE CROWDS! YOU... *UM*...MAKE ME SICK!
...
...
DO YOU... *UH*...WANT TO GO HOME IN A BODY BAG?!
YOUR... *UM*...
YOUR FAT MOMMA WILL BE WAITING!
MY MOM'S NOT FAT!!
THEN SHE'S A POOPY-PANTS!
POOPY-PANTS! POOPY-PANTS!
...?
THEY'RE JUST TALKING... ?

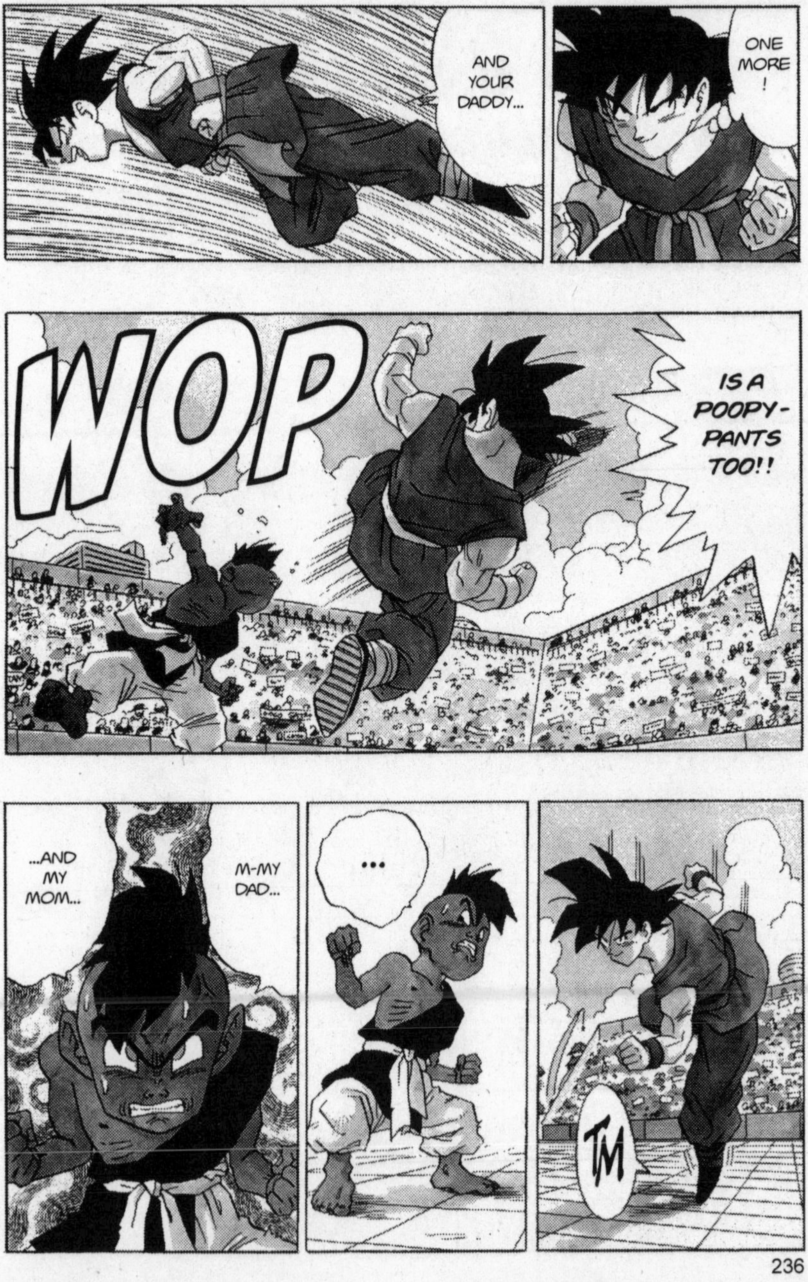
ONE MORE !
AND YOUR DADDY...
IS A POOPY-PANTS TOO!!
WOP
TM
...
M-MY DAD...
...AND MY MOM...

READ THIS WAY

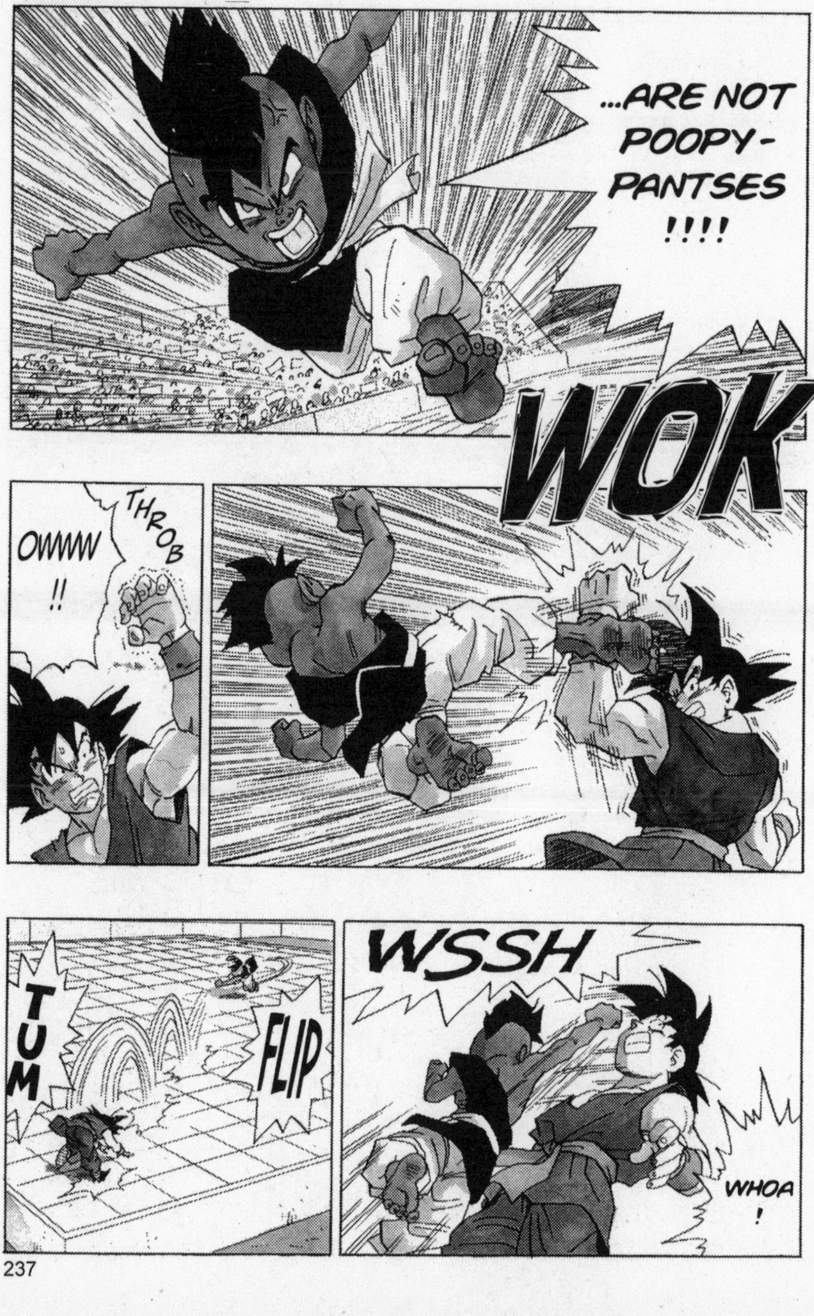
...ARE NOT POOPY-PANTSES !!!!
WOK
THROB
OWWW !!
WSSH
WHOA !
FLIP
TUM

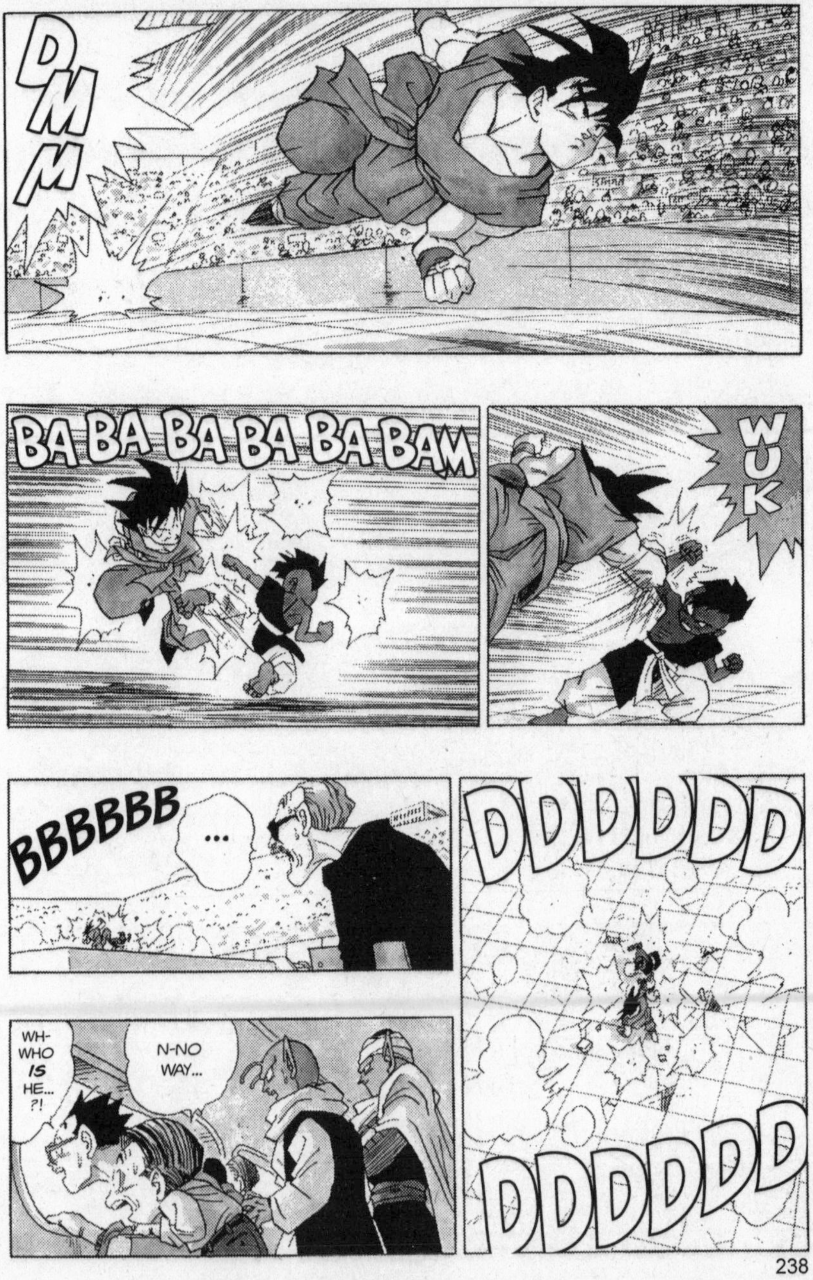
DMM
WUK
BA BA BA BA BA BAM
DDDDDD
DDDDDD
BBBBBB
...
N-NO WAY...
WH-WHO IS HE...?!

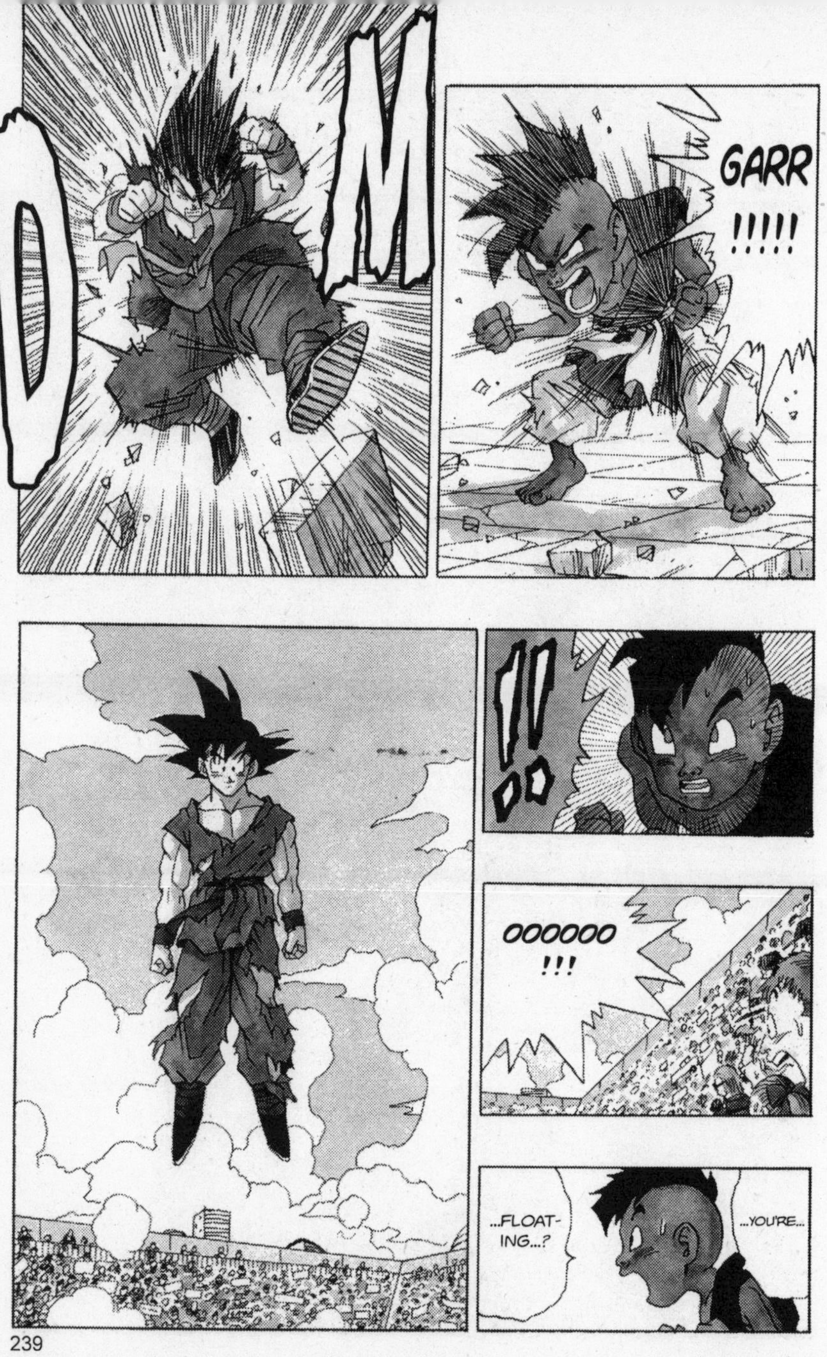
GARR !!!!!
D M
!!
OOOOOO !!!
...YOU'RE...
...FLOAT-ING...?

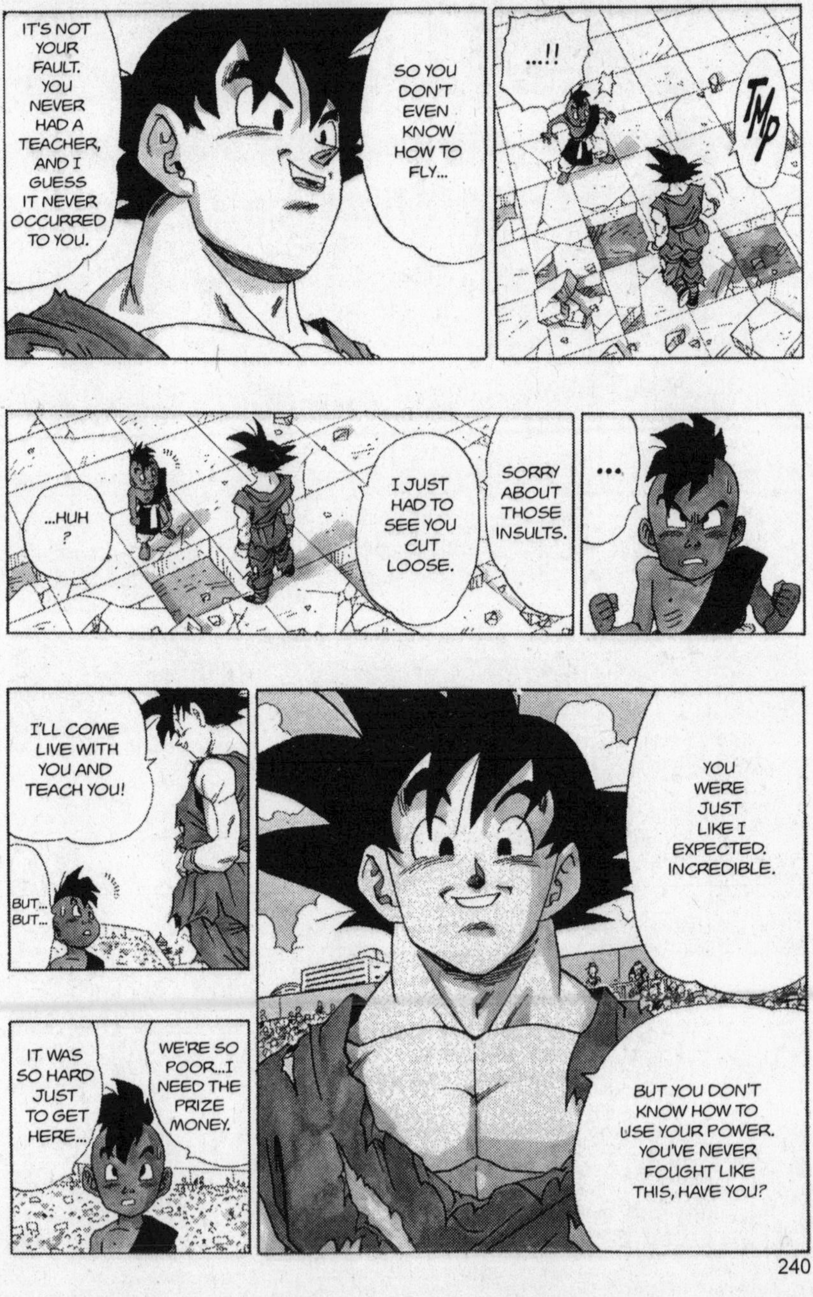
...!!
TMP
SO YOU DON'T EVEN KNOW HOW TO FLY...
IT'S NOT YOUR FAULT. YOU NEVER HAD A TEACHER, AND I GUESS IT NEVER OCCURRED TO YOU.
•••
SORRY ABOUT THOSE INSULTS.
I JUST HAD TO SEE YOU CUT LOOSE.
...HUH ?
YOU WERE JUST LIKE I EXPECTED. INCREDIBLE.
BUT YOU DON'T KNOW HOW TO USE YOUR POWER. YOU'VE NEVER FOUGHT LIKE THIS, HAVE YOU?
I'LL COME LIVE WITH YOU AND TEACH YOU!
BUT... BUT...
WE'RE SO POOR...I NEED THE PRIZE MONEY.
IT WAS SO HARD JUST TO GET HERE...

READ THIS WAY

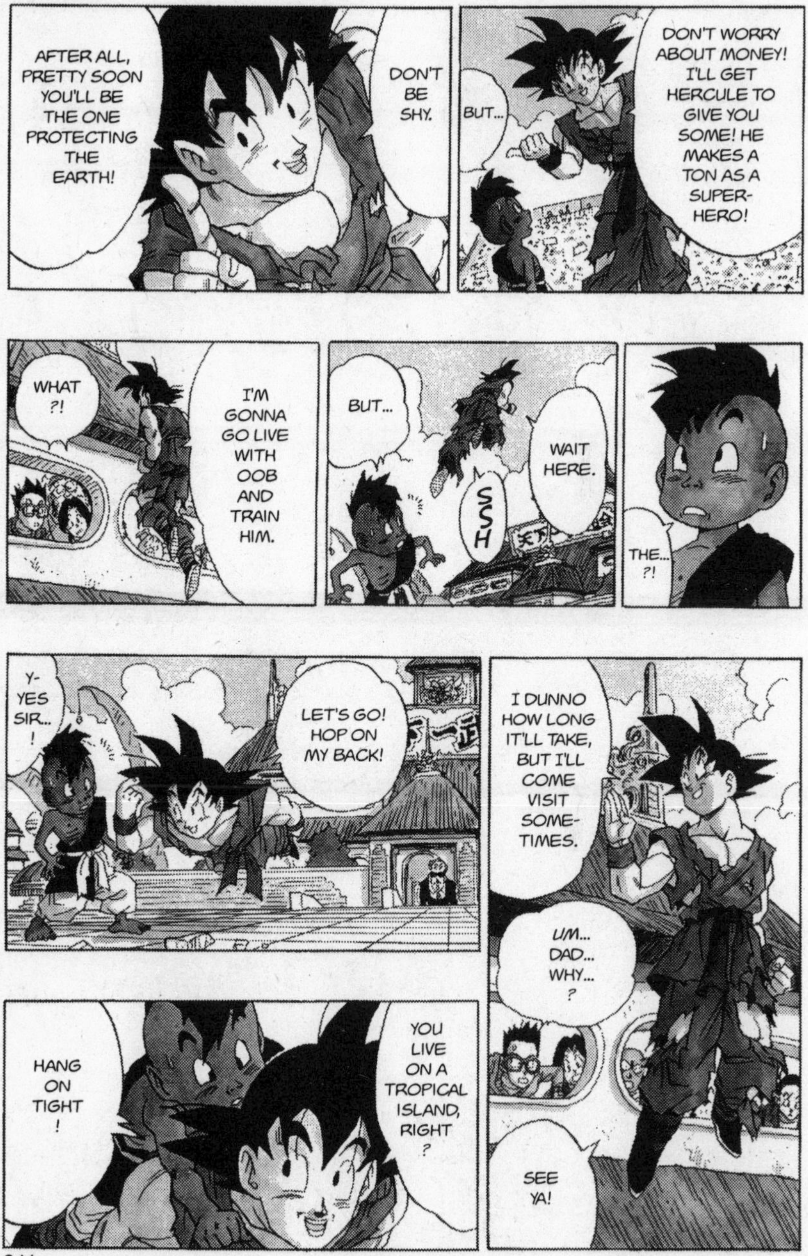
DON'T WORRY ABOUT MONEY! I'LL GET HERCULE TO GIVE YOU SOME! HE MAKES A TON AS A SUPER-HERO!
BUT...
DON'T BE SHY.
AFTER ALL, PRETTY SOON YOU'LL BE THE ONE PROTECTING THE EARTH!
THE... ?!
WAIT HERE.
SSH
BUT...
I'M GONNA GO LIVE WITH OOB AND TRAIN HIM.
WHAT ?!
I DUNNO HOW LONG IT'LL TAKE, BUT I'LL COME VISIT SOME-TIMES.
UM... DAD... WHY... ?
SEE YA!
LET'S GO! HOP ON MY BACK!
Y-YES SIR.. !
YOU LIVE ON A TROPICAL ISLAND, RIGHT ?
HANG ON TIGHT !

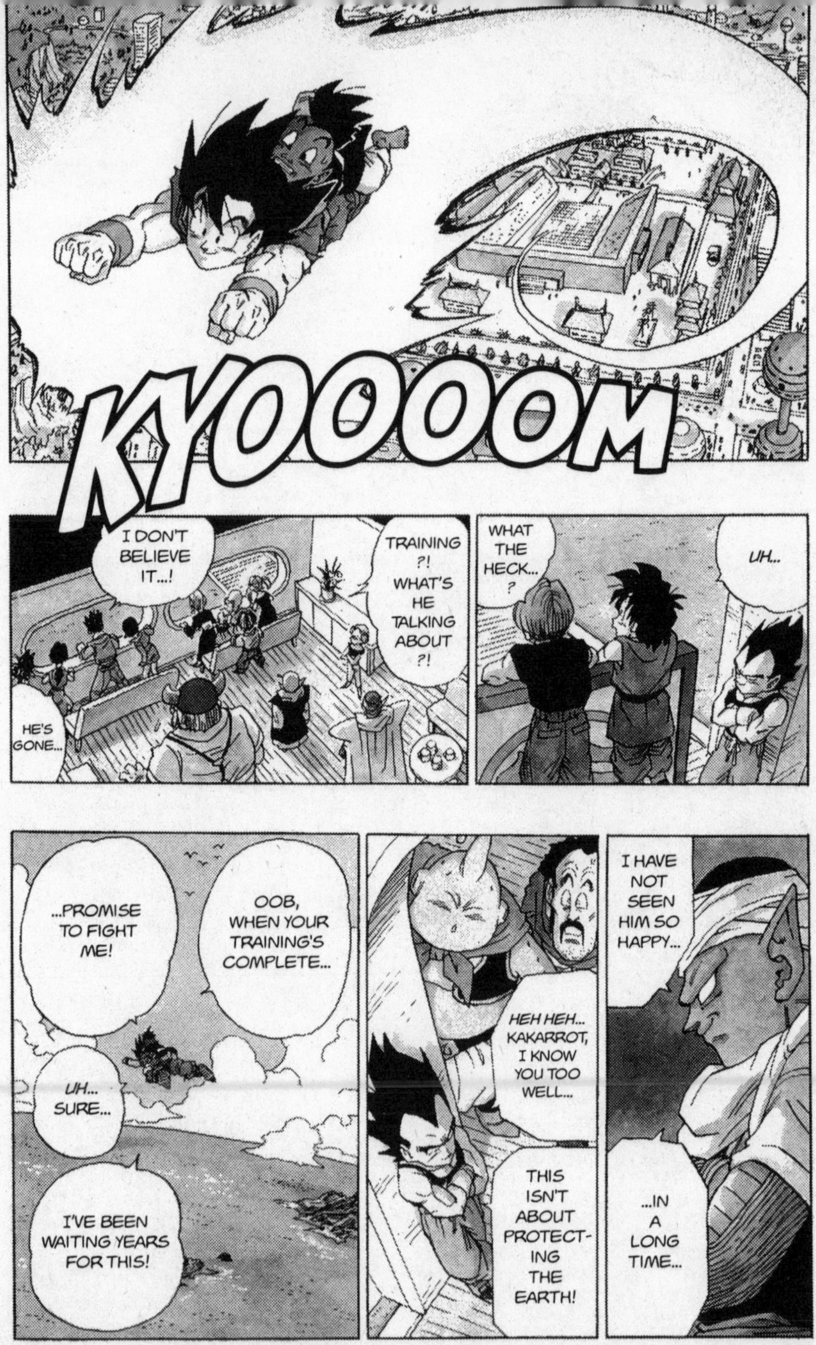
KYOOOOM
UH...
WHAT THE HECK...?
TRAINING?! WHAT'S HE TALKING ABOUT?!
I DON'T BELIEVE IT...!
HE'S GONE...
I HAVE NOT SEEN HIM SO HAPPY...
...IN A LONG TIME...
HEH HEH... KAKARROT, I KNOW YOU TOO WELL...
THIS ISN'T ABOUT PROTECT-ING THE EARTH!
OOB, WHEN YOUR TRAINING'S COMPLETE...
...PROMISE TO FIGHT ME!
UH... SURE...
I'VE BEEN WAITING YEARS FOR THIS!

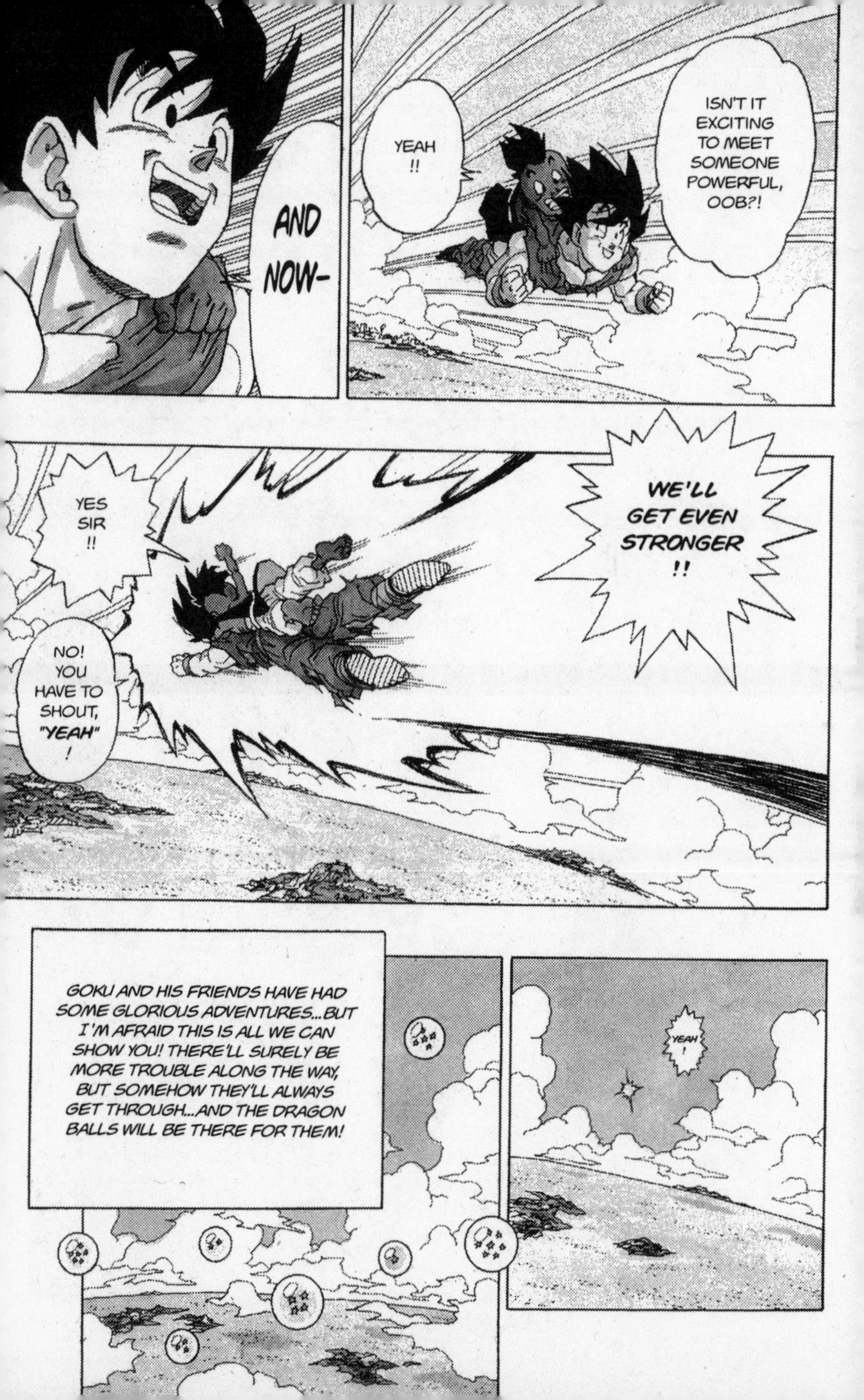

ISN'T IT EXCITING TO MEET SOMEONE POWERFUL, OOB?!
YEAH !!
AND NOW-
WE'LL GET EVEN STRONGER !!
YES SIR !!
NO! YOU HAVE TO SHOUT, "YEAH" !
YEAH !
GOKU AND HIS FRIENDS HAVE HAD SOME GLORIOUS ADVENTURES...BUT I'M AFRAID THIS IS ALL WE CAN SHOW YOU! THERE'LL SURELY BE MORE TROUBLE ALONG THE WAY, BUT SOMEHOW THEY'LL ALWAYS GET THROUGH...AND THE DRAGON BALLS WILL BE THERE FOR THEM!

THANK YOU!!
AND GOODBYE!!

THE-END
— FINIS —

TACKLE LIFE WITH AS MUCH ENERGY AS GOKU!! I'LL TRY TO DO THE SAME!

Thank you so much for reading **Dragon Ball** for all these years. I'm grateful for all the support you've shown me, right to the finish line! I've been planning this end for quite a while—I'm sorry that it had to be announced so suddenly. My editors have agreed to let me end this manga so I can take some new steps in life. It's time to take a break—although I may draw some one-shots here and there. I'm sure you'll see me again, and I'm sure it'll be fun (or at least, I hope so), so stay tuned! Until we meet again—so long!

—Akira Toriyama
May 1995

DRAGON BALL Z: THE END

DRAGON BALL

BALL FULL COLOR FREEZA ARC

After years of training and adventure, Goku has become Earth's ultimate warrior. And his son, Gohan, shows even greater promise. But the stakes are increasing as even deadlier enemies threaten the planet.

Goku and his friends journey to the planet Namek to confront the deadliest enemies Earth has ever seen—in full color!

Akira Toriyama's iconic series now in FULL COLOR!

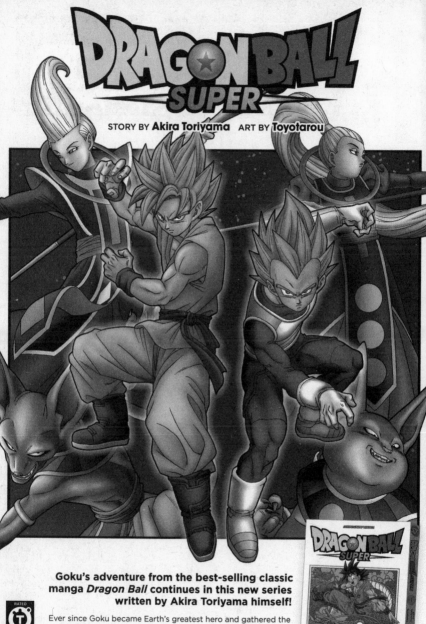

DRAGON BALL SUPER

STORY BY **Akira Toriyama** ART BY **Toyotarou**

Goku's adventure from the best-selling classic manga _Dragon Ball_ continues in this new series written by Akira Toriyama himself!

Ever since Goku became Earth's greatest hero and gathered the seven Dragon Balls to defeat the evil Boo, his life on Earth has grown a little dull. But new threats loom overhead, and Goku and his friends will have to defend the planet once again!

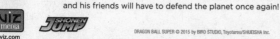

You're the Wrong Direction...

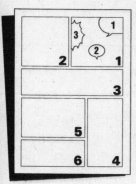

Whoops! Guess what? You're starting at the wrong end of the comic!

…It's true! In keeping with the original Japanese format, Akira Toriyama's world-famous **Dragon Ball Z** series is meant to be read from right to left, starting in the upper-right corner.

Unlike English which is read from left to right, Japanese is read from right to left, meaning that action, sound effects and word-balloon order are completely reversed… something which can make readers unfamiliar with Japanese feel pretty backwards themselves. For this reason, manga or Japanese comics published in the U.S. in English have traditionally been published "flopped"—that is, printed in exact reverse order, as though seen from the other side of a mirror.

By flopping pages, U.S. publishers can avoid confusing readers, but the compromise is not without its downside. For one thing, a character in a flopped manga series who, in the original Japanese version, wore a T-shirt emblazoned with "M A Y" (as in "the merry month of") now wears one which reads "Y A M"! Additionally, many manga creators in Japan are themselves unhappy with the process, as some feel the mirror-imaging of their art skews their original intentions.

In recognition of the importance and popularity of **Dragon Ball Z**, we are proud to bring it to you in the original unflopped format.

For now, though, turn to the other side of the book and let the adventure begin…!

—Editor